CONSTRAINTS
ON THE ECONOMIC
DEVELOPMENT OF ZAMBIA

CONSTRAINTS
ON THE ECONOMIC
DEVELOPMENT OF
ZAMBIA

edited by
Charles Elliott

NAIROBI
OXFORD UNIVERSITY PRESS 1971
LUSAKA DAR ES SALAAM LONDON

Oxford University Press, Ely House, London W. I.

GLASGOW NEW YORK TORONTO MELBOURNE WELLINGTON
CAPE TOWN IBADAN NAIROBI DAR ES SALAAM LUSAKA ADDIS ABABA
DELHI BOMBAY CALCUTTA MADRAS KARACHI LAHORE DACCA
KUALA LUMPUR SINGAPORE HONG KONG TOKYO

Oxford University Press, P.O. Box 72532, Nairobi, Kenya

Contents

v

vi

List of Tables

vii

viii

List of Maps and Figures

MAPS

FIGURES

I

Introduction

CHARLES ELLIOTT[1]

THIS introduction is divided into two sections. The first outlines the basic features of Zambia's economy and the implications of those features for its economic policy. The second section sketches the history of economic planning in Zambia and describes the emergence of a strategy for development in the years immediately before and after the achievement of political independence in 1964. This then sets the scene for the discussion in Part I of the main problems facing the country's principal industries.

But first it will be well to clarify a word that will inevitably recur many times in this book and which indeed forms the connecting theme of the individual contributions—namely 'constraints'. Most of the readers of this book will be familiar with the term in the context of linear programming, where a constraint determines the value of the objective function so that a marginal increase in the constraining factor will produce an increase in the objective function.[2] It is in a slightly less rigid form of this sense of the word that most contributors use it. It is either stated or implied that GNP or the output of the particular sector under discussion would have been higher had the relevant input been in greater supply. But three implications should be emphasized. First, the responsiveness of output to changes in inputs is of course not proportional. A given degree of shortage (as measured for instance by the proportionate difference between the very short-run and long-run equilibrium prices) in different inputs may have widely different

---

[1] Assistant Secretary of the Committee on Society, Development, and Peace of the World Council of Churches and the Pontifical Commission Justice and Peace; formerly Reader in Economics and Head of Department, University of Zambia.

[2] Those familiar with linear programming techniques will see that a number of assumptions—e.g. independence of inputs—are implicit in this simple formulation.

effects on the achievable level of output. A shortage of bricklayers has more effects on the level of output than an equally grave shortage of economists. This suggests that from the point of view of the economist the significance of a constraint is the output foregone per unit shortfall of the constraining input.

Second (a point given lengthier treatment by Richard Jolly in Chapter 2) no constraint can be adequately defined without reference to the market. If a shortage exists—i.e. the market is not in equilibrium—the price of the input will tend to rise, and in the long run supply will tend to increase. Obviously the elasticity of supply—both in the short run and the long—then becomes a key concept, for it determines both the scale of the short-run price rise and the new long-run equilibrium price. As normally expounded, however, it says nothing about the *rate* of increase of prices or supply. Government intervention, trade union structure, the fragmentation or integration of industry, the scale of the disequilibrium in the relevant market, and a wide range of institutional factors—all these determine the speed of the response to market disequilibria. The rate of increase in supply may be affected by the development of shortage in other sectors: shortage of construction capacity may only be made good when transport capacity is increased.

Third, a factor shortage can only be interpreted in the light of an existing technology. Again, in a linear programme this is self-evident, but in the context of this volume it needs emphasis since a change in technology may be a more practicable method of increasing output than an increase in one or more factors currently in short supply. This is particularly true in agriculture, where the productivity of land and labour can be rapidly increased by relatively minor and cheap changes in techniques. In industry, too, more substantial changes in technique can so alter the labour-input mix that a shortage of one type of labour —e.g. skilled craftsmen—can be overcome. The difference between these two cases should, however, be noted: in the first case, a change in technology leads to an increase in productivity of a given factor through greater intensity of use, while in the second it allows one factor to be substituted for another in short supply.

This raises the last general point that can usefully be made at this stage. The availability of close substitutes for given inputs in short supply is clearly a key determinant of the 'strength' of a constraint stemming from the shortage of a particular factor or service. Oil can replace coal in copper smelting (at a cost) and aircraft can replace railways (at a high cost), but unskilled labour cannot replace skilled nor domestic currency foreign exchange. Thus the specificity of a constraining factor affects both the 'strength' and the duration of the implicit loss of output. In the limiting case of an entirely specific input of which the supply cannot physically be increased except in the very long run, the constraint becomes absolute and can be accurately costed as the output foregone as a result of the constraint.

I

An appreciation of the structure of Zambia's economy inevitably begins with emphasis upon the dominant position occupied by the copper industry. The following table shows for the years 1964 to 1967, the proportion of GDP, export earnings,[3] direct government revenue, and employment originating in the industry. It must be emphasized that these figures refer directly to the output of the copper companies and exclude the multiplier effect of expenditures originating either from capital formation or wages earned in the sector or from government expenditures financed by tax revenues from copper companies. These indirect effects are almost as important as the direct effects in explaining the central position in the economy occupied by the mining industry.

TABLE 1.1

Percentage contribution of copper industry to principal economic variables

	1964	1965	1966	1967
GDP[1]	47[2]	38	37	32
Exports	92[3]	93	95	95
Government revenue	53	71	64	56
African employment	18	17	15	15

[1] At factor cost.
[2] Copper and cobalt.
[3] All mining and quarrying, thereafter mining only.

Sources: National Accounts, and *Copperbelt of Zambia Mining Industry Year Book, 1967,* Copper Industry Service Bureau, Kitwe.

An important result of the dominant position of the copper industry is that the level of copper production is sufficient to earn foreign exchange and generate tax revenues on a scale that is not far short of, and may until 1968–9 have been well in excess of, the absorptive capacity of the

[3] In only four African countries does the proportion of total exports accounted for by the leading sector exceed that in Zambia: Libya (petrol), Mauritania (iron ore), Mauritius (sugar), and Gambia (groundnuts).

economy as a whole. The following table compares the value of exports and the value of government revenues as percentages of the GNP for a number of African countries and for India, which provides a useful contrast.

TABLE 1.2

Exports and government revenue as percentage of GNP

	Revenue as % of GNP[1]		Exports as % of GNP	
Tanganyika	12.2	1953–4	45.3	1967
Uganda	12.1	,,	40.0	,,
Kenya	24.5	,,	22.6	,,
Nigeria	8.4	,,	16.8	1960
Ghana	22.2	,,	30.7	1962
Zambia[2]	40.0	1967	63.1	1967
India	8.3	1953	5.1	1960–1

[1] GNP at factor cost.

[2] The Lewis-Martin figures appear to be central government only. The equivalent figure for Zambia would in this case be 36% (cf. Table 1.1).

Sources: Column 1: A. Martin and W. A. Lewis, *Manchester School*, 1956. Although the data are old, they serve as a guide to the order of magnitude, though in some countries, notably India, the situation has changed substantially since 1953. Zambia: *National Accounts*.
Column 2: E. Africa: P. Ndegwa, *The Common Market and Development in East Africa*, East African Publishing House, Nairobi, 1965. Ghana: W. Birmingham, I. Neustadt, and E. N. Omaboe, *Study of Contemporary Ghana*, Vol. II, Allen and Unwin, London, 1966. Nigeria: *National Development Plan*, 1962–68, Lagos, 1962. Zambia: *National Accounts*, 1968.
India: M. Singh, *India's Export Trends*, Allen and Unwin, London, 1964.

This suggests (although it does not prove) that, compared with the other countries in the table, Zambia was relatively free of the two principal bottlenecks to development. This was reflected in the surpluses on both the balance of payments and on the government current account in the early years after Independence. Partly as a result of the increased absorptive capacity of the economy after the initial infrastructure had been supplied in the years immediately following Independence, and partly as a result of a fairly rapid rate of internal inflation, these surpluses had begun to disappear by 1968.

On the other hand, the domination of the economy by the copper industry did not produce a substantial level of supply of locally produced inputs for the mining industry. Chapter 9 analyses the reasons for this and shows how the copper industry has traditionally had a low level of linkage with the manufacturing and service sectors. Partly as cause and partly as effect, the level of manufacturing output in the economy has been small.[4] Table 1.4 compares the proportion of GNP originating in the manufacturing sectors of a number of African countries. This shows that, by comparison with East but not West Africa, Zambia's manufacturing development has not been commensurate with the industrial base offered by the mining sector. This is further suggested by Table 1.3 which gives a comparison between the structure of the manufacturing industry in Zambia and the pattern predicted by the Chenery-UN model on the basis of Zambia's population and *per capita* income.[5] The general conclusion is that in metals the degree of industrialization is, by comparison with the 'norm', very high, but in every other industry Zambia is 'abnormally' under-industrialized. The food sector is worth particular reference.

TABLE 1.3

Patterns of 'normal' and achieved industrial output in Zambia, 1967

	Actual	'Normal'	Actual % 'Normal'
	(US$ m.)	(US$ m.)	
Food, beverages, tobacco	33.4	55.9	60
Textiles	1.19	10.2	11
Clothing and footwear	4.9	9.4	52
Wood products	4.0	6.5	61
Paper products	3.2	2.0	55
Printing and publishing		5.8 { 3.8	
Leather	—	2.9	0
Rubber	0.9	1.3	69
Petrochemical and coal products	3.4	7.2	47
Non-metallic minerals	8.1	10.5	77
Basic metals	66.7	1.9	436
Metal products		15.3 { 13.4	
Others	0.3	1.3	23
	126.0	126.1	

Sources: From A. Young's article in *Eastern Africa Economic Review*, Vol. 1, No. 2, December 1969. See, too, M. D. Steuer and C. Voivodas, 'Import Substitution and Chenery's Patterns of Industrial Growth', *Economia Internazionale*, 1962.

[4] This is partly the result of treating smelting and refining as mining rather than manufacturing. The reclassification of these activities naturally increases the proportion of GDP originating in manufacturing.

[5] H. B. Chenery, 'Patterns of Industrial Growth', *American Economic Review*, 1960, Vol. LI, No. 4, pp. 624-54. *A Study of Industrial Growth*, UN Depart-

Quite apart from the low linkage effect of the copper industry, there are a number of reasons for this slow development. Foremost among these must be counted the policy of the Federal government, which was to establish the manufacturing base of the Federation of Rhodesia and Nyasaland in Southern Rhodesia and to give only minimal encouragement to manufacturing industry north of the Zambesi. Membership of the Federation robbed the territorial government of the right to impose tariffs within the territory, since the whole Federal area was a customs union and the expense and difficulty of transport failed to act in the same way as a tariff, since any domestic industry was heavily dependent upon imported raw materials and capital goods. Further, the market was not only small but so divided[6] that an industry in which the economies of scale are at all important was rendered uncompetitive with the industry of Southern Rhodesia or even of South Africa and Britain. It was only when the market, protected by adequate tariffs, expanded very rapidly after the growth of employment and earnings, and more particularly the rise in government demand after Independence, that the manufacturing sector was able to grow substantially. This is further discussed in Chapters 7 and 11.

TABLE 1.4

Manufacturing output percentage of GNP at factor cost

	%	date
Uganda	7.5	1963
Tanzania	8.1	1963
Kenya	13.3	1963
Nigeria	1.3	1960
Ghana	5.0	1960
Zambia	7.4	1965

Sources: E. Africa: P. Clarke, *Development Planning in East Africa*, East African Publishing House, Nairobi, 1965.

Nigeria: *National Development Plan, 1962–68*, Lagos, 1962.

Ghana: W. Birmingham *et al.*, *Study of Contemporary Ghana*, op. cit.

If the foreign exchange and tax revenue bottlenecks have hardly started to operate in Zambia and if the market constraint on

ment of Social Affairs, New York, 1963. The 'norms' are obtained by applying a series of regression equations, derived from a cross-sectional study of over 50 countries, to Zambian data on population and income per head.

[6] Analytically, there were four subdivisions of the main market: European urban and rural, and African urban and rural.

industrialization has been much weakened, there is still one formidable constraint that was obvious as soon as political Independence for Northern Rhodesia became a real possibility and which remains much in evidence five years after Independence: namely, manpower. It is worth quoting the opening paragraph of the *Manpower Report* published in 1966, already a classic in its field:

Most African countries were, in terms of education, poorly prepared for Independence, but in Zambia educational facilities for Africans were even more deficient than elsewhere. During the colonial era African education was not given high priority; in spite of comparative wealth, during most years far more was spent on education for the few Europeans than on all forms of education for the African population. From 1954-1963, European education had been a Federal responsibility financed from Federal taxation, which tapped the main sources of revenue in Zambia, Malawi, and Rhodesia. In contrast, African education was a territorial responsibility relying entirely on local funds. The result was that African education, to a large extent, was cut off from the major sources of Zambia's wealth, revenue from copper. Secondly, in spite of Zambia's comparatively advanced industrial structure, opportunities for apprenticeship and on-the-job training of Africans were hindered by racial discrimination. Until 1959, no African was permitted by law to be apprenticed in Zambia. Thirdly, the discrimination of various sorts inside the Civil Service, in trade unions and in the private sector limited the opportunities for Africans to gain practical experience and responsibility in many types of work. Of course, there were exceptions, and many individuals and institutions had laboured for many years to right these injustices. Indeed, without their tireless efforts, Zambia would have remained an educational desert. But the lack of priority, the general shortage of funds for education and the limitations of training opportunities meant that steps that were taken in other countries during the crucial decade before Independence, were not taken in Zambia. Zambia was less prepared than most other African countries in the north, east, and west of Africa.[7]

The coincidence of the shortage of educated, skilled and trained manpower and the implementation of the ambitious development plans inevitably led to an acute crisis in the labour market. A distinction ought to be made between the three labour markets. First is the European market dominated by the copper companies' employment of 7,000 Europeans.[8] The growth of demand for European skills, however, came not from the copper industry in which there was, in fact, a substantial fall in the number of Europeans employed between 1964 and 1968, but from the

---

[7] *Manpower Report*, Government Printer, Lusaka, 1966, p. 1.

[8] Quantitatively as important but more diffuse and therefore less organized are the 7,000 Europeans employed in the commercial sector and an equal number in 'other services'.

construction and manufacturing industries which experienced very rapid rates of growth over this period and in which the stock of supervisory skills in the country in 1964 was small. Difficulties and delay over the granting of work permits and entry visas meant that growth of the already inelastic supply of this category of labour was rendered even more sluggish. The result was that the Europeans with the right kind of skills already in the country were able to demand and receive salaries that, skill for skill, would be difficult to match anywhere in the world. In the skilled African labour market the position was not fundamentally different. Skilled and semi-skilled workers were in such short supply that they were able to secure very substantial increases in earnings over the period. However, the shortage of housing for skilled Africans implied a stickiness in the labour market which may have gone some way towards moderating the free play of market forces on the wages of African skilled and semi-skilled workers. On the other hand, the pressure on employers to accelerate the promotion of Zambians to higher posts, particularly in the mining industry after the publication of the Brown Commission's report on wages and conditions of service in the copper mining industry, implied an artificial rate of growth of demand for this scarce resource.

In the unskilled market the position was perhaps a little more complicated. On the one hand there is some evidence that the rate of urban drift increased markedly after Independence for a complicated series of reasons ranging from political education during the Independence struggle to the attraction offered by rapidly rising wages in the urban sector. To this extent the supply of unskilled labour was probably increasing more rapidly than the demand for it, which was itself reduced by the tendency already discernible by 1965 for entrepreneurs to substitute capital for labour as a result of the manpower shortage and rapidly rising labour costs. In a perfect market therefore one would not have expected the wages of unskilled labour to rise rapidly. However, like labour markets anywhere else in the world, the unskilled labour market in Zambia is far from perfect and the inevitable imperfections were increased substantially by the implementation of the Brown Commission's Report in 1966 and the subsequent extension of substantial wage increases to other sectors of the economy.

The other effect of the whole manpower situation, allied to the political necessity for rapid Zambianization not only in the civil service but throughout the economy and particularly in the mining industry, was the alleged deterioration in labour productivity caused by lack of discipline, drunkenness, incompetence, and a whole complex of problems in the industrial relations field. Although Zambianization was blamed by both foreign and local observers, and latterly by some senior politicians, for the deterioration in labour productivity, this was only one amongst many reasons for the restlessness of the labour force reflected in quantitative and qualitative deterioration in work performance.

But the problems of the industrial labour force, though clearly most important from the point of view of the industrial development of the country, hardly compare quantitatively with those of the rural population. For by far the most essential feature of the economy that must be emphasized in an introduction is the fact that Zambia is still a rural society. Over 80 per cent of the population live in the rural areas and of these the vast majority earn their living, in either cash or subsistence terms, from the land. It is no surprise therefore that the political philosophy of the government, namely Zambian Humanism, like Ujamaa, stems very largely from a conception of rural society. Nor is it surprising that the policy area that has caused the government most anxiety has been rural development, for by any definition Zambian agriculture is inefficient. Though it is easy to exaggerate the suitability of the Zambian climate and conditions for intensive agriculture, the fact that in 1966 over 20 per cent of Zambia's food was imported from abroad owes less to the natural environment of agriculture than to ineffective agricultural policies before and after Independence. The structural inefficiency of this sector is reflected in its inability to provide a large and rapidly growing market for home-produced goods, its oversupply of labour to the urban sector, its absorption of private and public capital, often with very little effect on output, and consequently its inability to generate either from cash savings or from direct labour input adequate productive assets to ensure a satisfactory rate of growth and a flexible pattern of agricultural output. The implications of this structural inefficiency for the rest of the economy are brought out in the chapters that follow. But without prejudice to the discussion that follows it is worth commenting immediately that it is almost certainly true that no country in Africa faces such a contrast between, on the one hand, an urban industrial sector that is growing and developing very rapidly, and on the other, a semi-stagnant rural economy which seems to defy, often at very considerable expense, all attempts at restructuring it in the process of growth.

II

Although both Federal and territorial governments had attempted to frame development plans, these were crude and conservative forerunners of the two major planning documents that have been produced in Zambia since Independence.[9] In some ways more significant, however, than either the Transitional Development Plan or the First National Development Plan published in 1966 was the Report of the UN/ECA/FAO team, headed by Dudley Seers, which was made available to the government in 1964.[10] This report established the basic strategy of development to be pursued in Zambia by both the Transitional Development Plan and the First National Development Plan, and is therefore of the first importance. Recognizing the main features of the economy as presented above in section I, the Seers Report developed a basic strategy of development based on the rapid establishment of import-substitutive manufacturing industries and the transformation of African agriculture by the application of modern techniques. By these means urban employment was to be increased, the dependence of the economy on the copper industry reduced, regional disparities in income and level of living moderated, and *per capita* income and consumption raised. To realize this broad strategy, the report developed four main tactics. Firstly, fiscal reforms would produce a substantial increase in government revenue and expenditure which would form the main source of new demand in the economy. Secondly, huge expenditures were recommended on education and transport: the former to breach the manpower bottleneck in the medium term and the latter to widen the impact of the cash economy on the rural areas and thus increase the supply of agricultural products and demand for manufactured goods. Thirdly, the use of foreign exchange reserves was seen as a necessary measure to increase the level of supply until the envisaged investments became productive. Fourthly, substantial investments were to be made in the rural economy: credit was to be made more readily available, mechanization was greatly to be accelerated, and marketing and extension services much improved.

---

[9] An Emergency Plan was prepared in 1963 to provide a framework for government expenditures until the publication of the Transitional Development Plan in 1965.

[10] UN/ECA/FAO, *Report of the Economic Survey Mission on the Economic Development of Zambia*, Falcon Press, Ndola, 1964.

The policy of diversification is not as unassailable as it might at first seem, and elsewhere I have advanced some arguments against it.[11] In the present context three points should be made. The first is that the early stages of diversification do not lead to any decrease in the dependence of the economy as a whole nor more particularly, of government revenue, on the copper industry; the second is that diversification in manufacturing and agriculture necessarily implied a rapidly increasing demand for all factors of production but particularly skilled and semi-skilled workers much before supply could be increased; the third is that diversification in both spheres to the exclusion of the rapid development of copper production, underplayed but not overlooked in the report, not only takes a specific and not wholly realistic view of changes in comparative advantage but also implies a rate of growth of demand for tax revenue and foreign exchange greater than the probable rate of growth of supply. Thus the policy implies the gradual elimination of surpluses on both government account and the balance of payments. This effect was already discernible in 1968 and resulted in the modestly deflationary budget of January 1969.

The Transitional Development Plan and the First National Development Plan sought to put this strategy and these tactics into effect. The Transitional Development Plan allocated funds between sectors in accordance with Table 1.5.

From the table it may be seen that the Transitional Development Plan adhered fairly closely to the priorities outlined by the Seers Report. The relatively high expenditure on administration, defence, and internal security was a necessary result of the new legal status of the country. Education and agriculture between them accounted for nearly a third of the total expenditures; if we add the K 5.0 m. (1 kwacha = 58 p. sterling) of the transport, communications, and power allocation which was to be spent on roads,[12] then the total allocation serving the basic objects of the Seers Report rises to well over one third.

The Transitional Development Plan marked a new era of planning in the country in so far as there was an attempt in the plan to calculate the demands made by each project on the scarce resources of the

11 Essay in W. Tordoff (ed.), *The Politics of Zambia*, Macmillan, Londno, forthcoming 1972.
12 Much of the balance of the K 19.2 m. was for improved telecommunications and postal services in the rural provinces, but more particularly external connections to East Africa and the north, motivated very considerably by political considerations.

TABLE 1.5
Approximate expenditure, by sector, during transitional plan
(*K m.*)

Sector	Carry-overs	New projects 'A'	'B'	Total
Administration, defence, and internal security	4.8	6.8	2.4	14.0
Education and training	4.0	9.8	0.8	14.6
Agriculture and natural resources	4.6	4.4	10.0	19.0
Services to industry and mines	—	0.4	1.4	1.8
Transport, communications, and power	10.6	7.0	1.6	19.2
Health and social welfare	3.4	1.0	2.6	7.0
Housing and local government services	11.2	5.0	—	16.2
	38.6	34.4	18.8	91.8
less 10% ⎫	3.8			
less 25% ⎬ implied shortfall		8.6		21.8
less 50% ⎭			9.4	
	34.8	25.8	9.4	70.0

Notes: 1 As is evident from the last three rows, the title of the columns indicates order of priority in execution.
2 In this as in all similar tables in this volume, currency has been converted to kwacha. 1 kwacha = 58 p. sterling.

Source: Transitional Development Plan, Lusaka, 1965.

economy. These were recognized as skilled labour and construction capacity. But the very small statistical base from which the compilers of the plan had to work limited the application of a scarce-resource approach to planning to the crudest guesses of the supply of and demand for resources implicit in each project. One of the most damaging criticisms that can be made of the First National Development Plan published eighteen months later than the Transitional Development Plan is that it failed adequately to continue the transition already evident in the TDP from financial budgeting to scarce-resource planning.

The First National Development Plan accepted the strategy of both the Seers Report and the Transitional Development Plan, giving great weight to the development of education, of transport, and of the twin elements of diversification: agriculture and industry. Table 1.6 gives the sectoral distribution of funds under the First National Development Plan.

The writers of the FNDP had absorbed the Seers strategy more carefully, and thus the first of the eight objectives of the plan was

TABLE 1.6

First National Development Plan: capital expenditures by sector and province
(K'000)

Sectors	Northern	Western	Eastern	Central	Southern	Barose	Luapula	North-Western	Total
Agriculture	6,206	4,632	4,904	10,958	8,198	4,030	4,058	4,228	47,214
Mining	14	50	64	1,004	4,794	2	86	36	5,750
Manufacturing	776	11,188	438	36,028	9,254	442	704	418	59,248
Construction	80	70	80	124	74	70	66	50	614
Electricity and water	2,840	328	3,052	25,294	23,800	2,690	1,600	2,322	61,926
Commerce and finance	700	1,098	534	1,114	314	602	586	684	5,632
Transport and communications	26,906	5,918	11,152	50,818	14,434	936	1,456	4,372	115,992
Government services:									
” Agriculture	1,950	1,718	1,790	4,952	4,442	1,696	1,100	976	18,624
” Health	2,888	4,614	1,906	5,052	1,736	1,098	1,844	528	19,666
” Education	9,332	8,200	8,322	27,756	10,042	6,220	5,796	3,064	78,732
” General	8,102	37,592	6,982	56,666	14,682	6,090	4,858	4,308	141,280
General Services	1,058	52	696	3,860	2,528	52	62	534	8,942
Total	60,852	75,460	40,020	225,626	93,998	23,928	22,216	21,520	563,620

'the diversification of the economy, so that the copper industry is not the only employer in the economy and so that a great proportion of domestic demand is satisfied by domestic production from a large industrial base'.[13] The plan thus called for an increase of 146 per cent in manufacturing output based on import-substitutive industries, and proportionate increases in output of other sectors as shown in Table 1.7.

TABLE 1.7

Industrial origin of GDP: projected expenditure from FNDP (K m.—1964 prices)

	1964	1970	% Increase
Agriculture	18.2	31.2	+ 71
Mining	237.6	386.2	+ 63
Manufacturing	26.2	64.4	+146
Construction	20.4	60.6	+198
Commerce	45.0	97.6	+117
Transport	20.6	39.2	+ 90
Services	69.0	170.2	+147
Total	437.0	849.4	+ 94

Source: *First National Development Plan, 1966–70*, Office of National Development and Planning, Lusaka, July 1966.

Between the preparation of the final draft of the FNDP and its publication in 1966, the full extent of the economic repercussions of Rhodesia's illegal unilateral declaration of independence in November 1965 became clear. To this extent the First National Development Plan was outdated before its publication. By mid-1966 it was clear that it would be impossible to meet the extremely ambitious targets of the plan either in real or in financial terms and it was also obvious that, failing massive aid from Britain and other friendly powers, considerable resources would have to be diverted from the objectives of the plan to the new objective of surviving as a nation and simultaneously maintaining a reasonable rate of growth within the economy. As far as financial resources were concerned the worst of the embarrassment was deflected by a substantial and sustained rise in the price of copper, reinforced by the prolonged American strike in 1967. From the point of view of real resources, however, the situation was more critical. We have already mentioned the difficulties of recruiting skilled manpower. This was matched by difficulties of importing raw materials and finished products as a result of a precipitate political decision to switch transport routes

---

[13] *First National Development Plan, 1966–70*, Office of National Development and Planning, Lusaka, July 1966, p. 5.

away from the south to the north, either through the Congo or through Tanzania. Simultaneously efforts were made to keep the rate of expenditure detailed in the plan up to schedule, with the inevitable result that the FNDP's fourth objective, 'to maintain reasonable price stability', went unfulfilled as the total level of supply of the economy either contracted or failed to grow at a sufficient pace to meet the growth in demand. Only those who had exceptional skills or strong monopoly bargaining positions were able to defend themselves against the rise in prices. Nonetheless the rise in wages, reported in the *Economic Report* of 1968 to be 30 per cent in the urban economy, was matched by an increasing tendency to substitute capital (and skilled labour) for labour and thus endanger the plan's second objective, namely an increase in employment of *at least* 100,000 jobs during the course of the plan.

Nevertheless by 1967 much had been achieved. Table 1.8 shows that investment had risen spectacularly over the period.

TABLE 1.8
Gross fixed capital formation at market prices
(K m.)

	1964	1965	1966	1967
Agriculture, forestry, and fishing	5.0	7.3	9.2	10.3
Mining and quarrying	27.0	25.0	27.1	28.3
Manufacturing	5.4	9.5	15.8	23.0
Construction	1.0	8.6	9.4	13.4
Electricity and water	3.0	5.7	6.0	7.0
Trade	2.8	9.8	6.5	12.2
Financial institutions and insurance	0.8	1.3	2.5	4.8
Real estate	4.0	13.2	17.8	18.2
Transport and communications	6.0	7.8	19.5	25.8
Community and business services	2.6	} 5.7	} 4.3	} 6.1
Personal services	1.2			
Total private & government enterprises	58.8	93.9	118.1	149.5
Total central & local government	17.4	26.4	57.7	68.6
Total gross fixed capital formation	76.2	120.3	175.8	218.1

Source: Economic Report, Lusaka, 1968.

Predictably this was especially strongly marked in manufacturing, agriculture, transport, and the public sector. By contrast, the level of investment in mining was nearly constant.

TABLE 1.9
Industrial origin of GDP of Zambia at factor cost
(K m.)

	1964	1965	1966	1967
Agriculture, forestry and fishing	53.3	54.8	60.5	64.4
Mining and quarrying	220.8	208.9	240.1	235.5
Manufacturing	28.2	40.0	60.2	78.9
Construction	20.0	39.4	54.0	63.3
Electricity and water	5.0	5.3	7.4	8.9
Trade	45.8	71.3	78.3	96.4
Financial institutions and insurance	0.6	10.7	11.5	16.9
Real estate	10.6	9.2	15.2	14.9
Transport and communications	20.6	32.4	32.4	47.9
Government administration	21.2	30.4	35.7	39.4
Community and business services	19.6	34.1	34.6	51.3
Personal services	19.6	12.2	14.6	15.6
Gross domestic product at factor cost	465.3	548.6	644.5	733.4

Note: The discrepancies between the 1964 figures in this table and Table 1.7
are accounted for by revisions to the figures undertaken by the CSO
after the publication of the FNDP and by the fact that in Table 1.9 sales
from African agriculture and a notional figure for subsistence agriculture
are included, whereas they are excluded from the FNDP figures.

Source: Economic Report, Lusaka, 1968.

Table 1.9 shows how this investment increased production, with the
really dramatic rises coming in manufacturing, construction, and the
public sector. Despite its statistical weakness Table 1.10 shows how
successful the policy of diversification had been by 1967. In the case
of every sector except services (excluding agriculture) the plan targets
had been exceeded, with particularly significant rises in manufacturing,
construction, and commerce. Although still by far the largest sector,
the dominance of the copper industry had been much reduced.

It was against this economic background that the famous
Mulungushi Reforms were announced in April 1968. The effect of
the reforms, described in detail elsewhere,[14] was to nationalize twenty-
three leading companies, to limit the repatriation of profits, deprive
non-Zambians of bank credit except under special circumstances,
and force non-Zambians (largely Asians) out of the retail and petty
building sectors to make room for Zambian co-operatives and individual

[14] See B. de Gaay Fortman (ed.), *After Mulungushi: the Economics of Zambian
Humanism*, East African Publishing House, Nairobi, 1969.

TABLE 1.10
Percentage industrial origin of GDP[1]

	1964	1967	1970 Plan projection
Agriculture	11.5	8.4	(3.6)[2]
Mining	47.8	31.0	45.5
Manufacturing	6.1	10.6	7.6
Construction	4.3	8.7	7.1
Commerce	12.2	17.9	11.5
Transport	4.4	6.7	4.6
Services	14.2	16.5	20.0

[1] Following the extremely crude procedure of the plan, for comparative purposes copper output is valued at 1964 prices. The latest figures of 1964 value added by sector differ substantially from those in the plan. The distribution implicit in the GDP figures published in the *Economic Report* for 1968 has therefore been used for 1964 and 1967. The plan projections have been left unmodified.

[2] Commercial agriculture only.

Sources: FNDP; *Economic Report*, Lusaka, 1968.

entrepreneurs. In July 1969 the process was taken a step further by the state's purchase of 51 per cent of the equity of the mining companies.[15] It is too early to assess the full impact of the reforms, but apart from diminishing, probably temporarily, the inflow of foreign capital and increasing substantially the proportion of the non-mining economy directly controlled by the state (through the Industrial Development Corporation), the effects on the basic features of the economy are unlikely to be dramatic. From the longer-term viewpoint, however, the aggressive—and some would say reckless—approach of the Industrial Development Corporation is likely to ensure that at least the plan targets on growth of manufacturing output will be met. The concomitant loss of efficiency was already evident from the 1966 input-output matrix.

The introduction of a mildly deflationary budget in January 1969, attended by strikes on the Copperbelt in protest against the extension of taxation to the economic élite of employed Africans, marked not so much a turning point in Zambia's development[16] as a recognition of

[15] The 'nationalization' of the copper companies was announced as this volume went to press. It has not been possible therefore to incorporate a discussion of its effects.

[16] As well as control of inflation, a rationale of the budget was that copper prices were likely to fall heavily (an entirely reasonable but wrong view) and that therefore government revenue and foreign exchange earnings would be deficient.

the over-zealous scale of the FNDP, of the supply inelasticities within the internal and external economy and of the fact that Zambia is still very heavily dependent upon economic forces over which she has no control. To that extent, the period in which the financial constraints could be ignored was ended.

Part I
GENERAL CONSTRAINTS

2

The Skilled Manpower Constraint

RICHARD JOLLY[1]

I INTRODUCTION

THERE are two reasons for giving particular attention to the shortage and scarcity[2] of skills as a constraint to development in Zambia. Firstly, because the lack of skills and education in Zambia was the major constraint to expansion in the years after Independence. Secondly, because this lack was so extensive in comparison with that in other developing countries that Zambia's experience serves as the pathological condition from which to study the symptoms of acute scarcity of manpower in the process of development.

The main reasons for this acute scarcity of skills in Zambia are easy to explain. At Independence, Zambia had fewer skilled and educated citizens than virtually any other ex-British colony. There were in 1963 in total under 100 Zambian graduates and under 1,000 secondary school graduates—comparable to the numbers of African secondary school graduates in Ghana in 1943, in Uganda in 1955, in Kenya in 1957, and in Tanzania in 1960. Zambia's deprivation was the result not of poverty but of priorities. In spite of her wealth and revenue from copper and of considerable expenditures on primary and all levels of

---

[1] Richard Jolly is a Fellow in Development Economics at the Institute of Development Studies, University of Sussex, England.

This chapter, the major part of which was prepared for a staff seminar at the Institute of Development Studies in October 1969, draws heavily on the two basic publications on skilled manpower in Zambia: *Zambian Manpower* and *Manpower Report*, published respectively in 1969 and 1966 and available from the Government Printer, Lusaka. The author is grateful for comments and criticisms on an earlier draft of this chapter by Chris Brown, Chris Colclough, Charles Elliott, Len Joy, Emmanuel de Kadt, Charles Shackleton, John Weeks, and Geoff Wood. The author is solely responsible for the views expressed.

[2] These terms are defined in section IV of this chapter.

non-African schooling, secondary and higher education for Africans were held back in Zambia over the crucial period when they were being rapidly expanded in other colonial territories elsewhere in Africa.[3] Nor was this lack of formal education offset by Zambia's exceptional capacity for industrial training: restrictive legislation made it illegal for any African to be apprenticed until 1959.

Quite apart from the scarcity of skilled Africans, the total supply of persons with higher levels of skills and education has been extremely scarce since Independence, relative both to the supply of other key resources and to the rapidly rising level of demand. This is analysed in detail later in the chapter but the main reasons can be mentioned here. On the side of supply, the number of expatriates, though still large (about 80,000 in total, of whom about 30,000 are employed), has declined and many have for long wavered on the point of leaving, inevitably diminishing morale and commitment and leading to higher turnover rates, higher wages (and other costs), and less local experience (even if probably some increase in the level of skill of persons newly recruited). In this respect both Independence and the Unilateral Declaration of Independence (UDI) by Rhodesia have tended to polarize attitudes leading to the departure of many expatriates. Some have been replaced, often by staff on OSAS and technical assistance arrangements with Britain. But Britain, in spite of her close involvement and acknowledged responsibility for both Zambia's colonial past and Rhodesia's UDI, felt it necessary in 1968 to put a financial ceiling on the amount of manpower aid she was willing to extend to Zambia over this critical period, thus adding a new and important restriction to Zambia's most important source of overseas recruitment.[4]

---

[3] Trevor Coombe has assembled in great detail the pre-war evidence on this aspect of Zambian educational policy. Anyone tempted to dismiss the backwardness of secondary education in Zambia as an unfortunate oversight by colonial authorities will find it enlightening to refer to his thorough analysis of the conflicting interests of the parties involved, many very conscious of the issues under discussion. See Trevor Coombe, 'Origins of Secondary Education in Zambia', Parts I, II and III, *African Social Research*, June & December 1967, June 1968, Institute of Social Research, University of Zambia and Manchester University Press.

[4] In 1967, British OSAS and technical assistance staff working in Zambia represented 22 per cent of *all* such British staff working abroad and nearly 11 per cent of Britain's total expenditure on bilateral technical assistance. The financial ceiling placed on the British programme to Zambia in effect acted to limit the flow of personnel (even if Zambia had been willing to finance them)

In parallel with these restrictions on the side of skilled manpower supply came dramatic increases in demand, the result of a considerable expansion in the economy and important structural changes accelerated by the challenges of UDI. This expansion was fuelled by unprecedented increases in government revenue and foreign exchange which grew three or four times in as many years under the influences of mounting copper prices, new taxation arrangements, and the reversion to government of copper royalties formerly paid abroad to the BSA company. For the public sector, this made possible a series of ambitious development plans, aiming at both expansion and structural change in the economy. Particularly important was the enormous expansion of secondary and university education, which greatly added to the demand for teachers.[5] For the private sector, the expansion of government demand added many opportunities to those already opened up for local manufacturing by the termination in 1963 of the Federation with Rhodesia and Nyasaland, which had primarily operated in the economic (and political) interests of Rhodesia. Even without UDI, the structural changes (and the additional demands for skilled manpower which they brought) would have been considerable. Added to all these factors, Zambia's response to UDI greatly increased and accelerated its demand for skills at the same time as the political and social repercussions of UDI threatened the continuation of even that supply of expatriate skills on which, for all its inadequacies, the country depended.

II MANPOWER CONSTRAINTS

In at least four major ways, manpower can act as a constraint on economic and social development. First, the scarcity of skilled and educated persons can hold back growth and distort its pattern. Second, the scarcity of unskilled labour, at least at some seasons and in certain areas, can limit the supply of available human effort and thus limit what can be achieved. Third, a fast rate of population growth creates various

because the process of recruitment was so closely linked with the financial administration of aid and technical assistance.

[5] A detailed account of Zambia's ambitious educational plans after Independence has been given by the person most directly responsible, the former Minister of Education, the Hon. J. M. Mwanakatwe. See his book, *The Growth of Education in Zambia since Independence*, Oxford University Press, Nairobi, 1968.

problems, some of which tend to slow the rate of growth and job creation. Fourth, if only a few women have reasonable levels of basic education, this will limit advance in the home and in traditional agriculture, and severely retard the preparation and development of the future generation.

This chapter deals only with the first of these constraints in Zambia, partly in order to concentrate its theme and partly because some of the others are taken up elsewhere in the book. But it is important not to lose sight of the last three, since they also operate in Zambia. Indeed, they comprise essential dimensions of Zambia's manpower constraint which in the preoccupations with the scarcity of skills and education have often been neglected, both in analysis and in policymaking.

Unskilled labour, for instance, is rarely thought of as a scarce resource in Zambia, in view of the large number who are unemployed and seeking jobs in the towns. But compared with most other African countries, a higher proportion of Zambian men are in urban wage-earning employment and, thus, a lower proportion are directly dependent on the land. Furthermore, the population density in Zambia is low compared with other developing countries. The result is that even with existing agricultural practices, labour can be scarce in some rural areas.

A decade ago, Barber estimated that over half the adult males were absent from the rural areas and that if more labour was withdrawn, agricultural output would fall.[6] Since that time, the number of adult males has grown much faster than wage employment, in both rural and urban areas. Even so, it is likely that unskilled labour is still scarce in relation to land and other resources at least in the more sparsely populated regions, particularly at times of planting and harvesting. In this respect, the unemployed in the towns are more a sign of a maldistribution of labour, the result of a distorted pattern of wages and other incentives rather than a sign of unlimited labour throughout the country.[7] Thus, even today, it seems likely that unskilled labour is a

---

[6] W. J. Barber, *The Economy of British Central Africa*, Oxford University Press, London, 1961, p. 230.

[7] Admittedly, this begs the question as to whether the unemployment would remain if the distribution were improved, particularly since 6.8 per cent of the males over 16 in the rural areas were recorded by the 1963 census of Africans as seeking paid work. But evidence of the numbers seeking paid work is ambiguous as soon as one takes account of distorted incentives. This point is treated more fully in section IV of this chapter, in the discussion of the meaning of scarcity.

scarce resource in certain areas of Zambia and acts as a constraint on development.

Given this scarcity of unskilled labour it may seem contradictory to argue that a high rate of population growth forms a second constraint on Zambia's development, particularly when the total population is little more than four million and population density is low. But the rate of increase of a country's population can be too high even when the present size of its population is, in some respects, too small. Zambia's high rate of population increase, about $3\frac{1}{2}$ per cent per annum, means that an exceptionally high proportion of its population is under 15 years old. This high 'dependency ratio' has increased the social costs of education and other child services, and lowered the amount of government expenditure available for more immediately productive investment. This in turn has lowered both the growth rate of the economy and of wage employment and, at the same time, increased the numbers of young persons looking for jobs.

Finally, there are the problems created by inadequate levels of education among women. This, of course, is much more than a question of education, but education is an important factor and serves as a reminder of two more basic things. First, that general improvements in the standard of *family* living are part and parcel of economic and social development whether or not included within gross domestic product as conventionally defined. Second, that in Zambia improvements in rural life depend crucially on the women in their roles as mothers raising children and as rural workers responsible for a large part of peasant agriculture. Yet in 1963, 85 per cent of adult Zambian women in the rural areas had never been to school. Of the 15 per cent who had any schooling, only 3 per cent had more than 4 years—markedly less than men in the rural areas or women in towns.

Too little is known about the precise effects of this educational deficiency on the quality of rural life or its preparedness for change. But there is no doubt that production and health suffer in a number of ways and that maternal illiteracy will prevent most rural children from developing as fully as children in the towns, thus tending to perpetuate the rural-urban divisions. The consequences of illiteracy and under-education among women in the rural areas will thus be a serious handicap to modernization for many years ahead, and is a strong argument for wide major programmes of education and rural extension for all age groups.

III THE SCARCITY OF
SKILLED MANPOWER IN ZAMBIA

But, however important these other manpower constraints, it is the scarcity of educated manpower which has been so frequently emphasized in Zambia in the years since Independence. 'In terms of high level manpower', stated the UN Economic Survey Mission in 1964, 'Zambia is one of the least-educated countries in a most under-educated continent.' 'Skilled and educated manpower', stated President Kaunda in 1966, 'is Zambia's scarcest resource.' These points have been repeated many times in government, the mines, industry, and the rest of the private sector.

Some figures may help to quantify the position described. Table 2.1 gives the broad structure of output and employed manpower in 1965, showing separately total employment and employment of persons with or requiring secondary schooling or above.

TABLE 2.1

Output, employment and educated manpower
by economic sector in Zambia, 1965

Sector	Value[1] added	Employment		
	£ m.	Total ('000s)	Persons with or requiring secondary education or above ('000s)	Col. 3 as % of col. 2 %
Agriculture: subsistence	21.7	500[2]	—	—
non-subsistence	5.5	25.4	1.2	4.7
Mining	148.7	53.7	8.8	16.4
Manufacturing	20.0	34.5	6.0	17.4
Construction	17.3	44.6	3.3	7.4
Commerce and finance	43.6	24.4	9.1	37.2
Transport and communications	11.6	11.5	3.6	31.3
Services: government[3]	29.9	64.0	20.5	32.0
domestic	3.8	35.0	—	—
other	5.8	12.8	3.4	26.6
Total	303.9	805.9	56.0	6.5
of which modern sector	282.2	305.9	56.0	18.3

[1] GDP at factor cost.

[2] Estimate of adult males in rural areas without paid employment.

[3] Includes all government production and employment including that for specific sectors.

Source: Manpower Report, Lusaka, 1966, p. 13, which see for other notes.

Table 2.1 indicates the sharp division of Zambia's dual economy: between agriculture and non-agriculture, rural and urban, subsistence and non-subsistence. The dividing line is slightly different in each case and the contrasts are somewhat overstated since a good deal of government activities and employment is directly concerned with the rural sector. But even making allowances for this, under 10 per cent of the educated manpower employed and of the order of 10 per cent of the output produced was in agriculture. Yet agriculture is the sector which involves two-thirds of the labour force and on which the vast majority of the Zambian population—men, women and children—depend for their income and welfare.

Outside of subsistence agriculture and domestic services, it is noteworthy that agriculture and construction, the two most labour-intensive sectors (in terms of total employment per unit of output) are also the two which employ the smallest proportions of educated manpower.

Although the proportion of educated manpower employed by government is high, it is under half the proportion in Botswana, Uganda and Nigeria, the other countries for which recent comparable data are readily available. A similar picture emerges from comparing two other characteristics of the Zambian situation indicated by Table 2.1. The proportion of total population in the rural areas dependent on agriculture is lower in Zambia than in most other African countries and the proportion in urban wage-earning employment is considerably higher.

A very high proportion of Zambia's educated manpower is expatriate and it is this dependence which most obviously reveals the shortage of skilled and educated Zambians. Table 2.2 shows the breakdown of employment by race. In 1965–6, all but 4 per cent of high-level manpower with degrees and all but 12 per cent with School Certificates were non-Africans. Very few of these non-Africans were citizens. Even at the lower secondary (Form 2) level, over two-fifths of those employed were expatriate. In spite of enormous expansion of education and training in the 1960s the number of educated Zambians at the end of the decade was still too small to reduce very significantly the chronic dependence on non-citizens over almost the whole range of the country's most skilled and influential occupations.

Table 2.3 puts these figures in perspective by comparing them with those of other countries in West, East, and Southern Africa. With the exception of Botswana, Zambia in recent years has been far more dependent on expatriate manpower than Kenya, Tanzania, Nigeria, or the Sudan, a representative selection of East and West anglophone

TABLE 2.2

*Actual educational qualifications of the Zambian employed
labour force, 1965–6*

Actual educational level	Africans	Non-Africans	Total	Percentage non-Africans
Degree	150	3,500	3,650	95.7
Diploma or 'A' level	500	5,900	6,500	92.0
Secondary School Certificate	1,500	12,000	13,500	88.8
Form 2	7,300	11,400	18,700	61.0
All other	261,700	1,900	263,600	0.7
Total	271,100	34,800	305,900	11.4

Note: Due to rounding, some totals are not exact.

Source: Manpower Report, p. 14.

Africa. The contrasts between Zambia and the other countries exist at all levels from graduate to middle secondary school. Even though the Zambian data refer to a later period than for most of the other countries, Zambia had at all educational levels far less local manpower than Nigeria and the Sudan and at all educational levels except graduates much less than Tanzania and Kenya.

TABLE 2.3

*Percentage of expatriates in high-level posts in selected
African countries*

Manpower category[2]	Botswana 1967	Kenya[1] 1964	Nigeria 1964	Sudan 1967	Tanzania 1964–5	Zambia[1] 1965–6
Degree level or equivalent	n.a.	77	39	12	82	96
Post School Certificate, 1–3 years formal education or training	96	25	5	6	23	92
School Certificate	81	54	0	2	31	88
Middle secondary school level	37	18	0	0	9	41
Total[3]	31	48	13	3	31	62

[1] Refers to all non-Africans.

[2] Some differences exist in the categories used by different countries but the categories quoted are broadly comparable.

[3] Weighted average all middle secondary school level and above.

IV DEFINITION OF MANPOWER SCARCITY

A heavy dependence on imported, expatriate manpower is only one symptom of a scarcity of skilled and educated manpower. Indeed, in itself it provides only evidence of a scarcity of educated citizens, not of educated manpower in general. Although there is additional evidence of a general scarcity of skilled and educated manpower in Zambia, it is necessary to define one's terms rather carefully if one wishes to quantify the extent of this general scarcity and to assess its effects as a constraint on development.

To those familiar with the numerous vacancies, the endless advertisements and the daily difficulties of almost all employers in recruiting and keeping skilled and educated staff in Zambia, the wish to define terms may seem somewhat academic. Surely this obvious and continuing experience is enough to establish the point?

There are, however, important contradictions between recent Zambian experience and simple interpretations of the scarcities of manpower. It is claimed, for example, that skilled and educated manpower is Zambia's scarcest resource, far scarcer than in most other African countries, let alone elsewhere. But at the same time, many sectors of the Zambian economy have since Independence grown much faster than at any other period during the previous decade and considerably faster than in most other developing countries. This apparent contradiction deserves some careful analysis.

The need for clear analysis is even greater if one wants to consider the ways in which the scarcity of skilled and educated manpower has held back development. This question requires in principle a comparison of two situations—the development which did occur against the development which would have occurred had educated manpower not been the constraint that it was. But what does it mean for educated manpower not to be the constraint that it was? That it should be no constraint at all? This would be a situation with an unlimited supply of skilled manpower—surely an unrealistic standard of comparison? That Zambia should be self-sufficient in educated manpower, free from 'excessive' dependence on expatriates? This could no doubt be a desirable political condition, but does it have economic meaning and, if this situation came about, would it eliminate the manpower constraint? And at what point does the manpower constraint give way to other constraints? Or do some or all constraints operate together? Clearly there is a need for careful analysis.

As a starting point, it is useful to distinguish (1) scarcity; (2) shortage; (3) relative scarcity (or long-run shortage).

In economic terms, skilled manpower is almost always scarce, in the sense that it has a positive marginal social product: the potential to produce things that people want. Scarcity is thus the typical condition in which almost all goods, services and economic resources are found. In this sense, skilled manpower in Zambia is obviously scarce, but, since almost every other economic resource is too, it is hardly surprising and not very noteworthy.

Shortage, in contrast, is a market condition. At given prices (of skilled manpower, and of all other goods and services and with the existing distribution of income), a greater quantity of skills is demanded than the quantity supplied. In economic terms, the quantity of skilled seeking work falls short of the given number of skilled jobs available at the going wage and fails to reach the equilibrium given by the interaction of the short-run demand and supply schedules. Economists tend to identify the failure to reach equilibrium with a failure of prices to adjust, but as suggested later, this is only one of the reasons why shortage may exist. At any rate, shortage in this case refers to a short-run disequilibrium situation, in which the market has failed to reconcile the demands and supplies for the resource in question, and thus symptoms of shortage—overtime, vacancies, rising turnover rates, etc.—appear. Clearly, skilled manpower in recent years in Zambia has been in severe shortage in this sense, although so, of course, have other resources. Indeed, any resource which is scarce (in the sense defined earlier) can usually be thrown into shortage simply by forcing down its price.

Shortage can be illustrated in terms of the short-run supply and demand schedules familiar to economists. Shortage exists whenever, as in Figure 2.1, the quantity of skilled labour demanded (OL_{DI}) exceeds the quantity supplied (OL_{SI}) at some given wage (OW_1). In the figure, the shortage or vacancies (L_SL_D) would disappear if the wage rose to the equilibrium wage ($L_{SI}L_{DI}$).[8]

FIGURE 2.1
Short-run disequilibrium in the labour market

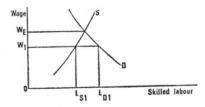

Relative scarcity—the third condition—is defined in terms of optimal balance over the long run in relation to specified objectives. The resource in greatest scarcity is the one in which present supply falls furthest short of what would be optimal. In order to make this definition workable, a number of ambiguities need to be settled.

First, one must specify the nature of the objectives in mind. In principle, the objectives can be general (e.g. to maximize output or economic growth, etc.) or highly specific (e.g. to provide a doctor-population ratio of 1:5,000 by 1980). In practice, the more specific the more risk of them being based on rigid, conflicting, or unreasonable targets. There is thus a great need to check on the mutual consistency and feasibility of the objectives as well as to check the assumptions for translating them into optimal manpower demands.[9]

Second, one must decide whether the objectives refer to the present or the future. If to the present, the question of scarcity refers to whether *past* investments in training and educating skilled manpower have been optimal in terms of *present* objectives. Under certain very restrictive assumptions, this boils down to the question of whether the economic rate of return on past investments in education and training is greater

Harvey Leibenstein provides a stimulating discussion of supply and demand conditions in relation to skilled manpower in 'Shortage and Surpluses in Education in Underdeveloped Countries', in C. A. Anderson and M. J. Bowman, *Education and Economic Development*, F. Cass, London, 1966. The above discussion refers to the supply and demand of particular types of skilled or educated persons in the *whole* economy where one would expect the supply and demand schedules to be well behaved, with the supply fairly inelastic (affected only by changes in migration and participation rates), and the demand with an elasticity somewhat less than unity. The latter follows because a high proportion of skilled and educated manpower tends to be employed in government and teaching and a lower proportion in private services and industry. The number of skilled and educated persons government can afford to employ—from any given revenue—will vary indirectly with their level of wages, implying *cet. par.* a price (wage) elasticity of about unity. The elasticity in the private service sector is probably somewhat lower and in the industrial sector extremely low, approaching zero. Although no study of the elasticity of demand for educated manpower in Zambia is available, I would estimate that the combination of these factors would lead to an overall elasticity for broad categories of educated labour of between $-\frac{1}{2}$ and -1.

[9] Economists tend to emphasize economic feasibility but it is, of course, only one of the dimensions involved. Lack of political or social feasibility can just as quickly lead to a failure to implement a programme (in the present sense of failing to translate objective into effective economic demands for skilled manpower) as lack of economic feasibility.

or less than the return on other investments. If objectives refer to the
future, then the question is whether *present* investments in education
and training are optimal in terms of meeting *future* objectives. Although
under certain circumstances, optimality for present objectives will be
the same as optimality for future ones, in principle they are different
questions and should be treated separately.

Once objectives are defined, together with the optimal balance of
resources required to implement them, it is possible to construct future
demand and supply curves and to make the concept of relative scarcity
operational. Figure 2.2 illustrates the position, showing short-run
demand and supply curves for the base period (as in Figure 2.1)
together with the demand curve for some future date and the future
supply curve corresponding to future short-run supply in optimal
balance with the supply of other resources. Relative scarcity refers to the
amount by which present supply falls furthest short of future optimal
supply relative to the shortfalls of other resources.

FIGURE 2.2

Long-run disequilibrium in the labour market

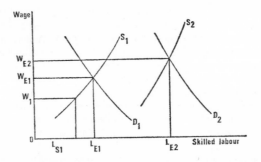

At this point further ambiguities must be considered. Should long-
run shortage be defined in terms of the *absolute* or the relative increase in
supply required to move from the present to the future position? And
should the base line from which to measure the required shift in supply
be the optimal (OL_{EI}) or the actual (OL_S) quantity of the scarce resource
at present supplied? These are important distinctions as Figure 2.2 shows.

In principle, the most satisfactory measure would be based on the size
of the relative shift required in the whole supply schedule. This would
ensure that the definition and measure of supply change was not affected by
whether or not the initial or final situations were actually in equilibrium.

If this is accepted, the resource in greatest long-run shortage or scarcity would be the one for which the required shift in the short-run supply schedule was proportionally greatest over the period considered. In order to avoid ambiguity, the shift in the supply schedule would have to be measured (like an income elasticity) as the proportional change in supply and *for some defined* and *constant* level of prices and other inputs,[10] possibly those corresponding to market equilibrium in the short run.

At this point one may contrast the above definition of long-run shortage with an alternative version, based on relative rates of return. In principle the starting point from which to derive this alternative definition would be similar,[11] based on supply and demand schedules for

10 With difference in prices, etc. the relative shift in supply schedules might well be different, and thus also the rank ordering of resources in long-run scarcity. In Figure 2.2 for example, the measurement of relative shift of the supply schedules from S_1 to S_2 will be different if

$$\frac{OL_{S2}}{OL_{S1}}$$ is measured at the wage level W_1, W_{E1} or W_{E2}.

11 It is worth stressing this point, since a great deal of confusion has been engendered by the debate on manpower forecasting versus rate of return techniques. As techniques for future planning, both approaches in principle attempt to forecast optimal points of intersection on future supply and demand curves. But each approach involves short cuts and approximations, which can be illustrated by reference to Figure 2.2. Manpower planners have tended (with exceptions) to concentrate on shifts in terms of required balance between the quantity demanded and the needed supply. Rate of return proponents have tended to concentrate on the present price (wage) structure, to assume that future wages (sometimes more cautiously that the future *relative* wage structure) will not be different (i.e. ignoring *shifts* in the supply and demand curves—or at least all but shifts which leave relative wage and price relationships unchanged), and to expound their methodology in terms of the costs and benefits of adjustments along the schedules which raise or lower the return on education relative to the marginal return on other investments. This assumes in principle variable factor proportions, though in practice the calculations have been based on constant proportions, since wages have been assumed unchanged on the assumption that only marginal changes were being considered. Ideally for non-marginal changes over time (the essence of the problem) one would take account of both *movements along* the demand curve over time, together with departure of the (market) demand curve from the curve of social marginal product. In practice economists are still in the era of making crude approximations to this ideal. The choice between manpower planning and rate of return methods hinges largely on whether shifts in the demand curve are quantitatively more important than movements to the optimum along it (from the present actual wage position) in contributing to the total increase in the optimum quantity of manpower demanded.

both the present and future periods, though in practice its proponents are usually more trustful of the market and less inclined to derive future demand curves from plan targets. But the big difference is in the definition of relative scarcity. This would be defined in terms of the relative rates of return on investment in additional future supplies of each scarce resource. Since the marginal product of additional supply depends on the position and elasticity of the future demand curves as well as on the quantity supplied, this definition could well give a different ordering of scarcity from the first. Indeed, resources in equal long-run shortage by the first definition would be valued by the second definition in order of the relative inelasticity of their demand curves, the one with the most inelastic demand being the scarcest in supply. While there is a certain logic in this ordering since it corresponds to the highest return for marginal short-run changes, it is less convincing over longer periods, when larger changes in supply are involved. Moreover, when market imperfections are important, the meaningfulness of such calculations is highly questionable.

V THE EVIDENCE FOR SHORT-RUN SHORTAGE AND LONG-RUN SCARCITY

Having defined terms, we can now consider the evidence for shortage and scarcity of skilled manpower in Zambia over the period since Independence.

Without any doubt, skilled manpower in Zambia in the last few years has been in exceptionally severe shortage in the sense of short-run market disequilibrium. The number of unfilled Division I and II vacancies for government reached nearly 4,000 in 1966, equivalent to over a quarter of all government posts at this level. Skilled vacancies reported in the private sector in the 1965–6 Manpower Survey amounted to only about 2.7 per cent of total skilled employment but the enormous number of job advertisements and the open frustrations of many employers unsuccessful in their attempts to hire additional staff leaves no doubt that actual vacancies were much greater. Moreover there is evidence to suggest that skilled shortage became increasingly more severe. Over the period 1963–8, the number of vacancies in skilled jobs registered with the labour exchanges rose from about half to nearly twice the number of persons seeking skilled jobs. At the beginning of this period, over three-quarters of registered job vacancies were filled within the year. By 1968, the proportion was scarcely a quarter.[12]

As expected, these extreme skill shortages led to sharp competition for such supplies of skilled manpower as were available and to various somewhat haphazard attempts to strengthen or expand recruitment from other countries. In some parts of the labour market, competition took conventional forms—employers bidding up wages or increasing fringe benefits, wage scales, or the point along the scale at which any individual or skill group would start. In the government or the mines, where open wage competition was limited by unified scales and various rules, competition usually took the form of offering persons more rapid promotion, often to more senior jobs in another ministry or department, sometimes also upgrading the new job, in order to make it senior enough to be attractive. It is not at all clear that this round of promotions served any useful purpose, since it did little to improve the allocation of skilled manpower (as opposed to altering it) and it did virtually nothing to expand the total supply. Even promotion by shifting was in time in part controlled within government by the establishment of a civil service manpower committee with power to veto transfers within government departments and place a ceiling on the numbers of Zambian school leavers which the mines would be allowed to recruit each year.

All of this set limits on the extent of competition, and forced many employers and government ministries to live with their shortages. Although wages rose rapidly, increases were general and widespread, differentiating little between particular skills or occupations and heavily influenced by the major salary revisions within government and the mines in 1966, following from the Brown and Whelan Commissions. The clearest indication of these imperfections in the labour market is that earnings for the unskilled rose so much faster than for the skilled, in spite of growing urban unemployment.

Unfortunately data are not available to document exactly the rise in wages of skilled manpower. Table 2.4 shows the nearest information available—increases in average earnings of Africans and non-Africans.

[12] This occurred concurrently with a marked decline in the number of vacant jobs registered, suggesting that many employers no longer found it worth their while to use the labour exchanges to try to find skilled staff. Increasing use was, however, made of the labour exchanges for hiring unskilled labour, possibly so that private employers could be seen to be expanding employment in as fair a way as possible and so defend themselves against government pressures to expand unskilled employment even faster.

Data on non-African earnings are poor proxy for skilled earnings but the figures leave no doubt about the very large increases which occurred. Non-African wages increased at an accelerating pace from 1963 to 1966, the rate averaging 8.9 per cent per annum over the four years 1963 to 1967, compared with 2.8 per cent per annum over the previous decade.

TABLE 2.4

Annual increases in wages and prices in Zambia, 1963–8

(% *per annum*)

	1963–4	1964–5	1965–6	1966–7	1967–8	Average 1963–4 to 1966–7
Non-African earnings (mainly skilled labour)	3.9	6.2	16.9	9.0	(5.4)[1]	8.9
African earnings (largely unskilled labour)	19.4	12.0	12.1	38.8	(5.1)[1]	19.5
Imported capital goods[2]	—	-7.7	+35.2	+1.4	—	8.5
Consumer price index[3]	3.8	5.9	7.9	5.1	9.9	5.7
GDP (factor cost current prices)	13.3	18.1	17.4	13.8	—	15.7

[1] Preliminary estimate.

[2] F.o.b. index for machinery and transport equipment, adjusted to include a c.i.f. component, on the assumption that total expenditure on c.i.f. is allocated among all imports in proportion to their value.

[3] Index for both low- and high-income groups. Low-income group index rose slightly faster, high-income slightly slower, averaging 4.6% per annum from 1963–7.

Source: Calculated from data in Tables 4, 23, 50, 56 and 58, *Monthly Digest of Statistics*, Government Printer, Lusaka, 1969.

Although only the broadest order of magnitude can be gauged by these figures, the effects on demand and supply are fairly clear. On the demand side, the large rise in skilled earnings was accompanied by an even larger rise in unskilled earnings, averaging over 19 per cent per annum, and a fluctuating but also sizeable increase in machinery prices averaging nearly 9 per cent per annum. Thus, far from the rise in skilled earnings representing an increase in the price of skilled manpower relative to other factors, it in fact meant little change in relation to the price of capital[13] and a considerable decrease in relation

[13] The price of capital is a notoriously tricky concept, let alone statistic. In this case, it refers to the price index of imported machinery given in Table 2.4.

to the price of unskilled labour. The net result almost certainly increased the pressure on private employers (increasingly exerted over the previous ten years), to substitute skilled manpower and capital for unskilled labour, rather than the reverse. Thus, if anything, the effect of price changes would have been to *increase* slightly the demand for skilled manpower (relative to other *factors*) rather than to reduce it.

Far more important than any substitution in the *pattern* of demand for inputs was the increase in the general *level* of demand due to the enormous expansion of production in the economy. In economic terms, the rightward *shift* in the demand curve for skilled manpower (linked to the expansion of output) far outweighed any move *along* the curve (due to changes in relative factor prices). Gross domestic product at current factor cost expanded by an average of 15.7 per cent per annum from 1963 to 1967. Although a constant price series is not available, it is unlikely that the expansion in real output was less than about 10 per cent per year[14] over the period, and the rate was probably higher during 1965 and 1966, as government spending accelerated under the impetus of the development plans and the emergency expenditure of the UDI crisis. Since much of this expenditure occurred in the sectors which used high proportions of skilled and educated manpower, especially manufacturing and education, the shift in the demand for skilled manpower must have been considerable, an increase of at least a quarter and more likely of about a third over the three years following Independence.[15]

On the supply side, the main changes have almost certainly been due to migration, education, and training, the result of general changes of economic policy and institutions, rather than of changes in short-run price and market conditions. But before turning to these longer-run

[14] The physical index of mineral production fell by 4 per cent from 1964–7. GDP in all sectors other than mining rose by 115 per cent which, after deflation by the consumer price index, for all its imperfections, gives an average increase of 21.3 per cent p.a. Combining these two indices gives an estimate of the real increase in output of 11.6 per cent p.a.

[15] It is of course difficult to be precise about the size of this increase in demand. There is no statistical series on skilled employment over time and even if there were, it would show only the shift between points of disequilibrium, not the movement of the equilibrium points of the demand schedules. Since the points of disequilibrium are as much given by the supply of skilled manpower as by demand, and supply increased little over the period (as shown later), the actual increase in skilled employment must also have been fairly small.   (*Continued overleaf*)

factors, the effects of changes in hours of work and labour force participation rates should be considered.

The increase of 8.9 per cent per annum in average skilled earnings was accompanied by an increase of 4.6 per cent in prices—giving an average increase of 4.3 per cent per annum in real terms. It is not possible to be sure how much of this corresponds to an increase in average earnings per hour and how much to an increase in the number of hours worked. Hours of work for many government officials remained at $37\frac{1}{2}$ hours per week, a remarkably low level in view of the shortage of skilled manpower and probably a reflection of a general weakness of management and incentives within the civil service. In the private sector, skilled staff generally worked longer hours than in the public sector, and as the pressures built up, the hours were sometimes lengthened considerably either in formal overtime or in other ways. (And, of course, in government many individuals worked longer hours on a voluntary basis, particularly at the senior levels.)

In contrast to the increase in hours, the proportion of all skilled persons employed in the labour force shows no clear trend. Over the two years from 1963 to 1965, the participation rate of the non-African population in the wage-earning labour force increased slightly from 37.4 per cent, but then dropped to reach 35.4 per cent in 1968. Given all the uncertainties of the data, and the changing age, sex, and national composition of the expatriate population, this fluctuation is difficult to interpret.[16]

The shift of roughly a quarter to a third in the demand schedule is based on the same methodology as the 1965–6 Manpower Survey; broadly assuming that the shift in each demand schedule for skilled manpower (secondary school leavers and above) is the same as the sectoral increases in output, but in this case over the period 1964 to 1967. The demand for teachers and other public sector manpower was estimated directly from government programmes. Even this methodology embodies an assumption which underestimates the shift in demand since it is based on the growth in economic production which actually took place, not the growth which would have taken place had the supplies of skilled manpower been in equilibrium and not in shortage and relative scarcity.

[16] It is interesting to note that the labour force participation rate for non-Africans in 1954 was 42 per cent higher than at any period since Independence. Without a sample survey, it is virtually impossible to calculate the participation rate of skilled and educated Africans. But the size and rapid expansion of full-time secondary and higher education means that the labour force participation rate for Africans in this group will be low, in spite of the pressures for Africanization and the relatively low proportion of females in this group.

But as mentioned already, the main influences on the supply of skilled manpower have been education, training, and migration. In economic terms all of these lead to shifts in the short-run labour supply schedule, possibly influenced by relative changes in earnings, but mainly by changes in education, training, and recruitment policy.

Enormous programmes of education and training were undertaken in Zambia after Independence. Secondary school intake increased three-fold in two years (1966 and 1967). The University of Zambia in its first year enrolled more Zambians than had ever attended university before. Technical education and teacher training were expanded and there was hardly a specialist institution without additional facilities and an enlarged intake. Table 2.5 summarizes some of the figures.

TABLE 2.5
General[1] educational expansion in Zambia,
1963–8
('000)

	1963	1964	1965	1966	1967	1968
Primary—final year enrolments	10.4	13.0	31.0^2	36.1	41.9	49.2
Secondary—total enrolments	7.1^3	13.9	17.2	24.0	34.1	42.4
University enrolments	(4)	(4)	(4)	0.312	0.504	0.688

[1] Excludes technical teacher training and adult education.
[2] The full primary course was shortened from 8 to 7 years in 1966, giving two cohorts to terminate their education in 1965.
[3] Excludes enrolments in non-African schools which became multiracial fee-paying schools in 1964.
[4] Various university students were studying abroad, but their numbers are not available.

Source: Ministry of Education Statistics, 1968.

Because of the time lag between providing education and obtaining its benefits, the post-Independence expansion had little impact on the supply of skills to the labour force. Educated job seekers up to 1969 were almost all Zambians who had started their secondary, technical, or university education before Independence. And the number joining the labour force from the secondary schools, let alone completing university or other post-secondary education, did not add more than a few per cent to the total stock of such persons. Moreover, those who did complete their education were young, thus further limiting their net addition to effective supply in the short run. Training and experience were probably more significant than formal education in their effects on the supply of skilled manpower over this period. There must have been a considerable increase in skills due to formal and informal training for upgrading persons already employed in the labour force. By its very nature, this is notoriously difficult to measure, and comprehensive data are not available. But in 1966, some form of in-service training was provided for about 60 per cent of persons in private sector jobs requiring secondary education or above, and for perhaps half of government employment at the time. It is difficult to assess the impact of this on the level of skill and competence of the labour force over this period since it depends on the effectiveness of the training actually provided, not on the number of employees for whom training was potentially available. Moreover, formal training, like education, is only part of basic job preparation and opportunities for gaining experience and learning on the job under efficient supervision are probably the most important, though least easily measured, factor.

Although it is not possible to be precise about the quantitative changes in the supply of skilled manpower, one can summarize the order of magnitude of all these effects. At the end of 1965 the number of Africans in jobs requiring secondary education or above was 2,200. However considerable the short-term training or upgrading programmes, by the end of 1967 they could not have added more than about 2,000 to 2,500 to the stock of educated manpower. Although proportionately very large, in relation to the stock of educated Africans this would represent an increase of only 8 or 10 per cent in the total numbers employed (African and non-African) at this level.

Moreover, over the same period, the total number of non-Africans in employment declined by about 2,300, in parallel with the decline in the total non-African population of the country. Probably the bulk of these were in low-skilled posts which had been localized. In addition, with the continuing turnover of expatriates, there was probably some increase in the level of posts for which expatriates were recruited and a good deal of rapid promotion of expatriates already in posts. The extent to which this really raised the average skill level of expatriates employed is debatable, though it may well have risen slightly. But after taking account of all these factors, it seems unlikely that the effective number of skilled and educated expatriates can have risen by more than a few per cent. Speculative though it is, the overall increase in the supply of skilled manpower from 1964 to 1967 could not have been more than at most 10 or 15 per cent, markedly less than the outward shift in demand over the same period.

This evidence on changes in the supply and demand for educated manpower can now be summarized in relation to the question of relative long-run scarcity, defined by the amount by which supply at any one period falls short of what is optimal for long-run objectives. Over the period considered, evidence suggests that the demand for skilled manpower increased rapidly, and certainly faster than the supply. If, therefore, skilled manpower was in long-run scarcity or even optimal supply at the beginning of the period, it would have been in long-run scarcity by the end.

At this point, it would be nice to have firm evidence that skilled manpower was in fact in optimal supply or in long-run scarcity at the beginning of the period, in order to clinch the argument. But although there is ample evidence that local supplies of skilled manpower (i.e. African or potential Zambian citizens) were continuously in long-run scarcity for some years, there is no direct evidence of the total supplies of skilled manpower from which to judge the overall position, except in 1965–6.

But at least for 1965–6, admittedly after two years during which the demand for skills moved ahead of supply, one can compare the Zambian position with that for a number of other countries, developed and under-developed, for which comparable data are available. The results, summarized in Table 2.6, reveal an extreme situation.

In comparison with up to 12 developed and 12 less developed countries, for all of which data were available, Zambia's ratio of skilled labour to capital was the lowest and the ratio of skilled labour to output almost the highest. These are both characteristics one would expect to find in a country in which skilled manpower was scarce relative to capital and labour. In comparison with other LDCs, Zambia's capital-labour ratio is high, even though in comparison with more developed countries it is the lowest.

Too much cannot be read into these comparisons since they neglect structural differences in the mix of outputs, inputs, and techniques between countries. In effect, the comparisons are based on the assumption that all countries operate on the same production function. One can qualify this assumption in a few ways and show that the conclusions still hold, but ultimately some such assumption will be implied whenever the comparisons are to be treated as meaningful. If account is taken of the level of output per worker in the comparisons, the above conclusions are generally strengthened: the skill-capital ratio would not only have to rise but would have to rise more rapidly than output

TABLE 2.6

Comparison of factor input and output ratios in Zambia with ratios in certain other developed and less developed countries

Ratios	Symbol	No. of countries in comparison		Zambia ratio in relation to	
		LDCs	DCs	other LDCs	DCs
Skilled manpower / Total employment	$\dfrac{S}{L}$	9	12	Average in whole economy; low in manufacturing sector; high in transport sector	Low in whole economy and manufacturing sector; average in transport
Skilled manpower / Output	$\dfrac{S}{O}$	6	10	Very low	Very low
Capital stock / Total employment	$\dfrac{K}{L}$	5–12	5–12	Very high	Very low
Skilled labour / Capital stock	$\dfrac{S}{K}$	(1)	(1)	Low	Average

[1] No direct data available: calculated from $\dfrac{S}{L}$ and $\dfrac{K}{L}$ ratios.

Note: Most of the above conclusions are based on a number of different comparisons for different types of skilled manpower stock defined either by educational level or occupational group. In most cases, the various comparisons point to the same conclusion, summarized in the table.

Source: Calculated from tables given in OECD, *Occupational and Educational Structure of the Labour Force and Levels of Economic Development*, OECD, Paris, 1969.

per worker if Zambia is to reach ratios comparable to those of more developed countries.

Nor can these differences be explained solely in terms of the high productivity of Zambia copper mining. Separate data for the manufacturing sector are available for Zambia and certain other countries: these data in no way contradict the above conclusions.

Further support for the argument that total supplies of skilled manpower were increasingly in long-run scarcity in relation to other factors is found by referring to relative costs and prices. The costs of skilled labour relative to the cost of capital, or even more strikingly to the cost of unskilled labour in Zambia, must be significantly above the comparable ratios in most developed countries. Although exact comparisons are difficult, the level of average earnings in Zambia in 1965–6 can be shown in relation to comparable figures for other countries, as given in Table 2.7.

TABLE 2.7

Average annual earnings of males in Zambia, India and the UK by level of education (£ per annum)

Level of education	Zambia[1] 1965		India[2] 1961	UK[3] 1964–5
	African	Non-African		
Degree level	1,368	2,359	} 311	1,540
Diploma or 'A' level	572	1,992		1,278
'O' level	622	1,589	185	1,177

[1] Private sector only.
[2] Urban workers only.
[3] Sample of workers in electrical engineering.

Source: Zambia: *Manpower Report*, p. 69.
India: Blaug, Layard and Woodhall, *The Causes of Graduate Unemployment in India*, Penguin Books, London, 1969.
UK: Blaug, Peston and Ziderman, *The Utilization of Educated Manpower in Industry*, Oliver and Boyd, London, 1967. Calculated from data p. 34.

From the figures it seems clear that the cost of educated labour in Zambia must have exceeded that in many developed countries by an amount comparable with or greater than the margin by which transportation and other charges raised the cost of imported capital. The evidence given earlier on rapid rise in salaries and the larger number of vacancies makes it clear that even these prices must have been well below the short-run market equilibrium prices.

The significance of the data on African earnings is not that they indicate short-run marginal cost (which because of absolute supply limitations they do not) but that they show the direction in which future costs of educated manpower in Zambia may tend. With the increase in local supply, at least in the long run, the relative cost of skills in relation to capital may be expected to be reduced considerably. And at that stage, the relative scarcity of skilled and educated manpower will give place to a more optimal relationship with other factors.

In view of these long-run prospects, it may be useful to end this section with a more formal summary of the long-run picture, based on projections of Zambia's growth and manpower demand until 1980, given in Zambia's 1966 *Manpower Report*. The basic data and assumptions for these projections are given in Appendix A of the report. Table 2.8 summarizes the implied growth rates from 1965–6 to 1970 and 1980.

TABLE 2.8

Projected increases in GDP and manpower inputs to
reach 1970 and 1980 plan targets in Zambia
(annual percentage increase from base year)

	GDP constant prices	Total wage earning employment	Skilled manpower Total	Locally trained citizens
1965–6 to 1970	11.0	7.0	13.0	n.a.
1965–6 to 1980	7.6	n.a.	10.1	30.5

n.a.=not available.

Source: Calculated from data in *Manpower Report*, Appendix D.

Table 2.8 shows dramatically how skilled manpower is in extreme long-run scarcity relative to all labour and, by implication, to capital. The required growth over the 15-year period in locally trained skilled manpower is four times the growth in GDP and even more as a multiple of the growth of total employment. Although no projections are available on capital requirements over the whole period, it seems inconceivable that capital requirements could rise so rapidly in relation to economic growth. For example, even if the capital-output ratio were to double over the period from its relatively high level of about 4 in 1965–6 to the extremely high figure of 8 in 1980, the required growth in the capital stock would still be only 13.7 per cent per annum, well under half the required growth in locally educated manpower.

This conclusion of course largely reflects the starting position of so few Zambians in high-level posts and the planning decision to reach virtually complete localization in 1980.[17] But even if one considers the

---

[17] One reader of an earlier draft thought that this target date for virtually complete localization ought to be questioned, in view of the extremely rapid expansion in education which it required. In the light of the economic effects of employing large numbers of expatriates, analysed in section VI, one might well question whether on economic grounds an even earlier date was not preferable. But whatever the economic costs and benefits of earlier or later target dates, it should be clear that localization, like other policies closely related to educational expansion, is only in part an economic question. Objectives and implications of localization can thus be properly assessed only within a much broader framework of analysis.

required growth in *total* supply of educated manpower, without regard for nationality, the rate is high in relation to the likely growth of labour or capital. This is particularly true if one accepts that the high ratios of skills to capital and labour which existed during 1964-7 will gradually be reduced as the supply of lower-cost manpower increases and dependence on high-cost imported manpower decreases. If the skill-capital ratio is to be reduced in this way, the growth of skilled manpower will clearly have to exceed the growth of capital. This again confirms the view that skilled manpower *in general* is in long-run scarcity in Zambia, even if in less extreme scarcity than locally educated manpower.

VI THE EFFECTS OF SHORTAGE AND SCARCITY OF SKILLS AND EDUCATION

Behind the statistics of the earlier sections lies a remarkable paradox. Skilled and educated manpower in Zambia over the period was both in extreme shortage and relative scarcity, not only in comparison with other key resources in Zambia but also in comparison with the relative scarcity of skilled manpower in other developing countries. Yet at the same time the rate of economic growth in Zambia was exceptionally rapid, not only in comparison with earlier periods in Zambia but in comparison with growth rates achieved in other countries. Clearly this rapid growth was called forth by the opportunities and ambitious plans after Independence and in large part fired by the mounting levels of foreign exchange and government revenue made available from the high value of copper exports, royalties, and taxation. But whatever its origins, the rate of growth embodied exceptionally rapid expansion of physical production in almost every sector outside of the mining industry. How was this possible, given the concurrent and exceptional scarcities of skilled educated manpower?

In brief, there are two main explanations. First, that growth, though rapid, was not as rapid as it would have been if skilled manpower had been in optimal balance with other resources, instead of in shortage and relative scarcity. Second, that growth as measured by statistics of output and national income[18] misses out a great deal of what is important for assessing change in the quality and standard of living as

[18] See data on pp. 15–17.

well as change in the economic, political, and social structure on which future development will depend. Thus both in respect of consumption and investment, Zambia's growth of national income over recent years probably overstates the changes that have taken place.

This final section of the chapter considers further these two explanations in their effects on:

(a) the rate and structure of growth, particularly in the rural areas;

(b) the 'quality' of growth, particularly in education and other services;

(c) the distribution of income and strategic political choices.

The rate and structure of growth, particularly in the rural areas

On the assumption of decreasing marginal returns to factors, it is a simple matter to show that sub-optimal supplies of skilled manpower will lead to a lower output, and a lower potential rate of future growth than would be the case if all factors were in optimal balance. And at a general level, this is the explanation of why Zambia's growth rate, rapid though it has been, has, in fact, been less than it might have been given the other resources available.

This general explanation can be illustrated by a few examples of the particular ways in which the growth and structure of the Zambian economy have been held back by the shortages and scarcities of skills.

The obvious ways in which the combination of too little skill with too much capital and other resources has shown itself are in wasteful use of raw materials, inadequate maintenance and repair of capital, excessive imports, neglected entrepreneurial opportunities, poorly cultivated land, and so forth. Examples of inefficiency in the use of resources can be found of course in any economy, but in recent years such examples have occurred throughout Zambia to a degree and at a frequency which is exceptional. Most striking of all perhaps has been the waste of trucks, tractors, and agricultural equipment destroyed or damaged by unskilled operation and inadequate maintenance. The 'hell run' along the road from Tanzania to Zambia blazed a trail of damaged vehicles, rusting reminders of the enormous cost of skill shortages, compounded by the urgencies of a national emergency.

Skill scarcities have also been at least partly responsible for excesses in many building projects, excessive standards, excessive use of materials, and a poor quality of finished product relative to cost, the combined result of shortages of skill and of expertise in design, decision-making and implementation. And weaknesses in construction projects have been paralleled by rising costs and inefficiencies in manufacturing. Where there has been quality control, the rate of rejections will have risen; where there is no quality control, the standard of the final product will have fallen, not invariably but often.

In the mining industry it seems that rough use over long hours with inadequate maintenance has reduced the expected life of some underground machinery from 10 to 4 years. Yet the quality of management, and indeed the supplies of skilled manpower at all levels within the mining industry, have probably been maintained much more adequately than in other sectors of the economy. This is the result partly of a massive training and upgrading programme, partly of a skilful reallocation and some subdivision of job requirements and responsibilities, partly of a continuing programme of expatriate recruitment, though increasingly from sources outside Southern Africa.

It is important to emphasize that this wasteful use of materials and capital has often gone far beyond what could be described as an economically optimal increase in the use of capital and materials to offset sub-optimal numbers and levels of skilled staff. In economic terms, the shortage of skills has generally *not* been balanced by a rational calculation of how much additional capital and other inputs to use, but has led to a marked decline in the application of rational management in the allocation of resources. This is not meant pejoratively, but as an objective description of the results of extreme skill shortages. Ample illustrations could be given in the day-to-day administration of the railways, private firms, government ministries and departments, provincial and rural headquarters. It is, to repeat, in no sense a unique situation: but the shortage of skills at Independence, the inevitable delays in local training, the bottlenecks in recruitment from abroad, the rapidity of growth, the surge in the government revenue and foreign exchange, the structural changes arising from Independence and UDI all produced these symptoms of skill shortage in much more acute form in Zambia than in most other countries, developed or developing.

Apart from its effects on growth, the shortage of skills severely distorted the economic structure which has developed. When skills are limited, where they are deployed becomes doubly significant. In Zambia, the rural areas inevitably lost out in the competition for the skills which were available. Within the United National Independence Party, within government administration, in the allocation of administrators, mechanics, doctors or building foremen, planners and professional expertise, the rural areas usually received lower priority than the towns. The result is that a disproportionate part of growth and development has been concentrated in the Copperbelt and Lusaka. Again this tendency can be found in most developing countries, but in Zambia in exceptional form. The rural areas received fewer and lower quality staff than the towns, in spite of the Cabinet's priorities and genuine efforts to the contrary. The result was that in comparison to urban developments, rural projects and programmes were, in size and number, slower to start, took longer to implement, and were often severely delayed before completion.

An important exception was in the secondary school building programme, where a deliberate attempt was made to locate schools in the rural areas and to build them of a size large enough to attract construction companies with their equipment and skilled staff (often recruited from abroad). But these were an exception, and the inadequate designs and high costs of the schools (even after allowing for some hasty cost reductions made at the late design stage) show the toll which skill shortages took, even though their net benefit to the rural areas will hopefully be considerable.

A second major distortion in structure followed almost inevitably from the employment of such a dominant number of expatriates in so many of the skilled and educated positions in both the public and private sectors. These expatriates, mainly from Britain, Rhodesia, or South Africa, contributed not only their skills but the far-reaching influence of their attitudes, their political views and priorities. One need not be racialist or chauvinist to recognize that these were often sharply at variance with those of the majority of Zambia's citizens, to say nothing of her political leaders. And the contrast was made even greater by the polarizing effects of the illegal declaration of independence by Rhodesia and the successive but ineffective attempts by Britain to deal with it.

Some examples may show the wide variety of aspects encompassed by these expatriate influences. First, in consumption standards: in 1967, the average earnings of non-Africans were 23 times the *per capita* income of Zambia, roughly ten times the ratio of skilled earnings to *per capita* income found in developed countries. Such incomes were spent on large houses, cars, boats, clothes, radios, food, holidays to Rhodesia and South Africa—all obvious forms of consumption that strengthened the sense of inequality between expatriate and local, white and black. The result was local ambitions and expectations far beyond anything that could be generally within the nation's grasp for several generations. Again this phenomenon is not unique to Zambia and it is impossible to tell to what extent it was responsible for the higher wage demands and wage levels which followed. But undoubtedly expatriate living standards have had important effects in many African countries, and greater effects in Zambia where the proportion of expatriates is larger, the differentials greater, and the sense of racial injustice among urban Africans probably greater than in most other independent African countries.

Probably the most important effect of these wide expatriate/local differentials was in inhibiting government from taking a strong stand on wage claims in mining, government, and elsewhere. Rapid increases in the general level of wages and salaries[19] raised consumer imports and opened up throughout the economy differentials which have already limited growth, distorted the distribution of income, and which will raise severe structural problems for many years ahead.

This point is so central that a further comment is in order. From an extremely favourable position in both the balance of payments and government revenue just after Independence, Zambia had by 1968 moved to a position of near deficit in the balance of payments and great pressures on government revenue, reprieved somewhat by an upturn in copper prices. Much of the blame for this was attributed to the size of the government's programme,[20] which was accordingly cut in the 1969 budget, with predictable effects on investment, growth, and employment, particularly in the construction industry. Yet an examina-

---

[19] See the detailed analysis by J. B. Knight in Chapter 4, particularly the discussion of the Brown and Whelan Commissions (which recommended increases of 22 per cent for many workers in mining and government in 1966) and the repercussions on wages throughout the rest of the economy.

[20] Although not strictly relevant to the argument of this section, it may be useful to deal with the argument that the size of the government's programme (and the 1966–70 development plan in particular) was primarily responsible for the resulting pressures on government revenue and foreign exchange and should have been smaller. There are two replies. First, it seems clear from the evidence of expenditure increases, relative price increases, and the structure of imports that the rise in consumer demand has been a more important influence on price inflation and import increases than the rise in investment demand, let alone plan expenditures. It is also clear that by far

tion of the figures shows that almost all the rise in imports was not the result of a rise in import coefficients but of an expansion in the level of demand, in which the increase in consumer demand was greater in absolute amount than the increase in investment demand. Most of the rise in consumer demand and at least part of the rise in investment demand was the direct result of the enormous and largely autonomous increases in the level of wages and salaries. Without these increases, it is clear that the favourable position in both the government budget and the balance of payments would still persist. Such is the cost which, at least in part, must be attributed to the distorting influence of expatriate salary and consumption levels.

Less obvious are the expatriate influences on standards. Many of these are direct transfers from life in a more industrialized society, including indeed the abilities and expertise for which the expatriate is wanted and employed. But others are more debatable—ranging from ways in which the employment of an expatriate leads to the transfer of

the greater part of the rise in consumer incomes is due to the increase in the average level of incomes, not in the numbers employed. For the reasons given in this chapter it is also clear that these wage increases, particularly among the unskilled but in certain respects also among the skilled, were usually the result of cost-push rather than demand-pull factors. In this sense it is incorrect to place primary blame on the size of the plan rather than wage increases for the resulting increases in imports and prices.

A more subtle variation of the argument is that the plan was too big, not because it alone would have put undue pressure on the government revenue and foreign exchange available but because it was predictable that the plan would be accompanied by large wage increases and that, together, the plan plus the wage increases would exceed the resources available and lead to an inflationary rise in prices and imports. At this point the argument hinges on the objectives and strategy of government. Given the objective of raising the share of investment in the economy, a large investment programme was essential; if this could have been achieved with only small wage increases, this would obviously have been preferable; but even if with large wage increases, a large investment programme with inflation would be better for economic growth than to sacrifice investment for the sake of (some) price stability and a (somewhat) reduced level of imports.

Even with a smaller investment programme, it is by no means clear that price or import increases would have been greatly reduced (in view of their major causes), particularly as the large plan did at least make it clear that there was a real conflict between investment and consumption. Without this sense of conflict, the government's willingness to agree to large wage and salary increases might have been even greater, and their use of taxation and other anti-inflationary instruments even less than it has values from a different culture, society, or nation to the way it injects or strengthens the narrower interests of a higher income group, a different class, or a different race. Again the argument is not that a mixture of cultures or even interests is not healthy for a society, but that in Zambia these values and attitudes of expatriates and non-citizens have assumed an exceptional form due to the predominant position of expatriates in the higher levels of skills and occupations. Two examples may illustrate the range of issues affected.

A major problem after independence in any country is to adapt the style and structures of public administration to the new priorities of government. This is a difficult task in any situation, involving skilful judgements about how best to localize the *objectives, procedures,* and *structures* of the civil service and not merely its personnel. Localization in the first sense is more difficult than in the second, since it involves *selective* innovation and exploration of new approaches, new styles of administration, new training methods, not merely the replacement of expatriates with local staff trained in the old ways. Yet the very nature of the problem makes it a task for local citizens fired with a vision of the opportunities and challenges of independence, and having a long-run stake in the country. There must be local leadership at the political level.

Of course, this has happened in Zambia, as in other countries. But the task has been more difficult, and may prove to have been slower and less thorough than elsewhere, owing to the much smaller and less experienced number of Zambians available. Even though the statistical rate of Zambianization has been impressively rapid, the limitations in education, training and experience of many of the Zambian personnel

been. Sooner or later the conflicts between investment, consumption, and the distribution of incomes must be faced; the large investment programme brought this point forward.

None of this is to argue that the government's investment programme did not contain a number of badly designed or even misguided projects and programmes. But this is to be explained in part by the shortage of skills (especially in the administrative machine) and in part by the urgency for action. It is not clear that the *proportion* of inadequate projects would have been less with a smaller investment programme, let alone that their cost would have been reduced if part of the smaller programme. Even with all the misguided projects, it seems clear that most parts of the government's programme have made a greater contribution towards its general objectives than have the increases in private consumption arising from the increases in the level of wages and salaries.

available, particularly at the middle levels, has meant that the sizeable number of expatriates still employed have inevitably retained much more influence. And almost as inevitably, this has carried with it the tendency to perpetuate pre-Independence 'standards' and even on occasion to adopt new standards borrowed directly from the developed countries or elsewhere, rather than to assess them from within the new Zambian situation and innovate where necessary.

A particularly obvious example was the perpetuation of colonial conditions for long leave (with travel paid to Europe or South Africa): these conditions were applied to many Zambian civil servants for long after Independence, partly in order to minimize differences which might appear discriminatory between expatriate and local conditions. Less obvious but more important were certain features in the style of administration, not necessarily irrelevant or counterproductive, but often accorded a priority which conflicted with the new emphasis on development. One of the main mechanisms through which inappropriate standards were maintained was in the processing of vacancies, the grading of posts, and the qualifications required by the Establishments Division of the civil service. Architects, for example, could not be employed unless they possessed British qualifications, in spite of exceptional shortages. Housing standards also operated to inhibit recruitment by specifying a standard of housing to which each level of civil servant was entitled. The demand for housing soon exceeded the supply available, introducing a crucial constraint on further recruitment from abroad.

A second example of inappropriate standards can be drawn from a more technical field—medicine. Here again there is a tremendous need to work out styles of medical care appropriate for mass application in the rural areas. In spite of important efforts to extend rural facilities, the bulk of expenditure on both practice and training has gone to hospital care, frequently in large and expanding hospitals, as in the medical school in Lusaka. Clearly this is not just the result of expatriate pressures in any simple sense, but it is arguably the effect of external rather than local standards in the general sense.[21] At considerable

---

[21] This is important to recognize since the external influences are likely to continue, even when the Zambian medical service is fully localized. The influence of professional standards in the developed countries has a pervasive effect on medical practice in almost all developing countries, which contributes an internal brain drain of talent and effort away from the pressing health problem of the majority of the population.

cost, facilities have been built, a style of service strengthened, and doctors and staff given training in a type of system which will leave many Zambians without effective treatment.

In both these respects, inappropriate standards have distorted the structure of growth, and reduced both its present value and its suitability as the foundation for further growth. Again it is difficult to be precise and clearly the influences are by no means wholly unfortunate. But there seems little doubt that on balance over the long run the employment of a dominant proportion of expatriate staff has entailed real costs (in terms of lower growth and distorted structure) considerably above what would have been incurred had skilled local manpower been in optimal supply.

Quality of output

Besides reducing the observed growth rate, the shortage and scarcity of skills has reduced the effective quality of output, in ways which often do not show up in the national income statistics.[22] In this respect, the symptoms of skill shortage (as opposed to skill scarcity) bring their own particular biases which tend to overstate the quality of output. On the one hand, extreme market shortage leaves so many job opportunities open that many middle-level staff spend a significant amount of time reading job advertisements and making applications—both more difficult to control when skilled supervision is inadequate. Too many jobs chase too few skilled persons, to the point where turnover rates rise and many persons stay in a job too short a time even to gain much useful experience, let alone to be very productive. At the same time, competition between employers, desperate for additional staff, takes the form (particularly in government where salary scales are fixed) of upgrading the level of the post and thus the level of salary which it commands. Both these tendencies reduce the quality of output in ways which national income statistics do not reveal. The first effects tend to overstate the amount and quality of work which any individual does;

---

[22] Government services, for instance, are measured by valuing the inputs into them rather than the output, i.e. in terms of the wage bill paid to the government servants. At times when average wages have been rising more rapidly than consumer prices, the value of services appears also to rise. The development of a special price deflator for government services is possible, but few countries have achieved anything that satisfactorily reflects changes in output rather than inputs.

the second artificially inflates the number of persons employed in the higher grades (though often not doing work of that quality) and thus tends to overstate output in the service sector, even when apparently measured in constant (real input) prices. Both ways tend to overstate output in the service sector.

Perhaps more important in Zambia has been the deterioration in educational quality, particularly in secondary schools, resulting from younger, less qualified teachers staying shorter periods, in new schools, often with the support of hardly any staff with previous experience. With the surge of new secondary schools and the sudden need for additional teachers,[23] the position was rapidly reached when in some schools the most experienced teacher was an expatriate headmaster in his early twenties with less than two years' experience. The situation was in no major sense the fault of the government, let alone of the individual teachers themselves. It was the direct result of Zambian educational deficiencies at Independence, coupled with the enormous and rapid programme of expansion to deal with it. Yet the result was a serious decline in educational standards (judged by examination results) and a questionable relevance of what was taught (with too little time for teachers to work out something more relevant). It was extremely difficult for the schools to put a strong emphasis on collective values and nation building, since the expatriate teachers were the least equipped politically, culturally, or socially to do this. This loss of quality may be judged either as a lower standard of relevant education or, more economically, as a decline in the potential productivity of secondary school leavers. In the long run, this decline in quality is likely to have serious effects by carrying into the future many of the skill deficiencies (particularly of quality, increasingly less of quantity) of the present.

A further example of the repercussions of skill scarcity can be found in the operation of justice and the law courts. The number of Zambian Africans with legal qualifications was very small and none had sufficient years of experience to be a high court judge under the rules in force until 1969. In a situation already racially tense with recent memories of severe racial injustice, it was inevitably difficult for justice to appear to be done, in courts where so many of the key actors were white and expatriate. Even in lower courts, where African citizens

---

[23] The position was made worse by the very small proportion of expatriate teachers who renewed their contracts after the first two years—about 10 per cent in Zambia compared with about 30 per cent in Kenya and 50 per cent in Uganda.

predominated, problems were caused by inadequate training and experience, particularly among members of the police force giving evidence. Often reasonable cases did not succeed, because of poorly prepared or presented evidence, sometimes introducing a sense of uncertainty and arbitrariness about the whole proceeding. Respect for law and justice inevitably suffered, with major repercussions on the social and political framework of the whole country.

The distribution of income and strategic political choices

It will already be clear how much the distribution of income has been affected by the influence of manpower scarcity and the employment of expatriates. Absolute differentials within the wage and salary structure have increased enormously. Inequalities have also increased between those with wage-earning jobs and those without—the unemployed in the towns and those dependent on agriculture in the rural areas. This has been the result partly of the widening gap in earnings but also of the slow growth of employment and of the decline in the quality and distribution of government services. In short, the bulk of the wage increases went to paying employed people more than into employing more people and this, in effect, limited the numbers of persons able to enjoy the benefits of wage increases.

Less obvious were the indirect effects of scarcity and quality deterioration on the effective distribution of government services. The distortions of economic structure, already discussed, brought with them distortions in income distribution not only away from the rural areas in general but very unevenly within the rural areas. The upshot was not only greater inequality in the present, but the creation of a situation making for greater inequality in the future. The persistent scarcity of skilled and educated manpower will thus only continue the difficulties of remedying these imbalances.

Once again the tendencies towards inequality are in no sense unique to Zambia, but the exceptional scarcities of manpower exacerbate them. The key points in a society's structure on which inequality feeds include access to education and the ownership of property. This whole essay in one sense is a description of the *long-run* effects of inadequacies in Zambian education—which may well persist even longer, due to growing weaknesses in the quality of the now-expanded secondary and higher education systems. Since the Mulungushi Declaration in 1968, major moves have been taken to deal with the second source of long-run inequality: the ownership of property. Government is participating in the ownership of key industries, including the mines. There can be no doubt that in terms of the ideals of Mulungushi these were desirable moves. But to be a reality, participation means much more than a majority holding in the shares of a company or representation on the board of directors. It means the active representation of national interests in decision-making. In terms of effective participation, the continuing scarcity of skilled manpower may well delay for some while the time when these moves will achieve their full objective.

The effects of manpower scarcity on implementing the Mulungushi Declaration within the country raise even wider questions about the external objectives of the government. This is to refer to Independence, UDI and the massive attempts to reorient the country away from Southern Africa and towards the north. The major task of external reorientation forced by the irreconcilable division between Zambian values and those of apartheid and white supremacy presents Zambia with continued challenges in many fields. These include trade and political relations, discussions on the Kariba dam, the drawn-out wrangles over the railway, the border violations, and guerrilla attacks. In all of these, Zambia's objectives and ideals come into continual conflict with those of the southern countries. Little of the conflict has so far been open—for many reasons—but in part because the peace has been preserved through a lack of power, the effect of Zambia's manpower scarcity. In this respect, there is a parallel in the role of education in internal and external security of the countries to the south. Internally within these countries, the inequalities and control of education serve (with other factors) to maintain the position of the dominant white minorities within the country. Externally, the borders are guarded by the inadequacies of past education and the present dependence on expatriates in countries to the north, particularly Zambia and Malawi. In Zambia, the extreme scarcity of skilled manpower not only limits her freedom to deal with this situation, but makes her vulnerable to all the pressures and manoeuvres which follow from it. Thus the political cost of manpower scarcity is the postponement of an important degree of independence. No one acquainted with the political events of Southern Africa in the last few years or alert to their implications for the future of Africa will underestimate this cost.

3

Industrial Relations
in Zambia, 1935-69

K. QUINN, S. J.[1]

INTRODUCTION

In what sense can industrial relations be said to be a constraint on
Zambia's development? The question itself is ambiguous because if we
define development in a wider sense than the narrowly economic, good
industrial relations may be thought to be a product of the process of
development itself. Certainly in Zambia's case, economic development
and progress towards a more just and humane society can scarcely fail
to remove some of the causes of friction and bitterness—racial
discrimination, tribal and political feuding, unjust wage scales—which
have characterized a society in which industrial harmony has been
almost impossible. So when we consider the improvement of industrial
relations as a factor contributing to more rapid *economic* development,
we should bear in mind that satisfactory relationships at his place of
work is to the employee one mark of a just and, in an important sense,
developed society.

If by industrial relations we mean the whole complex of relationships, both individual and collective, which arise directly or indirectly
from organization for production or exchange, it is easy to sketch out the
connection between industrial relations and economic development.
We may distinguish between the relationships that exist between
employee and employee, between groups of employees, between
employee and employer (usually in some collective form on both sides),
and finally between employers in Chambers of Commerce, employers'
federations, or some kind of inter-industry organization. We may then
rephrase our opening question by asking whether it is true that a
restructuring of any of these relationships would lead, or would have

---

[1] Formerly Senior Lecturer in Economics, University of Zambia.

led in the period under review, to more rapid growth in any of the indicators of development. To help pinpoint the issues, we may pose some specific questions referring to each of the groups of relationships outlined above. If tribal and racial antagonisms had been less marked since Independence, would output per employee have been higher? If there had been one strong, well organized union representing all employees of the copper industry, would less output have been lost through strikes? If a mutually satisfactory pay scale had been introduced by the management and accepted by the employees of the copper industry in, say, 1962, would the very rapid rise of wages in the period 1966–8—contributing as it did to a slower rise in employment and strong inflationary tendencies—have been avoided? If employers throughout Zambia had adopted a common and progressive attitude to Zambianization in the early 1960s, would the manpower crisis that developed in 1965–6 have been less serious? These are the kind of questions we must face in this chapter. Not all of them can be answered, for quantification of opposite effects is seldom possible in this subject. But to appreciate the complexity and tenseness that are the hallmarks of industrial relations in Zambia, a fairly lengthy historical account of their development is essential.

HISTORICAL BACKGROUND

Early obstacles to the formation of unions

1 The African labour force

Until 1966, Zambia was a source of unskilled labour for Rhodesia, South Africa, the Belgian Congo, and to a lesser extent Tanzania. For example, the *Annual Report* for the year 1947 of the Northern Rhodesia Labour Department stated that 47,413 Zambians were employed in Rhodesia and a special labour officer was resident there to look after their interests, particularly in compensation claims arising from accidents and silicosis in the mines. In 1966 the Rhodesian authorities refused entry to Zambians seeking work for the first time. Only those who were returning to their previous employment were admitted, and only then provided that their absence did not exceed five months. The latest figures available estimate that in 1965 5,741 Zambians were working in the Rhodesian mines, but there are no reliable figures for the number of Zambians who are still working on Rhodesian farms. A special organization, the Witwatersrand Native Labour Association (WNLA) was licensed to recruit Zambians from the Barotse Province for work in the Rand gold mines. The contracts of work were for twelve months but could be extended for a further period not exceeding six months. It was estimated that as a rule about one-third of the workers extended their contracts. In the early sixties the number recruited was 6,800. On 14 October 1966, by government order, recruiting by WNLA came to an end—at that date there were 4,572 workers on contract.

Other countries to use imported Zambian labour were the Congo and Tanzania. In 1946 there were over 4,000 Zambians working in the Congo and 2,500 in Tanzania. Almost all of the latter came from the Northern Province and worked in the gold mines and on the sisal estates. The *Annual Report* of the Labour Department for 1948 stated:

Migration to other territories, chiefly the Congo and Tanganyika, was again on a small scale. Only 9 per cent (about 3,000) of the employees of the Union Minière Company in the Congo are Northern Rhodesian Africans. Twenty years ago the figure was in the neighbourhood of 50 per cent.

The general picture is that until recent years Zambia was exporting large numbers of unskilled workers. There was, however, the paradox that at times non-Zambians migrated in equally large numbers to seek work in Zambia, particularly in the mines. Appendix IV of the *Annual Report* of the Labour Department, 1959, gives a total of 16,562 non-Zambian Africans employed in the country: this was one-sixth of the 96,331 Africans in employment. Of the non-Zambian Africans 10,470 were employed in mining, of whom 5,236 came from Malawi and 2,709 from Tanzania. There was a decrease in subsequent years, so that in 1966 the number was 9,284, of whom 4,937 came from Malawi and 2,407 from Tanzania. The presence of such a large number of non-Zambians made the problem of forming trade unions in some ways more difficult, owing to the great diversity of tribes and countries of origin. It must be said, however, that the first strike by Africans in the mining industry was greatly helped by the Malawians, of whom quite a number held clerical or other relatively elevated posts.

The large number of Zambian workers abroad should not lead one to think that the Zambian easily took to employment for cash. From the earliest days the government used taxation as a means of inducing the young adult males to enter the labour force. Taxes had to be paid in cash, hence the need of employment for money. A further incentive was the existence of professional recruiters. Orde Browne summarizes the 1929 Employment of Natives Ordinance provisions concerning recruitment as follows:

> Recruits are licensed by the Secretary of Native Affairs. Bond (amount fixed by the Governor) at present £100 for Rhodesia, or £250 for foreign contracts. Licence must specify district of recruitment, and employers served. . . Labour Districts may be gazetted under Ordinance 41. Medical inspection of contract labourers is compulsory . . . Foreign contracts must be specially prepared for work outside Rhodesia; penalty for enticing a native without contract £100 fine or one year's imprisonment.[2]

In spite of prohibition of unlicensed recruiting, there were regular complaints in the *Annual Reports* of the Labour Department about such recruiting for farm work in Southern Rhodesia.

In the late twenties the flow of Zambian labour was mainly seasonal, the workers usually returning home from April to June to harvest their crops. C. F. Spearpoint estimated that the average period of African employment in the copper industry was only about six months.[3] There was no agreed policy among the mining companies on the question of a stable African labour force. For example Nkana made only two-year contracts; other companies tended towards a more stable labour force. The close contact of the worker with his village of origin did, however, accidentally have one good effect in the depression of the thirties which hit very hard the newly opened copper industry in Zambia. In 1930 there were 30,000 Africans in mining and development work. The number fell to 13,900 at the end of 1931 and 7,000 in 1932. That such a contraction of employment did not have serious social results was due solely to the fact that the displaced workers simply returned to their villages. An improvement took place in the second half of the thirties and World War II assured the future of copper mining. The African workers numbered 14,000 in 1937, 27,000 in 1941, and rose to 36,147 in 1953. By the 1940s the turnover rate had fallen to around 5 per cent per month. But as late as 1947 the average period of employment for those leaving the mines was only 15 months.[4] Stabilization

---

2 G. St. J. Orde Browne, *The African Labourer*, F. Cass, London, 1933, reprint, 1967, pp. 159–60.

3 'The African Native and the Rhodesian Copper Mines', *African Affairs*, July 1937, p. 53.

4 R. E. Baldwin, *Economic Development and Export Growth—a Study of Northern Rhodesia 1920–1960*, University of California Press, Berkeley, 1966, p. 110.

increased during the 1950s and the monthly turnover rate fell to 2.6 per cent; the percentage of African labour in mining employed for less than two years fell from 71 per cent in 1937 to 39 per cent in 1959. This trend has continued to the present time. In 1967 the percentage of the Zambian labour force in copper mining having two years of service or less was 14.8; those with 3 years or less represented 22.7 per cent, while only 30.3 per cent had served four years or less.[5] The average length of service in years rose from 6.5 in 1960 to 8.4 in 1967.[6] The monthly turnover fell steadily from 1.9 per cent in 1961 to 0.6 per cent in 1966.[7]

Statistics are not available on labour turnover in other Zambian industries but the overall picture is that it has fallen in recent years. Many factors have contributed to this, notably higher wages, better prospects of advancement, improved educational, medical and recreational facilities, and the catch-all category 'The attraction of the bright lights'. The situation can be summarized as follows: over the years the Zambian has acquired experience and skills in industry; he has become much less mobile in his switches from employment in the money economy to self-employment in subsistence agriculture. There remains, nevertheless, a large amount of job-switching in the money economy among unskilled workers. Gradually the Zambian industrial worker is becoming conscious of himself as an integral part of the economy. In his working life he has accepted money as the criterion of success, but in his social and family life tribal traditions are still quite strongly active. Obstacles to a sense of purposeful unity among the workers are such things as the relatively large proportion of non-Zambians in the work force, the different tribal and provincial origins of the unskilled who are illiterate and resent the promotion of younger men who have had the advantage of a full primary schooling.

2 The European labour force

As the first trade unions in Zambia were set up by and catered exclusively for Europeans, it may be useful to give some figures of the growth of the European population. From 1,497 in 1911 it grew slowly

---

[5] *Copperbelt of Zambia Mining Industry Year Book, 1967*, Copper Industry Service Bureau, Kitwe, Table 15, p. 48.
[6] ibid., Table 16, p. 49.
[7] *Statistical Year Book 1968*, Central Statistical Office, Lusaka, Table 4.12.

to 3,624 in 1921. The development of copper mining led to a large influx of immigrants, and in 1931 the European population numbered 13,846. World War II slowed down the rate of growth, and the number was 21,907 in 1946. Thereafter growth was spectacular: 37,079 in 1951, and 65,277 in 1956. The European population reached its highest point in 1962 at 77,000. Since that year there has been a small annual decline, until in December 1966 it was estimated to be 67,400.

Prior to the development of copper mining, the three main sources of paid employment for Europeans were the civil service, the railways, and the Kabwe (formerly Broken Hill) lead and zinc mine. In the 1921 census one-third of the adult European males were farmers and only 133 were employed in mining. In such conditions there was little scope for trade union activity; wage scales were determined by those paid to craftsmen working on the railways.

Europeans employed in mining numbered 3,098 in 1941 and 5,879 in 1953. This big increase is due not just to the greater economic activity that came after the war. In the early years mining was a hard life, diseases such as malaria were endemic, medical facilities were poor. Over the years disease was wiped out, hospitals of a very high quality were provided by the mining companies, good housing and schools became available, first-class recreational facilities were provided, and the Copperbelt became a most attractive place in which to live and work. The European worker no longer considered Zambia to be a place to be endured for the sake of high pay. Many of these workers intended to make Zambia their home and that of their children. They had become settlers. Others decided to stay in Zambia for the duration of their working lives. These two categories had now a vested interest in preserving their jobs, particularly in preventing their being replaced by lower-paid African labour.

The advent of trade unions

European railway employees in Zambia were catered for by the Rhodesia Railway Workers' Union and were able to slow down African advancement. In mining there was no colour bar and many African workers became carpenters, bricklayers, or semi-skilled tradesmen. The depression made it imperative that the companies should reduce costs, and one way was to replace expensive Europeans by local workers with a certain amount of experience. In 1932 a group of mine officials from the Rand considered the Zambian 'almost if not wholly equal in efficiency to the average worker on the Rand'.[8] Some unskilled and semi-skilled Europeans lost their jobs. Consequently the idea of setting up a trade union was frequently mooted. It was not, however, until after the African strike of 1935 that it was taken in hand seriously. In 1936 Charles Harris of the South African Mine Workers' Union visited the Copperbelt, where he considered that African workers had invaded the preserve of skilled labour. A branch of SAMWU was founded on the Copperbelt and supported by the Railway Workers' Union, aiming at making Zambia a 'white workers' country' by ensuring that only union men would be employed in copper mining. The branch of SAMWU became the autonomous Northern Rhodesia Mine Workers' Union in 1936 and was recognized by the companies in 1937—but its objectives were unchanged. By July 1938 it claimed to have 1,000 members, i.e. about 50 per cent of the European daily paid workers. In that year it made a 'gentleman's agreement' with the companies under which 'the relation between white and black will not be interfered with for a period of another two years'. In brief, there would be no further substitution of Zambian for European labour. Thus one of the problems of present-day industrial relations in Zambia—the need to promote Zambians—originated prior to World War II.

The second major problem of industrial relations was present from the earliest days—the low pay of the unskilled rank and file. In 1935 the average wage of Africans was £1 3s. per month, housing was poor, and workers were often physically ill-treated by white supervisors. Resentment was brought to a head by an increase in the tax on industrial workers in 1935. In May of that year there was a series of strikes at Mufulira, Nkana, Roan. A riot broke out at Luanshya in which 6 Africans were shot dead and 23 wounded. A commission of enquiry was set up to investigate the disturbance, but the African workers gained little from the strike. It did show, however, that they were capable of organizing in defence of what they believed were their rights, even though they did not have the benefit of a trade union to direct their actions.

At government level, African workers' interests were looked after, not very effectively, by the Native Industrial Labour Advisory Board until 1940, when a Labour Department was instituted. At the level of the mine their industrial, social, and family problems were dealt with by

---

[8] Quoted in R. Gray, *The Two Nations*, Oxford University Press, London, 1966, p. 93.

a committee of tribal elders under the general surveillance of the compound manager. This was in line with the government's effort to govern through tribal control. In spite of this, as urbanization grew, the worker's contacts with his native village weakened. In 1942–3 tribal elders were elected by the workers instead of being appointed by chiefs. At the same time the industrial interests of workers were, at each mine, transferred to a boss boys' committee (a boss boy was a sub-foreman responsible for a small group of workers). The tribal elders' sphere was reduced to dealing with social and family problems, and in 1951 the workers voted to end the tribal elder system altogether.

In 1940 the average European wage was £40 per month. In spite of an agreement not to strike in order to keep the war effort going, the European workers struck for higher pay and better conditions in March 1940 and won acceptance of almost all their demands, including a 5 per cent increase in wages and the closed shop system. Seeing the success of the European strike, the Africans followed suit at the end of March. Their claim was for a wage of 5s. to 10s. per day, and an end to ill-treatment by European supervisors. As proof that they were worth the proposed increase they offered to produce more ore in a shift than a gang of Europeans working on a comparable face. The companies offered them a flat 7 per cent temporary cost-of-living bonus; this was an average of 2s. 6d. per month. The offer was rejected and on 3 April 1940, a riot broke out at Nkana. Army and police fired on the crowd, killing 17 and wounding 69. The resulting Forster Commission of Enquiry gave a 2s. 6d. per month increase in wages, free protective clothing, overtime rates, and better housing for married workers. The most important recommendation for securing industrial peace was that: 'The mine managements should consider with representatives of the Government and the Northern Rhodesian Mine Workers' Union to what positions now open to him the African worker should be encouraged to advance'. This remained a dead letter. European pressure, industrial and political, was too strong. In 1942 when Roan opened a third reverbatory furnace Europeans were put in charge of the African workers who had previously worked the other two. Finally in 1946 the union won an agreement that effectively established a colour bar in the copper industry.

It had thus become clear that a trade union was essential for African workers. Late in 1943 an African Shop Assistants' and Tailors' Committee was formed in Kitwe. Similar organizations were set up at Ndola, Mufulira, Luanshya, and Chingola, and at the end of 1947 they united to form the first African trade union in Zambia, the Shop

Assistants' Trade Union. In mining, small unions were set up at four mines in 1948 and they united in 1949 to form the Northern Rhodesia African Mine Workers' Union, the strongest union in Zambia. The objectives of all the African unions were quite clear: (1) higher pay for the unskilled members, and (2) the freedom to obtain the highly paid jobs that were now under the control of European unions. Their methods were equally clear. Since Africans had no political power they had to rely on negotiation backed by the threat of strike. Often only by making the threat a reality were they able to gain concessions.

In 1947 the first breakthrough had been made when the Dalgleish Commission was set up to discover, *inter alia*,

(1) what posts, not now occupied by them, Africans are capable of filling immediately; and (2) what training facilities should be made available to Africans to enable them to advance to more responsible and skilled posts in industry and how these training facilities should be provided.

The Commission found that African mine workers were capable of doing twenty-eight different kinds of jobs hitherto confined to Europeans and recommended that these jobs be 'transferred to Africans as early and as unprovocatively as possible'. [9] The discussions between the companies and the European union ended in a deadlock and no effective steps were taken until 1955. In the meantime a second African union had been set up in 1953, the Mines African Staff Association (MASA), which was registered in 1954 and recognized by the companies as the negotiating union for African staff. NRAMWU objected strongly, claiming that it was sponsored by the companies in order to weaken the bargaining position of the African Mine Workers' Union. This dispute between the African unions continued until 1966 and greatly weakened their effectiveness.

As a result of an approach by the companies, quadripartite discussions began between the companies, NRMWU, the Mine Officials and Salaried Staff Association (formed in 1941), and the African NRAMWU. When the discussions ground to a standstill over the application of 'equal pay for equal work and responsibility', a Board of Enquiry was set up in 1954 under the chairmanship of Sir John Forster who had been Chairman of the Commission that enquired into the riots of 1940. In its reports the Board rejected the European union's interpretation of 'equal pay' and wrote:

9 Dalgleish Report, Government Printer, Lusaka, 1948, p. 7.

We are satisfied that a reasonable degree of African advancement will be achieved only by making available, at rates of remuneration duly related to the African wage structure, work which, having been simplified by the fragmentation of some of the European jobs, will provide, as the apt analogy of the African Staff Association suggested, some missing rungs in the African industrial ladder . . . The satisfactory solution of the difficulties rests squarely on the parties concerned.[10]

The Board did not list, as did the Dalgleish Commission of 1947, the jobs that could be taken over by Africans. Instead it made much use of the idea of fragmentation and proposed in embryo a principle that was to cause much trouble in later years, i.e. 'rates of remuneration duly related to the African wage structure'. This would seem to imply that the wages for the new jobs should be built up from below, i.e. related to the existing African wage structure without any necessary relationship to the wages of Europeans. This idea later found its full expression in the Hadow Report of 1963-4.

Forster to Brown

The European unions were reluctant to make any concessions to implement the recommendations of the Forster Board. It was not until the Roan Selection Trust group of companies terminated their recognition agreement with NRMWU that a compromise was reached in September 1955. The union agreed to release from Schedule 'A' (the name given to those jobs which were represented solely by the European union) certain jobs of low content together with certain 'identical' or 'ragged edge' jobs done by Europeans in some mines and by Africans in others. For their part the companies accepted the rate for the job for those jobs remaining in Schedule 'A' and recognized the European union as the sole representative of all employees doing Schedule 'A' work irrespective of their racial origin. Some 24 jobs were released. Some of these were fragmented (the total thus became 40) and in addition the companies created 35 intermediate jobs with a higher job content than jobs of a similar kind already being done by Africans. Of the 75 jobs now available for the first time to Africans only 11 fell to the African Mine Workers' Union, 62 went to the newly formed MASA and 2 went to the Mines African Police Association. The agreement of 1955 provided that an independent firm of industrial consultants should make an analysis of the job content of Schedule 'A' positions. This was done and in 1959

[10] Forster Report, Government Printer, Lusaka, 1954, pp. 28-9.

in a new agreement the European union released a further 38 jobs of low content.

The African workers were now in a position to ascend through the released jobs to Schedule 'A' jobs and to European rates of pay. Those who were able to benefit from these concessions were but a small proportion of the African labour force and they belonged mostly to MASA. The African Mine Workers' Union resented this and there was open hostility between the two unions. The African Mine Workers' Union called a strike on 3 January 1955, for increased wages and improved conditions in which 33,000 African workers out of a total of 37,000 were out until 4 March. The strike collapsed, and the workers returned on their pre-strike pay and conditions of service. The members of MASA remained at work during the strike.

In March 1955 the companies informed MASA that they were prepared to recognize it as a negotiating agent. This naturally required an amendment of the agreement with NRAMWU which up to this time had been the sole negotiator for African mine workers. Several fruitless meetings took place and on 12 May 1955, the companies gave six months' notice of the termination of their agreement with the union. The union wanted individual African employees to have the choice of which body should represent them. This was turned down by the companies.[11]

May to September 1956 was a period of great unrest. Some NRAMWU leaders said the companies were trying to break the union. Mr. H. Nkumbula, General President of the African National Congress, declared on 11 June in Lusaka, 'It looks at the moment—and I have checked this up—as if they are trying to undermine Union leadership. They are taking all the intelligent and well-informed young miners into the Salaried Staff Association and using them to break down Union strength'.[12] Strikes became the order of the day: Nchanga, 23–24 May; Nkana, 18 June; General Strike of 25,000 workers, 20–24 June; Rhokana, 2–8 July; Mufulira, 3–5 July. Further discussions between the companies and NRAMWU took place on 10, 14, 19, 23 and 25 July without any positive results. The Supreme Council of the union

---

11 One crucial point was the position of NRAMWU leaders who were eligible for membership of MASA. The number of union leaders was 138 and 66 were involved as their jobs had become supervisory and staff jobs. The companies found jobs in NRAMWU categories for 64 of them without loss of pay.

12 Branigan Report, Government Printer, Lusaka, 1956, p. 20.

called a series of two- to three-day strikes at each mine in succession ('rolling strikes') between 30 July and 23 August. In addition there were several assaults by AMWU members on members of MASA. Finally on 11 September 1956, a State of Emergency was proclaimed on the Copperbelt, 32 Africans were arrested, among them the General Secretary of AMWU and 25 members of the Supreme Council.

There followed the Branigan Commission to enquire into the disturbances. Three of the arrested leaders—who were detained at Mumbwa—gave evidence before the Commission: M. D. Nkoloma, General Secretary of AMWU, M. R. Mwendapole, Branch Secretary, Nchanga, and J. M. Chapoloko, Branch Secretary, Roan Antelope. The Commission concluded that the cause of the unrest was 'the irresponsible opposition of NRAMWU to MASA.'[13] The Commission was not satisfied from the evidence that any person or organization outside the mining industry had caused the unrest. Some members of the African National Congress had publicly expressed opposition to MASA and 'appeared to be motivated by a desire to limit the representation of African employees . . . to one union'. It also declared that the internal organization of AMWU had seriously deteriorated since early 1955 and that its finances were in a bad state.

The events of 1956 had brought an important new element into Zambian industrial relations: the activities of African political parties. There has not yet been a full study of the relationship between trade unions and political parties in Zambia prior to Independence.[14] The African National Congress was the first fully effective political party in Zambia, but its efforts to secure close co-operation with the trade unions had little success. The chief reason for this was that Lawrence Katilungu, head of AMWU since its foundation and also President of the African Trades Union Congress, believed that politics and trade unionism should not be confused. Katilungu was the biggest figure in trade unionism and his union with its huge membership was the only one that had sufficient financial resources to be of value to ANC. When ANC called a strike in April 1953 as a protest against Federation,

---

[13] ibid., pp. 49–51.

[14] The most complete account available is in D. C. Mulford, *Zambia, the Politics of Independence, 1957–1964*, Oxford University Press, London, 1967. Other works with less detail are: R. I. Rotberg, *The Rise of Nationalism in Central Africa*, Oxford University Press, London, 1966; R. Hall, *Zambia*, Pall Mall Press, London, 1965; R. Gray, *The Two Nations*, Oxford University Press, London, 1966.

Katilungu, though a member of ANC, refused to call out his members. This made him many enemies inside the union and the trade union movement; such activists wanted closer links with ANC and a more militant union programme. The opposition was led by Robinson Puta, Vice President of the African Trades Union Congress and Chairman of the Chingola branch of NRAMWU and an official of ANC, M. D. Nkoloma, General Secretary of both ATUC and AMWU, and D. Konkola, President of the Northern Rhodesia African Workers' Trade Union and an active ANC organizer. Other opponents to Katilungu were J. M. Chapoloko, M. R. Mwendapole, G. Chindele (all were AMWU branch secretaries), and Justin Chimba, Organizing Secretary of the Northern Rhodesia General Workers' Trade Union. By August 1955 the opposition had gained control of the ATUC. Konkola replaced Katilungu as President, Puta and Nkoloma retained their positions as Vice President and General Secretary, Chimba and Chapoloko became Executive Committee members. A sub-committee of nine was formed to deal with political matters; almost all the members were the more militant politically oriented union members.

Katilungu's position as President of AMWU was safe but to forestall the ATUC group's attack he unexpectedly resigned in November 1955, only to be re-elected with a greater strength early in 1956 while Puta lost his position as Vice President. During the 'rolling strikes' of 1956 Katilungu moved nearer to Nkumbula while at the same time the militant members of ANC became more hostile to Katilungu. In the March 1959 general election Katilungu was defeated as a candidate for the Copperbelt constituency. This setback and a visit to Nairobi, where he appears to have been influenced by the late Tom Mboya, led him to become a supporter of combined trade union and political action. Here, however, he found Nkumbula too erratic and he returned to his previous position of non-cooperation. When the final split in ANC took place in October 1959 there was no unified trade union policy concerning the new party UNIP, as Katilungu was overseas for two months prior to the fission. His activities as a trade unionist were further restricted in 1960 when he became a member of the Monckton Commission that was set up to review the Federal constitution. As UNIP had decided to boycott the Commission this only increased the opposition to him by the UNIP trade unionists. ANC's general meeting in December 1959 backed UNIP's boycott of the Monckton Commission and even though the effort to oust Katilungu as President failed, Mwendapole, one of his AMWU opponents, was elected

General Secretary of ATUC. In February 1960, just before he joined the Commission, J. Chivunga, President of the Union of Commercial and Industrial Workers, and A. Kalyati, General Secretary of the same union, denounced him at an executive meeting. Katilungu's reply was to expel UCIW and a number of smaller unions from ATUC on the grounds that they had not paid their annual fees to ATUC, thus leaving only two unions in ATUC—MASA and AMWU.

Chivunga and Kalyati, joined by Mwendapole, who resigned from ATUC, formed the smaller expelled unions into the Northern Rhodesia Reformed Trades Union Congress (RTUC). Even though it could not draw on the resources of AMWU, RTUC became a centre for the opponents of Katilungu and was closely connected with UNIP. Katilungu joined forces with ANC in October 1960 and a month later was deprived of his position as President by the Supreme Council of AMWU. His successor was J. Chisata, a former AMWU Mufulira chairman. This destroyed Katilungu's power in ATUC and the two opposing congresses united in February 1961 as the United Trades Union Congress (UTUC). UTUC included AMWU and MASA and was a victory for the opponents of Katilungu. Chivunga was elected President and Kalyati, Mwendapole, and W. Chakulya, former RTUC officials and members of UNIP, filled key posts. UNIP had a large number of the twenty members of UTUC's general council.

This internal struggle for power has been described in detail because it shows that politics had become a vital factor in trade unionism; it directed the unions away from their former functions; it also gravely weakened the whole labour movement. Above all, the names of the trade unionists involved practically represent a roll call of the men in top positions in government and business today. They are now lost to the movement, and the weak position of trade unions today is largely due to the fact that there were few with ability and experience to succeed them. Katilungu became ANC's Deputy National President in March 1961; he was an able organizer and during Nkumbula's nine months in prison he reorganized the party's structure and finances. He was also a potential threat to UNIP because he still retained a large following among trade unionists and had given a more acceptable image of ANC to the European voters for the coming elections in 1962. His death in a car accident in November 1961 was a severe blow not only to ANC but also to the trade union movement.

Within UTUC there was constant strife between the various factions. Throughout 1963 J. Chisata, President of AMWU and a UNIP member

of the Legislative Council, was under fire both from UNIP and his
trade union rivals. Eventually J. Chimba, who had become Minister of
Labour and Mines after UNIP's success in the January 1964 elections,
ordered Chisata and two other prominent trade unionists, Jonathan
Chivunga and Wilson Chakulya, to sever their connections with the
labour movement. Chisata and Chivunga were made parliamentary
secretaries in the new government. The disputes in UTUC eventually
produced a split and the consequent formation of two separate groups.
Subsequently the two sides met under the chairmanship of S. M.
Kapwepwe, the then Minister for Home Affairs, settled their differences,
and elected new officials to lead the congress. The disputes continued,
however, and on 31 October 1965, UTUC was dissolved and replaced
by the Zambia Congress of Trade Unions (ZCTU). The new congress
was set up under the provisions of the Trade Unions and Trade
Disputes Ordinance (Amendment) Act 1965 and the minister appointed
its first executive in November. N. Tembo was appointed President
and A. Nkumbula General Secretary.

While AMWU and UTUC have had a predominant part in this
survey of African trade unionism, there was a steady growth in the
number of unions and in their membership. In 1959 there were eight
African registered unions, only three of which had a membership of
over 1,000. The following year the unions numbered eleven, and five
had a membership of over 5,000. In addition there were fourteen
unregistered unions. In 1964 registered unions numbered nineteen,
with thirteen having over 1,000 members. Since then the number has
fallen. The latest figures available are for 1967, when there were only
thirteen registered unions. The decrease is due to the removal of some
unions from the register and to amalgamation among some competing
unions. In 1967 there were three amalgamations: (1) the National
Union of Transport and General Workers and the Zambian Long
Distance and Heavy Haulage Union formed the National Union of
Transport and Allied Workers; (2) the Zambia Railways Amalgamated
Workers' Union was a combination of the Railway African Workers'
Union and the Zambia Railway Workers' Union; (3) the Mineworkers'
Union of Zambia (the strongest union, with 44,256 members out of a
total of approximately 105,000 African unionized workers) was formed
from the Zambian Mineworkers' Union (a later name for AMWU),
the Mines Local Staff Association and the Zambia Mines African
Police Association.

The increase in the number of unions had its drawbacks. There were demarcation disputes between rival unions, personal and political rivalries between leaders, sudden changes in alliances and in officials. An outstanding example of a union that has suffered from too-frequent changes of officials arising from internal rivalries is the Zambia National Union of Teachers. Another great source of weakness was that subscriptions were not regularly paid and even some big unions were not able to handle their finances properly.

The belief that there should be only one union in each industry began to gain adherents. Where this could not be achieved by amalgamation, as in the case of road transport, some unions attempted to go it alone. A particularly important instance of this occurred in 1963 when the Mines African Staff Association changed its name and its constitution. It became the United Mineworkers' Union (UMU), claiming to represent all workers in the industry. This was a direct attack on ZMU. The companies refused to recognize UMU and cancelled its 'check off' system of collecting union dues. In spite of having the support of certain important members of UNIP the new union had to accept defeat at the end of 1964 when it amended its name and constitution and became the Mines Local Staff Association.

AFTER INDEPENDENCE

Political Independence had created great expectations among all Zambians. The workers believed that it would bring them higher wages, better working conditions, better housing, and rapid promotion to the jobs and salaries previously held by Europeans, thus closing the gap between Europeans and Zambians. Before any of these objectives could be achieved it was necessary to abolish the 'closed shop' of the European mining workers' union and to overcome their resistance to job fragmentation. In February 1964 the European union changed its name to the Mine Workers' Society (MWS) and all its members were transferred to staff conditions of service. The union won several benefits in exchange for the agreement.

The next move of the companies began in August 1964. Under the Advancement Agreements of 1955 and 1960 the European union members had been guaranteed employment. This is effect would mean that Zambians could not replace Europeans when they were qualified to do so. The companies now proposed (1) that new expatriate employees would be on a fixed-term contract; (2) that present incumbent expatriates would, when displaced by a Zambian, receive in compensation six months' basic salary plus one month's salary for each twenty-four months' continuous service. There were other benefits including air fares and £100 p.a. per child who was being educated outside Zambia. Through hard bargaining, the unions secured in addition an allowance of 7 per cent of basic pay. This was the price the companies had to pay for two key changes—the temporary nature of expatriate employment in the mines and the expatriates' acceptance of their obligation to train the Zambians who would eventually replace them. The final stage was achieved in March 1966. All expatriate workers, except those whose job life expectancy was less than two years, were put on fixed-term contracts. Again a price had to be paid—another expatriate monthly allowance at the rate of 6 per cent of basic pay.

The practical effect of these wage gains by the unions can be illustrated by considering the example of the rockbreaker. Prior to February 1964 he earned a minimum wage of £112 10s. per month; in April 1966 he received £177 11s. per month, in addition to a number of benefits for house rent, education, and leave payments. The European unions had greatly enhanced the salaries of their members.

To help the progress of Zambianization the mining companies changed their manning structure. In place of a European ganger in charge of a crew of virtually unskilled labour, they substituted a supervisor working with trained operators. The supervisor directed and co-ordinated; the operators were responsible for specific jobs and were provided with the necessary helpers and labourers. Mechanics were trained in certain parts of the skilled artisan's jobs. By early 1966 there were about 2,300 miners each responsible for his own 'end', or small section of the mine face, and there were 150 section bosses,[15] supervising the work of the operators.

The companies have for many years run very extensive courses of training for workers of all categories. In evidence to the Brown Commission they stated that between 1 January 1964 and 31 March 1966, 23,334 Zambians had undergone training, of whom 891 withdrew from the courses, 1,494 failed, 18,491 passed and 2,458 were still in training. The biggest groups being trained were 11,728 partially skilled workers and 7,002 semi-skilled. The recurrent costs during 1964-6 were £6.2 m.[16] As far as possible the companies try to give

15 The number is expected to rise to 450 by 1970. In the same period the number of mechanics is expected to rise from 1,012 Zambians to 2,178.
16 *Report of the Commission of Inquiry into the Mining Industry* (Chairman:

training to existing employees instead of bringing in new ones. Here a difficult problem arises from the educational standards of the employees: 34.33 per cent are illiterate; 41.83 per cent left school between Standards I and IV (lower primary); 19.32 per cent are upper primary; 3.7 per cent are Form 1–2, 0.62 per cent are Form 3–4. Training schemes are also being run by the government, local authorities, railways, and banks.

By 1964 some Zambians were capable of taking over jobs hitherto reserved for Europeans; others were being trained to do sections of these jobs. The crucial point was: were wages and salaries to be those of the displaced expatriates? Earlier we referred to the Forster Report (1954) which spoke of 'rates of remuneration duly related to the African wage structure'. The terms of reference of the Hadow Commission, 1964, included the following:

> To review the salaries and conditions of service of the Northern Rhodesia public and teaching services ... and to make recommendations having particular regard to ... the need to devise salary levels for the local civil service and for the teaching service which the public revenue and the economy of the country will be financially capable of sustaining in the long term.[17]

The Seers Report observed:

> Africans moving into European jobs naturally expect to be paid the same high salaries. Yet if this were the general practice, a highly unequal distribution of income would develop amongst the citizens of Zambia. This would make it more difficult to get other sections of the population to agree to wage stabilization and in the long run it would prejudice both economic advance and political stability.

There was thus a consensus among the experts that African wages should not be related to those of expatriates.

The Hadow Commission recognized that salaries of local officers should be related to what the economy of Zambia could sustain in the long run. They recommended a reduction of salaries in the higher levels of the existing local salary scale and large increases at lower levels. Concerning expatriates they wrote: 'We believe it to be important that there should in future be only one salary structure in the Service and that this should be salary scales proposed for the local civil service'.[18]

Roland Brown), Government Printer, Lusaka, 1966, p. 170.

[17] *Report of the Commission appointed to Review the Salaries and Conditions of Service of the Northern Rhodesian Public and Teaching Services* (Chairman: Gordon Hadow), Government Printer, Lusaka, 1969, p. i.

[18] ibid., p. 38. By 'local' the Commission meant 'African'—cf. p. 16.

Expatriates would in addition receive personal pensionable allowances which added to their basic salaries would equal their existing salaries. It should be noted that a large proportion of the additional personal allowances were paid for by the United Kingdom government.

When the mining companies came to deal with salaries they almost inevitably settled on a basic scale for Africans, and set up a dual wage scheme: a lower one for Zambians and a higher one for expatriates. The fundamental reasons as given to the Brown Commission were the need to induce expatriates to come to Zambia and the temporary nature of their employment. Their first efforts to deduct the inducement and compensating elements from the existing European scales met with failure because these scales were worked out in hard bargaining by workers who considered themselves as settlers. Further, the European scales had many anomalies because when the local scale was built up by job evaluation from the base of the existing African jobs the differential between the local and expatriate rate for the same or similar work varied from 24 per cent to 103 per cent.[19]

It is one thing to devise a new manning structure and wage scale and another to get it accepted by the workers and their unions. At the end of January 1964 the Zambia Mineworkers' Union asked for a big wage increase. The companies countered by asking the union to approve of the new manning structure and the principle of the dual wage. Several fruitless meetings took place. Matters were precipitated by the action of MASA in forming UMU and claiming to represent all workers in mining. The ZMU leadership was under pressure and on 16 May told the companies that an agreement must be reached quickly. Finally the union accepted a general increase of 12n per shift. The problem of staff and supervisory grades was complicated by the fact that the mines refused to recognize UMU and so there was no organization to represent these workers. As noted previously the UMU effort failed and the reconstructed Mines Local Staff Association was not recognized until March 1965. The price of recognition was acceptance of the dual wage scheme by the union.[20] Subsequent negotiations resulted in certain improvements in the wages and conditions of ZMU and MLSA members but the dual wage system remained intact.

Those Zambians who had advanced into European jobs, Schedule 'A', with European rates of pay and those who had got the jobs released

19 Brown Report, Government Printer, Lusaka, 1966, p. 23.
20 ibid., pp. 26-7.

under the 1960 Advancement Agreement and wages related to European pay were an anomaly in a structure based on African conditions. Accordingly they were 'localized', i.e. transferred to the African scale. The numbers involved in Schedule 'A' jobs were 117, of whom 103 transferred to local terms and got compensation of six months' basic salary plus one month's salary for each 24 months' service, and 12 workers left the mines under the same condition. Two transferred to local terms and took a personal allowance of the difference between their former wage and the local scale but at every general increase in wages one-third of the income was deducted from the personal allowance.

The local scale was built up from the base of existing jobs with the aid of job evaluation. This at least avoided the anomalies of the European wage structure but it divorced African wages from any connection with European wages. They were responsive to local economic factors.

This approach . . . tended to discount a local factor of tremendous importance in Zambia—the acute shortage of workers of any race or colour capable of undertaking skilled or technical work. It is this factor which accounts for the high wages which European workers were able to secure in negotiations with the companies. African workers who have acquired skills comparable to their European colleagues cannot easily be persuaded that what they have to sell to their employers is worth less because the colour of their skin is black.[21]

Dissatisfaction with the dual wage system and the wages of the lower workers became widespread, so that early in January 1965 ZMU presented what in fact amounted to a demand for a general wage increase; in particular it wanted the shift differential for all employees to be that of the European MWS, leave for Africans and Europeans to be based on rank only, Africans and 'local Europeans' with similar qualifications to be employed on the same terms and conditions.[22] These proposals were tantamount to a fundamental revision of the June 1964 agreement which the union said it had signed under pressure of inter-union rivalry. Negotiations broke down in September 1965 and the union wrote to the Registrar for permission to hold a strike ballot. He replied that the officers had not been properly elected—this was the election in which many UNIP candidates had been elected. New elections did not take place until March 1966. The union held

21 ibid., p. 23.
22 ibid., p. 158.

meetings with the companies on 15–19 January 1966, and signed an agreement giving increased pay for all: 11 per cent at the bottom of the scale, 8–9 per cent higher up, 30 days paid sick leave each year, a small percentage increase in shift differential, and a £5 bonus in lieu of back-dating. Again under the pressure of internal rivalry the union had rushed a settlement which they later regretted. In the meantime the concrete results of the agreement enabled the union leaders who had negotiated it to be returned to office in the March 1966 elections. The rank and file did not remain satisfied for long. ZMU members went on strike at Nchanga. The strike spread to Bancroft on 29 March, Luanshya on 31 March, Rhokana, the Copperbelt Power Company, Chibuluma, Chambeshi, and Mufulira on 2 April, and the Ndola Copper Refineries on 4 April. Of a labour force of 42,000, 23,000 were on strike. The return to work was not complete until 14 April.

The Brown Commission, set up on 5 April 1966, to enquire into these strikes, was given very wide terms of reference, to:

(1) Enquire into the conditions of service, including wages, housing, leave, and social facilities of employees in the mining industry serving on local conditions of employment evolved by the mining companies, whether through negotiations with employee organizations or otherwise.

(2) Enquire into the disparity which exists between the conditions of service, including the aforesaid matters, of employees in the mining industry serving on expatriate conditions of employment and of employees in the mining industry serving on local conditions of employment.

(3) Determine whether the disparity referred to in paragraph (2) hereof should be eliminated or reduced having regard—
   (a) to the national interest;
   (b) to the consequences, whether financial, economic, social, or otherwise, which would result from such elimination or reduction; and
   (c) to the improvement in industrial relations which might be expected to follow from such elimination or reduction.

(4) Examine the procedures which may exist in the mining industry for Zambianization and determine the effectiveness of such procedures.

(5) Examine any other aspect of industrial relations in the industry.[23]

The Commission was to enquire into dualism in wages, hospital, housing, and social facilities as well as Zambianization. That the objection to dualism was not confined to miners is evidenced by the terms of reference of the Whelan Commission set up on 22 April to review the salary scales of the civil service, teachers, police, prison

[23] ibid., p. v.

officers, Zambia defence forces and non-civil service employees of the government, which included 'the need to bring the existing dual salary and wage structure to an end as soon as possible'.[24] The Brown Commission rejected the dual wage system, because it ignored the scarcity value of skilled African labour and because it was unacceptable to African workers as a return of distinctions based on race and colour.[25] It also rejected the suitability of the expatriate wage scale for the mining industry as creating an inflationary effect and thus causing serious damage to the economy of Zambia. Faced with the necessity of setting new rates at some point between the local wage and the expatriate wage, the Commission looked at the top of the existing local scale and took a job that was in both scales, namely that of shift boss. The local rate was £110 per month and the expatriate rate £181 16s. The Commission

... reached the conclusion ... that a proper basic rate for both local and expatriate shift bosses would be the existing local rate increased by one-third of the difference between the two rates on the existing scales. One-third of the difference is £23 8s. 8d. which would represent an increase on the local scale of approximately 22 per cent.[26]

Wage increases

The expatriate scale had many anomalies whereas the local scale based on job valuation was consistent and straightforward. If the Commission awarded one-third of the difference between the local and expatriate scale for each job it would distort the scale by introducing the European anomalies. Consequently it settled for a flat 22 per cent increase on the existing local scale which included jobs ranging from worker to shift boss.[27] The local scale ran only as far as shift boss and the Commission recommended that the task of preparing a single wage scale covering all occupations in the industry should be undertaken immediately. Future expatriate employees would be allowed certain inducement allowances to be approved by the Ministry of Labour both in amount and form. Concerning existing expatriate employees the Commission wrote:

[24] *Report of the Commission appointed to Review the Grading Structure of the Civil Service, the Salary Scales of the Civil Service* ... (Commissioner: F. J. Whelan), Government Printer, Lusaka, 1966, p. 2.
[25] Brown Report, Government Printer, Lusaka, 1966, p. 42.
[26] ibid., p. 45.
[27] ibid.

We are aware that the companies have legal and moral obligations to expatriates already in their service. We do not suggest that these should be disregarded. However, where they are inconsistent with the proposals we have made, we recommend that a way should be found of discharging them on an agreed basis so that the new basic pay scale can be established for all workers without unnecessary delay.[28]

The Commission also considered that trade unions for expatriates were inconsistent with their status and should be replaced by something akin to a civil service senior staff association.

The 22 per cent increase was accepted by the government and the companies. The Whelan Report made roughly the same increase, though with larger amounts for lower-paid and smaller for higher-paid workers. A general movement of wage increases spread throughout industry in the second half of 1966 and early 1967. The Commission in addition recommended that a start should be made immediately on preparing a single wage scale based on job evaluation methods in which the unions would participate by retaining a reliable firm of industrial consultants to advise them on what was being done. No more was heard of this proposal until early 1969. Apparently there were difficulties, chiefly financial, in getting suitable consultants, and the companies went ahead with the task of job evaluation. Hitherto their work had dealt only with the operative grades but in the two years they believed that they had worked out a technique that would cover operatives, clerical, technical, and administrative occupations.

In August 1967 the Mineworkers' Union of Zambia raised the question of the single wage scale applicable to all employees. This wage scale had in the meantime acquired the title of Industry Basic Pay Scale (IBPS). The matter came up again in January 1968 when the union complained of the delay in introducing the IBPS. The companies' reply that the IBPS was the present salary schedule of the local employees was not acceptable to the union. At a meeting of the Mining Joint Industrial Council on 26 June 1968, the union said the IBPS for the higher workers should be two-thirds of the expatriate rate. The companies' refusal was based on the following arguments: (1) that this would introduce the distortions of the European scales to the new structure, and (2) that this would involve considerable wage increases at a time when government ministers were calling for wage restraint. The two opposing positions were held at further meetings in October and December. Finally, on 17 March 1969, the union informed

[28] ibid., p. 50.

the Ministry of Labour and Social Services of a dispute with the copper mining companies and requested the appointment of a conciliator.

On 28 March 1969, a Board of Conciliation was set up to deal with the dispute over the union demands for:

1. the elimination of the 19- and 21-day leave settlements; in effect this would make 22 days the minimum leave;
2. recognition of the fact that the local salary scale was not acceptable as the IBPS;
3. a revaluation in the number of grades; and
4. a progressive salary scale for operative grades.

The conciliation proceedings ended in agreement. Both sides agreed that the future integrated wage structure and the IBPS should be based on job evaluation. A new advance was the clause that a job evaluation consultant was to be appointed by the union to participate in preparing the new ranking schedules and to report on them to the union. This was the first time that a union had agreed to participate in job evaluation.

Zambianization

The Brown Commission accepted that the companies' programmes were a major, sincere effort to deal with the problem of training Zambians. It added, however, that decisions about training programmes and the rate of replacement of Europeans must involve government participation. The reasons were that: (1) the scale of operations in the mines raises the issue to a national level; (2) there is often a tendency among expatriates to underestimate what Africans can do; and (3) 'the good faith of the companies is not accepted by the workers . . . This is regretted but must be faced. It is a consequence of the deplorable history of African advancement during the Colonial era'.[29]

In December 1966 the Minister of Labour set up a Zambianization Committee for the mining industry. The Minister of State for Presidential Affairs, Mr. A. Milner, was chairman until September 1967, when he was succeeded by Mr. H. Mulemba, Minister of State for the Cabinet and Public Service. Later Mr. Milner returned as chairman. The other members are the Minister of State for Technical Education, the Secretary to the Cabinet, the Permanent Secretaries

[29] ibid., p. 74.

of the Ministries of Labour, Lands and Mines, the Staff Development Adviser (Cabinet Office), the Director of Civil Service Training, a representative from each of the two mining groups, the President and General Secretary of ZMU, and the Chairman of the Zambia Expatriate Mineworkers' Association.

From the start the members got an understanding of the problems by visiting the mines: meetings were held on the mines rather than in distant boardrooms. The aim was 'to lay down a programme of Zambianization which would not only satisfy the legitimate aspirations of Zambians working in the mines, but ensure the maintenance of high standards of productivity and safety in the interests of the nation as a whole.[30] Because of this approach and the outlay by the mines of K 10 m. a year on training courses, Zambianization has gone faster and with less friction than in any other sphere apart from government. Zambianization at the high levels depends on the availability of graduates and 'O' level school leavers and the committee has been able to get a bigger allocation for mining.

The report underlines two problems in this field. At present young Zambians are being promoted rapidly.

> Once Zambians have filled the higher posts there will be no programme to replace one Zambian by another except as a result of retirement, resignation, or other allied cause ... The post-Zambianization pattern of career advancement may well be as slow as—or even slower than—the colonial norm, for the succession to a senior official who is still relatively young in years is certain to be slower than if he had attained his post only as the culmination of long years of gradual advancement. It may well be a generation before normal balance between length of service and career opportunity is finally achieved.[31]

There is some evidence that the rate of promotion is slowing down in the civil service, causing some dissatisfaction among the younger and sometimes better technically qualified recruits.

The second cause for concern is the instability of trainees for professional and technical posts. The demand for their services, together with the offer of better salaries and conditions, is such that they change jobs instead of remaining set and gaining experience. The committee was really outspoken on this matter, since it affects many other industries, especially the banks and railways which have set up training schemes.

---

[30] *The Progress of Zambianization in the Mining Industry*, Ministry of Labour, Lusaka, 1968.
[31] ibid., p. 5.

The result is a growing number of individuals who are half-trained in many fields but fully competent in none, who have turned the virtue of job mobility into the vice of job instability. (The) Committee now proposes to take firm measures to curb this unhappy trend before it grows out of all proportion. Zambia has not set out to produce a cadre of qualified men only to see them veer from one opportunity to another for monetary and prestige reasons which have nothing to do with the national interest or the social contribution which it is within their power to make.[32]

Productivity

Questions have been raised even in Parliament about some of the results of Zambianization. Serious allegations have been made of inefficiency in the railway industry in particular. But it is hard to judge whether this arises from Zambianization or from the general decline in discipline. For instance, the *Annual Report* of the Department of Labour, 1966, considered that the deterioration of discipline on the mines was a threat to the success of the Zambianization programme.

Expatriate supervisors were completely demoralized and unwilling to exercise authority for fear of arousing the resentment of local workers and being unjustly labelled as racialist, with the possible threat of deportation. Discipline therefore became lax, with consequent adverse effects on production. Zambian supervisors, on the other hand, were anxious to prove their keenness and ability to exercise their newly acquired authority. Their zeal was sometimes resented by their fellow countrymen in subordinate positions and a number of incidents occurred involving local supervisors and workers, particularly at Bancroft and Nchanga.[33]

Things had become worse in the following year:

Both expatriate and local supervisors were subjected to intimidation resulting in a complete breakdown of authority at the supervisory level, with the consequent effect upon safety, efficiency, and production. Those expatriates who, in spite of intimidation, exerted their authority and insisted on maintaining production were accused of being racialists. Local supervisors were threatened with physical violence or with witchcraft.[34]

A special conference was called by the Minister of Labour, Mr. M. Sipalo, comprising labour and trade union officials and employers, to discuss the problems of indiscipline and low productivity. Among the causes of the latter it listed lateness, insubordination, absenteeism, drun-

[32] ibid.
[33] *Annual Report* of the Department of Labour, 1966, Government Printer, Lusaka, p. 13.
[34] ibid., 1967, p. 9.

kenness on duty, inciting others to strike, and unjustified provocation.[35]

There are no detailed studies of the extent of these causes of low productivity. A survey in the building industry in Lusaka at the end of 1966 and early 1967 recorded an incidence of 30 per cent absenteeism.[36] Addressing a seminar on 'The Importance of Industry in the Economic Development of Zambia' on 28 February 1969, the Minister of Trade, Industry, and Mines, Mr. J. Chimba, said that standards of discipline were appalling, and had resulted in 369 derailments on Zambia Railways between mid-1967 and mid-1968. Many of these accidents were caused by gross negligence and drunkenness. He added that to a lesser extent the same conditions were to be found throughout Zambian industry.[37] Further figures were given by President Kaunda on the same occasion. He contrasted the big percentage increase in wages with the alarming slump in labour productivity:

> In the construction industry, for instance, a drop in output per man is estimated at 22 per cent. At the same time, there was a decline in labour productivity of about 3 per cent in motor vehicle repair and a shattering 56 per cent drop in the textile industries.[38]

The President attributed the drop in productivity to absenteeism, drunkenness, indiscipline, indolence, unconstitutional strikes and deadlocks, as well as bad management.

Strikes

Fluctuations in the number of strikes or lock-outs per year give a useful indication of the state of industrial relations. Table 3.1 shows the number of stoppages in seven industries chosen either because of their importance in the economy or because of the frequency of disputes leading to a cessation of work.

The following figures are the totals for 1959, 1960, and 1961, which were relatively free from the political elements that complicated the situation just before Independence.

	Number of stoppages	Number of man-days lost
1959	23	2,185
1960	61	7,507
1961	65	19,640

[35] *Report of the Livingstone Labour Conference, 1967*, Ministry of Labour, Lusaka, p. 4.
[36] ibid., p. 11.
[37] Mimeographed report.
[38] Mimeographed report.

TABLE 3.1
Industrial stoppages

Industry	1964		1965		1966		1967	
	Number of stoppages	Number of man-days lost	Number of stoppages	Number of man-days lost	Number of stoppages	Number of man-days lost	Number of stoppages	Number of man-days lost
Metal mining	22	69,234	10	2,065	32	549,383	16	983
Clothing manufacture	6	469	10	243	13	546	11	1,446
Construction and civil engineering	39	14,294	35	1,208	64	15,266	40	8,430
Light and power	2	68	2	27	1	3	8	417
Railways	3	16,147	3	13,651	1	111	4	1,033
Other transport	5	517	2	63	12	1,574	22	4,089
Government services	12	15,286	2	124	16	1,282	17	13,791
Other	62	9,723	50	5,112	102	11,241	104	15,899
Total	151	125,738	114	22,493	241	579,406	222	46,088

Source: Derived from *Annual Reports* of the Department of Labour.

Even when one makes allowances for the increased economic activity and its concomitant increase in employment in the post-Independence years, Table 3.1 shows that strikes have increased greatly in frequency. To keep the figures in a proper perspective it should be recalled that the total employed labour force rose from 268,700 in 1964 to 347,050 in December 1967, which means that the number of man-days lost was a relatively small proportion of the possible man-days worked. For example, in 1966, the worst year for strikes, the total number of man-days lost was 579,406; with a total employed labour force of roughly 300,000, the possible man-days worked was of the order of 90 million, so the proportion of man-days lost was approximately 0.6 per cent. As a matter of fact, the number of man-days lost through strikes was actually less than the number lost through the addition of two extra public holidays.

When we turn to particular industries, however, the picture becomes much blacker. In 1966 there were approximately 50,000 persons employed in mining. Allowing for Sundays and holidays, the working year is approximately 300 days, so the number of man-days lost was over 3 per cent of total man-days. Such calculations do not, however, give the true situation in Zambia. No account is taken of the indirect loss of production and of the fact that mining is the chief source of foreign exchange and one of the main sources of government revenue. Likewise strikes in transport cripple a land-locked country that depends on foreign trade for all its essential commodities. Consequently it is not surprising that the government sometimes took very strong measures against strikes. Thus in January 1967 when some European workers continued a strike at Mufulira in spite of an appeal from President Kaunda for national unity in face of the problems caused by Rhodesia's UDI, the Mufulira branch chairman was restricted to the remote Mporokoso district. At the same time an extension to the Preservation of Public Security Regulations made it an offence to withdraw labour on the mines. In the same year, when the Zambian miners went on strike to secure that the Zambia Mines Local Pension Fund be wound up and that the workers receive back their contributions a number of strike leaders were restricted to rural areas. A ban was imposed on all public meetings on the Copperbelt and certain operations in the mines were declared essential services. More recently the Vice President intervened in a strike of some Lusaka municipal workers by ordering them back to work on the next day and threatening to call out the military and police if any attempt was made to interfere with those ready to return to work.

Legislation

Trade union law is based on three fundamental principles enshrined in the British system, namely (1) freedom of association; (2) the right to bargain collectively and, in certain circumstances, to withdraw labour; and (3) minimum participation and interference by government. Uneasy at the increase in the number of strikes due partly to the growth in the number of unions and to squabbles between contending unions, the government made important changes in the Trade Unions and Trade Disputes Ordinance which became effective early in 1965. To discourage 'splinter' unions a minimum of 100 members instead of the previous 7 is now necessary before a union can be registered. Any unregistered trade union must dissolve and every official is liable to a penalty not exceeding £5 for every day that it remains unregistered. A common phenomenon after Independence was the setting up of new unions by 'professional' organizers, who found that a union gave them prestige and finance. The amended law now declares that to qualify for election as an officer of a trade union a person must have worked for three years in the particular occupation or industry with which the union is directly concerned. If the union has less than 500 members an official must be actually employed in the industry. Under sections 15, 15A, and 15B of the Ordinance the Registrar of Trade Unions must be given an annual audited statement of the financial affairs of every union. Section 9 compels a union to hold a secret ballot for a number of matters including the election of delegates to a general meeting, the election of the general officers of a union, calling a strike, the imposition of a levy, and the increasing of the subscription paid by members.

The greatest weakness of Zambian unions is that they rarely have the finances to pay enough capable officials. To remedy this, section 20A empowers the minister to make orders regarding the deduction of union subscriptions by employers from the pay of their employees for payment to the union. Many unions have 'check-off' agreements with employers on a voluntary basis. The present law goes further than this. If the minister is satisfied that a union is 'sufficiently representative of the employees concerned' he may make an order compelling an employer to deduct the union dues. Such an order is known as a 'Dues-Stop' and binds the employer to deduct subscriptions from all his employees, whether they are union members or not. Before such an order can be made the number of union members must exceed 60 per

cent of those employed either in the industry or in a particular undertaking. A 'Dues-Stop' order is not granted unless the union is a member
of TUC, and under an amendment of 1967 20 per cent of the dues
received must be transmitted by the union to TUC. This is aimed at
remedying TUC's chronic lack of funds.

An indirect effect of the 'Dues-Stop' is a strengthening of the
congress's power over the individual unions through section 9A of
the Ordinance. When a union is affiliated to congress certain 'prescribed
decisions' must have congress approval before they can have effect.
The 'prescribed decisions' are:

1. to hold a strike ballot or call a strike;
2. to dissolve a trade union;
3. to reconstitute a trade union as two or more unions;
4. to amalgamate with one or more trade unions;
5. to affiliate to a federation of trade unions;
6. to impose a levy;
7. to increase or decrease the subscription or entrance fees of
    members; and
8. to alter or amend the rules of a trade union or to change its
    organizational structure.

Union difficulties

The need of congress approval to hold a strike ballot would at first
sight seem to be a strong force against strikes. In practice it has been
completely ineffectual. It would appear that in 1967 the approval of
congress was not asked in a single one of the 222 strikes that took place.
Every one of them was unconstitutional, i.e. carried out without the
union's approval and/or without the approval of congress, and often
without going through the agreed channels. The reasons for this are
complex. ZCTU under Mr. Chakulya is a strong supporter of the
government's plea for wage restraint, so the unions feel that approval
would not be given. The union leaders themselves are being constantly
reminded by ministers and party officials to concentrate more on
productivity than on wage claims so they are very reluctant to give
official approval to strike action. In very many cases the strikers were
not even aware of the recognized procedures. Whatever the causes may
be, the present situation is that the unions have little control over their
members. A wide gap is opening up between the rank and file and the
top union officials.

Works committees sometimes become the organ through which workers express their discontent.

Works committees would have been more successful had the quality of leadership been better at plant level. Unfortunately, those who talked most tended to be elected to these committees irrespective of whether they are suitable or not. Furthermore, many of the committee members, like some branch officials of trade unions, did not take the trouble to familiarize themselves with procedures for the channelling of grievances and many of them failed to explain the role of the committee itself in relation to management. As a result many works committees, instead of playing a constructive role, became a source of trouble. Members adopted a dictatorial attitude towards management and set themselves up as workers' watch dogs above company discipline.[39]

A committee set up in 1964 at the Chambeshi Open-Cast Mine was dissolved in 1965 on the advice of the Ministry of Labour owing to the excessive militancy of the worker members.[40] The 1964 Report said that at times union officials were suspicious of works committees where they were not directly represented 'on the grounds that the influence of the trade union was being undermined'.[41]

A further source of union uncertainty is sometimes euphemistically called 'outside interference'. This is not a matter that is frequently discussed. The Livingstone Conference in 1967 recommended that:

Only labour officers, trade unions, and managements should look into industrial relations. Outside interference in industrial matters should stop and only trade unions and the Ministry of Labour should be left to handle such matters.[42]

The Department of Labour *Annual Report*, 1967, stated that 'external interference by unqualified persons continued to aggravate the position'. This refers primarily to UNIP local officials. Not infrequently it happened that in a dispute the workers turned to the UNIP branch to get support for their claims while the employer called in the local labour officer. Such uncertainty about the extent of the powers of party officials had a bad effect on the morale of both labour officers and trade union officials. At the seminar on 'The importance of industry in the economic development of Zambia' in February 1969, the Vice President, Mr. S. Kapwepwe, stressed that while labour leaders and political

[39] *Annual Report* of the Department of Labour, 1967, Government Printer, Lusaka, p. 11.
[40] ibid., p. 18.
[41] ibid.
[42] *Report of the Livingstone Labour Conference, 1967*, Ministry of Labour, Lusaka, p. 19.

leaders were partners in the struggle for political independence they were now at loggerheads and divided. In the course of the seminar the unions said that their work was hampered by the interference of political parties in trade disputes. The ministers and government delegates present replied that this interference arose from the weakness of the leadership of the unions and took place only to secure a return to work so that negotiations could continue. The labour leaders also pointed to the lack of regular consultation between government and unions on labour matters. An outstanding example of this was the First National Development Plan, which was prepared and published without consultation with labour.

Outlook

The achievements of unions have been considerable in securing better wages and higher jobs for their members. Their present weakness and difficulties make one ask whether a trade union movement based on English law and practice is viable in a developing country. Instead of striving for a bigger slice of the cake they are reminded over and over again to make the cake bigger by raising productivity levels and to consider the interests of the country as a whole. Productivity, safety, and service are expected to replace wages and promotions. It is doubtful if the unions, no matter how well led, can realistically be expected to make such a fundamental change within the existing framework. For instance those who say that the unions should give better services to their members seem to forget that in mining the industry provides medical, social welfare, recreational, and social facilities for its workers. Those who preach wage restraint as one of the great needs of Zambia today should read paragraph 120 of the Brown Report:

> We believe that the time has come, and indeed is overdue, for the movement of wages in the mining industry to be guided by a policy on wages, incomes and profits which can only be formulated by the government itself. A measure of wage restraint will not be achieved by economists writing about it in their reports, still less because it is enthusiastically espoused by the mining companies as their own policy.

Those who blame the weakness of the unions on the poor quality of local leaders ignore the fact that men of ability and education can earn far higher salaries than the unions can pay. The cry for better educated leaders and members is genuine, but is it fair to put the whole onus of doing this on the unions? The position and activities of unions in modern Zambian society are a national issue which cannot be resolved unless and until the government becomes directly involved.

4

Wages and Zambia's Economic Development

J. B. KNIGHT[1]

INTRODUCTION

CAN wages constrain economic development? There was no doubt in the minds of the members of the Seers Mission:

> The wage and salary question is perhaps the most serious problem facing the government; its decision on the wages and salaries it pays itself, and the way it exercises its influence on wages and salaries in the private sector, may be decisive in determining whether Zambia will become during this century a modern developed country.[2]

However, one might argue that wages are not in themselves a *constraint* on Zambia's development, but that they can tighten or loosen a number of the potential constraints examined in this volume: the savings constraint, the foreign exchange constraint, the public finance constraint, the skilled manpower constraint, the market constraint, and the constraint imposed by foreign competition at a given exchange rate. The effect of wage-behaviour then depends on which of these potential constraints is actually effective. Consider briefly the mechanisms by which wage-behaviour may retard or accelerate development.

At least four categories of income recipient should be distinguished

[1] Fellow of St. Edmund Hall, and Research Officer at the Institute of Economics and Statistics, Oxford University, England. The author wishes to express his gratitude to the Institute for Social Research, University of Zambia, for according him affiliate status during his stay in Zambia, to the many government and mining company officials who gave him their time and access to information, and to his wife for her help with the computations. He wishes to point out that he alone is responsible for the views expressed. The paper was completed in February 1969.

[2] UN/ECA/FAO, *Report of the Economic Survey Mission on the Economic Development of Zambia*, Falcon Press, Ndola, 1964, chapter 2, section 53.

in Zambia: peasantry, wage-earners, salariat, and profit-recipients. The peasants are the poorest and largest group. By comparison, the unskilled wage-earners are a privileged minority. In turn the salariat of skilled and educated employees bears the same relationship to the wage-earners as the latter bear to the peasantry. Profits are distributed only to a handful of Zambian residents, most profits being repatriated abroad.

What is the effect of an increase in earnings from employment on the distribution of income among these groups? If firms are unable to raise prices, the burden of increased wage costs is borne directly by profits, although the reduction in profits may affect all groups indirectly by reducing the incentive to invest and produce. If firms are able to raise prices in response to the increase in costs, the effect is to redistribute real income from the peasantry to the modern sector of the economy by altering the terms of trade between these sectors. However, the fall in peasants' real income may be insignificant if they spend only a small proportion of it on the products of the modern sector.

The savings constraint

Lack of savings can act as a constraint on development if development expenditure is limited by the fear of inflation created by demand pressures. The effect of earnings behaviour on the savings constraint depends on the redistribution of income it causes and the marginal propensity to save of each income group. If the savings propensity rises with average income per recipient, then in so far as increased earnings reduce profits they reduce the savings ratio and tighten the savings constraint; but in so far as they reduce peasants' real incomes by worsening their terms of trade, they increase the savings ratio and so loosen the savings constraint. The question must be settled empirically.

The foreign exchange constraint

Each of the four classes of income-recipient has a certain propensity to import. As with the savings propensity, we can assume that the import propensity is directly correlated with income per recipient. Many of the salariat are expatriates temporarily in Zambia and many profit-recipients are resident abroad, and the repatriation of their income is equivalent to importing. If the increased earnings reduce profits the foreign exchange constraint is slackened; if they reduce peasant incomes it is tightened. If wage increases raise domestic costs and prices they discourage exports and encourage imports, so worsening the balance of trade. Wage increases can have a further effect on the propensity to import. Most capital goods taking the form of machinery and equipment have to be imported into Zambia from developed countries. An increase in the cost of labour relative to capital may encourage the use of more capital-intensive techniques (i.e. involving a higher capital/output ratio), so increasing foreign exchange requirements.

The market constraint

These four categories of income-recipient may also have different propensities to consume domestically produced consumer goods. In particular, they may have different propensities to consume domestic industrial goods, in the production of which there are important internal and external economies. Let us assume that the marginal propensity to consume these goods rises initially with income per recipient, but since they are necessarily simple products, it eventually declines. Then a rise in wages and salaries, whether at the expense of profits or of the peasantry, is likely to increase the demand for locally produced industrial goods. If the size of the market is the effective constraint on industrialization, increased earnings, especially of unskilled workers, may accelerate the pace of industrialization.

The public finance constraint

If there exists a Central Bank able to engage in 'deficit finance' there is no public finance constraint separate from the savings constraint: deficit financing is limited by the inflationary pressures resulting from deficient saving. However, there is a limit to which resources can be diverted for public development expenditures. The main source of revenue for public development expenditure in Zambia is government saving, i.e. government current revenue minus government current expenditure. Wage and salary increases reduce government saving by raising current expenditure on wages and salaries. Since many government current expenditures have a high wage and salary content, government saving is sensitive to wage and salary levels. Moreover, many public development expenditures involve construction work with a high labour content: wage increases raise the cost of these development projects and so tighten the public finance and saving constraints.

The skilled manpower constraint

There is within the wage-employment sector in Zambia a very wide dispersion of earnings from employment based on skills, education, and country of origin. This wide dispersion reflects in part the extreme scarcity of skilled and educated manpower, which enables it to earn a 'scarcity rent'. Variation in salaries will not alter the supply of educated local people unless they are permitted to join the world market: their supply is fixed in the short run and determined by government educational expenditure in the long run. However, many of the skilled and educated workers in Zambia are foreigners who have been attracted to Zambia from developed countries: their opportunity cost is the world price; their salaries have to be kept in line with the world market rate. Increases in their earnings as their opportunity cost increases may be necessary to prevent the educated manpower constraint from tightening.

The cost constraint

Given the current Zambian exchange rate, only certain industries can profitably withstand foreign competition. Zambia can and does of course protect infant industries against imported substitutes, but in future she may not be able to do so. One way of overcoming the limited size of market for industrial products is to join a common market with other African countries: in 1967 Zambia applied to join the East African Common Market. But a common market implies freedom of trade between partner countries. If labour costs are higher than in partner countries, and other costs of production are not lower, Zambian products are uncompetitive. Wage cost increases may tighten the constraint on industrialization and production for export imposed by foreign competition at the existing exchange rate.

These suggested relationships are no more than hypotheses to be tested; and it is the purpose of this chapter to test some, but not all, of them.[3] After a brief examination of the reasons for recent wage increases, a study is made of the relations, first, between wage costs and economic development and, second, between wage incomes and development.

---

[3] For a more comprehensive study of Zambian earnings, on which this chapter draws heavily, see a forthcoming study by the author.

WAGE BEHAVIOUR

The Zambian labour market has two main features: a wide dispersion of earnings—between educated and uneducated, mining and other sectors, African and non-African; and a rapid increase in average

FIGURE 4.1

African average earnings by sector, 1954-66

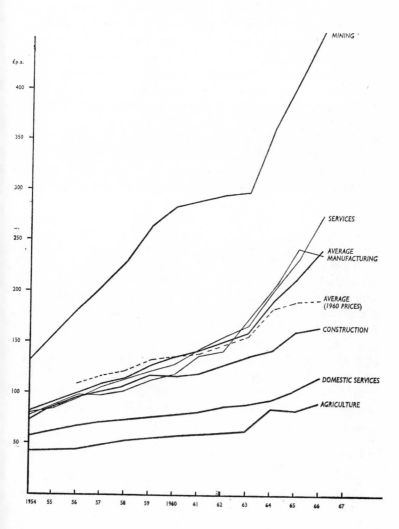

earnings over the last decade. As we shall see, these features are not unrelated.

The rapid increase in African earnings is clear from Figure 4.1 showing actual average earnings in each year, and Table 4.1, showing the annual average percentage increase in both actual and real average earnings over the period 1954–66. African average earnings rose from £78 to £240 per annum; by almost 10 per cent per annum in money terms and by more than 6 per cent per annum in real terms. African average earnings in mining and quarrying rose at a percentage rate only slightly faster than the average, from £132 to £467 per annum; being more than double the average earnings of Africans in the rest of the economy. African average earnings rose fairly steadily until the year of Independence, 1964, when there was an acceleration in the growth of money wages but not of real wages.

Over the same period, non-African average earnings rose less rapidly, by 4.3 per cent per annum in money terms and by 1.3 per cent per annum in real terms (see Table 4.1). Nevertheless, the average earnings for all sectors exceeded £2,000 per annum in 1966, being as much as £3,300 in mining and quarrying. The ratio of non-African to African average earnings fell from 15.9 in 1954 to 8.5 in 1966.

However, it would be wrong to assume that the earnings differences are due simply to race. Table 4.2, referring to the private sector (excluding mining) in 1965, shows that earnings also vary considerably with the level of education. African university degree holders received 6.9 times as much as the average earnings of uneducated Africans (i.e. those of whom no post-primary education was required) and Africans with a complete secondary education (i.e. 'O' level qualifications) 3.2 times as much as the uneducated. Moreover, the difference between African and non-African earnings at the lower levels of education is partly due to the greater training and experience of non-Africans. Had Africans at each educational level been paid the average non-African earnings for that level,[4] their average earnings would have been £305. On this criterion only 6 per cent of the difference in average earnings between Africans and non-Africans is due to factors other than education.[5]

[4] On the assumption that non-Africans in jobs not requiring formal education would have the same earnings as Africans in that category.

[5] It is of course true that race had an indirect effect on earnings through education, since access to education before Independence depended mainly on race.

TABLE 4.1
Average cash earnings by sector and by race, 1954 and 1966

	African				Non-African				Ratio of Non-African to African earnings	
	Actual earnings £ per annum		Real earnings Percentage increase p.a.		Actual earnings £ per annum		Real earnings Percentage increase p.a.			
	1954	1966	1954–66	1954–66	1954	1966	1954–66	1954–66	1954	1966
Agriculture, forestry and fishing	41	95	7.3	4.0	803	1,520	5.5	2.4	19.6	16.0
Mining and quarrying	132	467	11.1	7.7	2,120	3,299	3.8	0.8	16.1	7.1
Manufacturing	76	239	10.0	6.6	1,080	1,778	4.2	1.2	14.2	7.4
Construction	74	166	6.9	3.7	1,094	1,954	5.0	1.9	14.8	11.8
Electricity, water and sanitary services	65	228	11.0	7.6	1,179	2,464	6.3	3.3	18.1	10.8
Commerce	73	244	10.6	7.2	750	1,449	5.6	2.6	10.3	5.9
Transport and communication	86	344	12.2	8.8	1,024	2,231	6.7	3.6	11.9	6.5
Domestic services	56	124	6.8	3.6	540	—	—	—	9.6	—
Other services	77	263	10.8	7.4	829	1,368	4.3	1.3	10.8	5.2
All sectors	78	240	9.8	6.4	1,237	2,045	4.3	1.3	15.9	8.5

Note: To obtain the increase in real earnings the African and non-African earnings are deflated by the consumer price index for lower incomes and higher incomes respectively. The lower income index goes back only to 1956: the percentage annual increase 1956–66 was assumed also to apply to the period 1954–66.

Source: Manpower Report, Government Printer, Lusaka, 1966, Table B5, *Monthly Digest of Statistics*, Government Printer, Lusaka, April 1968 and other issues.

TABLE 4.2

Annual average cash earnings of males
by education and race, 1965
(£ per annum)

Education qualification	African	Non-African
Degree	1,368	2,359
Diploma or 'A' level	572	1,992
'O' level	622	1,589
Form 2	392	1,529
Less than but requiring Form 2	359	1,236
Other	197	—
All levels	204	1,668

Notes: 1   The public sector, mining, and domestic service are excluded.
2   No non-Africans were reported in the category 'other'.

Source: Manpower Report, Lusaka, 1966, Table B7.

Political factors played an important part in changing the earnings structure during the period under consideration. After Federation in 1954 there were halting steps to break down the colour bar which prevented Africans from rising to skilled and educated jobs, and the principle of common scales was established in mining in 1960 and in the civil service in 1961, although the number of Africans in skilled and educated posts was still very small.[6] But with Independence, those non-Africans who did not opt for citizenship—the vast majority—lost their settler status. The independent African government introduced in the civil service the principle of common basic scales plus an additional payment to expatriates[7] to induce them to remain in their posts until they could be replaced by citizens. Citizens were placed on the new basic salary scales, considerably lower than the scales to which they had been eligible. The same reversal of policy took place in the mining industry.

It is government policy to encourage the formation of trade unions and the practice of voluntary collective bargaining. Where trade unions are well organized, as in mining, free collective bargaining takes place. Where industries are partly or ineffectively organized, provision exists for agreements reached in joint industrial councils or wages

---

[6] Even after a year of independence, less than 3,000 of the 23,000 jobs 'requiring' at least 'O' level qualifications were filled by Africans.

[7] *Report of the Commission appointed to Review the Salaries and Conditions of Service of the Northern Rhodesia Public and Teaching Services* (Chairman: Gordon Hadow), Government Printer, Lusaka, 1964.

councils to be given legal effect. The government also set up a wages board in 1960 to prescribe statutory minimum wages applying to the remaining unorganized sectors of the economy, unless specifically excluded.

In the mid-fifties there was little trade union organization in Zambia. In 1957 trade union membership was 22,100, of whom only 8,900 were Africans, almost all in the mining industry. However, African union membership grew, first in mining and then elsewhere, until by 1965 there were 105,300 union members in 27 unions, of whom 39,500 were in mining. But pressures for wage increases do not operate only through official union action. The urban labour force, although small in number, has a political power disproportionate to its size. Urban workers are politically aware, close to the politicians, conscious of the wide dispersion of incomes within the urban sector, and vocal.

Workers in the copper industry are in a peculiarly good position to secure wage increases. The African miners were made militant by the great inequalities between black and white within the mining sector; and being geographically concentrated and socially unified, they became organized in the early fifties. They were well placed to disrupt the industry and indeed the economy. Nor have the mining companies always been loth to grant wage increases. It is a highly profitable industry, and very capital-intensive, so that African wages are only a small proportion of total costs (9.4 per cent of gross output in 1964). They have therefore been able to pay wage increases of the magnitude experienced without much effect on profits, costs, and production. They have been willing to buy good industrial relations, and anxious to guard against charges of 'exploitation'. Productivity in mining rose rapidly, by 7 per cent per annum, between 1955 and 1964. Probably this productivity growth was in part a response to wage increases,[8] but there is also reason to expect some response of wages to productivity, i.e. it was possible for the companies to accommodate the rise in earnings per employee of 7.7 per cent per annum over this period without wage costs cutting significantly into the share of profits.

These wage increases did not occur in a vacuum. A widening of the existing gap between mining and other earnings caused discontent among workers in other sectors, so producing pressures on the government as an employer and on its wages board, and influencing wage negotiations elsewhere in the economy. Evidence of 'wage-leadership'

[8] See below, p. 111.

is obtained from a least-squares regression analysis of earnings in mining and elsewhere over 13 years. The two best equations (both significant at the 1 per cent level) were:

$$N_t = 2.844 + 0.289 \, M_t \qquad (R^2 = 0.632)$$
$$(0.070)$$
$$N_t = 2.023 + 0.329 \, M_{t-\frac{1}{4}} \qquad (R^2 = 0.601)$$
$$(0.089)$$

where M is the annual absolute change in average earnings in mining, N the annual absolute change in average earnings in non-mining, and t indicates the year of change. Thus, for instance, the second equation implies that an annual increase in mining earnings was associated with a change in the annual increase in non-mining earnings about one-third as large, with a time lag of three months.[9] The mining sector acted as a 'wage-leader' for the rest of the wage-employment economy.

The pressures on employers and the government for wage increases are well illustrated by the events which led up to and followed on the Brown Commission in 1966.[10] In 1964 the African miners' union (Zambian Mineworkers' Union) accepted the principle of a differential between the earnings of citizens and expatriates in the same job, in return for the introduction of a new manning structure, which made possible the upgrading of many unskilled miners, and a general wage increase equal to over 10 per cent in the case of the lowest paid workers. But this reversal of policy, and its illogical application,[11] coming at the time of Independence, smacked to the African miners of racialism and was resented; the leadership lost support. In January 1966 the mining companies and the ZMU—its leaders facing union elections—negotiated an agreement which gave an 11 per cent increase in rates at the bottom of the scale and averaged over 8 per cent. But the rank and file felt cheated, and their discontent rapidly showed itself in a general un-official strike. According to the President in his broadcast to the nation during the strike, 'the recent agreement entered into by those who purport to represent local miners obviously falls short of their members' expectations and cannot be a basis for industrial peace on the Copper-

---

[9] The lag is introduced by weighting annual data.

[10] *Report of the Commission of Inquiry into the Mining Industry* (Chairman: Roland Brown), Government Printer, Lusaka, 1966.

[11] The non-African earnings structure, which in part reflected the bargaining strength of non-African miners rather than the scarcity of skilled manpower, was not replaced by a local scale plus expatriate allowance.

belt.'[12] Clearly the Brown Commission, in proposing increases in local rates equal to 22 per cent in the case of lowest paid workers, was concerned primarily to achieve industrial peace.[13]

The way in which the wage increase in mining spread to the rest of the economy is summarized in Table 4.3. The Brown Commission made its recommendations in August 1966, to be effective from October. The following month the Whelan Commission recommended increases for central government employees, and these increases were extended to local government employees.[14] Within three months of the wage increase for 43,500 miners, over 50,000 other workers had a rise. The various wages councils, joint industrial councils, and wages boards all agreed on increases, and in the next eight months at least a further 70,000 workers were affected. In almost every case the increase for lowest-paid workers was at least 22 per cent (see Table 4.3). Industrial unrest at this time was fairly general, and in addition to the increases listed in the table there were others negotiated at the firm level.

WAGE COSTS AND ECONOMIC DEVELOPMENT

Wage costs have different effects on production and prices in different parts of the economy. One distinction lies between goods and services produced mainly for export to world markets and those produced mainly for sale to local markets. In the latter case we should distinguish between those subject to and those free from foreign competition. These categories correspond very approximately to the primary, secondary, and tertiary sectors of the economy respectively. Mineral production accounted for 92 per cent of exports in 1965, and there were some minor agricultural exports. Export prices for these products are determined on world markets over which Zambian producers have little control. The effect of increased wages is therefore to reduce production, the reduction being greater the greater the wage component of final product and the greater the elasticity of supply. In 1965 only about 6 per cent of manufactured products were exported. Nevertheless,

---

[12] Written evidence of the ZMU to the Brown Commission, Appendix.

[13] Brown Report, pp. 43–8.

[14] *Report of the Commission appointed to Review the Grading Structure of the Civil Service, the Salary Scales of the Civil Service (. . .)* (Commissioner: F. J. Whelan), Government Printer, Lusaka, 1966.

TABLE 4.3

Wage increases after the Brown Report

Sector	Authority	Date effective	Percentage increase for lowest-paid workers	New wage for lowest-paid workers £ p.m.	Number of employees affected
Mining	Brown Commission	1.10.66	22	27.3	43,500
Central government	Whelan Commission	1.1.67	20–80[3]	13.5	35,800
Urban local government	Negotiation	1.1.67	4	14.1	8,900
Rural local government	Ministry of Local Government	1.1.67	20–80[4]	13.5[5]	2,400
Shopworkers	Wages Council	1.11.66	25–21[1]	13.1–15.0[1]	5,900
Building	Joint Industrial Council	1.4.67	33	13.7	14,000
Civil engineering	Joint Industrial Council	1.4.67	33	13.7	7,000
General minimum wage	Wages Board	1.4.67	33	13.7	17,000
Hotel, clubs, restaurants	Wages Council	1.5.67	35–55[2]	14.0–18.0[2]	4,100
Agriculture	Wages Board	21.8.67	29	7.2	30,000

[1] After 5 years' service.
[2] After 8 years' service.
[3] According to area, being greater in rural areas.
[4] Before 1967, rural local authorities normally paid the central government rates in their area.
[5] Raised to £15 three months later.

these are the products which Zambia would hope to export were it to enter the East African Common Market, and they are also the products which would be subjected to competition from substitutes produced by partner countries. Increased wages would deter the location of manufacturing industries in Zambia; the deterrent being stronger the greater the wage component of final product and the greater the price-elasticity of demand. There are some products (e.g. construction and most services) which enjoy a geographical protection from imported products. Here industry-wide wage increases are likely to be passed on as higher prices. Prices increase more the greater the wage cost as a proportion of total cost and the smaller the price-elasticity of demand. For *all* categories of commodity there is less upward movement of the supply curve the greater the elasticity of substitution of other factors for labour in response to the increased relative price of labour: with high elasticity the main effect is on employment rather than production or prices.

In Table 4.4 Zambian production in 1965 is classified into the 18 sectors of the input-output table for that year.[15] Imports of final products plus total exports, expressed as a proportion of domestic production, are taken as a crude 'index of external competition'. The fact that the overall index is 0.8 indicates that Zambia has an extremely open economy. The commercial primary producing sectors show average values of the index, and the secondary sectors some extremely high values; whereas it appears from this rough measure that in services and construction the degree of external competition is very slight. Given a fixed exchange rate and a prohibition on import restrictions, only in services and construction is it possible to pass on an increase in wage costs in the form of higher prices.

To indicate the importance of labour costs in each sector, wages may be expressed as a proportion of gross output (Table 4.4). However, these estimates may understate the importance of labour costs for two reasons. For one, gross output may exceed total costs including normal profit. For the other, the estimates include only the direct labour costs and exclude the wage component of intermediate goods used in production. Therefore they show the increase in costs resulting from a doubling of wages in only one sector at a time. However, by inverting the matrix of the input-output table it is possible to include these indirect wage

15 *National Accounts 1964–65 and Input-Output Table 1965*, Central Statistical Office, Lusaka, 1966, table facing p. 34.

TABLE 4.4
The wage component of costs, 1965

	Earnings per employee £p.a.	Direct wage cost as % of total cost	Direct and indirect wage cost as % of total cost	Index of external competition
Peasant farming, forestry, fishing, quarrying	} 107	1	1	0.0
Commercial farming		36	40	0.6
Metal mining	741	21	27	1.2
Food	332	12	33	1.5
Beverages and tobacco	517	11	18	0.3
Textiles and clothing	236	15	18	6.8
Sawmills, printing and publishing	331	25	34	0.7
Rubber and chemicals	552	21	28	5.7
Mineral products	306	18	30	0.5
Basic metals and metal products	473	21	27	0.7
Machinery, other manufactures	553	26	32	10.7
Construction	239	25	34	0.0
Electricity and water	482	7	42	0.0
Trade	} 515	22	33	0.0
Banks, real estate		20	35	0.2
Transport	502	39	44	0.5
Other services	300	82	84	0.2
Unspecified	—	—	33	0.2
Total	386	25	34	0.8

Notes: 1 Total cost is taken to be gross output.
2 The 'index of external competition' is imports of final products plus total exports divided by value added at a factor cost.
3 'Indirect wage costs' are the wage component of domestically produced intermediate goods.

Source: National Accounts 1964–65 and Input-Output Table 1965, Central Statistical Office, Lusaka, 1966, Tables 3, 9, 10, p. 34; *Monthly Digest of Statistics,* Central Statistical Office, Lusaka, April 1967, Table 4.

costs as well[16] (Table 4.4). This is the best estimate of the effect on costs of a doubling of average earnings throughout the economy. (The

[16] The following set of equations was solved for all x:

effect of a 10 per cent increase in average earnings is of course obtained simply by moving the decimal point one place to the left.) On average, costs rise by a third, but there is considerable sectoral variation. The percentage increase is high for commercial farming and naturally low for peasant farming, and less than average in copper mining. It varies between 17 and 34 per cent for manufacturing and exceeds the average for construction. It is relatively high in all services and particularly high (84 per cent) in 'other services', a category which comprises mainly public and domestic services. On this criterion, commercial farming, construction, and services suffer most from a rise in wages while mining and most manufacturing come off lightly.

It would appear, therefore, that in most of the sectors which are subject to foreign competition wage costs are a small proportion of total costs, so that costs rise, and production falls, only slightly; and in most of the sectors for which the wage component is large there is little foreign competition, so that the effect is to raise prices rather than reduce production. The sectors in which production is likely to be most sensitive to wage increases are commercial farming and the following manufacturing industries: food processing, textiles and clothing, sawmills, printing and publishing, rubber and chemicals, machinery and other manufactures.

The fact that prices of some goods and services rise in response

$$x_1 = \alpha_1 w_1 + \sum_{j=1}^{n} \beta_{1j} x_j$$

$$x_2 = \alpha_2 w_2 + \sum_{j=1}^{n} \beta_{2j} x_j$$

.
.
.

$$x_n = \alpha_n w_n + \sum_{j=1}^{n} \beta_{nj} x_j$$

where x_i = the percentage increase in total cost of the ith industry;

α_i = the wage component of total cost in the ith industry;

w_i = the percentage increase in wage cost, here assumed to be 100 per cent in each industry;

β_{ij} = the cost to the ith industry of intermediate goods from the jth industry, as a proportion of total costs; on the assumption that the prices of intermediate goods increase by the same percentage as their total cost.

to wage increases affects both the distribution of income and the pace of development. The change in relative prices redistributes real income from the peasants to the modern sector; and the increased price of public services and construction projects reduces the volume of public expenditure financed from limited revenues and the volume of profitable investment.

In 1966 the public sector (central government, local authorities and statutory bodies) had a payroll of 64,960 employees (30 per cent of total wage-employment) and a wage bill of £23.7 million, implying annual average earnings per employee of £365.[17] Table 4.5 shows the wage component of current expenditures by the public sector in 1965. It exceeds 50 per cent in general services and social services, and is particularly high in the subsectors general administration, justice and police, sanitation, fire and water, education and health.

It may be important to consider the effects on costs if the earnings of unskilled employees were increased while those of the educated élite were held. In 1965 the public sector employed 11,700 people with at least Form 2 education and 52,250 with less than this terminal level of education. Earnings data are not directly available, but estimates of earnings in the private sector excluding mining, adjusted for the racial composition of the public sector, suggest that the educated were paid 55 per cent of the total earnings bill, at average earnings of £1,230 per annum, and the uneducated 45 per cent of the earnings bill, at average earnings of £230 per annum.[18] Therefore a doubling of the earnings of uneducated employees would raise total wage costs by 45 per cent.

It is true that public saving (current revenue less current expenditure) was no less than 37 per cent of current revenue, and that public saving was more than double public gross fixed capital formation in 1965 (see Table 4.5). Saving was not a constraint on development expenditure in the public sector, so that wage increases could have been met without curtailing public services. But the favourable revenue position in 1965 provided no guarantee against the future operation of a financial constraint.

The Zambian government applied for admission to the East African Community in 1967. The main benefit to be gained from joining this

---

[17] *Monthly Digest of Statistics*, Central Statistical Office, Lusaka, April 1967, Tables 3 and 4.
[18] *Manpower Report*, Lusaka, 1966, Tables B7 and C12.

TABLE 4.5
Wage costs in the public sector, 1965

	Wage bill £m.	Wage bill as % of expenditure	Expenditure as % of current revenue
Current expenditure:			
General services	10.0	52	19.7
of which: general administration	4.4	58	7.8
justice and police	4.2	69	6.2
Community services	1.9	44	4.4
of which: sanitation, fire and water	0.6	75	0.8
Social services	9.3	59	16.1
of which: education	6.8	73	9.5
health	2.0	46	4.5
Economic services	1.8	21	8.6
of which: transport and communications	0.2	50	0.4
Unallocable	1.0	7	14.5
Total current expenditure	24.0	39	63.3
Public saving			36.7
Current revenue			100.0
Capital expenditure			40.1
of which: gross fixed capital formation			16.2

Note: The public sector is defined as central plus local government.

Source: National Accounts 1964–65 and Input-Output Table 1965, Lusaka, 1966, Tables 14 and 18A.

common market is the increased demand for the products of Zambian industry. The reverse of the coin is that the Zambian market will be opened to competition from East African industrial producers. Table 4.6 shows the average earnings in 1965 by sector for Zambia and the three East African countries and for East Africa as a whole, and also the ratio between Zambian and East African earnings. By comparison with East Africa Zambia has a 'high-wage economy'. Average earnings in Zambia are almost double those in East Africa. Moreover, apart from the special case of mining, the earnings differential is greater in manufacturing than in any other sector. Will the fact that average earnings in Zambian manufacturing are more than double the East African average deter firms from setting up or continuing to produce in Zambia?

There was a census of industrial production in 1964 in two of these countries, Zambia and Uganda. It is therefore possible to make a closer study of the effects on costs of earnings differences in the industries of these two countries. Since average earnings in the manufacturing

TABLE 4.6

Annual average earnings by sector in Zambia and East Africa, 1965

	Uganda (£)	Kenya (£)	Tanzania (£)	East Africa (£)	Zambia (£)	Zambia (East Africa =100)
Agriculture, forestry and fishing	80	61	82	71	107	151
Mining and quarrying	184	174	204	192	741	386
Manufacturing	173	210	176	193	421	219
Construction	120	207	122	131	239	182
Electricity and water	—	440	185	274	482	176
Commerce	330	359	267	336	515	153
Transport and communications	207	354	214	290	502	173
Services	211	236	192	221	300	136
Total	170	274	138	202	386	191
Legal minimum wage, 1968	90	105	90	—	160	—

Sources: Uganda Government, *Statistical Abstract 1966;*
Republic of Kenya, *Statistical Abstract 1966;*
United Republic of Tanzania, *Statistical Abstract 1965;*
Republic of Zambia, *Monthly Digest of Statistics, April 1968.*

Notes: 1 The unit of currency in East Africa is the shilling. The East African data are converted into Zambian pounds at the current exchange rate of sh. 20=£1.
2 The legal minimum in the capital city is given in each case.

sector of Uganda fall short of the East African average, our results may overstate these effects. On the other hand, because it is necessary to neglect the wage component in the cost of intermediate goods, there is also a tendency to understate the effects of earnings differences. Gross output is taken to indicate total costs, and this too may lead to understatement. In only two products, textiles and bricks, is Zambia not at a cost disadvantage (see Table 4.7). It matters little whether the cost difference attributable to differing earnings is expressed as

	Average earnings			Direct wage costs as proportion of total costs				Proportion of costs attributable to earnings differences	
	Zambia (£p.a.)	Zambia (Uganda =100)	Uganda (£p.a.)	Zambia (%)	Zambia with Ugandan average earnings (%)	Uganda (%)	Uganda with Zambian average earnings (%)	Zambian costs (%)	Ugandan costs (%)
Grain mill products	349.8	241	145.2	8.0	3.3	3.3	7.9	4.7	4.6
Bakery products	319.6	189	169.1	19.2	10.2	12.4	23.5	9.0	11.1
Other food preparations	309.1	238	130.1	10.6	4.5	3.9	9.3	6.1	5.4
Breweries and soft drinks	515.1	156	330.7	13.2	8.5	15.7	24.4	4.7	8.7
Textiles and clothing	225.6	90	250.9	14.7	16.4	18.2	16.4	1.7	1.8
Sawmills	194.4	187	103.8	39.5	21.2	25.5	47.7	18.3	22.2
Furniture and fixtures	256.8	178	144.6	19.5	11.0	28.5	50.7	8.5	22.2
Printing and publishing	637.7	221	288.9	46.5	21.1	29.1	64.2	45.4	35.1
Rubber products	447.8	142	314.7	23.5	16.5	16.8	23.9	7.0	7.1
Structural clay products	135.4	98	137.6	50.0	50.8	32.2	31.7	0.8	0.5
Non-metallic mineral products	369.0	188	196.8	19.7	10.5	17.0	31.1	9.2	14.1
Iron and steel, and metal products	465.2	196	237.4	24.4	12.4	5.8	11.4	12.0	5.6
Electrical machinery	506.3	227	222.7	24.2	10.6	28.2	64.1	13.6	35.9
Transport equipment and repair	492.4	187	263.8	44.9	24.0	28.9	53.9	20.9	25.0
Total manufacturing	369.9	170	218.2	19.4	11.4	11.6	19.6	8.0	8.0

Notes: 1 Only those industries common to both countries are shown in the table, but 'total manufacturing' includes all industries. The ISIC code descriptions of an industry are not always identical for the two countries.

2 Gross output is taken to indicate total costs.

Sources: Republic of Zambia. Census of Production 1964, 1966; Uganda Government, Survey of Industrial Production 1964, 1966.

a proportion of Zambian or Ugandan costs. The cost difference amounts to 8 per cent for total manufacturing in both cases, and the average of the two estimates exceeds 10 per cent for bakery products, sawmills, furniture and fixtures, printing and publishing, non-metallic mineral products, electrical machinery, and transport equipment. It appears that the high earnings paid to labour place Zambia at a significant disadvantage relative to her potential partners in the East African Community.

This conclusion is subject to two qualifications. First, it is possible that differences in labour costs are offset by other cost advantages. Differences in transport costs may be important, although these may well accentuate the Zambian disadvantage. Moreover, it is clear from the differences in labour cost per unit of output in the two countries that the higher Zambian earnings per employee are not offset by higher Zambian productivity per employee. Second, Zambia may be protected from the harmful effects of entry to the Common Market by two 'measures to promote balanced industrial development'.[19] One is a system of 'transfer taxes'. These can be imposed on other members' products by partners which have a deficit in interterritorial trade in manufactures, provided that the tax does not exceed half the external tariff and provided that the tax-imposing country produces the commodity on a significant scale. The other measure is the establishment of an East African Development Bank to which all partners subscribe equally but from which the industrially backward partners benefit most.

The effects of an increase in wage costs have been analysed on the assumption that the exchange rate remains constant. If the competitiveness of industrial products is eroded by wage increases, could it be restored by a devaluation of the currency? Given the high elasticity of demand for Zambian exports and high elasticity of supply of imports into Zambia, the devaluation must improve the balance on current account and can have no significant effect on the terms of trade. But it does produce a considerable redistribution of income within the economy. In terms of domestic currency the price of both exports and imports increases by the extent of the devaluation. Unless the government can tax away the windfall accruing to the mining industry, the miners' bargaining position is strengthened, and there is a greater likelihood of increased earnings in mining, subsequently spreading to other sectors of the modern economy. In 1965 total final imports and

19 *Treaty for East African Co-operation*, signed 6 June 1967.

final consumer goods imports were 26 and 18 per cent of gross national income respectively, and in 1966 the import propensity of African employees in Lusaka was on average 24 per cent.[20] Real incomes are cut through the increase in import prices, in proportion to the import content of consumers' income. Since the propensity to import probably increases with income, this in itself may improve the distribution of income. However, employees, by raising money wages, are in a better position to restore their real income than peasants. Not only are wage costs likely to increase but also the cost of materials. Imports of intermediate goods accounted for one-sixth of total costs in 1965, and, in the case of manufacturing alone, the import content of costs amounted to one-third.[21] This brief analysis suggests that, as a result of the ensuing increase in the cost of inputs, the competitive advantage gained is likely to be small relative to the size of devaluation.

Has the rapid increase in wages led to a corresponding increase in productivity and so offset the effect of increased wages on unit costs ? There is an association in two of the three sectors for which data of real output changes can be pieced together.[22] Whereas in manufacturing annual productivity growth lagged behind wage increases over the period 1955–64 (3 per cent compared with 9 per cent), annual growth of productivity and average earnings were closely in line for commercial agriculture (13 and 11 per cent respectively) and metal mining (7 and 8 per cent respectively). It does not follow from this association that the increased wages caused the increased productivity. Nevertheless it is possible, for the following reasons. First, an increased wage may improve workers' diet and so raise labour efficiency. Second, a higher wage may permit and encourage the stabilization of a migrant labour force, so raising the quality of labour. Third, the increased cost of labour relative to capital encourages the substitution of capital for labour.

Consider the argument that wage increases lead to improved nutri-

---

20 See Table 4.8.
21 Total costs are defined as GDP at market prices plus imports of intermediate goods. For the manufacturing sector alone total costs are value added at market prices plus imported intermediate goods plus intermediate goods from other sectors, and import costs are imported intermediate goods plus the import content of intermediate goods from other sectors.
22 Volume indices are used, except in the case of manufacturing between 1954 and 1961, for which the implicit price index for the Federation has to be used to deflate current values.

tion, leading in turn to improved health and hence to improved physical efficiency of workers. There are a number of possible weak links in this chain of reasoning: additional income need not be spent on food, or on nutritious food, or it may merely increase the average size of the urban family. Health may be impaired by diseases other than malnutrition, or malnutrition may have become chronic, and physical fitness need not be the constraint on the efficiency of labour. The recent household expenditure survey gives little support for this hypothesis: a cross-section analysis shows a marginal propensity to spend on food of one-third, and a marginal propensity to consume food per 'man unit' of less than 0.10.[23] On the other hand, the 1960 survey shows a systematic rise in calories consumed per 'man unit' from 2,590 calories per day for the lowest to 3,010 per day for the highest quintile income group, a range which could influence labour efficiency.[24]

A system of migrant labour lowers labour efficiency and deters firms from investment in the training of their workers. Since a ready supply of migrant labour depresses the market-determined unskilled wage rate, to break down a system of migrant labour it may be necessary to raise wages above the market rate. Moreover, there is evidence that, since the mid-fifties, labour has become more stabilized and the average size of the urban family has increased. A random sample of African employees in 1954 in Lusaka indicated that 65 per cent of households were 'family units' as opposed to single men,[25] and this figure rose to 84 per cent in 1960.[26] Average household size in Lusaka rose from 3.38 in 1954 to 3.90 in 1960 to 5.20 in 1966.[27] Moreover, the average household income for the surveys rose from just over £7 a month in 1954 to nearly £24 a month in 1966. However, the importance of stabilization during this period is limited by the fact that only a minority of African workers in Lusaka were migrants at the start of the period.

---

[23] *Interim Report on the First Three Months of the Lusaka Urban Budget Survey, October–December 1966*, Central Statistical Office, Lusaka, 1967.

[24] *First Report on Urban African Budget Surveys held in Northern Rhodesia May to August 1960*, Central Statistical Office, Lusaka, reprinted 1965, Table 26.

[25] D. G. Bettison, *Numerical Data on African Dwellers in Lusaka, Northern Rhodesia*, Rhodes Livingstone Institute Communication No. 16, 1959.

[26] *First Report on Urban African Budget Surveys held in Northern Rhodesia May to August 1960*, Central Statistical Office, Lusaka, reprinted 1965.

[27] *Interim Report on the First Three Months of the Lusaka Urban Budget Survey, October–December 1966*, Central Statistical Office, Lusaka, 1967.

The labour-intensity of production may be reduced either in response to changing relative factor prices or for reasons unrelated to wage increases, for instance technical progress embodied in capital goods imported from developed countries. To give an example from copper mining: was the decisive factor in raising productivity the increased wage (encouraging substitution of capital for labour and semi-skilled for unskilled labour) or relaxation of the colour bar (permitting substitution of semi-skilled for unskilled labour) or technical progress (in earthmoving equipment and mining methods) emanating from abroad? There is Zambian evidence to support both the 'factor substitution' and 'embodied technical progress' hypotheses. Relative factor prices moved in favour of machinery by 3.2 per cent per annum between 1954 and 1965.[28] On the other hand, it is true that 94 per cent of Zambian demand for 'machineries' in 1965 was met by imports.[29] An indication that factor substitution did not much offset the effect of wage increases on costs is the evidence of Table 4.7 that wages as a proportion of total costs are considerably higher in Zambian than in Ugandan manufacturing industries.

To summarize: it appears from the limited evidence that wage increases may have raised productivity, so tending to offset their effect on unit costs. However, the extent to which cost increases were offset in this way is unlikely to have been complete and possibly not even significant. Moreover, to the extent that wage increases raised productivity without also permitting higher production, they reduced employment, so aggravating the problem of urban unemployment and, by preventing peasants from entering the wage-employment sector, worsening the distribution of income.

WAGE INCOMES
AND ECONOMIC DEVELOPMENT

An increase in wages affects not only costs of production but also wage incomes and therefore expenditure. What effect does this change in income have on the demand for domestically produced goods, especially industrial goods, on the demand for imports and on savings?

[28] *Monthly Digest of Statistics*, Central Statistical Office, Lusaka, April 1967, Tables 3, 4, 47, 49.
[29] *National Accounts 1964–65 and Input-Output Table 1965*, Central Statistical Office, Lusaka, 1966, Table 3 and table facing p. 32.

In turn, what implications do these changes in the pattern of expenditure have for economic development, if the effective constraint on development is the demand for industrial products, or a shortage of foreign exchange or of savings?

The data available to answer these questions are an input-output table for 1965 and a sample household budget survey of the high-density, i.e. African, housing area of Lusaka in 1966.[30] The input-output table indicates for 63 consumption categories the proportion of expenditure on imports and on domestically produced goods and services by 40 sectors of origin.[31] The budget survey permits a breakdown of expenditure into 103 consumption categories for 8 household expenditure groups, grouped according to expenditure range.[32] Consumption in the two cases can be reclassified in 37 common categories. On the assumption that the source (primary, secondary, tertiary, or imports) of each consumption category is the same for all expenditure groups, it is then possible to find demand by source and by expenditure group, i.e. the proportion which each group spends on imports, on domestic products arising in the primary, secondary, and tertiary sectors, and retains in savings.

Making use of these cross-section data, it is possible to show the effect of wage increases on expenditure patterns. A 50 per cent increase in wage rates (non-wage income remaining constant) raises the average income of households in each expenditure group. The effect of this increased income on expenditure is calculated by regressing expenditure on income. A strong relationship (significant at the 0.1 per cent level) is found, of the form

$$C = 1.175Y - 123.5 \qquad (R^2 = 0.994)$$
$$(0.038)$$

where C is consumption expenditure and Y income.[33] This implies a negative cross-section marginal propensity to save![34] On the assump-

---

[30] ibid. and *Interim Report on the First Three Months of the Lusaka Urban Budget Survey, October–December 1966*, Central Statistical Office, Lusaka, 1967.

[31] In the unpublished version. The published table shows only 10 consumption categories (p. 33).

[32] The 4 groups exceeding £50 per month have been consolidated owing to the small numbers in each.

[33] Because free or subsidized housing is common, consumption excludes rent and income includes housing allowance minus rent.

[34] The negative savings of the higher income groups may result partly from the fact that Christmas bonuses, received by some of these households,

tions that the cross-section consumption function can be applied to households whose incomes increase, and that households are evenly spread within each expenditure range, it is possible to estimate the number of households moving into higher expenditure groups as incomes increase. In this way the expenditure, by source, of the African population of Lusaka before and after a 50 per cent wage increase can be estimated.

The results of this exercise are shown in Table 4.8. The allocation of income by the African population of Lusaka before and after the increase (columns (a) and (b) respectively) reveals (in column (g)) that expenditure on imports is the most income-elastic component of expenditure, followed by local services, then industrial goods (with an income-elasticity of 1.02), followed by local primary products; while the rate of saving falls and actually becomes negative. Therefore, if the effective constraint on development is foreign exchange or saving, a wage increase retards development. If the constraint is demand for domestically produced industrial goods, the effect of a wage increase is surprisingly slight; the increase in demand for the products of local industries being only 27 per cent of the wage increase in our example.

It is true that the high marginal propensity to import (42 per cent) provides greater scope for industrialization through import substitution, if necessary behind tariff barriers. Wage increases raise the demand for potential import substitutes, permitting the exploitation of economies of scale in their production, and reducing the degree of protection and hence the level of domestic prices necessary for the establishment of these industries. The benefits derived from reduced protection must then be weighed against the disadvantages of wage increases. However, such a policy for industrialization is likely to be incompatible with the alternative method of expanding the market for domestic industries, i.e. entry to a common market. And it is the latter policy which the Zambian government appears to be adopting.

A general wage increase can have secondary effects on the economy, for instance on employment. In so far as increased wage costs cut back

---

were spread over the year in the analysis of income but were spent mostly during December (*Interim Report*, sup. cit., p. 4). No indication is given of the quantitative importance of this factor. Unfortunately the final report of the Lusaka urban budget survey, covering a whole year, was not available at the time of writing.

TABLE 4.8

The effect of a 50 per cent wage increase on the allocation of income

	Original expenditure £'000 (a)	Expenditure after wage increase £'000 (b)	Expenditure after wage increase and employment decrease £'000 (c)	Original expenditure % (d)	Expenditure after wage increase % (e)	Expenditure after wage increase and employment decrease % (f)	(b)−(a) / (a) % (g)	(f)−(d) % (h)
Expenditure on imports	135.2	229.2	163.7	24.3	29.4	29.4	69.6	5.1
Domestic expenditure:								
primary	106.8	124.9	89.2	19.2	16.0	16.0	11.7	−3.2
secondary	143.5	204.2	145.8	25.7	26.2	26.2	42.3	0.5
tertiary	148.6	237.9	169.9	26.7	30.5	30.5	60.1	3.8
Total expenditure	534.2	796.2	568.5	95.8	102.0	102.0	49.1	6.2
Saving	23.3	−15.5	−11.1	4.2	−2.0	−2.0	−116.7	−6.2
Total income	557.4	780.7	557.4	100.0	100.0	100.0	40.1	0.0

Note: The data of columns (a)–(c) refer to the African population of the high-density areas of Lusaka.

Sources: Central Statistical Office, Lusaka; *National Accounts 1964–65 and Input-Output Table 1965,* 1966; *Interim Report on the First Three Months of the Lusaka Urban Budget Survey, October–December 1966,* May 1967; unpublished data.

production, they reduce employment, and in so far as the increased price of labour raises output per unit of labour input without raising output, it reduces employment. In either case the reduction in employment decreases the wage bill. On the assumption that the wage increase leads to an equal proportionate decrease in employment, and total non-wage income is unaffected, the initial level of income is restored. But this income is allocated in a different way (column (c)). The smaller labour force with the higher average earnings spends 5.1 per cent more of its income on imports, saves 6.2 per cent less, and spends only 0.5 per cent more of its income on local industrial products (column (h)). On these assumptions, the foreign exchange and savings constraints are tightened, and the market constraint on industrialization is loosened only very slightly.

The results of this exercise are no better than the assumptions on which it is based. For instance, it is dangerous to generalize from a three-month survey of African households in Lusaka. Also dubious is the assumption that the effect on expenditure of a general rise in incomes can be found from the cross-section analysis of expenditure patterns by income group. Moreover, the data refer only to urban wage-earning households, and exclude peasant incomes and profits. A wage increase reduces output, squeezes profits and raises prices in varying proportions, depending on such factors as the motivations of firms, their supply and demand curves, the degree of competition both domestic and foreign, and government policy. Wage-earners benefit at the expense of the peasants if modern sector prices increase, and of profits if prices are held down. In so far as peasants' real incomes or profits are squeezed, there are changes in the allocation of total income, with further effects on the pattern of demand. These qualifications must be borne in mind.

Nevertheless, the exercise suggests that an increase in wages, by causing a change in incomes and their allocation, is likely to tighten the foreign exchange and savings constraints, and to relax only marginally the constraint imposed by lack of industrial demand. Only if it is government policy to industrialize behind tariff barriers does the argument for wage increases as a spur to industrialization carry weight.

SUMMARY AND CONCLUSIONS

The mining industry is crucial to an understanding of recent earnings behaviour in Zambia. The bargaining strength of the miners (resulting from their power to disrupt the industry and the economy and their resentment of the vast racial income differentials in the industry), the technical conditions of the industry, and the attitude of the mining companies all helped to produce a rapid increase in average earnings in mining over the last decade. This increase then spread, through political and trade union pressures, to the rest of the economy. As a result Zambia is saddled with an earnings level double the average in East Africa. Moreover, whereas the increases could be accommodated by the mining industry without significant harmful effects, the consequences for the rest of the economy were more serious.

In raising costs wages may either decrease production or increase prices. Probably wage increases did not curtail production very much in Zambia over the last decade. In those sectors in which wage costs are a high proportion of total costs, i.e. increased wages have a large effect on costs, there is little foreign competition and it is more likely that prices rose than that production fell. In those sectors subject to foreign competition, i.e. where the impact of cost increases is on production rather than prices, wage costs are not a high proportion of total costs, so that output was little affected. Nevertheless, in manufacturing the difference in wage costs per unit of output between Zambia and Uganda is sufficiently great to put Zambia at a competitive disadvantage if it enters the East African Common Market. Construction and services are sectors in which a general wage increase is likely to be passed on in price increases. The increased price of construction work may have reduced the profitability of investment. The increased cost of public services and development expenditures can restrict their provision; but this is unlikely to happen in Zambia until the government is faced with a financial constraint.

Wage increases may have raised productivity (through their influence on health, labour stabilization and training, and choice of techniques), so helping to offset their effect on unit costs. However, the offsetting is unlikely to have been complete and may possibly not even have been significant. Moreover, the increased productivity probably reduced employment and so worsened the distribution of income.

It was argued that an increase in wages, by causing a change in incomes and their allocation, is likely to tighten the foreign exchange and savings constraints, and to relax only marginally the constraint imposed by lack of industrial demand. However, the wage increase does give more scope for industrialization by means of import substitution.

It is clear that, given a fixed exchange rate, high and rising wages are more harmful if Zambia enters a common market, so making it impossible to protect Zambian products against foreign competition, than if the country chooses to industrialize behind tariff barriers. Nevertheless, an increase in wages has harmful effects even in the latter case, both on growth and the distribution of income. Devaluation can offset the effect of wage increases, but the ensuing increase in the cost of inputs means that the competitive advantage gained is likely to be small relative to the size of devaluation.

It is important that the Zambian government devise an incomes policy which restricts the growth of wages to the rate of growth of peasant incomes. Yet such a policy has little hope of success unless it also tackles the main source of wage-earners' discontent: the wide dispersion of incomes within the modern sector of the economy.

5

Financial Constraints on Zambian Development

C. R. M. HARVEY [1]

INTRODUCTION

ZAMBIA is unusual among developing countries in that she has large resources of her own to finance development—almost exclusively derived from copper, of course. Thus, in the First National Development Plan 1966–70, total public sector expenditure (capital and recurrent) was estimated at K 1,241.6 m. for the four years. No less than K 1,049.6 m. of this, or 84.5 per cent, was estimated to be available from taxation, and only K 126.0 m., or 10.1 per cent, from external loans and foreign aid.[2] Most development plans as ambitious as this one depend very heavily on optimistic projections of the country's ability to procure aid and foreign loans.[3] The result of depending very heavily on such an uncertain source of finance is very often that plan targets are not met, and the government is forced to borrow from its central bank or in other very short-term ways, with inflationary results.[4]

It will be argued in this chapter that in spite of the very large sums already raised by the present taxation system, and the prospect of more,

---

[1] Lecturer in Economics, University of Zambia. Chapters 5 and 6 were written in mid-1968 before the quasi-nationalization of the copper industry (*ed. note*).

[2] The remaining finance was estimated to come from 'internal finance' (K 6 m.) and 'internal loans' (K 60 m.). *First National Development Plan, 1966–70*, Office of National Development and Planning, Lusaka, July 1966.

[3] See, for example, R. H. Green, 'Four African Development Plans', *Journal of Modern African Studies*, Vol. 3, 2, pp. 253–74, reprinted in E. H. Whetham and J. I. Currie, *Readings in the Applied Economics of Africa*, Vol. 2, Cambridge University Press, 1967.

[4] This probably happened in Ghana: see A. J. Killick, 'The Monetary Effects of Recent Budgets in Ghana', reprinted from the *Economic Bulletin of Ghana*, Vol. 9, 1, in Whetham and Currie, op. cit.

the economy will shortly be moving on to an inflationary course unless the tax base is widened and tax rates increased, or unless the government is willing to slacken its own rate of growth of expenditure.

In order to develop this argument the chapter will examine the banking system and other credit-giving institutions, non-bank sources of finance for the budget, personal savings generally, and the trends that have developed over the last three or four years with their implications for the future. Having made out a case, I hope, for widening the tax base and increasing tax rates, I shall examine the tax system both to see how this can be done and also to see if it is creating the right incentives in work, production, saving, and investment.

THE COMMERCIAL BANKS

At the end of 1965 the commercial banks in Zambia were in a position of considerable excess liquidity, with comfortable spare cash held with banks abroad, and a very substantial ability to increase their lending. At that time therefore there was no question of the availability of bank credit being a constraint on the expansion of the economy; in fact there must have been a deficiency of demand of the right sort. This last qualification is clearly important since the banks' criteria for selecting suitable borrowers could well, and indeed must, have left unsatisfied a number of would-be borrowers. This aside (it will be dealt with below), the banking system in 1965 had ample funds for a multiple expansion of credit, if borrowers of the right sort presented themselves, without any increase in the base of the money supply by the Bank of Zambia.[5]

In the following period, to June 1968, this is exactly what happened. During this period balances at the Bank of Zambia rose by only K 2.0 m. while deposits rose by K 62.9 m. and loans and advances rose by K 54.5 m. (using averages of end-month figures, as in Tables 5.1, 5.2, and 5.3).

By the middle of 1968, however, this source of finance had been

[5] For changes in the banks' position since 1965 see Tables 5.1, 5.2 and 5.3. Because individual months' figures can be misleading, especially when a few large customers can cause considerable distortions, averages of end-month figures have been used throughout. Because the banks' figures are made up at the end of the calendar month, when many large transactions, such as the payment of wages, take place, some distortions could remain; but it is unlikely that they could affect the overall picture presented here.

fully utilized. Net balances held abroad by the commercial banks had moved from K 7.8 m. in 1965 to the negative figure of $-$K 5.1 m.; that is, the banks were net borrowers from banks overseas, mainly, of course, their own head offices. In addition their internal position was pressing up against the limits represented by the official cash reserve requirements. These are that 8 per cent of demand deposits, and 3 per cent of savings and time deposits, must be maintained as balances at the Bank of Zambia. In 1965 these percentages came to only K 5.1 m. compared with bankers' balances at the Bank of Zambia of K 8.1 m.; that is, only about 63 per cent, or under two-thirds of bankers' balances at the Central Bank, were being used to satisfy compulsory reserve requirements—the remainder represented idle balances, which were available, and were in fact subsequently used, as a basis to expand the money supply.

By mid-1968 the position was very different. The amount of bankers' balances at the Bank of Zambia was K 10.1 m., but the amount of this needed to satisfy compulsory cash reserve requirements was K 9.4 m. In fact, for a brief period around the middle of the year the commercial banks actually borrowed (up to K 3.0 m.) from the Bank of Zambia, thus using for the first time the Central Bank's facilities as lender of last resort, and emphasizing the using up of their own spare cash reserves.

TABLE 5.1

Commercial banks: deposits and lending, 1965–8

| | Averages of end-month figures: K m. | | | |
	1965[1]	1966	1967	1968[2]
Demand deposits	53.6	72.4	86.9	100.4
Time deposits	28.6	32.6	41.9	44.7
Total deposits	82.2	105.0	128.8	145.1
Loans and advances	27.9	34.3	52.7	82.4
Bills of exchange	7.0	15.4	30.8	24.8
Total private sector lending	34.9	49.7	83.5	107.2

[1] Figures for 1965 are for last 9 months only.
[2] Figures for 1968 are for first 6 months only.

Clearly the banks still have considerable resources other than cash, with varying degrees of liquidity. Their note holdings, although as liquid as anything can be, are not really in this category. The cash reserve requirements laid down by the authorities relate only to balances at the Bank of Zambia, and thus exclude till money (banks' own note holdings). Not surprisingly, in these circumstances, the banks have economized on note holdings, so successfully that they have remained

TABLE 5.2

Commercial banks: private sector lending
as a proportion of total deposits

Averages of end-month figures: %

	1965[1]	1966	1967	1968[2]
Loans and advances	33.9	32.6	40.9	56.8
Bills of exchange	8.5	14.7	23.9	17.1
Total private sector lending	42.5	47.3	64.8	73.9

[1] Figures for 1965 are for last 9 months only.
[2] Figures for 1968 are for first 6 months only.

TABLE 5.3

Commercial banks: cash position

Average of end-month figures: K m.

	1965[1]	1966	1967	1968[2]
Net balances abroad	+7.8	+8.3	+2.5	−5.1
Balances at Bank of Zambia[3]	+8.1	+9.5	+9.6	+10.1
Balances required at Bank of Zambia by reserve ratios	5.1	6.8	8.2	9.4

[1] Figures for 1965 are for last 9 months only.
[2] Figures for 1968 are for first 6 months only.
[3] Net of amounts owing to Bank of Zambia.

at much the same level through the last two to three years. There is therefore unlikely to be any scope for actual reductions in order to boost balances at the Bank of Zambia, when the large rise in total deposits is considered (65 per cent in the two and a half years to June 1968).

There still remain, however, holdings of treasury bills (K 7.7 m.), bills of exchange (K 20.8 m.), and 'investments' (almost entirely locally-registered stock, K 8.5 m.). Given that there is almost no local capital market, these holdings might not be thought to be very liquid. In fact, however, the Bank of Zambia will discount treasury bills, and that proportion of bills of exchange which are eligible. What is more, holdings of Government of Zambia locally-registered stock may also be sold to the Bank of Zambia at prices which are published monthly by the bank, and which move in line with movements in its own discount rate. What this all amounts to, then, is that in spite of the absence of markets of the type that exist in the major capitals of the developed world, such as London, New York, and Paris, Zambian commercial banks can regard their fixed interest bearing assets in a very similar way as regards liquidity as would their counterparts elsewhere. That is, the shorter-dated the asset, the less likely is it to involve a bank in a loss if sold; and the longer-dated an asset, the more likely is such a loss. Thus by increasing its own discount rate, and at the same time lowering its buying prices for stocks, the Bank of Zambia can involve the commercial banks in substantial losses if they choose to try to improve their cash position by selling 'marketable' assets rather than by restricting advances to customers. The banks also have the choice of selling short-dated assets, such as treasury bills, which would minimize their immediate losses, but reduce their potential for doing the same again later (that is, reduce their overall liquidity); or of selling longer-dated assets with a higher immediate loss but less damage to their liquidity position.

In short, the pressures which the Bank of Zambia can put on the banks are really quite similar to those which, say, the Bank of England can put on commercial banks in London, the difference being that such pressure would be more direct in Zambia, working as it does through direct contact, rather than through the complicated and sensitive day-to-day movements in a market; but slower, since at present price movements occur only monthly.

A second possible source of additional bank finance could be the running down of advances to non-Zambians.[6] If this took the form of a reduction in the finance of consumption (presumably of consumer durables mainly) financed by means of bank credit, then there would indeed be a net increase in bank finance available for development purposes,[7] and there could in addition be a reduction in the demand for imports. In so far, however, as advances were withdrawn from non-Zambians who were using the loans in business, then it would not lead to any increase in funds for development. This source of funds is probably not large. The breakdown of bank advances by borrower groups is less up to date than other banking statistics, but in July 1967 only K 3.2 m. had been lent under the category 'personal accounts',[8] not all of which of course would be to non-Zambians. To the extent that there is a non-Zambian element in the other categories it would, as already argued, probably have to be re-lent to Zambians in similar undertakings.

The other possibility is a further increase in the net indebtedness of the banks to their head offices overseas. There is no compelling

[6] Under the terms of the Mulungushi Declaration, April 1968.
[7] Availability does not necessarily increase funds lent for development; the banks could lend to Zambians for consumption instead.
[8] The figure is a residual and so individual months' figures must be treated with particular caution—this one, however, looks to be in line.

reason why the big international banks should not be willing to allow head office overdrafts to branches in one part of the world, at the expense of course of branches somewhere else. Zambia has, in the last two or three years, moved from just such a position of net lending to the rest of the world, through the banking system, to one of net borrowing. Indeed it would be quite rational for the big international banks to channel funds in just this way to areas where the prospects of profit (calculated as gross yield on loans less any allowance for relative degree of risk) were greatest. This is just what the big banks with many branches do *within* a country.

There is, however, some evidence that the big international banks do not do this, but in fact try to avoid a position of international imbalance, except where there is a position of net lending by overseas branches *to* the head office. R. A. Sowelem has argued that a deterioration in the liquidity position of commercial banks of the Federation of Rhodesia and Nyasaland led to a 'marked slowing down in the expansion of bank credit'. [9] This interpretation is supported (as is also argued by Sowelem) in the evidence submitted by the British Overseas Banks Association to the Radcliffe Committee on the working of the monetary system. There it was clearly established that the big international banks were only prepared to make advances in one country, in excess of the deposits in that country, as a very temporary measure, for example for seasonal requirements, so that local branches could *not* regard head office overdrafts as a permanent source of funds.[10] A reason suggested by Sowelem for such behaviour by the big banks is their fear of exchange rate instability.[11] If a bank is in a position where lending in a country is financed by funds from elsewhere, there would be a risk of loss in the event of a devaluation. If this is so then the greater the risk of devaluation, the more quickly will the head office of a bank insist on the restriction of credit in a country which has overdrawn its head office account.

This attitude was confirmed in recent interviews. One bank official was in fact surprised at head offices having restricted imbalanced posi-

----

[9] R. A. Sowelem, *Towards Financial Independence in a Developing Economy: An Analysis of the Monetary Experience of the Federation of Rhodesia and Nyasaland 1952–63*, Allen and Unwin, London, 1967, pp. 230–31.

[10] *Minutes of Evidence of the Committee on the Working of the Monetary System*, Cmnd. 827, questions 4327–4520, HMSO, 1960, quoted in Sowelem, op. cit., pp. 231–2.

[11] Sowelem, op. cit., pp. 234–5.

tions in the past, but was very emphatic that imbalances would not be allowed in the future, because of the recent (1967) sterling devaluation, which was not followed uniformly by all the sterling area countries.[12] On that occasion some substantial losses were made, so that if it was likely in the 1950s that head offices would always try to correct a deficit position of branches in any one country, it must be much more likely now, when the sterling area is much less unified, and nearly all the countries in it are independent and pursuing independent monetary policies.

The implication of all this is that further net lending to the commercial banks in Zambia by their head offices abroad is unlikely. On the contrary, the head offices are likely to insist on the restoration of the present overdrawn position to one of net balance, which, without further help from the Bank of Zambia, would mean that the banks would actually have to reduce their present level of lending.

The possibility of borrowing temporarily from abroad does of course reduce the speed of operation of attempts by the Bank of Zambia to control the money supply; but provided that the big banks do in fact continue to act in the way described, then the Bank of Zambia can always exercise ultimate control, perhaps with some delay.[13]

THE BUDGET POSITION AND THE GOVERNMENT'S NEED FOR FINANCE

Having established that, broadly speaking, further increases in bank credit will depend on the willingness of the Bank of Zambia to permit further expansions in the banks' cash reserves, the question remains as to how great the pressure will be on the Bank of Zambia to do so unwillingly; that is, whether the need for government deficit finance, and an inability to raise it from the general public, may force the Central Bank to borrow on the government's behalf from the commercial banks, or even to finance the deficit itself.[14]

[12] Most, like Zambia, did not devalue; some, e.g. Malawi, devalued by the same amount as Great Britain; others, e.g. New Zealand, devalued by more.
[13] The possibility of such delays may be a small price to pay for the greatly added stability of the banking system arising out of the existence of overseas head offices on which they can overdraw temporarily.
[14] Roughly speaking, financing a deficit by borrowing from the commercial banks increases the money supply by that amount; borrowing from the

TABLE 5.4

Central government budget position 1964–5 to 1967–8
(K m.)

	1964–5	1965–6	1966–7	1967–8
Current revenue	+157.1	+217.4	+272.7	+292.5
Current expenditure	−101.4	−123.9	−162.5	−183.2
Current surplus	+55.7	+93.5	+110.2	+109.3
Capital expenditure	−30.6	−65.7	−93.7	−114.2
Overall budget surplus (+)/deficit (−)	+25.1	+27.8	+16.5	−4.9

Sources: *Monthly Digest of Statistics, Estimates of Revenue and Expenditure, Financial Reports,* Central Statistical Office, Lusaka.

Notes: 1 The 1966–7 financial year was extended for six months to December 1967. In order to give a comparable run of figures the 'years' in this table are all on a July to June base.

2 Current expenditure excludes 'Appropriations from revenue', which is a transfer of the current revenue surplus to capital account, and thus appears in this table as part of the current surplus.

3 Current expenditure also excludes estimates of repayment of loans, which is listed in the government's figures as part of statutory expenditure. Loan repayments were estimated to be K 4.2 m., K 15.5 m., K 7.8 m. and K 20.8 m. in the four years.

From Table 5.4 it can be seen that in the last four years the government has moved gradually from a position of substantial surplus in 1964/5 and 1965/6 to a position of having a small deficit in 1967/8. The biggest change in the government's position has occurred in this latest year when it moved from a surplus (on current and capital account taken together) of K 16.5 m. to a deficit of K 4.9 m., a net change in the overall budget position of over K 20 m.

The actual size of the surplus or deficit depends to a considerable extent on the definition of items that should be included in the budget (see the notes to Table 5.4). The figures given here exclude all financing items, that is, the redemption of earlier government borrowing, and the flotation of new loans, of whatever sort. The reason for taking this line is that basically one requires to know two separate things— the net financing *requirement* of the government as witnessed by the deficit (or surplus) in the government's receipts of revenue, and expen-

central bank increases the commercial banks' cash reserves by the amount of the deficit, and thus permits an expansion of credit much larger than the government deficit itself.

diture of all sorts; and the net amount *borrowed* by the government from the non-bank public.[15] The second figure is shown in Table 5.7, and is enough to cover the existing deficit; but there is no particular reason to expect a dramatic increase in non-bank lending to the government, so that a sharp deterioration in the budget position, other things being equal, is going to lead eventually to inflationary pressure.

The main cause of this change in the budget position has been a slowing down in the rate of growth of current revenue. From Table 5.5 it can be seen that although the rates of growth of current revenue, current expenditure, and capital expenditure have all decreased over the last three years, the rate of growth of revenue has fallen away most, to only 7 per cent in 1967/8.

TABLE 5.5
Annual rates of growth of recurrent revenue and
expenditure, and capital expenditure, by government

	1965–6	1966–7	1967–8
Current revenue	+38%	+26%	+7%
Current expenditure	+32%	+22%	+20%
Capital expenditure	+114%	+43%	+22%

Source: Monthly Digest of Statistics, Central Statistical Office, Lusaka.

Since between 60 per cent and 70 per cent of revenue derives directly from the copper mining industry, the amount of revenue is heavily dependent on the price of copper, which is outside the control of the Zambian government. Ways and means of increasing other types of revenue are discussed in the section on taxation. There is, however, another major factor affecting the size of the government's budget deficit, and that is the recent inability of the government to spend the amounts estimated at the beginning of each year (mainly on capital account).

Table 5.6 shows how the government has only been able to spend between 80 and 90 per cent of estimated expenditure in the last two years.

The reasons for this are difficult to identify precisely, but are probably mainly associated with delays in decision-making and in administra-

---

[15] The term 'non-bank public' is here used in the same sense as in the *Bank of England Quarterly Bulletin,* that is, to include any source other than the central bank and the commercial banks. It could therefore include, for example, quasi-government bodies such as the Post Office Savings Bank and quasi-banking bodies such as the merchant bank, as well as the rest of the private sector.

TABLE 5.6

Actual and estimated expenditures compared

Type of expenditure	1965–6 K m.	1966–7 K m.	1967–8[1] K m.
Current expenditure:			
estimated	109.4	156.7	192.1
actual	123.9	162.5	183.2
actual as % of estimated	113%	104%	95%
Capital expenditure:			
estimated	65.5	136.5	150.2
actual	65.7	93.9	114.2
actual as % of estimated	100%	68%	76%
Current and capital:			
estimated	174.9	293.2	342.3
actual	189.6	256.4	297.4
actual as % of estimated	108%	87%	87%

[1] The 'estimate' for 1967–8 consists of the estimate for the odd half-year July–December 1967 plus an arbitrary one-half of the estimate for the financial year 1968.

Source: *Estimates of Revenue and Expenditure* and *Monthly Digest of Statistics*, Central Statistical Office, Lusaka.

tion, and with major shortages of skilled manpower, both local and recruited from overseas. To some extent this has been offset by rapidly rising prices, which have enabled the government machine to spend more—in purely money terms—than would otherwise have been the case. Other hold-ups have occurred because of physical problems, such as the development of new supply routes from the coast. It seems probable that these constraints will ease in the future, as the administration becomes more experienced, as the huge spending on education begins to produce skilled people, and as the purely physical supply problems are solved.

There is one other special factor affecting the budget position in the current year, which is the inclusion in the estimate of capital receipts for 1968 of an expected further contribution of contingency aid from the British government, as an offset to additional expenditure arising because of sanctions against Rhodesia. After the budget estimates were published the British government refused any further aid under this heading, despite having intimated that it would provide it at the time of UDI. The sum provided for in the estimates was some K 46 m., and a large part of this will presumably not be received (about K 38 m.).

The money that *was* actually received from the British government during 1968 relates to the first British contribution, which had not all been paid by the end of 1967. This of course greatly eases the financing problem for 1968 (see Table 5.7), but does not alter the underlying change for the worse in the budget situation.

With all these factors taken into account, the position is that the government's overall budget position has recently swung into deficit for the first time, and the immediate prospects are that it will remain in deficit, with a real possibility that the deficit will increase. Given also that prospects for the copper price are poor,[16] then it becomes probable rather than possible that the deficit will increase. In answer to the question posed at the beginning of this section, as to whether pressure is likely to grow on the Bank of Zambia to allow further increase in the money supply, the answer must be in the affirmative, unless the government is able to borrow from the private sector, and thus transfer sufficient command over resources from the private to the public sector.

GOVERNMENT BORROWING FROM THE NON-BANK PUBLIC

Table 5.7 shows that the government has been able to borrow from non-bank sources in each of the last three years.

A fairly steady source of finance is the increase in the note circulation. In so far as this represents a normal increase in demand for notes for transaction purposes, it is a fairly stable source of government finance, with the additional advantage that it is interest-free to the government.[17] The slackening off in the growth of the note issue in 1967/8 is probably due to the changeover to decimal currency in January 1968, and is thus probably temporary. Some of the old notes held as hoards may have been paid in and not replaced. When the banknotes were changed in the UK in 1963 the note issue fell by some £90 m., or £2 *per capita*, so that the rise in the note issue that year was much smaller than usual. It resumed its normal increase in subsequent years.

---

16 Copper prices are appallingly difficult to forecast, but opinion is fairly widespread that they are likely to be lower in the medium term.

17 In fact the Bank of Zambia, like all central banks, holds interest-bearing government debt against the note issue, but since the bank is wholly owned by the government, the only real costs of this form of borrowing are printing and administrative.

TABLE 5.7

Changes in the financing of the budget 1965–6 to 1967–8

(*K m.*)

	1965–6	1966–7	1967–8
Budget surplus (+)/deficit (−)	+27.8	+16.5	−4.9
Non-bank financing:			
Increase in notes and coin	+5.7	+9.4	+6.4
Increase in small savings (POSB)	+0.5	+0.5	+0.6
Change in non-bank holdings of stocks and treasury bills	+7.2	−1.3	−5.1
Loans and grants, etc.	+0.3	+3.8	+19.9
Total non-bank financing	+13.7	+12.4	+21.8
Bank and external financing:			
Borrowing from the commercial banks:			
Stocks	+4.2	−9.5	+4.4
Treasury bills	—	+0.7	−1.5
Notes and coin	+0.5	−0.1	+2.3
Borrowing from Bank of Zambia	+1.1	+5.2	−5.2
Decrease (+) in government balances with the banking system	+3.9	−9.1 ⎫	
		⎬	−16.9
Decrease (+) in reserves; errors, etc.	−51.2	−16.1 ⎭	
Total: Financing items	−27.8	−16.5	+ 4.9

Notes: 1   Holdings of stocks and treasury bills by the non-bank public is a residual after deducting holdings by the banking system (including the Bank of Zambia) from the total outstanding.

2   The last financing item 'Decrease (+) in reserves; errors, etc.' is a residual, but is thought to be mainly a reflection of changes in the external position. It cannot be checked precisely with the balance of payments accounts, which are given on a calendar year basis only; but it is not inconsistent with the picture given there.

3   All the figures are as at end-June: since large variations may take place from month to month, and also at the end of the month, the figures should be treated with some caution.

Source: Monthly Digest of Statistics, Central Statistical Office, Lusaka.

If notes are being used for savings, this source of finance might prove to be unstable.[18] But a major change of social habits would have to occur if this fund of notes held by the public were to decrease;

[18]   There is some evidence that hoarding of notes does occur—see below, p. 143.

and such a change is unlikely to occur except over a longish period. In addition, if the government's savings campaign is successful in persuading people to save through government savings media (the Post Office Savings Bank and National Development Bonds), any fall in private hoards of notes, and thus in the note issue, would be immediately self-financing from the government's point of view. The increase in small savings with the Post Office Savings Bank is fairly small—the whole problem of savings is dealt with more thoroughly below.

The worrying part about the figures is the deterioration in non-bank holdings of stocks and treasury bills. With the expansion of the economy, and in particular the growth of local financial institutions such as insurance companies, one would have expected a steady growth of this figure. Instead it fell slightly in 1966/7, and by K 5.1 m. in 1967/8, offsetting most of the rise in other sorts of non-bank financing. In fact the only reason that total non-bank financing grew in 1967/8, over the previous years' figures, was that the government received the remainder of the British aid, already referred to; while it clearly helps to solve the financing problem in 1967/8, this is not a source of finance that can be relied on in the future.

The overall picture is therefore that *continuing* sources of non-bank finance actually deteriorated in 1967/8. Even if the position is restored to its earlier state, with, say, between K 10 m. and K 15 m. coming from this source, with a modest annual increase from notes, holdings of stocks, and treasury bills, and possibly small savings, there is absolutely no reason to suppose that the total will increase in the future at anything like the rate at which the budget position, and therefore the need for finance, has recently been deteriorating—and is likely to deteriorate in the future—unless there is a major increase in savings.

If this analysis is substantially correct, then the government must urgently consider tapping new sources of tax revenue, or it will be forced into the position of having to borrow from the banking system to finance its deficit, which would be inflationary.

GOVERNMENT BORROWING
FROM THE BANKING SYSTEM

Before discussing the possibilities of increased tax revenue, it is necessary to look at the government's *ability* to borrow from the banking system. In a developed economy, with established money markets, the government can always borrow from the banking system, since an increased deficit will always be reflected in increased banking system holdings of government stocks or treasury bills, if no other form of finance is forthcoming. In underdeveloped economies this is not necessarily so.

In Zambia the position is as follows. A government deficit will, in the first instance (and in the absence of other, non-bank, financing), increase the commercial banks' balances at the Bank of Zambia. Other things being equal this would enable the banks to expand advances and deposits by a multiple of the increase in their cash. But since the President's Mulungushi speech in April 1968 the banks have had to apply to the Bank of Zambia for exchange control permission to lend money to any non-Zambian, or to any company whose shareholders are not *all* Zambian citizens. Existing credit commitments were allowed to run on, but have to be submitted to the Bank of Zambia when they come up for review, which is normally annually. At first (for three months or so) agreements were all allowed to be renewed, but for six months only. Since then, however, the Bank of Zambia has begun to refuse renewal in some cases. This power of refusal is an especially large one, since very few companies of any size can be entirely Zambian owned. For example, the rule applied to all the companies partly owned by government through Indeco,[19] even where this amounts to a majority shareholding, if the remaining ownership has any non-Zambian elements.

Apart from giving the Central Bank the power to direct credit in a very detailed way (but only negatively—this power in itself does not allow positive direction of credit where it would not otherwise have gone), what this means is that an overall expansion of bank credit can be prevented by the refusal of a sufficient number of loans. The banks would then be left with idle funds on account at the Bank of Zambia which they would of course prefer to put into treasury bills or government stock. Either way the government will have financed its deficit. The result in a situation where all available resources are fully employed, such as is almost certainly the case in Zambia at present, would of course be inflationary, but not as inflationary as it would be if a *multiple* expansion of credit were permitted to occur through further increases in bank advances.

[19] The Industrial Development Corporation.

A disadvantage of this system, from the commercial point of view, is that it must reduce the flexibility of the banking system, by reducing the speed with which loans are granted, and by making it uncertain whether loans will in fact be available. Commercial and industrial firms will not be as sure of bank finance, when necessary, as they were before. In an economy where import delays, for example, are a part of commercial life, such inflexibility must be especially damaging, as must be any additional uncertainty in Zambian business life. The uncertainty could be partially reduced if the Bank of Zambia were to publish the guidelines used by them in deciding whether to permit banks to lend or not—but this the bank has not yet done. The principal advantage from the government's point of view is that it can limit the inflationary effects of its own deficit, if and when such deficits cannot be financed by borrowing from the non-bank public.

One other possibility should be mentioned: the commercial banks might prefer to transfer some funds, accruing to them because of a government deficit, to their head offices abroad. From the internal point of view this would be self-financing since a bank doing this would have to buy the relevant currency from the Bank of Zambia, which would then have additional kwacha to lend back to the government of Zambia. In such a case the deficit would effectively have been financed out of reserves of foreign exchange. It is unlikely that such a movement would develop on any significant scale, since it could be stopped fairly easily by the Bank of Zambia; the banks must know this and would presumably not want to incur the ensuing political unpopularity.

The actual *amount* of government borrowing from the banking system (including the Bank of Zambia) has in fact been very small in the last three years, as can be seen from Table 5.7. This is very much to be expected since throughout most of this period the government has had a budget surplus, and in addition has been able to borrow positive amounts from the public. In fact in the last two years, banking system holdings of stocks and treasury bills have actually fallen slightly; and at the same time the government's bank balances have risen.

THE PROBLEM OF LENDING
TO SMALL-SCALE BORROWERS

Reference has already been made to the difficulty which commercial banks have in lending to all would-be borrowers in countries such as

Zambia. Part of the trouble stems from the fact that most banks are branches of foreign banks and their staffs therefore have either been brought up (in the banking sense) in developed economic conditions, or have been trained by people who have such a background. But it is by no means simply a matter of adapting English banking methods to Zambian conditions, or of founding a purely Zambian bank. Most of the problems stem from the nature of banking itself, and the nature of Zambian conditions.

Banks take deposits, i.e. borrow money, on a promise to repay on demand, or at fairly short notice. It has therefore, quite rightly, long been regarded as sound banking practice for banks to lend money in situations where the loan can be expected to be self-liquidating. A classic example is the financing of imports, where the arrival of the goods automatically provides the bank's customer with the means to pay off the loan. Indeed, it was for the financing of foreign trade that banking was first developed in Central and East Africa, and it was long before they financed anything else.[20] Other sound banking principles include the taking of references, the securing of guarantees, the pledging of security (ideally highly marketable) or, failing all these, the certain knowledge of a steady future income from which to repay a loan. The ability to meet one or more of these criteria is a vital prerequisite for securing a bank loan in most countries. Nor should these sound banking practices be sneered at, since before they were firmly established, and widely practised, bank failures, with all the chaos and hardship entailed in them, were not uncommon; and they can still occur even nowadays.

But a quick comparison of these requirements with Zambian conditions reveals just how unsuitable they are if the aim is to increase the amount of credit going to small farmers, traders, businessmen, and the like. Zambian farmers do not, as a rule, own their land; and even if they did there is in many cases no market for it. It is thus of negligible use as security for a bank loan, even if banks liked mortgages as security, which they do not. Zambia, with its short period of contact with the modern economic world, has a very small supply of financial guarantors and referees. The fathers, uncles, ex-employers, and other types who may be expected to perform this function in other countries not only

---

[20] For a full discussion of this in relation to East Africa, see W. T. Newlyn, *Money in an African Context*, Oxford University Press, Nairobi, 1967, Chapter 4.

are not known to the banks, and would not be very suitable if they were, but they might not even have had their first contact of any sort with money until a few years ago. Add to this that backward farming technology increases the variability of yields, and therefore the risk of loss to a bank; that lack of education and experience are major handicaps in business and farming alike; and that lending small sums of money to large numbers of people is much less profitable than lending large sums of money to small numbers of people, because of the high cost of administration; and one can see that there are real problems in trying to lend successfully to the sort of people in Zambia who are currently unable to get bank credit, but need it badly.

These problems are common to many underdeveloped countries, although probably as bad in Zambia as anywhere. This is not to say, however, that money cannot be lent, and lent profitably, to emerging farmers, for example. Several firms in Zambia are successfully selling to small farmers on credit. One firm, African Farming Equipment (which is partly owned by government), does this by insisting on a down payment of 60 per cent (recently 50 per cent, but increased because of a growing credit shortage) with the remainder payable over a maximum of two years. An interest rate of 16–17 per cent has been high enough to cover bad debts and leave a reasonable profit. Only rarely is an open credit extended to anyone, and then only to someone who is already well known to the firm and has established his ability to repay debts.

The strong point of this system is that the down payment is good evidence of the borrower's ability to save significant amounts of money (credit is not normally given to a new customer for an amount less than K 200). Secondly, large items can in principle be repossessed—although no firm selling on credit likes to do this if it can be avoided. Thirdly, the firm arranges with marketing boards, where appropriate, to collect debts from crop proceeds. Fourthly, all applications for credit are dealt with centrally, so that firm and consistent criteria can be applied. In addition the firm enquires about the acreage farmed, equipment already owned, animals owned, and last season's yields. Managers of depots are local people, so such information is quite difficult to falsify.

There are of course weaknesses in such a scheme, not so much from the point of view of the firm selling equipment, etc., but from the national point of view. There may not be a large enough number of farmers who can raise the sort of sums necessary for down payments;[21]

[21] . . . although there may be considerable sums of money in the rural areas—

and frequently the sort of sum needed is too small to be handled in this way, or the item is not the sort that can be repossessed—for example fertilizer.

It is probable, therefore, that there remains an important number of people who need credit, but cannot be reached by conventional means on a profit-making basis. Or at least, no private organization is going to face the risks involved. Zambia has, in common with many other countries, recognized this and introduced a government financed and subsidized institution to fill the gap—the Credit Organization of Zambia (COZ). Formerly there were several separate institutions, for various categories of borrower, but they were all recently amalgamated into COZ.[22]

COZ is to some extent a misnomer, since much of the money distributed by it and its predecessors has been more of the nature of grants than credit. No down payments are required, there is no arrangement with the marketing boards to arrange for repayment out of crop proceeds, and in some cases there has been little care taken in obtaining postal and physical addresses of applicants. More important, the application forms make little attempt beyond enquiring the crop and acreage to be planted to assess the profitability of the venture which the applicant intends to finance with the loan.

Now it may be that there is a case for giving grants on a large scale to small enterprises of all kinds, including farmers of course, which are unable to obtain credit in conventional ways. Particularly if the grants are tied to the purchase of relevant things, such as ploughs and fertilizers, then it could be argued that this is a quick, and even moderately efficient, way of pushing out money on a large scale, getting it into the hands of those who want to do something enterprising with it, and ensuring at the same time that it is at least spent on the right things, even if there is insufficient skilled staff to follow up beyond this point. Such a thing would not be possible in countries with less money to spend than Zambia; but here it is at least arguable that any more conventional method of distributing government money to small businesses, especially farmers, would have increased the already

see below, pp. 142–4.

22 The Land and Agricultural Bank of Zambia, which lent mainly to farmers, was dissolved on 11 August 1967 and its assets and liabilities transferred to COZ under the terms of the Credit Organization of Zambia Act, 1967. COZ also lends to co-operative societies and other commercial and business projects (paragraph 28 of the Act).

large gap between the amount of development money going to large projects in the already developed sector, and that going to the less developed sectors of the economy. Especially as regards the rural sector, it could be argued that *only* by such a highly unconventional 'solution' could enough development be started off in the rural sector to satisfy the very urgent need there; and it is also possible that the political need to satisfy post-Independence aspirations among the majority of the people could only be satisfied in this way.

Thus it *could* be argued—but there are, as with all new solutions, a host of new drawbacks as well which should not be ignored. Firstly, it is surely a major psychological error to label distributions of this sort as 'loans' if there is inadequate provision for their recovery. Many of the recipients must have had little or no contact with monetary and financial dealings before, and if their first contact with a so-called loan is with a handout that turns out not to be repayable, it is going to be extremely difficult, if not impossible, to obtain repayment of loans which really *are* loans in the future.

Secondly, those recipients who *do* understand what a loan is, and are prepared and able to repay it, are going to be heavily discouraged from doing so by finding out that they are in a minority, and by finding out that no sanction attaches to default. In short, financial rectitude is actively discouraged where it exists, which must again be extremely unfortunate for the future, apart from being unjust in the present.

Thirdly, the amounts handed out to different individuals vary enormously. Thus while the whole scheme may be seen as a redistribution of income from the modern to the emerging sector, within the latter the scheme may in fact be creating new income inequalities of its own, based only partially (if at all) on the ability of the recipient to use the money productively, repay it, and leave a surplus for himself.

As COZ has not produced any audited accounts for two years, very little is known about the amounts of money lent out, amounts repaid, interest collected, or indeed any of the facts about its operations which would give some quantitative substance to the above discussion. All that is known is that the total amount lent to COZ (and its predecessors) by the government, by the end of 1967, was K 18.8 m.[23] Although nothing is known of the distribution of these assets since

---

[23] *Financial Report for the Eighteen-Month Period ended 31st December 1967*, Government Printer, Lusaka, 1968.

COZ took over from the Land and Agricultural Bank of Zambia, the latter's latest published figures gave the distribution of loans at end-March 1967 as in Table 5.8.

TABLE 5.8
Distribution of Land Bank assets, end-1964 to March 1967
(K m.)

	End-1964	End-1966	End-March 1967
Long-term loans: farmers	3.1	5.2	6.0
others	1.5	1.3	1.3
Short-term loans: farmers	2.5	4.7	5.6
others	1.6	1.7	2.1
Other assets	0.7	1.4	2.8
Total assets	9.5	14.4	17.8

Source: Monthly Digest of Statistics, Central Statistical Office, Lusaka.

What this amounts to, therefore, is that in the three years after Independence lending by the government to small[24] farmers and businessmen increased by about K 9 m., of which about two-thirds was to farmers. In addition various much smaller sums have been lent by various ministries as loans to co-operative societies, or as 'agricultural and rural credit' which probably amount to less than K 1 m. altogether.

The sums involved, therefore, although large, are small in relation to total government spending in the period (see Table 5.4), and especially in relation to government spending in the urban sector of the economy. As has been argued already, a case could be made for spending this amount of money; what is wrong is the enormous damage that has been done to the concept of lending and repayment. In addition considerable inefficiency has led to big delays, so that for example seasonal loans, in some cases taken over from the banks, have often been approved so late that any relevance to the current season has entirely lapsed.

OTHER FORMS OF CREDIT IN RURAL AREAS

It is a common phenomenon in many underdeveloped countries that the small farmer is heavily burdened by debt, at exorbitant rates of

[24] The maximum loan to any one individual is K 20,000 for farmers, K 10,000 for others (paragraph 33, COZ Act 1967).

interest, supplied by local moneylenders who are beyond the control of the authorities, and are almost wholly unaffected by monetary conditions elsewhere in the economy.[25] Such a situation can be a major hindrance to agricultural development, especially because it reduces the reward to greater effort and engenders feelings of hopelessness.

It is fairly certain that nothing of this sort exists in Zambia; certainly no evidence is available. Such lending as does take place is probably of a much simpler nature. Apparently practically all Africans owe or are owed small sums of money, at any point in time. People are unwilling to lend for normal consumption, but will lend for unexpected or unusual expenses such as a court fine, the need to make a journey to the funeral of a relative, and so on; that is, expenditure over which the borrower is considered to have no control. Men are considered creditworthy if they are working; otherwise people are much more willing to lend to women, who are thought to be more likely to repay, and can always raise small sums of money by brewing beer. The lender always tells his family of the loan to ensure repayment if he dies, and to ensure black-balling of the borrower in case of default.

The other form of informal credit available is that granted by local traders on purchases. Again, credit is not available for buying food, but is given up to 100 per cent for small items, say under K 10 or so, while bigger items require a 50 per cent deposit. There is no formal interest payable, but no cash discount is given on credit sales. As cash discount amounts to 15 per cent it is enough to cover bad debts (of 8-10 per cent or so) and leave a margin. Lending is almost entirely to wage-earners, and so shows little seasonal variation; security is based wholly on local knowledge of individuals.

The above description is based mostly on two districts of slightly above average prosperity, but what little is known of other areas suggests that it is reasonably typical of rural districts. The magnitude of such credit is not known since no statistics are available. Some idea can be got from an estimate that in one of these districts the total credit outstanding is less than K 20,000.

---

[25] See, for example, U. Tan Wai, *Organized and Unorganized Money Markets*, IMF, 1956, reprinted in G. M. Meier (ed.), *Leading Issues in Development Economics*, Oxford University Press, London, 1964; or F. Firth and B. S. Yamey (eds) *Capital, Saving, and Credit in Peasant Societies*, Allen and Unwin, London, 1964.

PROSPECTS FOR INCREASED
PERSONAL SAVING

Clearly Zambia suffers from a handicap common to all relatively poor countries: that it is extremely hard to save out of a small income. However, even in very poor countries, a low income per head can conceal extensive inequality in the *distribution* of income. Thus in Ceylon and Puerto Rico about 10 per cent of the population receive some 40 per cent of income. Where such income inequality exists there is clearly a much better prospect of extracting some savings than if everybody is uniformly poor.

It is no secret that Zambia has many of the features of a so-called dual economy. Using figures for December 1966,[26] 307,000 'Africans' were employed with an average annual wage of K 480; 29,000 'others' were employed at an average annual wage of K 4,090. While it may or may not be possible to save out of an annual wage of K 480, it clearly *is* possible on K 4,090; and the amount involved is large, since on the figures quoted the high-income group's total wage bill is not much less than that of the low-income group—K 120 m. compared with K 147 m.

But unfortunately for savings prospects the bulk of the high-income group are not Zambian, but expatriates, in Zambia on contract. As a result their savings are to a large extent repatriated to their countries of origin. This is mitigated to the extent that expatriates save at least temporarily in Zambia; and if this is an increasing fund, then increased resources are made available. But such a fund poses a constant threat to the balance of payments, and is not, therefore, one that is particularly reliable, or indeed desirable. The situation, that the high-income group saves mainly abroad, is also mitigated by the fact that some former foreign citizens have taken Zambian citizenship, and by the increasing number of Zambians who are themselves moving into the higher-income groups.

But there are further factors working against increased savings. The institution of the extended family can act as a sort of highly progressive income tax on the successful. Teachers, for example, often ask to be posted as far as possible from their home districts, when they complete their training, in order to avoid the descent of a hoard of relatives when they get their first job.

---

[26] *Monthly Digest of Statistics*, Central Statistical Office, Lusaka, September 1968, Tables 3 and 4.

Secondly, it is firmly established tradition that the way to cater for two of the main savings motives—precautionary saving against illness, loss of job and other disasters, and saving for old age—is to *spend* money, not to save it. Thus anyone with money above his immediate consumption needs, who wishes to provide for his own future, will spend money on his relatives and friends, in order that they will look after him, if and when his own turn comes. Zambians, one might say, invest in obligations rather than in financial assets.

Thirdly, there is certainly a big 'demonstration effect' in Zambia, caused by the very inequality of income already discussed, and possibly made more intense by a quasi-political desire to emulate the consumption standards of former political overlords, to prove oneself 'as good as' former rulers. An added factor in this demonstration effect against saving is that the expatriates remaining in Zambia will have an increasing standard of living *as a group*, as more and more of the lower and middle range jobs are filled by Zambians. To the extent, therefore, that the demonstration effect is created by expatriates as a group, rather than by the high-income group as a whole (which will include an increasing number of Zambians), emulation of consumption habits is going to be aimed at an ever-rising target.

Fourthly, there must remain, in a country which has had such a short contact with the rest of the world, a great number of people who have not grasped the most important discovery of the modern world: that it can be altered, in response to individual will. If a basic psychological attitude to one's surroundings is that they are immutable, then one of the most deeply-rooted motives for saving is removed.

Against this array of handicaps the government launched a savings campaign, in July 1967.[27] It is basically an educational effort at this stage, hoping first of all to promote the idea of individual savings. Secondly, and later in time, the campaign is hoping to promote the idea of institutional saving, so that the individual's money is safer, and made available for development. The campaign has used pamphlets, films, newspaper and television advertising, feature articles in the press, posters—in short, all the available communications media.

A second aspect of the government's savings campaign has been to offer tax relief on income from savings. In the 1968 budget the first

[27] For information about the savings campaign I am indebted to a paper presented by Mr. W. Herman to the Zambian Economics Club, and to private talks with Mr. Herman.

K 200 per annum income from savings was exempted from income tax; and *in addition* to this, interest on Post Office Savings Bank deposits is tax free, the first K 400 per annum of life insurance premiums is deductible from gross income before tax is assessed, and interest on the newly introduced National Development Bonds is also tax free. These provisions together amount to a very large exemption from tax for savers. The weaknesses of such provisions are that they provide no incentive to those whose incomes are too small to be liable to tax (and in Zambia exemptions are very high, so that this includes most of the population, *including* wage-earners); and secondly, that they rebate increasingly large amounts of tax as income rises, because of the progressive form of the income tax system. Thus National Development Bonds, which yield approximately 7 per cent (tax-free) if held for the full five years, yield about $17\frac{1}{2}$ per cent gross to someone who is liable to the top rate of income tax (60 per cent). In other words the government may be paying up to $17\frac{1}{2}$ per cent for its money, in interest and tax foregone.

There is naturally no evidence on who holds the bonds because they have only just been introduced, but an investigation some years ago into holdings of UK National Savings Certificates[28] revealed that over 75 per cent of them were held by people who had the maximum permitted holding (rather less than £1,000 per person); and whenever the limit is increased there is a temporary upsurge in demand as people buy up to the new maximum. What this indicates is that the certificates are mostly held by the wealthy, because of the tax exemption, and result in the government borrowing money at quite unnecessarily exorbitant interest rates. And, what is more, much of the money is quite probably switched out of other forms of government debt.

The short-term prospects for the savings campaign are undoubtedly poor. In the long term it may have some desirable educational effects; and in the long term some of the more important barriers to its success may break down, if the demands of extended families diminish, if spending for security and old age is replaced by personal saving, and if a more homogeneous society leads to a diminution of the demonstration effect. This last is the least likely to occur; and indeed if the gap between rich and poor countries continues to grow, then what Ragnar

[28] UK National Savings Certificates are very similar to Zambian National Development Bonds in that interest increases the longer they are held; and they are both free of all tax.

Nurkse has pointed out[29]—that the demonstration effect may be international—will serve to raise desired consumption levels and thus further reduce savings.

One major factor affecting savings has been neglected so far, and that is inflation. The Zambian savings campaign was in fact launched as part of a series of measures to combat inflation. In view of the above discussion it seems probable that the campaign, even if successful in some of its longer-term educational objectives, is extremely unlikely to have more than a negligible effect on inflation in the short term. But even if the difficulties already discussed did not exist, inflation itself would be a major disincentive to saving, probably the most important one of all. Thus there is to some extent a vicious circle operating: an increase in saving would help to curb inflation, but while inflation continues an increase in saving is unlikely. The way out of this vicious circle must be found, therefore, by some other route, most probably by an increase in taxation, which is in any case desirable for other reasons.

What of the second objective of the savings campaign, to persuade existing savings into savings institutions? To the extent that savings take the form of hoarding of goods, especially cattle, persuading people to exchange the goods for financial assets would be beneficial in several ways. It would increase the supply of goods, which would help to reduce inflation, and it would release the savings to be used for productive investment. Even an exchange of goods for bank notes would therefore be desirable. In the case of cattle hoarding it could even help in the very necessary process of improving cattle management, since one of the prime requirements of the latter is to think of cattle in financial terms. The saver would gain too by acquiring a safer and more durable asset, whereas animals eventually die from disease or old age.

In the case of exchanging notes for deposits in a savings institution or for National Development Bonds, the gain is not so obvious, since hoarding of notes does in fact release funds for development—increases in note holdings by the public are loans to the government. It could be argued that conversion of note holdings into savings deposits makes them a more stable form of borrowing from the government point of view, since the asset is less liquid and thus less liable to sudden spending, which would be difficult to control. But in fact most forms of savings

[29] R. Nurkse, *Problems of Capital Formation in Underdeveloped Countries*, Blackwell, London, 1964, p. 61 ff.

that are going to satisfy the precautionary savings motive *must be* fairly liquid, that is withdrawable on demand or at fairly short notice; and in fact most of them are—even National Development Bonds can be cashed in at short notice, although in this case there is a financial advantage in holding to maturity.

From the saver's point of view there is considerable advantage in a switch from notes to other forms of financial asset, *provided* the assets are liquid. What this means, in practical terms, is greatly increased provision of savings institutions in townships and rural areas, since liquidity in this context means physical ease of withdrawal (and deposit of course) as well as the legal right of withdrawal. If such facilities exist then the advantages to the saver are that his savings are safe from theft and fire (a major risk in rural Zambia), and possibly from scrounging relations too. In addition the interest rate, although unlikely to offset inflation fully, is a considerable improvement over notes, which are non-interest-bearing and therefore depreciate rapidly in real value.

Would the provision of a greatly increased number of savings institutions be worth while? In a country as large and as sparsely populated as Zambia the marginal benefit of additional savings banks is clearly going to diminish rapidly as the more densely populated areas are catered for. Nevertheless, the government is already committed to a savings campaign whose main benefits can only be long term; and the provision of banks and post offices yields other benefits as well as that of catering for savers. If the government really does want to encourage the savings habit as a long-term policy then savings institutions are an absolute necessity. It can even be argued that the provision of safe custody for people's money is in any case a necessary public service. And even the more densely populated areas are by no means adequately catered for at the present, so that there is plenty of scope for further provision before the marginal benefits fall away too sharply.

One possibility that has been suggested is that the Credit Organization of Zambia, which has widespread agents, should start taking deposits. Given the original conception of COZ this would have been a logical extension of its activities. But an organization that has produced no audited accounts for over two years, which has a widespread reputation for inefficiency and for making loans which it does little or nothing to recover, is hardly a suitable medium for collecting people's savings. Even with a government guarantee of deposits, which would of course be necessary, very few people would want to trust their money to such an organization; and indeed the mere soliciting of deposits by COZ would undo much of the good work of the savings campaign, since it would invite suspicion of all savings media.

Table 5.9 shows the main savings media, the amounts currently invested, growth in the last three years, and changes in the interest rates offered.

TABLE 5.9
Savings media 1965–6 to 1967–8

	1965–6	1966–7	1967–8
Building societies:			
Deposits at end–June (K m.)	38.2	42.5	47.3
Change on previous year (K m.)	+ 4.7	+4.4	+4.8
Percentage change on previous year	+14.0%	+11.3%	+11.3%
Post Office Savings Bank:			
Deposits at end–June (K m.)	6.2	6.7	7.3
Change on previous year (K m.)	+0.5	+0.5	+0.6
Percentage change on previous year	+9%	+8%	+9%
Commercial banks savings accounts:			
Deposits at end–June (K m.)	17.0	21.8	24.6
Change on previous year (K m.)	+1.9	+4.8	+2.8
Percentage change on previous year	+12.6%	+28.2%	+12.8%
Interest rates:			
Building societies savings shares	3%	$3\frac{1}{2}$%	$3\frac{1}{2}$%
Investment shares	$5\frac{1}{2}$%	6%	6%
Deposits	5%	5%	5%
Post Office Savings Bank	$3\frac{1}{4}$%	$3\frac{3}{4}$%	$3\frac{3}{4}$%
Commercial banks savings accounts	3%	$3\frac{1}{2}$%	$3\frac{1}{2}$%

Note: Dates of interest rate changes as follows: building societies investment and savings shares both raised in April 1967; POSB rate raised to $3\frac{1}{2}$% in January 1967 and to $3\frac{3}{4}$% in February 1967; commercial banks savings accounts rate raised to $3\frac{1}{4}$% in January 1967 and to $3\frac{1}{2}$% in February 1967.

Source: Monthly Digest of Statistics, Central Statistical Office, Lusaka.

The most striking thing about Table 5.9 is the relative success of commercial bank savings accounts and the building societies in attracting money, both in absolute amounts invested, and in recent rate of growth. To some extent this reflects the much longer period during which these private organizations have been advertising, in several cases extremely vigorously. Certainly it is not because of any great interest rate differential, since for some time the POSB has actually offered a slightly higher rate than, for example, commercial banks savings accounts.

Secondly, there is no sign of any acceleration of saving in these institutions since the savings campaign started, either generally, or in the government institution (the POSB). This is not at this stage a criticism of the campaign, since it has professedly long-term objectives. What it does reveal is that the high-income groups, who know all about savings and its possibilities, are probably influenced by advertising in choosing savings media; and that the wage-earners and other potential small savers may take a long time to influence, so that the savings campaign may have to continue a long while yet, and spend a lot more money, before it yields any discernible results—quite apart from the problem of inflation.

TABLE 5.10
Savings and price changes

	1965/6	1966/7	1967/8
Percentage change in 'personal savings'	+13.1%	+15.6%	+11.5%
Price changes: lower incomes index	+10.7%	+3.6%	+13.4%
higher incomes index	+5.1%	+4.8%	+9.6%

Note: 'Personal savings' is simply the sum of savings of the three institutional types itemized in Table 5.9.

Source: Monthly Digest of Statistics, Central Statistical Office, Lusaka.

The link between inflation and savings is demonstrated at a very simple level in Table 5.10. The three years shown are clearly not enough to demonstrate anything very rigorously, and it is not worth breaking them down into shorter periods, since inflation, in the nature of things, takes some time to register its impact on the saver. Nevertheless it is significant that the growth of savings, among those savers sufficiently sophisticated to put their savings in an institution and earn some interest, appears to be inversely correlated with the rate of increase in prices. The larger growth of savings in 1966/7 might be associated with the increase in rates offered in the latter part of that year, but the increase came too late to affect more than a small part of the year's figures, and the hypothesis is in any case not supported by the reduced rate of growth in 1967/8. Alternatively the inverse correlation may simply be because incomes do not keep pace with prices, and consumers maintain living standards during inflationary periods at the expense of saving. Whichever hypothesis is correct, inflation is bad for saving.

One further point: although the figures show an inverse correlation between the *current* rate of increase in prices and the *current* rate of growth of savings, the rational hypothesis would be that savings are adversely affected by expectations of *future* price increases, with current price changes used as the best available guide to the future. But one might expect savers to be influenced by a rising rate of increase in prices more adversely than by a high but steady rate of increase; and in 1967/8 the rate of increase in prices was significantly greater in the second half of the year than in the first.[30]

An interesting point arises in relation to the different savings media. Building societies seem to have been almost wholly unaffected in their ability to attract deposits by any of the factors discussed so far, whereas commercial banks savings accounts have been more volatile, accounting for all the variation in growth of savings. A possible explanation is that saving with building societies is most often connected with a desire for a loan to buy a house. A proven ability to save regularly, as witnessed by a steadily growing deposit, is the society manager's best indicator of ability to repay a loan, which is to him infinitely preferable to fore-closure of a mortgage as a means of getting his money back. Banks, on the other hand, although they may use past growth in a savings account balance as a criterion for granting credit, do not do so on such a well-publicized and consistent basis as the building societies.

If this suggestion is correct, then it has some very important implica-tions both for the future of savings and for the very tough problem of granting credit to small businessmen and farmers. It suggests that the way to encourage regularly increasing savings is to link them to the granting of credit; and that the way to grant credit to people who do not qualify according to 'sound banking principles' is to insist on regular savings first, as proof of ability to repay a loan. That this can be done is demonstrated by the success of African Farming Equipment already discussed in this chapter, and, in a much less specific way, by the universal success of hire purchase all over the world, which amounts to the giving of credit on principles that would make sound bankers turn in their graves.[31]

This is not a new idea, and has been put into practice on a limited scale elsewhere in the world, through savings co-operatives and bank loan schemes which are based on regular monthly savings *before* the loan

[30] The higher income index rose by 3.8 per cent and 5.6 per cent in successive 6-month periods to June 1968, the lower income index by 4.5 per cent and 8.5 per cent. There is also some reason to suspect that the indices understate the increase in prices so that the absolute figures quoted may be too small—there is no reason to suppose, however, that this bias has increased in recent months.

[31] In the UK, the banks did eventually move in on hire purchase, but indirectly through subsidiaries; and they proved rather bad at it, and got their fingers badly burnt.

is granted. An even more straightforward method is to sell agricultural equipment (for example) by normal hire purchase methods. All of these schemes are open to the objection that part of the problem is that people on low incomes cannot save or put down large deposits. But there exists considerable evidence that Zambian farmers can and do save substantial sums. Research in two rural districts suggests that some 75 per cent of farmers have significant sums of cash;[32] and the fall in the rate of increase of notes with the public at the time of change-over to the new decimal currency also suggests that there are considerable private note hoards.[33]

If the commercial banks are not capable of implementing such a scheme, because of their history and tradition, then there may be a case for a state-run organization to collect deposits and to issue loans on the basis of proven savings ability. This function could definitely not be performed by the Credit Organization of Zambia because of the damage already done by that institution to the concept of lending and repayment, but might be a suitable function for the proposed new Zambian commercial bank. In addition the government should be as generous as possible with credit for those institutions which are already giving credit successfully in the form of hire purchase facilities for buying productive equipment.[34] An essential prerequisite for the successful establishment of a bank that links savings to credit (and for the extension of hire purchase sales) is the reform or closure of COZ, since there is little incentive to save for the right to a loan, or for a down payment, if soft loans can be obtained elsewhere without serious effort (unless the individual is for some reason excluded from COZ credit).

SUMMARY

To sum up, the financial situation in Zambia seems to be as follows. The commercial banks have run out of surplus liquidity, and even owe

---

[32] Unfortunately not quantifiable at the time of writing.

[33] See above, the section on non-bank government borrowing. The existence of significant sums of cash in the rural areas is supported by gossip in many areas. In the nature of things it is extremely difficult to get hard evidence, since people are very naturally extremely unwilling to reveal their savings.

[34] African Farming Equipment, for example, had to increase their required deposit from 50 per cent to 60 per cent recently because of shortage of credit, and this had a marked effect on sales, as one might expect.

money to their overseas head offices; it is expected that these overdrafts will have to be repaid in the near future. Government expenditure is increasing much faster than government current sources of income, so that the budget situation is deteriorating rapidly. At the present rate of deterioration the deficit will shortly be larger than the government's ability to borrow from the non-bank public. The government has the technical means to borrow from the banks if it wants to, and could of course borrow from the Bank of Zambia. Some small increase in the banks' balances with the Central Bank may be justified, in order to allow the money supply to expand with the economy; but not on the scale that may be needed to cover the prospective deficit.

Meanwhile, although the commercial banks are able to supply the needs of the modern sector, the supply of credit to the emerging Zambian small businessman and co-operative, principally and most importantly in agriculture, has been largely taken over by a government body which has been granting a very relaxed sort of credit, the bulk of which is almost certainly not recoverable.

The prospects of increased personal savings are poor in the short and medium term, and business savings are not likely to be lent to the government.

The financial prospect therefore is for increasing inflationary pressure to build up, unless the government can reduce the rate of increase of its own demands on the economy, or unless there is an increase in tax rates and new sources of tax revenue are found. The next chapter therefore will examine the existing tax system to see if rates can be increased, or new taxes can be introduced, and also to see if the existing tax *structure* is in fact suited to the current stage of development, or whether it can be improved in this respect.

6

The Fiscal System

C. R. M. HARVEY[1]

INTRODUCTION

THE preceding chapter showed that Zambia is approaching a position familiar to most developing countries in which the ability of the government to spend money constructively on well-designed, carefully integrated projects and programmes exceeds its ability to finance such expenditure from existing sources and within the existing fiscal system. It is therefore necessary to examine critically the tax base of the economy to determine whether improvements in the system will help finance enlarged expenditures in the future.

Table 6.1 shows the estimated recurrent revenue of the central government in 1968. The dominance of the various taxes on the mining companies is obvious. They are expected to contribute over 55 per cent of revenue in 1968, and rather more than that percentage of taxation as such.

The actual size of the current yield of a tax is not of course the only guide to its importance. A protective import duty, for example, will yield less, the more successful it is. In Zambia, the current yield of the tax on company profits[2] is only about 5 per cent of the total, but its importance is much greater, since the detailed provisions of this tax will have great influence on the future structure of industry. It is, in fact, vital to get taxes as correctly structured as possible at an early stage in development, not only because of their influence on the future growth of the economy, but also because it is increasingly inequitable to make structural changes, the longer those changes are delayed. The present structure, including any concessions or loopholes, will be exploited to the full, quite rationally and legally. Businessmen,

---

[1] Lecturer in Economics, University of Zambia.
[2] Excluding the copper companies.

TABLE 6.1
Estimated recurrent revenue, 1968
(*K m.*)

				Percentage of total
Tax on mining companies:	income tax	37.6		15
	royalties	60.3		24
	copper export tax	41.1		16
	Total	——	139.0	
Income tax on non-mining companies			13.0	5
Income tax on persons:	self-employed	3.0		
	PAYE	16.3		
	other individuals	2.0		
	Total	——	21.3	9
Customs and excise:	customs duties	16.6		
	motor spirit tax	3.1		
	cigarettes	7.6		
	opaque beer	3.9		
	beer (other)	8.7		
	spirits	1.1		
	other	0.2		
	Total	——	41.2	16
Motor vehicle licences			1.9	1
Other licences and fines			1.5	1
Fees, payments for services, earnings of ministries			6.3	3
Overseas Service Aid Scheme (including compensation)			5.9	2
Bank of Zambia			1.6	1
Reimbursements of public debt expenditure			4.3	2
Interest			13.2	5
Other			0.9	—
Total estimated recurrent revenue			250.1	100

especially, rearrange their affairs substantially to take full advantage of the tax laws, and may therefore be involved in heavy loss if the laws are changed.

Having said this, it is nevertheless clear that it is vitally important to get the taxes on copper right, since, apart from their very large contribution to revenue, copper contributes about 95 per cent of export proceeds. Unfortunately the taxes on copper are hopelessly wrong, and this subject will be dealt with first. Copper company taxation is, incidentally, virtually the only area of Zambian taxation that has been examined at all thoroughly.[3] The foolishness of the pre-nationalization structure has even been officially recognized, to the point where President Kaunda announced that the royalty system would be changed 'in line with the wishes of the companies'.[4] The section that follows relates only to the system that existed up to August 1969. Thereafter a new tax formula was announced relating tax payable more closely to profits.[5]

TAXATION OF MINING COMPANIES

There were until mid-1969 three taxes on the copper mining companies: royalty, export tax, and income tax. The reasons for this unnecessarily complex system of taxation are mainly historical. Royalty used to be paid to the British South Africa Company, which owned the mining rights, and was transferred to the Zambian government at Independence. Export tax was introduced when the world's main copper producers decided to abandon the producers' price, in order to capture for the government a big share of the increase in price that followed. The income tax is the same as for other companies, and is paid on profits after the deduction of royalty and export tax. While it is reasonable to have a special tax system for the few companies that provide more than half the government's tax revenue, the system had undesirable effects, as can be seen from the following description.

Royalty was $13\frac{1}{2}$ per cent of the 'price' of copper less K 16 per ton produced. It was thus a tax on production, and ignored costs. It was also charged whether the copper was sold or not.

Export tax was 40 per cent of the 'price' of copper in excess of K 600 per ton exported. It was also of the nature of a tax on production, and, like royalty, ignored costs.

---

[3] See, for example, frequent articles in *Business and Economy of Central and East Africa*.

[4] Speech by President Kaunda at Mulungushi, April 1968.

[5] As this volume was in the press when the new arrangements were announced, it is not possible to analyse the present system in detail. However, the new tax system amounts in principle to a straight profits tax. Although the whole package deal announced at Matero in August 1969 is highly complex, because of the takeover of, and payment for, shares and because of changes in exchange control regulations, the *incentive* effects of the new system are basically those of a profits tax.

Finally, a profits tax was levied on profits remaining (if any) after the payment of royalty and export tax, at 37½ per cent on the first K 200,000 of profits and 45 per cent on the remainder. Until 1968 the rate of profits used to vary from mine to mine in an attempt to take account of varying profitability.[6] This was pointless, since a tax based on profits, at a uniform rate, already takes account of relative profits. The new system was an improvement, although there is little or no rationale in taxing small profits at a lower rate.

The system of export tax and royalty is inequitable since it takes no account of the difference in costs of the various mines, nor of changes in costs over time. The result is that the system may render some mines unprofitable, which are profitable before tax;[7] it may render some prospective mines unprofitable, which would be potentially profitable without the tax; it may render some grades of ore unprofitable to extract which would otherwise be profitable, and which may, for technical reasons, be impossible to extract at a later date, or only possible to extract (or process) at a later date at a much higher cost; and it causes low-profit mines to pay a higher proportion of their profits in tax than high-profit mines.

The system was based on absolute sums stated in money terms— royalty was not payable at all on a price less than K 98.00 per ton, export tax on a price less than K 600.00 per ton. This illustrates very well what happens when a tax is based on a figure which may be reasonable at some point in history, but which may be rendered quite irrelevant by the passage of time.[8]

The system was thus one which created the maximum amount of uncertainty in the minds of producers and potential investors (who may be the same people). Since the system was so inflexible, being unable to take account of any changes except in price, and since it might have rendered the whole of copper mining in Zambia unprofitable if costs rose sufficiently, the impression must have been that it would be changed, even before the Mulungushi speech. On the other hand a system which is adaptable to different circumstances, and to

---

[6] Income Tax Act 1966, Charging Schedule, Part III (p. 318).

[7] See Tables 6.2 and 6.3.

[8] Average costs per ton have risen to over K 400 per ton, which is higher than a long-term forecast for the price of copper by one of the companies only *two years ago*. With the pace of inflation accelerating, the cost of mining could have made K 600, the base point of the export tax, unsatisfactory in a few years.

TABLE 6.2
Tax system for the copper companies (until mid-1969)

A. Company with costs of K 300 per ton

Price K	Royalty K	Export tax K	Income tax (45%) K	Total tax K	Total tax as % of profit
500	51.5	—	66.8	118.2	59.1
600	65.0	—	105.8	170.6	56.9
700	78.5	40	126.6	245.2	61.3
800	92.0	80	147.6	319.8	64.0
900	105.5	120	168.4	394.2	65.7
1,000	119.0	160	189.4	468.4	66.9

B. Company with costs of K 400 per ton

500	51.5	—	21.8	73.2	73.2
600	65.0	—	58.8	123.8	61.9
700	78.5	40	81.6	200.2	66.6
800	92.0	80	102.4	274.6	68.7
900	105.5	120	123.4	349.2	69.8
1,000	119.0	160	144.4	423.4	70.6

C. Company with costs of K 500 per ton

500	51.5	—	—	51.5	(1)
600	65.0	—	15.8	80.8	80.8
700	78.5	40	36.6	155.2	77.6
800	92.0	80	57.6	229.6	76.5
900	105.5	120	78.4	304.2	76.0
1,000	119.0	160	99.4	378.4	75.7

D. Company with costs of K 600 per ton

500	51.5	—	—	51.4	(1)
600	65.0	—	—	65.0	(1)
700	78.5	40	—	118.6	118.6
800	92.0	80	12.6	184.6	92.3
900	105.5	120	33.4	259.2	86.4
1,000	119.0	160	54.4	333.4	83.3

[1] Mining unprofitable *before* payment of any tax, but some tax nevertheless payable.

changes in circumstances, and which therefore does not require frequent changes in the law, is much better for production and investment, since it aids the forward planning which production and investment require, by reducing uncertainty. While no country can give a guarantee that its tax system will not be changed, a country which has a system which is adaptable to changing circumstances, and therefore *need* not be changed, has a clear advantage over a country with a system such as the one under discussion which *must* be changed if costs go on rising, and which clearly ought to have been changed anyway—because of the additional uncertainty which the latter creates.

TABLE 6.3

Tax system for the copper companies (until mid-1969)
(Percentage of profit paid in tax at various prices and costs per ton)

	Cost per ton			
Price per ton	K 300	K 400	K 500	K 600
K 500	59.1	73.2	(1)	(1)
K 600	56.9	61.9	80.8	(1)
K 700	61.3	66.6	77.6	118.6
K 800	64.0	68.7	76.6	92.3
K 900	65.7	69.8	76.0	86.4
K 1,000	66.9	70.6	75.7	83.3

[1] Mining unprofitable *before* payment of any tax, but some tax nevertheless payable.

Notes: 1   It can be seen most clearly in Table 6.3 that the percentage of profit paid in tax actually *decreases* as the price of copper rises, in the case of the higher-cost mines, and this can even occur for certain price rises with lower-cost mines.

2   The reduced rate of income tax, $37\frac{1}{2}\%$, on the first K 200,000 of profits has been ignored—it makes very little difference to the figures in Tables 6.2 and 6.3 because of the size of the copper mining companies.

A further criticism of the system of royalty and export tax is that the 'prices' on which they were based were the monthly averages of eight prices on the London Metal Exchange (cash and forward for four types of copper) at the time of production, and of export, respectively. This average price bore little relation to the price actually received by the copper companies, and thus introduced an element of pure chance into the amount of tax payable. Either copper company or government may have gained from this in the most arbitrary way, if the copper price fluctuated very much. That this was a real, rather than an imaginary, possibility can be seen from recently published results in which a substantially unchanged revenue per ton received by the companies was accompanied by wildly different payments of royalty and export tax per ton.[9] Such a system made no sense, and might even have induced the companies to alter the timing of production and export in order to take advantage of it—any such action would have been a pure waste of resources.

Varying rates of profits tax created an additional complication and an annoying source of uncertainty, because of the rule that inter-

[9] See, for example, the quarterly reports of Bancroft Mines Ltd. and Nchanga Consolidated Copper Mines Ltd., for the quarter ending 30 September 1967.

company dividends were taxable in the hands of the receiving company at the latter's tax rate, gross of any tax already paid by the paying company.[10] This source of confusion would of course have been eliminated if all companies paid profits tax at the same rate; or if net dividends received bore no further tax. This problem is further discussed below in relation to the simplification of taxation there proposed.

The system outlined in the preceding paragraphs, and the criticisms made of it, suggest that it should have been very easy to devise a system which would suit both companies and government. There is, most unusually, a very wide area of agreement between the companies and the government over what the tax on the former should achieve: namely, that something of the order of 60 per cent to 70 per cent of profits should be paid in tax in some form or another; that the tax system should create the minimum of disincentive possible to production, investment, and the raising of finance for investment; and that the government should have a rather larger share of very high, or 'windfall', profits, created by abnormally high copper prices, than it should have of more 'normal' profits.[11] In addition it is in both parties' interests to have a tax system which does not *need* to be changed frequently—the government would of course always have the complete *right* to make any changes it desired.

Most of the above criteria could be met by a straightforward and conventional profits tax, at a high rate, of 60 per cent to 70 per cent. But this would not satisfy the requirement of creaming off a higher proportion of the exceptionally high profits generated by high copper prices. A scheme which would do this is outlined in Table 6.4.

TABLE 6.4
A proposed system of taxation for the copper companies

That part of profits per ton between:	Marginal tax rate
0 and K 100	50%
K 100 and K 200	60%
K 200 and K 300	70%
over K 300	80%

10 The importance of this factor has been greatly reduced by the changes in the 1968 budget.

11 This was the intention of the export tax, and to a lesser extent of the royalty— but the method was not even especially successful, and had disastrous side effects.

Clearly the actual figures chosen are a matter for discussion. In order to get an idea of order of magnitude, the system outlined in Table 6.4 would have yielded approximately the same amount of tax, in total, as in 1966/7; and the top marginal rate of 80 per cent is actually higher than under the old system (in which it was 74.4 per cent). Such a system would thus actually achieve the objective of the export tax to cream off 'windfall' profits to the government rather more effectively, but without the same disincentives for low-profit mines or prospective investment. In the meantime the proposed system would of course distribute taxation much more equitably by removing a serious disparity between the shareholders of different mines. While the two major *groups*, Anglo American and RST, would pay much the same in total taxation, they do not hold *all* the shares in the mines. Individual shareholders in the mines which under the old system earned a profit before tax, but earned nothing or sustained a loss after tax, would be treated more fairly, by the government allowing their mines to retain some post-tax profit. Conversely, individual shareholders in the most profitable mines would pay more tax, which would also be more equitable.

A 'disadvantage' (for the government) of the proposed system is of course that a mine making no profit would not be taxed at all, whereas under the old system a mine making no profit could be required to pay quite heavy tax. Since it would be in the interest of any company owning such a mine to close it down, it is not really in the government's interest to have such a tax. Every ton of copper sold earns valuable foreign exchange, and its production creates employment, even if it yields no tax revenue directly.[12]

A related disadvantage, for the government, of the proposed scheme is that revenue would be less, at very low copper prices. This is because the pre-nationalization tax system was extremely inequitable in taxing a larger proportion of the low profit generated when prices were low than of the high profit generated when prices were high. In fact if the price of copper had fallen substantially, that system of taxation would have crippled the copper companies because of the large rise in costs since the price was last low. It would not therefore have been in the country's real interest to have maintained that system of taxation if the price of copper fell, since the effect on the companies would have been to

---

[12] Considerable tax revenue would accrue from income tax on employees' earnings, indirect taxes on purchases of employees, etc.

choke off almost all profit, and thus prevent any exploration, expansion, or development. Indeed, the companies would have been acting perfectly rationally in closing 'unprofitable' (after tax) mines. A corollary of the proposed system is that the government would have to build up revenue reserves at times of high copper prices, in order to maintain expenditure at times of low copper prices, *to a slightly greater degree than under the old system*. Of course, the government already had to do this to a considerable extent, since even under the pre-nationalization system revenue fluctuated substantially with changing copper prices. That the difference would be surprisingly small can be seen in Table 6.5 where the percentage of profits taxed under the old and proposed systems are compared.

TABLE 6.5

Tax payable under proposed tax system compared with
tax payable under the pre-nationalization system

Cost/ton	K 300		K 400		K 500		K 600	
	A	B	A	B	A	B	A	B
Price per ton								
K 500	59.1	55	73.2	50	(1)	0	(1)	0
K 600	56.9	60	61.9	55	80.8	50	(1)	0
K 700	61.3	65	66.9	60	77.6	55	118.6	50
K 800	64.0	68	68.7	65	76.5	60	92.3	55
K 900	65.7	70	69.8	68	76.0	65	86.4	60
K 1,000	66.9	71	70.6	70	75.7	68	83.3	65

1 Mining unprofitable *before* payment of any tax, but some tax nevertheless payable.

Notes: A = Pre-nationalization system of taxation.
B = System proposed in Table 6.4.

The proposed system should of course be expressed in terms of profit as a proportion of cost per ton, not absolute profit per ton, since otherwise it would be open to one of the same objections as the old system, namely that a tax based on absolute figures in money terms may eventually become out of date. It would be easy to meet this objection. Table 6.3 was expressed in money terms to give the reader a quicker idea of orders of magnitude in present-day terms.

Under the proposed system individual mines would continue to pay different rates of tax, according to their profitability, so that under the present rule for the taxation of inter-company dividends one of the nuisances of the old system would continue. The rational solution is to treat inter-company dividends as tax paid in the hands of the receiving company. For example, if a very profitable mine holds shares in a relatively unprofitable mine, taxing the latter's dividend at the rate applicable to the profitable mine would amount to a high tax rate on a mine of low profitability—this is just what the proposed system is designed to avoid. If it is desired to increase the revenue from taxation, the way to do it is to increase taxation on the more profitable mine directly (that is, on its own mining operations), not on its already relatively unprofitable shareholding in a low-profit mine.

It has been suggested that the copper companies can alter their profits in order to avoid taxation, by selling at prices below the free market price to companies in which they have a financial interest. This has been put forward as a reason for basing taxation on the published world price. If this objection is taken seriously by the government,[13] then it would be possible to base the calculation of profit on the published world price for the type of copper actually sold by the company, and for the actual date on which sale took place. This would avoid the chance element in the existing taxes based on world prices (see above). A monthly, quarterly, or annual average of costs could then be taken and deducted from a (weighted) average of sales revenue. Such a system would avoid any possibility of this objection being valid.

It has also been suggested that the companies can alter their cost figures so as to avoid profits taxation. Against this one can point out that a vast number of people both inside and outside the companies would have to be in the know, and prepared to keep quiet; that the auditors would have to be dishonest or fantastically stupid, which is unlikely in a firm with a world-wide reputation which among other jobs audits the accounts of the Bank of England; and that the Commissioner of Taxes already keeps an extremely watchful eye on copper company accounts, in order to calculate profits tax, and would presumably continue to do so.

TAXATION OF NON-MINING COMPANIES

The present system

The taxation of companies other than the copper mining companies is basically sound in Zambia. Some of the detailed provisions require

[13] The author has no idea of its validity, and no way of checking.

criticism, however, mainly those intended to encourage investment by various types of tax relief.

The present system is as follows. Companies are currently (since the 1968 budget) taxed at $37\frac{1}{2}$ per cent on the first K 200,000 of taxable profits; and at 45 per cent on any further taxable profits.[14]

The provision for the carry-over of losses is very generous: they may be carried forward for tax purposes for an indefinite period, and may be deducted from the profit of the previous year (that is, the year previous to that in which the loss was incurred) if the taxpayer wishes.[15]

Currently, Zambia offers two main types of tax incentive for investment: firstly, there is a generous system of initial and annual depreciation allowances; secondly, a complete tax holiday is offered for periods of two years or more to firms qualifying for it under the Pioneer Industries Act.[16]

Initial and annual capital allowances are as shown in Table 6.6.

TABLE 6.6
Initial and annual allowances in Zambia

(%)

Type of investment	Initial allowance	Annual allowance
Industrial buildings:		
low-cost housing	10	10
other	10	5
Plant and machinery:		
prime moving machinery[1]	20	30
other	20	20

[1] Excavators, bulldozers, harvesters, tractors, etc.

The annual depreciation, or wear and tear, allowance is calculated on a depreciating balance method, that is, the appropriate percentage is deducted from the written-down book value of the capital equipment and is thus worth less each year (see Table 6.8 below for an illustration of this effect).

The initial allowance is deducted from the book value of capital equipment (in contrast to an investment allowance, which is not) and thus also reduces the subsequent effect of annual allowances. An initial allowance therefore has the effect of reducing tax liability in the year of capital expenditure, and increasing it subsequently; and

---

[14] Income Tax (Amendment) Act 1968, Section 26.
[15] Income Tax Act, 1966, Section 30(2).
[16] Pioneer Industries (Relief from Income Tax) Act 1965, No. 55 of 1965.

so amounts to an interest-free loan from government to the firm, or a postponement of tax liability, which is the same thing.

The Pioneer Industries Act allows any company to apply for pioneer status, and the Minister of Commerce and Industry may grant it if he is satisfied that expansion or initial development is in the public interest, that the industry is currently not big enough (or not being carried on at all), and that some encouragement is necessary.[17] The minister can impose any restrictions he wishes. For such companies (or products, since the minister can designate products as pioneer products), relief from income tax is granted for a minimum of two years; where the company spends at least K 50,000 on fixed capital, an extra year's relief is granted; and where more than K 100,000 is spent, an extra three years' relief is granted (making five in all).

In addition, all capital expenditure undertaken during the relief period is considered, for tax purposes, to have been spent on the day after relief ends, and is then eligible for all capital allowances. Tax relief is thus likely to extend well beyond the formal relief period. For example, a big firm, investing more than K 100,000 in fixed capital equipment, would in the sixth year of operation have some K 40,000 to K 50,000 (between 40 per cent and 50 per cent of the investment, depending on the proportion of prime moving equipment) to offset against profits, which would be unlikely to be as much as that, unless the investment was yielding a very high profit (that is, as much as 40 per cent). Total tax relief would thus extend over the sixth year at least, and probably even into the seventh or eighth year of operation.

Criticisms and proposed reforms

The Zambian system taxes low profits less than high ones, although the graduation is the simplest possible, with a single step at K 200,000. This provision is presumably intended to help small businesses. But it is an extremely crude way of helping them, distinguishing only two sorts of business. A business with K 199,000 of profits is not all that small; it may in fact be much more profitable than a business with higher absolute profits, and may therefore be much more capable of paying a higher rate of tax. Equally, of course, the situation might be reversed. Given that there is no better way of discovering taxable capacity than a

---

[17] For the exact terms, see the Pioneer Industries Act 1965, Section 3.

simple assessment of actual profit, then all companies should be taxed at the same rate. Nor is there any danger of discouraging the growth of very small companies by using a rate higher than the personal rate of the proprietor(s), since the proprietors need only to distribute the profits to reduce the tax rate. A more effective way to encourage growth is to give help through the tax system for expansion as such (not for the retention of funds), thus ensuring maximum effectiveness for such help. This is discussed more fully in the next section, on investment incentives.

If a single rate of tax were to be adopted for all companies, one might consider in the first instance what rate would raise the same amount of tax as previously; and, secondly, whether a higher rate would be significantly out of line with rates in neighbouring countries.

In calculating what tax rate would raise the same amount of revenue, one is handicapped by the lack of recent figures giving a breakdown of company profits by size. Using the most recent published figures, which are for the year 1962/3,[18] and excluding the copper mining companies, since their taxation should be dealt with separately, a tax rate of about 41 per cent would have raised the same revenue. The rates of tax in some neighbouring African countries are given in the following table.

TABLE 6.7

The taxation of company profits in some African countries
(%)

Country	Flat rate	Additional tax on undistributed profits
South Africa	40[1]	25[2]
Malawi	37½	22½[2]
Nigeria	40	—
Ghana	45	—
Kenya	40	—
Uganda	40	—
Tanzania	40	—

[1] Basic rate of 33⅓%, plus a surcharge of 3⅓% for 1968 tax year, plus a loan levy of 3⅓% which will be repaid 'in due course' with simple interest at 5%.
[2] Applies to private companies only.

It is apparent from the table that if Zambia adopted a flat rate of tax on company profits between say 40 per cent and 45 per cent it

[18] Income Tax Statistics, Assessments for the Income Year ended 31 March 1963, and raised to 30 June 1964.

would not be out of line with neighbouring African countries, and would not therefore endanger Zambia's competitive position in attracting capital. Minor variations in rate are not in the least significant, since the actual amount payable depends on detailed provisions in the tax laws, including, especially, the generosity or otherwise of capital allowances, and any other investment incentives offered by governments (all of which are discussed in this section). In fact there is a definite advantage to a system which has a slightly high flat rate, but an effective rate which is lower for growing companies through investment tax incentives, since this extracts the maximum revenue from stagnant companies and gives as much encouragement as possible for growth, so that other things being equal, 45 per cent or even 50 per cent would be better than 40 per cent.

The Pioneer Industries Act as described above is an extremely generous measure. The danger, as with all tax relief measures of this kind, is that it may be granted to firms which would have invested in the country anyway, and so may involve the country in an unnecessary loss of revenue. A second danger is that countries competing for investments may compete in offering tax relief, to the eventual advantage of none of them. A third danger is that dividends exempted from tax may be taxed in the country of origin, so that Zambian tax relief results in a gift of taxation revenue to that country.

The first danger can only be guarded against by the vigilance of the ministry in vetting applications for pioneer status. Unfortunately, once such an act has been introduced every prospective investor is going to claim its benefits, and will naturally insist that without them investment is out of the question; so that the ministry's bargaining position is undermined by the very existence of the act. The second danger may be at least partially prevented by international co-operation between countries who find themselves competing in this way, leading to agreement to limit the scope of offers of tax relief. Such agreement should not be too difficult to obtain, for example, with those of Zambia's neighbours with whom relations are good; nor need it wait on the country's entry into any common market. The third danger can be avoided by suitable amendments to double taxation agreements—this is already being tackled by the tax authorities.

A possible way of limiting the generosity of the Pioneer Industries Act would be to grant a tax holiday only for profits up to a certain maximum percentage of capital employed, and to charge tax on any profits in excess of this percentage. Thus if, for example, the percentage in question was 20 per cent, then a firm earning less than 20 per cent on capital employed would qualify for a tax holiday under the act. But a firm earning, say, 25 per cent on capital employed, would be charged the normal rate of profit tax on that part of profits in excess of 20 per cent on capital employed, that is, on a fifth of its profits in this example.

Such a scheme would amount to a tax on profitability, similar in principle to that already suggested for the copper mining companies. Such a tax is not feasible for all companies because of the insoluble practical difficulties of measuring capital employed in the long term. These practical difficulties are minimized, however, in the case of new enterprises; and where there is only a need for measuring capital employed for a maximum of five years, since after that the normal tax provisions would apply. The administrative burden would not be great, since capital expenditure is already measured for tax purposes, in order to apply the various capital allowances; and the assessment of profits for tax purposes is a normal process in the tax office.

The disincentive effect would probably be small since there would be no tax liability, as before, until profits had reached a very healthy level, and then only on the excess. As was suggested in discussing the tax proposal for the copper companies, a high marginal tax on a high rate of profit is not likely to discourage investment, since the investor will be only too pleased to think that such a high rate of profit is possible.

The advantage of introducing such a modification would be that enterprises which had little need of a tax holiday, that is, those making very high profits, would not escape taxation altogether; and the marginal firm which had relatively low profit expectations would be given the inducement that it needed, and increased possibilities for growth from its own retained profits.

There is another way for government to control excess profits earned by pioneer firms, or indeed other firms as well. Through the price controller the government can affect the price of outputs, and through import duties it can affect the price of a lot of inputs. Such control of profits is, however, rather limited. In general it will be easier to prevent price increases than to force prices down; control is hardly ever complete; and it is expensive in administrative resources. Furthermore, even if the government can prevent the making of excess tax-free profits by companies granted pioneer tax relief in this way, price control cannot compensate directly for loss of tax revenue; and there is also a danger of interfering with resource allocation.

The other main tax measure used in Zambia to attract and encourage investment is the system of capital allowances outlined in Table 6.7 above. The combined effect of annual and initial allowances is illustrated in Table 6.8, below.

TABLE 6.8

Annual and cumulative amounts of capital expenditure
allowed to be written off under the Zambian tax system of 1968
(%)

| Written off at the end of: | Plant and machinery | | | | Industrial buildings | | | |
| | Prime moving equipment | | Other | | Low-cost housing | | Other | |
	Annual	Cumu- lative	Annual	Cumu- lative	Annual	Cumu- lative	Annual	Cumu- lative
Year 1	50.0	50.0	40.0	40.0	20.0	20.0	15.0	15.0
Year 2	15.0	65.0	12.0	52.0	8.0	28.0	4.2	19.2
Year 3	10.5	75.5	9.9	61.9	7.2	35.2	4.0	23.2
Year 4	7.3	82.8	7.7	69.6	6.5	41.7	3.8	27.0
Year 5	5.2	88.0	6.1	75.7	5.8	47.5	3.7	30.7
Year 6	3.6	91.6	4.9	80.6	5.3	52.8	3.5	34.2
Year 7	2.5	94.1	3.9	84.5	4.7	57.5	3.3	37.5
Year 8	1.8	95.9	2.9	87.4	4.2	61.7	3.1	40.6
Year 9	1.2	97.1	2.3	89.7	3.8	65.5	3.0	43.6
Year 10	0.9	98.0	1.8	91.5	3.4	68.9	2.8	46.4

From Table 6.8 it can be seen that the present Zambian system allows a high proportion of capital expenditure to be written off quickly. Furthermore, the allowances are heavily concentrated in the early years, and can thus be expected to have the maximum effect on investors' calculations, since businessmen are known to have very short time-horizons. Zambian businessmen, with the additional uncertainties created by geographical position, recent political independence and so on, are most unlikely to be exceptions to this rule.

For the same reason—the short time-horizons of businessmen—the existing initial allowances are almost certainly preferable to British-type investment allowances. The latter allow an additional amount of capital expenditure to be written off in the first year; but this amount is *not* allowed to be deducted from the book value (for tax purposes) of the investment. This means that the firm is allowed to write off eventually more than 100 per cent of the investment, so that there is ultimately a loss of revenue to the government.

The write-offs permissible under any system of investment allowances in the first few years could be matched quite simply by a system of initial allowances. In order to contend that the investment allowances were a more effective incentive for investment, one would have to suppose that the prospect of being able to write off more of an investment in the more remote future years would induce sufficient *additional* investment to justify the loss of tax revenue involved.

So far, the argument suggests that Zambia has the right system of capital allowances. In itself this may be true but these are not the only investment incentives offered by the government. In addition to capital allowances the general effect of exemptions from import duties is to make capital goods, and to a lesser extent other industrial inputs, cheap in relation to imports of consumer goods. Since there is probably an indirect connection between what industry must pay its labour and what labour must pay for imported consumer goods, this also creates a bias against labour in production and investment. Finally, the Zambian National Provident Fund, whatever its main purpose, has the principal indirect effect of making labour more expensive, since each employee must pay 5 per cent of his wage, maximum K 4 a month, and this is matched by a similar amount paid by the employer.[19] The Pioneer Industries Act is neutral in this respect, but it only applies to a limited number of firms, and only to them for a limited number of years.

The net effect of the tax system is therefore to create a bias in favour of capital-intensive investment. In a country like Zambia this must surely be wrong. Even though there is a shortage of certain types of labour, much of which has to be imported at high cost at present, firms may choose a technique now which uses relatively little labour and be unable to change it later when Zambians with the right skills are more freely available. This bias in the tax system against labour is not uncommon in developing countries which have inherited a tax system which was transferred without sufficient thought (or without any) from a developed country.

It could be argued that since most capital *equipment* is imported in Zambia and, because of the country's remoteness, is more expensive than elsewhere, that the government is justified in making it cheaper through the tax system.[20] In addition the equipment is likely to last a shorter time because of relatively unskilled use, higher cost maintenance, the

---

19 Strictly speaking it would theoretically be possible for the employer to pass this backwards by pushing wages down or preventing wage rises that he would otherwise have allowed. Neither seems likely.

20 Transport costs are a real cost and so should not be offset by government for reasons of resource allocation, but in order to encourage investment.

poor state of the roads, and so on. This is undoubtedly true. But similar arguments apply to the supply of labour. Whereas in a developed country a prospective investor can expect to find a ready supply, at a price, of workers trained both in the general discipline of industrial work and in more specific industrial skills, and can expect them to be housed already, in a country such as Zambia he can expect no such thing, and must therefore expect to have to spend a lot of money on training for particular skills, on housing, and to get low productivity from both skilled and unskilled workers for an unknown period while they acquire experience. In short, labour costs, taken as a whole, are higher than they would be in many countries, in spite of nominally low wage costs. And wage costs are not even nominally low when compared to other developing countries. Finally, it is well known that skilled foreign labour costs more in Zambia than in its country of origin.

Various solutions have been suggested. The simplest is to give whatever subsidy is available to firms in the form of a direct payment in proportion to labour costs or numbers employed;[21] and to render the rest of the tax as neutral as possible in this respect. An alternative, which would be a far less drastic revision of the tax system and the Zambian National Provident Fund, would be to introduce some subsidy for the employment of labour to compensate for the present capital bias.

At present the tax system makes only one concession to labour costs, which is the accelerated depreciation allowances for low-cost housing. This concession is all to the good. But even so, it takes six years to write off half the cost of such housing against tax (see Table 6.8), so that with present tax rates rather more than three-quarters of the cost of this housing must be borne by the company in these first six years.[22] Thus even this expenditure, for which some tax concession has been made, can be a considerable burden on a developing company. Other housing does not have this concession, and does not even qualify as an industrial building.

There are other ways in which the government can redress the balance. The running costs of formal training schemes (but not necessarily the capital costs) are already deductible for tax purposes, as

[21] See, for example, A. R. Prest, *Fiscal Survey of the British Caribbean*, HMSO, 1957, p. 102; and J. E. Meade, 'Mauritius: a Case Study in "Malthusian" Economy', *Economic Journal*, September 1961.

[22] To the extent that companies can obtain loans, from building societies for example, then the company need only bear the cost of a down payment, and the continuing cost of a mortgage.

a cost. As with low-cost housing, this still leaves the company, especially in its early years when it can probably least afford it, with a considerable additional financial burden. The government should therefore consider making direct cash grants to help with the cost of training schemes. This proposal, if adopted, would not only help redress the bias in favour of capital, but would encourage more of such formal training schemes than would otherwise have been started. In other words, it would reduce the initial and continuing labour costs of those firms which would have undertaken training schemes anyway, and would induce the more reluctant firms to start proper training schemes. It would have two further advantages; first, that the government, by meeting some of the costs, would acquire the right to exercise some control over training schemes, and ensure that they were in the best interests of the trainee, the company, and the country; second, the proposal would leave the country with a real net long-term gain in the form of a better-trained labour force, should the company not succeed in establishing itself, or should it decide not to continue after the period of tax relief had ended.[23]

The argument could be taken a stage further. Apart from formal training for specific skills, the general lack of experience of the disciplines of industrial working among Zambians, added to the universal problems of getting a work force together and adapting it to new processes, would normally be expected to result in very low productivity in the early stages of a new enterprise (or indeed of the expansion of an existing one). There is therefore a case for the government offering some direct subsidy for increases in the employment of Zambians, either in the very early stages of an enterprise, or following the expansion of an existing one. Such a subsidy should taper off very rapidly after the first year. Again this would have the dual advantage of partially offsetting a very real additional cost which must be a grave disincentive for investment, and of partially restoring the balance of choice between capital- and labour-intensive techniques. There would have to be a compensatory clause for the repayment of tax rebate when employment fell, in order to avoid giving a rebate to a firm with fluctuating output every time output and employment rose which would not be returnable when output fell.

If, on the other hand, the government was prepared to undertake a more drastic reform, then it could adopt something on the lines of the

---

[23] This latter possibility is a very real risk with tax holiday schemes such as the Pioneer Industries Act.

Chilean copper taxation, with a reduction of the rate of profits tax for increases in output on some sort of sliding scale. This would be neutral as regards techniques of production, if annual depreciation allowances only were permitted for writing off capital at rates which approximated as nearly as possible to expected life. If the government wished to go further and positively encourage labour-intensive techniques it could make the sliding scale depend on increases in employment instead.

Finally, the cost of providing housing, which is in any case an exceptional expense, should be allowed as a cost for tax purposes, for *all* types of labour, that is, high-cost as well as low-cost housing. As a general principle of company taxation, all legitimate expenses should be allowed; and this reform, even if it temporarily favoured foreign labour, would lessen the likelihood of a choice of technique in investment being made because of a temporary shortage of skilled labour. For example it would be a pity for large commercial firms to install computers now when a large supply of clerical staff will soon be emerging from the schools.

DIRECT TAX ON PERSONS

The present system[24]

The existing direct tax system has the following prominent features:

1. To arrive at annual taxable income for income tax purposes, the following principal allowances are deducted from gross income:[25]

	K
Single persons	800
Married persons	1,600
For each child	240
Life insurance premiums, contribution to maximum of	400
Maximum allowances:	
single person	1,600
married person	3,600

[24] This section was written in 1968: some small changes were introduced to the system in 1969 and 1970. For one aspect of the 1969 measures, see C. R. M. Harvey, 'A note on the 1969 Zambian budget and the administrative constraint on further tax reform', *Zambia Law Journal*, Lusaka, January 1970.

[25] For the complete set of allowances see Income Tax Act 1966, Charging Schedule.

2.   The rates of income tax on taxable income, arrived at after the deduction of the above allowances, are as follows:

First K 1,040 of annual taxable income .	5%
Next K 1,040 ,, ,, ,, ,, .	$22\frac{1}{2}$%
Next K 2,080 ,, ,, ,, ,, .	$27\frac{1}{2}$%
Next K 2,080 ,, ,, ,, ,, .	$32\frac{1}{2}$%
Next K 2,080 ,, ,, ,, ,, .	40%
Next K 2,080 ,, ,, ,, ,, .	50%
Remainder ,, ,, ,, ,, .	60%

3. In addition to income tax there is a personal levy administered by local government authorities. The maximum rate is K 5 on incomes over K 400 per annum. Incomes below K 120 per annum for males and K 400 for females are exempt. Incomes of males between K 120 and K 400 per annum can be charged at rates up to K 5 per annum at the discretion of the local authority.

4. The Ministry of Local Government and Housing amended the Personal Levy Ordinance in 1968 to increase the rates of personal levy, but introduction of the new rates was postponed until 1969. The new rates are as follows:

Annual income	Personal levy
Between K 120 and K 200	K 1.25
,, K 200 and K 300	K 2.50
,, K 300 and K 400	K 4.00
,, K 400 and K 600	K 8.00
,, K 600 and K 800	K 12.00
,, K 800 and K 1,000	K 16.00
Over K 1,000	K 20.00

Provision was made for those paying K 8 or more per annum to spread the payments over the year, the detailed provisions for payment to be arranged by local authorities.

5. The method of assessing liability to personal levy is more difficult to comment upon generally, since it must inevitably vary greatly in different parts of the country. Each authority (township, city, or rural council) has to set up an assessment committee, supposedly from

among local persons of some standing and repute. This committee has then to estimate the income of every adult male in the district. As far as could be discovered, the committees only attempt to assess cash income, that is, wages in the case of employed persons (which creates no difficulty), sales of produce for farmers, and trading income for traders. No attempt is made to impute income where the farmers' own produce is consumed, or to assess the value of housing. The problem of assessing income is not very severe at present with the very low rates of personal levy and very small graduations in the rates. For example, almost all traders can be assumed to be making more than K 400 per annum, and farmers living off their own produce entirely and selling none can be assumed to be earning below K 120 per annum in most districts. Furthermore, if an error is made, the amount of tax involved is unlikely to be more than a kwacha, so no great injustice is likely to be done. In fact it is clear that the present system causes little controversy, since many authorities have not even appointed the appeals committee allowed for in the regulations. This will no longer be the case, however, when the proposed new rates are introduced; in fact some further thought will have to be given to assessment methods.

Criticisms

The income tax system has been taken, with few alterations, from the English system. Even the level of exemptions is more suited to English conditions, being actually higher in absolute money terms. Not surprisingly, therefore, the system is ill-suited to Zambia, in several ways.

The overall tax burden created by the system results in Zambian residents paying less tax than those of any of the neighbouring African countries. This is true at all levels of income, and for all categories of taxpayers, almost without exception. This is demonstrated in Tables 6.9, 6.10 and 6.11.

The gap between Zambian and other tax burdens is probably understated at the higher income levels because of the very generous life insurance allowance in Zambia, and because of the generous Zambian provision for income from savings.[26]

---

[26] Interest on Post Office Savings Bank deposits and National Development Bonds is tax-free and *in addition* the first K 200 of other unearned income is also tax-free.

TABLE 6.9

Comparison of annual tax payable by a single man in Zambia with that payable in various African countries and the UK

(All amounts to nearest kwacha)

Annual income	Zambia	Ghana	Nigeria (Lagos)	Malawi	Kenya	Tanzania	Uganda	South Africa	United Kingdom
400	5	8	6	12	4	4	42	4–6	—
800	5	36	26	36	64	64	130	32–34	57
1,200	25	74	46	86	130	130	210	84–90	154
1,600	45	124	86	160	198	198	286	136–146	283
2,000	93	174	136	230	256	256	356	206–218	488
2,400	183	234	206	335	312	312	426	261–278	539
3,000	325	330	342	503	466	466	616	348–370	733
4,000	599	548	566	835	742	742	942	510–538	1,051
5,000	876	834	866	1,188	1,072	1,072	1,322	684–710	1,371
6,000	1,201	1,182	1,166	1,551	1,446	1,446	1,746	992–1,032	1,692
8,000	1,923	2,018	1,916	2,294	2,354	2,354	2,754	1,918–1,992	2,385
10,000	2,811	3,120	2,842	3,073	3,384	3,384	3,884	3,006–3,120	3,260
12,000	3,891	4,320	3,992	4,106	4,512	4,512	5,112	4,212–4,370	4,280
16,000	6,291	7,120	6,292	6,707	7,068	7,068	7,868	6,770–7,024	6,590
20,000	8,691	9,920	8,592	8,907	9,768	9,768	10,768	9,650–10,386	9,440

Notes: 1 It was not always possible to obtain the latest figures; since the trend is for increased rates and lower exemptions, the figures of tax payable may be understated for some countries.

2 The South African figures include a special loan levy for 1968, repayable 'in due course' with simple interest at 5%. Provincial governments raise differing amounts of income tax; the figures show the range covered by the various provinces.

3 The figures for Malawi and the UK are adjusted for devaluation at the new official exchange rates.

4 Zambian figures include the personal levy—K 5 at all the income levels shown. For the effect of the proposed increased personal levy, see Table 6.14.

TABLE 6.10

Comparison of tax payable by a married man with no children in Zambia with that payable in various African countries and the UK

Annual income	Zambia	Ghana	Nigeria (Lagos)	Malawi	Kenya	Tanzania	Uganda	South Africa	United Kingdom
400	5	8	6	12	4	4	42	0–2	—
800	5	36	6	25	18	18	84	6–7	9
1,200	5	74	26	31	64	64	115	34–38	89
1,600	5	124	46	41	132	132	190	80–88	197
2,000	25	174	86	96	190	190	260	122–134	326
2,400	45	234	136	168	240	240	330	182–195	454
3,000	138	330	252	303	320	320	434	252–268	646
4,000	379	548	476	596	596	596	730	384–404	967
5,000	654	834	746	934	874	874	1,054	526–546	1,288
6,000	941	1,182	1,046	1,289	1,250	1,250	1,460	820–854	1,608
8,000	1,603	2,018	1,766	2,024	2,104	2,104	2,390	1,716–1,784	2,302
10,000	2,411	3,120	2,656	2,787	3,086	3,086	3,480	2,776–2,882	3,142
12,000	3,411	4,320	3,762	3,713	4,108	4,108	4,670	3,922–4,070	4,160
16,000	5,811	7,120	6,062	6,075	6,712	6,712	7,350	6,392–6,632	6,450
20,000	8,211	9,920	9,362	8,474	9,564	9,564	10,250	9,244–9,592	9,290

Notes: See foot of Table 6.9.

TABLE 6.11

Comparison of tax payable by a married man with two children in Zambia with that payable in various African countries and the UK

Annual income	Zambia	Ghana	Nigeria (Lagos)	Malawi	Kenya	Tanzania	Uganda	South Africa	United Kingdom
400	5	8	6	12	4	4	42	0–2	—
800	5	36	6	25	18	18	84	6–7	—
1,200	5	74	14	31	34	34	114	10–13	—
1,600	5	124	34	41	72	72	140	14–19	50
2,000	5	174	62	46	130	130	212	33–40	147
2,400	21	234	106	84	180	180	282	78–84	275
3,000	51	330	200	189	256	256	388	138–150	468
4,000	255	548	422	441	464	464	624	284–301	788
5,000	522	834	674	747	740	740	848	426–444	1,111
6,000	797	1,182	974	1,111	1,070	1,070	1,316	720–749	1,431
8,000	1,435	2,018	1,676	1,838	1,876	1,876	2,208	1,617–1,680	2,122
10,000	2,211	3,120	2,546	2,595	2,854	2,854	3,278	2,676–2,778	2,972
12,000	3,171	4,320	3,624	3,466	3,932	3,932	4,448	3,822–3,967	3,900
16,000	5,523	7,120	5,924	5,779	6,388	6,388	7,090	6,296–6,529	6,155
20,000	7,923	9,920	8,224	8,179	9,088	9,088	9,990	9,276–9,579	8,975

Notes: See foot of Table 6.9.

The high initial exemptions, ignoring the personal levy which is very small, have several effects. The number of income taxpayers is very small—about 50,000 people out of a population of 3.8 million and an employed population of over 300,000. More specifically, very few African wage-earners pay income tax. For example, among African employees of the copper mining companies, often referred to as the best-paid labour force on the African continent, only a handful (between 100 and 200) pay any income tax at all.[27] To put this another way, a Zambian does not begin to pay tax (apart from the small personal levy) until his income as a single man reaches some 10 times the *per capita* national income; and a married man with two children pays no tax before his income reaches a minimum of K 2,080 per annum, which is some 13 times the *per capita* national income, and about 139 times the *per capita* income in the rural sector.[28] As a point of comparison, the married man with no children in the UK begins to pay income tax when his income reaches a point rather more than half the *per capita* national income.

Another alien feature of the tax system is the fairly elaborate provision made for the differing family circumstances of taxpayers. It is worth considering whether *any* sort of allowance system is suitable in Zambian society at present, especially if exemptions were lowered so as to include the bulk of wage-earners.

With the extended family system, and customary marriages, it would be extremely difficult to discover, for many people, just exactly what their family responsibilities were. Nor would it be equitable to do so, since to give allowances to the man whose wife was legally married to him and who was bringing up his own children, would be unjust if the same allowances were not given to a man who had had a customary marriage, or was bringing up some nephews and nieces. His responsibility for the latter would be just as great, under present social customs, as it would be for his own children.[29]

In Western societies, a complex system of allowances is introduced into the income tax system in order to try to *increase* equity between taxpayers. Its introduction into African society is likely to reduce

[27] Actual figure quoted in an interview with the Commissioner of Income Tax. The order of magnitude can be confirmed from Table 4(e), *Ministry of Labour Annual Report*, Government Printer, Lusaka, 1966.

[28] Income in the rural areas is notoriously difficult to calculate; but the point is indisputable that it is extremely small in relation to the basic exemptions in the Zambian income tax.

[29] See, for example, Dr. K. D. Kaunda, *A Humanist in Africa*, p. 27.

equity as much as to increase it. Every man with a job in Zambia is well off, relative to the bulk of his compatriots; he is thus almost certain to acquire responsibilities for others, whether these be of a formal, legal nature, provable to the tax authorities, or not. Probably the most equitable way, therefore, to treat wage- and salary-earners as regards tax is simply to assume that they *all* have some family responsibilities, which are both difficult to discover exactly, and impossible to distinguish one from the other; so that the fairest thing to do is to treat them all the same for tax purposes.

The adoption of a system in other countries does not necessarily recommend it for use in Zambia; nevertheless it is interesting to note that allowances differing for differing family circumstances have been abolished at all levels of income in Ghana and Sierra Leone, and that the same system is effectively in force for lower incomes in, amongst others, Malawi and the East African countries. The principle has, of course, been adopted already in Zambia, in a very small way, in the application of the personal levy.

In fact there is precious little rationale in marriage allowances even in a Western society. After all, what is the rationale in giving allowances? It is that the state should try to alleviate the unavoidable additional expenses that come with family responsibilities. But in a modern age, when women without children are expected and able to work, why is there a generous marriage allowance? The position of two working people before and after marriage is essentially the same; there is therefore no clear reason why their tax position should change. Their expenses *may* increase, for example, if they were both previously living with their parents and must now set up a separate establishment; on the other hand their expenses may decrease, if previously they were maintaining two establishments. But just as the state does not tax bachelors differently according to whether they live with their parents or not, so with married people without children the state does not have a general rule as to whether expenses are greater or less, and so should take a neutral position, and tax them the same as before they were married. The rationale for a marriage allowance is probably obscured somewhere in English history, at a time when a 'gentleman' was expected to maintain his wife in idleness, by social custom; this rationale is no longer applicable even in England, and should certainly have no bearing on the Zambian tax system.[30]

---

[30] The separate taxation of married women would also greatly facilitate the

The point at which expenses *do* increase, and, more important by far, when income is drastically reduced, is when a wife has to stop work to have her first child. In fact the reduction in joint income is so great (up to or more than 50 per cent if the wife earns as much as or more than her husband) that no compensation in the tax system can possibly afford to be more than very minor in comparison. However, this is the point at which an allowance, *if any*, should become operative and it should remain operative until the mother's family responsibilities cease, that is, when her children finish their full-time education.[31] At that point any allowances should cease, and the woman, if she works, should of course again be taxed separately.

Even in a Western society, therefore, the allowance system has not kept pace with changes in social behaviour. As a result Zambia has inherited a tax system obsolete even in the countries from which it came, and wholly inapplicable here.

One final point should be made about the various allowances. They are so designed that their value to the taxpayer increases as his income rises, since they reduce his tax liability at the top marginal rate of tax. Thus the additional K 800 allowance deductible by the married taxpayer (on top of the K 800 allowed to all taxpayers) is worth nothing if his income is K 800 per annum or less, and increases in value to K 480 at an annual income of more than K 12,000. Similar effects occur in the application of the children's and life insurance allowances. While it could doubtless be argued that it costs a wealthy man more to maintain a wife or child, it seems extremely doubtful, to say the least, whether this should be recognized by the tax system.

The result of the high exemptions, the low rates, and the small number of taxpayers is that the government is taxing incomes much more lightly than it need; that the benefits of high income elasticity of a progressive income tax are being derived from only a small sector of the population; that the government's direct control over private spending is limited to the small tax-paying sector; and finally that Zambians who are by any standards well off compared to most of their compatriots contribute nothing directly from their incomes to the government's efforts to develop the country. One should perhaps add that, because

administration of PAYE. An enormous amount of administrative time is currently spent in discovering the 'correct' rate to apply to working married women.

31 It could be argued that a woman with children of school age can work, but it is doubtful whether this should be officially encouraged by the tax system.

of its complexity, the tax system needs a relatively large number of skilled administrators, who are extremely scarce in Zambia.[32] This has the additional result that a lowering of exemption limits without simplifying the present system is out of the question, for administrative reasons, for many years to come.

Suggested reforms

It appears that the government is in the fortunate position of being able to reform the income tax in such a way as to meet most of the above criticisms. If it wishes to widen the tax base and thereby increase its control over spending power, and especially over inflationary tendencies, then exemption limits must be lowered dramatically. Because of the administrative constraint this can only be done if at the same time the tax is drastically simplified. But, it is argued, a drastic simplification is in any case desirable, since, far from reducing equity as might be the case in a Western industrialized society, it would actually *increase* the equity of the system.

The sort of system that is suggested, therefore, is a monthly with-holding tax on all workers, including married women, who would be taxed separately from their husbands. The sort of rates that might be used for small incomes are shown in Table 6.12.

TABLE 6.12

A proposed system for taxing all salaries of up to K 200 a month (K 2,400 a year)
('*System A*')

Incomes:	Per month (K)	Per year (K)	Rate (%)	Tax on each slice of income (K)	Total tax at upper limit (K)
Up to	20	240	—	3	3
From	20– 40	240– 480	5	12	15
From	40– 70	480– 840	7½	27	42
From	70–130	840–1,560	10	72	114
From	130–200	1,560–2,400	15	126	240

The system of taxation in Table 6.12 (henceforward referred to as System A) contains a minimum rate of K 3 a year, on all salaries under K 20 a month. (This should not be confused with a minimum tax on all adult males—we are here discussing only those in employment.) This

---

[32] The Commissioner of Income Tax is currently only able to fill about half of his established posts; and training is a long process—in the UK, for example, it takes a *graduate* a further three years to qualify as a tax inspector.

TABLE 6.13

Tax payable under the system in Table 6.12 (compared with the 1968 system
(All figures annual)

Annual income (K)	Tax payable Amount (K)	As % of income	1968 system Single (K)	Married (K)	Married with 2 children (K)
400	11	2.7	—	—	—
800	39	4.9	—	—	—
1,200	78	6.5	20	—	—
1,600	120	7.5	40	—	—
2,000	186	9.3	88	20	—
2,400	240	10.0	178	80	16

is suggested because the collection of smaller sums than 25n a month per employee would be administratively expensive, even though it would b up to the employer to transmit the sum to the tax authorities. The sum is a small one, and would not be an unduly inequitable burden on any one in full-time employment.

The first rate of tax, 5 per cent, is rather low, and it could be argue that the sums of revenue raised by such a rate would not be wort collecting. Two points need to be made against this argument: first that the incomes involved, K 20–40 a month, are pretty small and would thus be harsh to tax them very severely; second, that one of th main reasons for introducing a scheme like System A would be t involve as many people as possible as directly as possible in thei country's affairs, and in paying for development. This inevitabl involves taking rather small sums from large numbers of low wage earners. In due course, they will, one hopes, move up the wage scal and become liable for larger tax payments. System A would thu establish a framework for the future, and by accustoming all wage earners to the payment of some tax, lay the ground for large increase in tax revenue as wages and employment rise.

The tax could be collected monthly, with no reassessment at th end of the year and therefore no annual tax returns needed. At presen income tax in Zambia is assessed on an annual basis, although fo regularly paid employees tax is actually deducted at source monthly under the PAYE system. The latter is potentially a great saver o administrative time, but is not currently being used to its best advantage since even those who have tax deducted monthly from their salaries still have to make an annual return—which creates work for th administration.

A side-effect of this arrangement is that non-Zambians who arrive in the middle of the tax year 'escape' a great deal of tax. Because in most cases the same system applies in their country of origin, they are eligible for large tax rebates there; and because their *actual annual* income in Zambia in this first year is below their annual *rate* of pay, their tax liability is lowered. There is no rationale in this. A man's standard of living, when in regular employment, is dictated by his *rate* of pay—a man being paid at the rate of K 4,000 a year who arrives in Zambia with six months of the tax year elapsed does not live at the level of a man earning K 2,000 a year, his pay for the next six months, but at the level of a man earning K 4,000 a year. He can thus be taxed accordingly. A further reason for taxing at the proper rate immediately on arrival (or immediately upon an increase in monthly salary) is that the taxpayer will otherwise suffer a sudden increase in monthly tax deductions after the beginning of the next tax year, after having become used to relatively low monthly deductions. This appears illogical and unfair to most taxpayers, and thus causes the maximum amount of taxpayer disaffection, which is something every tax system should try to avoid. It is always far better, from this point of view, to tax an increase in salary immediately, since it is easier to share an increase with the government than to become used to a higher rate of net pay, and then suffer a decrease.

Regarding the increases in personal levy, they will tax incomes above K 1,000 per annum at a rate of K 20 and make this payment an addition to income tax, where this was payable. This will give rise to the rather absurd situation where a married man has a rising tax payment up to K 1,000 a year, but above that level his tax payment remains the same up to K 1,600 if he has no children, or K 2,080 if he has two children. Thereafter, his tax payment rises again. If the government wishes to tax lower incomes then surely it is better to do so on a logically progressive basis throughout the whole income range, rather than on a piecemeal basis.

Secondly, the taxation of personal income through an extension of the personal levy would involve taxpayers in two different payments of tax. There is widespread evidence that the 'double taxation' of incomes in this way causes particularly strong resentment among taxpayers. If the objective is to raise additional money for local authorities, then this could easily be done by remitting to them an agreed proportion of the centralized income tax raised in their areas.

Thirdly, two systems of taxation require two administrative organizations, which is hardly something that Zambia can afford.

Fourthly, the proposed rates seem to be rather low. Only the merest handful of workers had incomes over K 840 a year in 1965, apart from mine workers. It is therefore likely that very few now have incomes over K 1,000 a year. Yet the proposed increase in personal levy would result in those in the highest income bracket for African wage-earners being taxed only about 4 per cent of their incomes. A stronger system is needed.

So far the suggested reforms have considered only the taxation of wages and salaries, which is relatively easy compared with the taxation of private income from investments, rural income, and the income of the self-employed.

If a system of taxing salaries monthly at source is adopted, then there is no need for annual tax returns, except for those with taxable income from sources other than their employment. Since every taxpayer would not be making a return as a matter of course, it would be necessary to ensure that the onus was on the taxpayer to make a return if private income made this necessary. The simplest way to do this would be to deduct a high rate of tax at source from dividend, interest, and other payments liable to tax, say 50 per cent. Then all taxpayers with a marginal rate of tax below 50 per cent would be able to reclaim some tax at the end of the year. Any taxpayer with a marginal rate of tax above 50 per cent would be assumed to be likely to have private income, and receive a tax form from the tax administration as a matter of course; the number involved would be small. Such a system would have the additional advantage that instead of the bulk of taxpayers with private income owing the government money for long periods, the government would owe the taxpayer instead; or put another way, the government would get a free loan instead of the taxpayer. The system would also reduce the amount of tax made irrecoverable by bankruptcy, etc.

The machinery for the taxation of rural incomes already exists, and is presumably intended to be used far more extensively when the increased rates of personal levy are introduced. The method of assessment could be improved, however; the following recommendations apply equally whether a unified tax system is adopted, or whether the personal levy proposals are introduced.

The most successful way of taxing incomes in African rural areas is the one which has been developed in Uganda.[33] There are local

[33] The following description is taken mainly from J. F. Due, *Taxation and*

committees, rather on the lines of those in Zambia, which make a list of all sources of income and wealth in their area, for example from farming, fishing, cattle, goats, chickens, milk and beer sales, trading, transport, wages, salaries, pensions, etc. The committee then converts each item to an annual income. Thus a cow might be assumed to earn its owner K 1.50 a year, a coffee tree 30n a year. For trading, the committee can assume a ratio (say 2:1) between income and stock. The sources of income are aggregated for each person, and tax is then assessed on *taxable capacity*. Thus tax is assessed on a man's *potential* income, rather than his actual income. The system has proved very successful in Uganda where it raises about 80 per cent of local government taxes, and this amount is about the same or slightly more than is raised by the central government income tax.

Thus if such a system were used in Zambia potential incomes would be roughly estimated in the way described, and the rates used could be as follows:

Assessed income from	Tax
K 120 – K 240	K 3.00
K 240 – K 360	K 6.00
K 360 – K 480	K 12.00
K 480 – K 600	K 19.50

and so on, using the same rate as in Table 6.12 for the middle income in each K 120 range.

The committee would thus only have to assess potential income to the nearest K 120; at the same time the system would fit into the proposed income tax system for employed persons. The minimum exemption is in line with that in the present personal levy system, and would probably exclude all farmers without any cash income, that is, those growing entirely for their own consumption. On the other hand, the use of potential income for assessment would mean that the part of output consumed by the farmer himself, where 'income' exceeded K120 a year, would be included.

Further advantages of the system are that because the marginal rate on increased *actual* income is zero, the incentive to increase production is unimpaired, and the farmer who manages to produce more than the average gains the full benefit.[34]

Economic Development in Tropical Africa, The MIT Press, Cambridge, Massachusetts, and D. Walker in E. F. Jackson (ed.), *Economic Development in Africa*, Blackwell, Oxford, 1965.

[34] The 'average' should in fact be set a little on the low side in order to encourage production.

Secondly, such a system would be a considerable encouragement to farmers to treat their assets as income-earning. For example a farmer would be taxed on the income he *could* be earning from a herd of cows, whether he was obtaining such an income or not, and would thus be encouraged to treat his herd in a commercial way.

Finally, assessment of potential income is rather easier than assessment of actual income. A locally-based committee should have enough knowledge of local conditions to assess the yield of various assets within the limits of accuracy required by the system; and this is considerably easier than assessing actual income, which requires a knowledge of both consumption and sales by the farmer. In addition, a tax based on cash income is in fact a direct disincentive to sales of produce, since increases in sales should lead to increases in tax.

The other major problem of lowering exemption limits is the taxation of the self-employed. There is no easy way to tax professional men, unincorporated businesses, etc., and lowering exemption limits would bring in a mass of people who would be much harder to assess even than existing taxpayers, because of inadequate or non-existent accounts, mobility, for example among itinerant traders, and so on. However, there is considerable scope for putting the onus on the taxpayer by imposing arbitrary assessments slightly above the likely true assessment, and thus obliging the taxpayer to submit evidence that his liability *is*, in fact, less. There is also great advantage in assessing on a current year basis, that is, assessing the taxpayer, for, say, a quarter of the previous year's payment, every three or four months, and settling up the balance at the end of the year. Again this has the advantage that the government waits less time for its money.[35]

As an administrative aid to tax collection, particularly with regard to the self-employed, the tax administration could introduce certificates of tax having been paid, which taxpayers would be required to produce at other points of contact with the government's administrative machine, such as applying for exchange control permission, or passports, or on leaving the country. This would encourage the prompt payment of tax, and prevent evasion.

If something like the proposed scheme for low incomes were adopted, then some increase in the taxation of existing taxpayers would be implied. That some such increase is feasible is clear from Table 6.14

---

[35] Both these are already done, to some extent (Income Tax Act, Section 76(2) and Ninth Schedule).

below, which summarizes the information in Tables 6.9, 6.10 and 6.11.

TABLE 6.14

Zambian direct tax as it would be with the increased rates of personal levy, as a percentage of the average direct tax payable in 7 African countries (as in Tables 6.9, 6.10 and 6.11)

1	2	3	4	5	6	7	8	9	10
	Single man			Married man, no children			Married man, 2 children		
			col. 2			col. 5			col. 8
Annual income		7	as		7	as		7	as
		country	%		country	%		country	%
	Zn	av-	of col.	Zn	av-	of col.	Zn	av-	of col.
	tax	erage	3	tax	erage	6	tax	erage	9
(K)	(K)	(K)		(K)	(K)		(K)	(K)	
400	4	12	33	4	11	36	4	11	36
800	12	55	22	12	27	44	12	26	46
1,200	40	111	36	20	53	38	20	44	45
1,600	60	173	29	20	107	19	20	71	28
2,000	108	232	46	40	160	25	20	113	18
2,400	198	300	66	100	214	47	36	160	22
3,000	340	440	77	154	307	50	66	243	27
4,000	614	700	88	394	547	72	270	450	60
5,000	891	1,008	88	670	790	85	537	698	77
6,000	1,216	1,364	88	956	1,170	82	812	1,042	77
8,000	1,938	2,235	86	1,618	2,000	81	1,450	1,850	78
10,000	2,826	3,253	87	2,426	2,980	81	2,226	2,830	78
12,000	3,906	4,372	89	3,426	4,050	84	3,186	3,900	81
16,000	6,306	7,002	90	5,826	6,550	89	5,538	6,350	87
20,000	8,706	9,688	90	8,226	9,280	89	7,938	9,040	88

The simplest reform would be to continue the system already proposed (see Table 6.12) for taxing low incomes, with a gradually increasing rate structure, and no allowances. It might be, however, that this would involve too abrupt an increase of the tax burden on those who have been generously treated by the present system. This sort of action is always bad tax policy. In the short term then the government could continue a modified system of allowances for family circumstances, involving a cash rebate equal for taxpayers at all income levels, to be reclaimed at the end of the year by the taxpayer. Thus the simplicity of a uniform system of deductions from wages and salaries would not be lost. In the long term the government could work towards a unified system with no allowances.

One final reform might help to counteract the demonstration effect already referred to in the section on saving. At the moment the taxation of terminal benefits, that is, lump sums received at the end of contract periods by expatriate employees, is in a transitional stage, which will be over in 1970. The opinion has been expressed, however, especially by the mining employers, that terminal benefits are not successful in attracting and keeping labour. They smack of paternalism in that the amount saved is determined by the employer; as savings, they do not carry interest; and there are doubts about changes in the law, either on taxation or exchange control.

The alternative is to offer a tax incentive for salary saved and sent out of the country. The objection to this is that it is bad for the balance of payments. But so are terminal benefits, which must normally be sent abroad, in that by definition the worker has no chance to spend them in Zambia. The other alternative, that the money be spent rather than saved, will normally result in additional imports, especially as the spending in question will be mainly on non-essentials, if it is an alternative to saving. Thus although it is true that a tax incentive for externalized saving is bad for the balance of payments, so are the alternatives. And since such a tax incentive is more attractive to contract workers, for the reasons already given, it would be the most effective way of reducing the gap in living standards; and would also effectively remove the possibility of retrospective legislation. If such an incentive were introduced, then money brought into the country by taxpayers who had taken advantage of the concession would have to be taxed as current income, in order to prevent people sending savings abroad at reduced tax rates and then bringing them back again to spend, free of tax.

Conclusion

The main point of these criticisms of the present income tax, and of the reforms suggested here, is that the system badly needs Zambianizing. It is not just that the government needs greater control over personal spending power, although this is important if inflation is to be controlled; nor is it simply that the government badly needs new sources of revenue to cover its expenditure requirements, although this too is urgent. It is that at the moment the great majority of revenue comes from the copper companies, and from an income tax which falls mainly on non-Zambians. It seems alien to the country's political philosophy that Zambians themselves should, in the great majority, be contributing nothing directly to the government's development effort, especially those relatively well off, with jobs in the urban areas. Thus, not only is it desirable that as many Zambians as possible should make a contribution, however small, to development; it is also important that the framework for such contributions be established as soon as possible, since it is much easier to do so now, with the copper price high and considerable prosperity all round, than it will be in less prosperous times. At the same time, there seems to be no need to let the expatriate off more lightly than is absolutely necessary. Clearly Zambia must compete internationally, since expatriate skilled labour is, almost by definition, extremely mobile internationally. But this means no more than that Zambian tax rates should not be noticeably above those of her neighbours and competitors.

7

Zambia's Markets: Problems and Opportunities

BASTIAAN DE GAAY FORTMAN[1]

INTRODUCTION

THERE can be no doubt that the existence of well-established markets gives a major impetus to economic growth and development. To overcome bottlenecks in supply an incentive is needed: the incentive of a good and secure market for the products in question.

A market consists of two essential components: first, demand—dependent of course on income, preferences, and prices—and, second, the possibility of supply reaching demand at a profitable price. Markets may grow through rising income or through increased availability and/or lower prices following improvements in transport and communication. Further, when markets are growing, increased specialization and internal and external economies of scale may give rise to further growth of income, which in turn may lead to increased public expenditure on transport and marketing facilities. But when markets are very restricted this whole self-stimulating process will not start at all. It is thus perhaps not too much to say that the market constraint is the most general constraint on development.

In a very simple economy, the most immediate opportunities for increasing supply are usually in the field of agriculture. The farmer is, however, not likely to take these opportunities unless he is sure he can sell his crop. Hodder, in a general study of economic development in the tropics, has put this very strongly:

> . . . a tropical farmer is unlikely to increase his production unless an increased demand is there, is seen to be there, and is easily accessible. Improved seed,

---

[1] Senior Lecturer in Economics, University of Zambia. The author wishes to express his gratitude to Mr. David Steeds, Food and Agriculture Organization, Bujumbura, for his helpful comments.

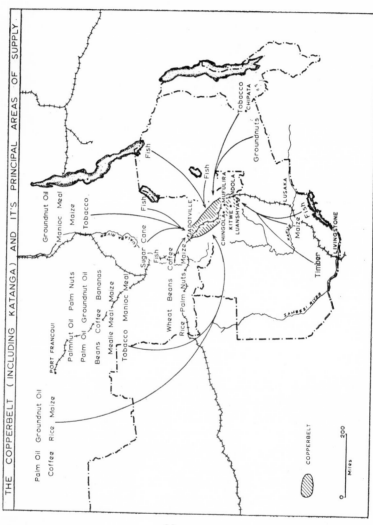

Map 7.1

fertilizers, and better irrigation facilities: a tropical cultivator is unlikely to use these to increase his total production unless the market for his increased production is first seen to exist and is accessible.[2]

Zambia has only a short history of local trade. 'There is no evidence to support a contention that African markets existed in Northern Rhodesia, or on its borders, much before 1930,'[3] Rotberg has noted. The explanation is not difficult to find: Zambia has a very low population density, is landlocked, and has no natural means of communication. Before the arrival of Europeans in the country its population density must have been between two and three people per square mile. In such a situation markets do not develop naturally and the pattern of subsistence agriculture is not easily broken.

The impetus to development in Zambia came from primary product export. The country appeared to be fortunate in possessing large copper deposits which could be profitably worked for the world market. This created income, and with it came *demand*. However, as we have already observed, the existence of demand as such is not enough: supply must also be able to reach it; only then can we speak of a *market*. The higher the level of demand, the more incentive suppliers have to reach the market. Thus the Copperbelt created a large market complex in Zambia and some of its neighbouring countries. Miracle, who wrote a study of the Zambian and Congolese (Katanga) Copperbelts, considering them together as one big centre of economic activity, has stated for example:

> The Copperbelt . . . has created what is unquestionably the largest market complex in Central and Eastern tropical Africa, with markets that draw a good portion of their commodities from 600 and notable amounts from as much as 900 miles distant.[4]

As can be seen from Map 7.1, the Copperbelt provided a profitable market for European farmers along the Zambian line of rail which runs from Livingstone to the Congolese border and which connects the country with South, West, and East African sea ports. But unfortunately it did not lead to considerable African economic develop-

---

[2] B. W. Hodder, *Economic Development in the Tropics*, Hutchinson, London, 1968, p. 202.

[3] R. I. Rotberg, 'Rural Rhodesian Markets', in P. Bohannan and G. Dalton, (eds), *Markets in Africa*, Evanston, New York, 1962, p. 582.

[4] M. P. Miracle, 'African Markets and Trade in the Copperbelt', in P. Bohannan and G. Dalton (eds), op. cit., pp. 698–9.

ment. A government marketing monopoly for grain and grain products, intended to support European farmers, and a prohibition on the sale or hawking of a few other necessities in market places, intended to protect storekeepers (mostly Europeans and Indians), prevented Africans from trading in products like maize, millets, sorghums, grain meals, salt, sugar, coffee, and tea.[5] Because it was difficult to compete with farmers along the line of rail or even in Rhodesia and South Africa, the Copperbelt market did not result in much commercial agriculture in the areas away from the line of rail. Groundnuts and tobacco from the Eastern Province were the most important agricultural imports from the so-called 'rural areas'. The development of African agriculture in areas near the line of rail showed, however, that the African farmer too is highly responsive to commercial incentives.[6] But the most important Copperbelt submarket for Africans appeared to be the *fish market*. Fish was—and is—transported to the Copperbelt from Lake Kariba, Lake Bangweulu, Lake Mweru, and even from as far afield as Lake Tanganyika.

Thus, apart from the development of fish markets along the lakes in Luapula Province (for tobacco and groundnuts from the Eastern Province the main outlet is the export market), the large Copperbelt market has not led to much economic development in the Zambian rural areas. The rural areas import from, rather than export to, the line of rail. The fact that freight rates from the outlying provinces to the line of rail are often as little as a third of the rates on transport in the other direction illustrates this clearly. Earners of money income in the rural areas spend only a small proportion of this on goods produced in these areas themselves.[7] Two important conditions for the development of local trading, namely a high density of population and location on or near long-distance trade routes (good trunk roads),[8] are only

---

[5] ibid., p. 707.

[6] cf. for example R. E. Baldwin, *Economic Development and Export Growth: a Study of Northern Rhodesia 1920–1960*, University of California Press, Berkeley, 1966, pp. 163–5.

[7] The new Urban African Budget Survey, carried out by the Central Statistical Office, Lusaka, will include figures for Mongu and Chipata. It will be interesting to see what proportion of their income African inhabitants of these rural towns spent on locally-supplied goods. The survey will be published in 1970.

[8] cf. e.g. Hodder, op. cit., p. 203. As for population density, Hodder mentions a figure of at least 50 persons to the square mile.

rarely fulfilled in places away from the line of rail. Zambia's prosperous copper production has created a large indigenous demand. This demand has attracted some local supply but the potential in income generation has by no means been fully developed. The country's economic development is definitely hindered by a market constraint arising chiefly from a badly developed system of transport and communication in a sparsely populated country. The density of population was 13.4 people per square mile by the end of 1966. Zambia has only 1.5 miles of railroads per 10,000 population, as against 8.5 miles in South Africa, a country about five times more densely populated. (For the whole Federation of Rhodesia and Nyasaland the figure was 3 miles.) Canada and Australia, which are developed countries with a low population density, have 32.4 and 24.98 railway miles respectively per 10,000 population. It is true that Zambia has 70 miles of roads per 10,000 population—for Canada and Australia the figures are 232 and 398 miles respectively—but of these less than 4 miles have been paved. In the rainy season few roads are easily passable. (A journalist recently reported that from Lusaka one could travel more quickly to Peking than to certain areas on the western border with Angola. [9])

During the time that the country was ruled by colonial and Federal governments—the latter residing in Salisbury—it was not a matter of concern that Zambia imported agricultural products from the South. But for independent Zambia the main development strategy seemed obvious: import substitution, in the first place for agricultural products but also as far as possible for manufactured products. Thus one of Zambia's principal aims is to exploit its own domestic market, i.e. to stimulate local supply of the goods it needs, directly as well as through improving marketing opportunities. In this chapter I shall first discuss the possibilities of Zambia's domestic market. Next opportunities in export markets will be examined. Finally, I will deal with some possibilities of expanding markets through economic integration. It should be emphasized that our topic is very wide. It is not possible in a chapter of this length to give anything more than an introduction to Zambia's market problems and opportunities.

---

[9] See *Business and Economy of Central and East Africa*, Lusaka, Vol. II, No. 8, p. 29.

THE HOME MARKET

Agriculture

The market

Zambia imports considerable amounts of food. Quite naturally at a time in which both exports and imports are increasing very rapidly, the proportion of total imports that is spent on food commodities is decreasing (see Table 7.1, column 11), but the absolute value of food imports is still rising. In 1967 Zambia imported food worth K 21.4 million and in 1968 the figure was probably about K 3.5 million higher.

It may be admitted that Zambia's policy of meeting her food demands more and more from domestic commercial sources has been partially successful. Table 7.1, column 7, indicates that the proportion of total food consumption for which supply came from domestic commercial farming and manufacturing of food products increased from 36.4 per cent in 1964 to 43.3 per cent in 1966. But this change appears to be purely the result of a *commercialization* of domestic agriculture and not of expanding import substitution. The proportion of total food consumption that came from imports remained almost the same: 20.4 per cent in 1964 and 20.1 per cent in 1966. The proportion supplied by subsistence agriculture, however, decreased from 43.2 per cent in 1964 to 36.5 per cent in 1966. The rise in commercial food supply is just keeping pace with the rate of urbanization.

Table 7.1, column 3, shows that food consumption as a percentage of total private consumption remained more or less constant—about 28 per cent—in the period 1964-6. We may assume here that the relative decrease of food consumption in the high-income groups was offset by a relative increase in the low-income and non-wage-earning groups. In the present stage of population growth and urbanization the latter groups are growing faster than the former. However, the present difference in average food consumption between African and non-African consumers[10] illustrates Engel's Laws in the Zambian context. It is likely that if income continues to rise, a certain critical point will be reached above which the proportion of income spent on food will fall. But since this will happen only gradually, it is probably safe

---

[10] In 1967 the average yearly income for Africans was K 666. For non-Africans the figure was K 4,458.

TABLE 7.1
Zambian food consumption

Year	1 Total private consumption	2 Total food consumption	3 Total food consumption as a % of total consumption	4 Consumption of own food products[1]	5 Consumption of food products as a % of total food consumption	6 Domestic commercial food consumption =(2)–(4)–(8)	7 Domestic commercial food consumption as a % of total food consumption	8 Food imports	9 Food imports as a % of total food consumption	10 Total imports	11 Food imports as a % of total imports
	(K m.)	(K m.)	(%)	(K m.)	(%)	(K m.)	(%)	(K m.)	(%)	(K m.)	(%)
1964	251.8	69.5	27.6	30.0	43.2	25.3	36.4	14.2	20.4	156.4	9.1
1965	300.2	82.7	27.5	31.7	38.3	34.5	41.7	16.5	20.0	210.7	7.8
1966	349.4	98.3	28.1	35.9	36.5	42.6	43.3	19.8	20.1	246.1	8.0
1967[2]								21.4		306.3	6.9
1968[3]								12.4		177.3	7.0

[1] African rural household consumption of own food products.
[2] Figures for imports only.
[3] Import figures only for the first half of the year.

Sources: *National Accounts 1964–1966*, Central Statistical Office, Lusaka, July 1968;
Monthly Digest of Statistics, Central Statistical Office, Lusaka, December 1968.

TABLE 7.2

Composition of food consumption

| | 1964 | | 1965 | | 1966 | |
	K m.	% of total food consump- tion	K m.	% of total food consump- tion	K m.	% of total food consump- tion
Bread and cereals (including mealie meal)	28.8	41.4	36.5	44.1	42.3	43.0
Meat and meat products	10.6	15.2	12.3	14.9	14.4	14.7
Fish and fish products	3.5	5.0	3.0	3.6	5.3	5.4
Milk, cheese, eggs and fats	6.7	9.8	9.8	11.9	13.1	13.3
Fruit, nuts and vegetables	13.9	20.0	14.3	17.3	14.3	14.6
Sugar and confectionery	4.0	5.8	3.8	4.6	4.9	5.0
Coffee, tea and cocoa	0.8	1.1	1.4	1.7	1.6	1.6
Other food	1.2	1.7	1.6	1.9	2.4	2.4
Total	69.5	100.0	82.7	100.0	98.3	100.0

Source: National Accounts, 1964–1966, Central Statistical Office, Lusaka. July 1968.

to say that for many years to come a rising national product in Zambia will imply increasing demand for food commodities.

Apart from the expected rise in income, market opportunities for other foodstuffs depend chiefly on four factors: (1) the proportion of income spent on the commodity in question; (2) the income elasticity of demand; (3) the rate of population growth; and (4) present imports of the commodity, i.e. the scope for import substitution.

Table 7.2 shows the composition of food consumption in Zambia for the years 1964–6. It appears that the bulk of total food expenditure is spent on bread and cereals, i.e. mainly mealie meal. Considerable amounts of money are also spent on fruit, nuts, and vegetables; meat; milk, cheese, eggs, and fats; sugar; and fish.

It would be dangerous to compute income elasticities of demand on the basis of Table 7.2. The amounts spent on meat, fish, fruit, and

[11] It should be noted that food consumption remained an almost constant percentage of total private consumption in the years concerned; see Table 7.1, column 3.

vegetables, for example, may be highly influenced by bottlenecks in supply. If supplies of these goods were unlimited, the proportion of income spent on them might be considerably higher and increasing, and the proportion spent on bread and cereals might be lower and decreasing. The only reliable conclusion with regard to elasticities that can be drawn from Table 7.2 is that income elasticity of demand for milk, cheese, eggs, and fats is considerably above unity.

TABLE 7.3

Urban African income elasticities of demand for food commodities

1 Commodity	Income elasticity of demand	2 Commodity	Income elasticity of demand	3 Commodity	Income elasticity of demand
Liquid milk	2.4	Bread	1.0	Mealie meal	0.4
Tinned and other milk	2.7	Sugar	1.2	Dried fish	0.3
Margarine and butter	2.3	Meat	0.8	Beans	0.1
Rice	1.8	Fresh fish	0.7	Cabbage	0.3
Potatoes	2.8	Cooking oil	0.8	Sausage and bacon	0.4
Poultry and eggs	2.1	Tomatoes	0.7	Tinned meat and fish	0.2
Buns and biscuits	1.9	Fruit	0.9		
Tea	1.6	Onions	1.0		

Source: Calculated on the basis of the *Second Report on Urban African Budget Surveys*, Central Statistical Office, Lusaka, 1960.

Generally more reliable computations of income elasticities can be made on the basis of the *Second Report on Urban African Budget Surveys*,[12] as has been done in Table 7.3. Here changes in the expenditure pattern were calculated on the basis of data collected for one year: 1960. It was assumed that income of each family and of each employed single person would increase by K 2 per month and that they would then adjust their expenditure pattern to that of the higher income group as revealed by the Budget Survey. Dividing the resulting increase in expenditure on each commodity by the assumed increase in

[21] Central Statistical Office, Lusaka, 1960, Appendix, Table II, p. 16.

income, income elasticities of demand were calculated. In Table 7.4
these are grouped according to whether they are above unity, around
unity, or below unity. It should be noted again that the possibility of
bottlenecks in supply may have limited expenditure on certain commodities—this would make the distribution over the various income groups
highly dependent on the 'first come, first served' principle—which
would render especially the lower elasticities rather unreliable. (It is
unlikely, however, that there were bottlenecks in the supply of mealie
meal in the towns concerned.) Besides, the general rise in income since
1960 may have changed certain income elasticities of demand.

TABLE 7.4

Projection of demand for selected food commodities in 1970

Commodity	Unit	Projection index	Apparent cons. 1963	Projected cons 1970
Maize	tons	151	253,200	382,300
Meat	tons	137	16,550	22,670
Fish: dried	tons	150	9,500	14,250
fresh	tons	150	3,600	5,400
Wheat products	tons	144	28,000	40,300
Sugar	tons	143	15,800	22,700
Liquid milk	gals	116	3,372,000	3,911,500
Tinned milk	tons	146	1,610	2,350
Cooking oil	gals	149	850,000	1,266,500
Margarine, butter	tons	114	1,780	2,030
Tea	tons	134	390	520
Rice	tons	143	1,500	2,150
Sausage, bacon	tons	114	1,240	1,410
Poultry	tons	110	580	640
Eggs	dozs	111	2,000,000	2,220,000
Tinned meat/fish	tons	135	1,130	1,530
Tomatoes	tons	111	2,200	2,440
Potatoes	tons	118	6,900	8,140
Onions	tons	125	1,500	1,870
Vegetables	tons	130	7,000	9,100
Fruit	tons	148	8,500	12,580

Source: A. H. Tooke, 'A Projection of the Demand for Selected Food Commodities in Zambia from 1963 to 1970', *Monthly Economic Bulletin of the
Ministry of Agriculture*, Lusaka, February 1965.

Table 7.4 shows a projection of demand for some food commodities
in 1970 which Tooke made in 1965.[13] Tooke calculated his projection

13 A. H. Tooke, 'A Projection of the Demand for Selected Food Commodities
in Zambia from 1963 to 1970', *Monthly Economic Bulletin of the Ministry
of Agriculture*, Lusaka, February 1965.

index on the basis of the income elasticities of demand which follow from the Urban African Budget Survey in 1960 and the *Preliminary Report of the Federal European Family Expenditure Survey* of October 1960. Furthermore he used the same assumptions with regard to population growth, movement from the subsistence to the cash income sector, and growth of gross domestic product and subsistence production as were made in the Seers Report. It appeared that projected increases in African demand were due largely to increases in population rather than to increases in *per capita* income working through income elasticities of demand. (In the case of the commodity with the highest elasticity, potatoes, only 20.4 per cent of the projected increase in demand from 1963 to 1970 was due to the demand elasticity.) In fact the increase in real income from 1963 to 1968 has been much above the Seers Report assumption of a 6 per cent growth of gross domestic product per annum.[14] This much higher growth of domestic purchasing power has increased the expansion of the food market considerably. The difficulty of predicting future copper prices makes growth estimates of the Zambian national product almost impossible: it is therefore not unreasonable to base long-term projections of demand for specific commodities on the assumed population growth only. In any case such long-term projections cannot be very reliable.

A safer assessment of the market for agricultural products can be made on the basis of external trade statistics. In view of the high transport rates—see Table 7.5—and the low unit value of most food commodities, the opportunities for import substitution seem good in agriculture. Food imports can be transported most cheaply from the South, but Zambia wants to terminate her dependence on Rhodesia and South Africa. It seems probable that for many commodities import substitution would be preferable to a change to another route for which transport rates would be more than four times as high.

Table 7.6 lists the sixteen most important foodstuffs imports. It appears that opportunities for import substitution are greatest for wheat, meat, sugar, oils, milk, sorghum, rice, and vegetables. Of these only the production of wheat has been neglected because of supposedly adverse climatic conditions.[15] The other commodities are all supplied locally but not in sufficient quantities to meet domestic

[14] See the Introduction, p. 16.
[15] In fact new types can and have been grown under irrigation.

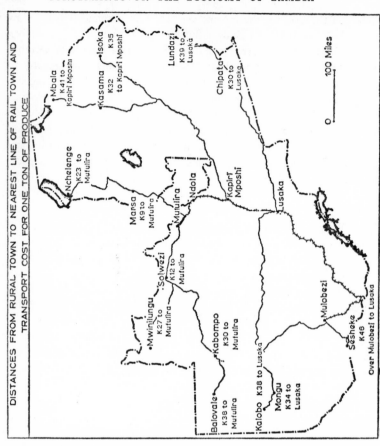

Map 7.2

TABLE 7.5
*Approximate transport rates to Lusaka for
selected commodities via different routes*

Place of loading	Means of transport	Type of goods imported via route	Transport rate/short ton
Beira/Johannesburg	Rhodesia Railways	Food commodities (wheat, etc.), fertilizer, salt, etc.	K 8
Beira/Johannesburg	Rhodesia Railways	Steel supplies	K 18
Beira/Johannesburg	Rhodesia Railways	Machinery	K 44
Lobito Bay	Benguela Railways	Machinery, food-stuffs, groceries	K 44
Dar es Salaam	Great North Road	Clothing, piece goods	K 34
Dar es Salaam	Zambia Air Cargoes	Luxury goods	K 140

Note: Transport rates from Beira and Johannesburg are about the same.

Sources: Rhodesia Railways Tariffs Book; Benguela Railway Tariffs Book; Zambia-Tanzania Road Services Ltd. Rates Pamphlet; Zambia Air Cargoes Rates Pamphlet.

demand in full. Import figures suggest that their production could be considerably expanded.

The market constraint

The foregoing analysis has shown that the Zambian market for agricultural products is fairly large and expanding. Since large economies of scale are only seldom involved, it seems that domestic demand should induce a big increase in local supply. We must not, however, forget the second component of markets: the possibility of meeting demand at a profitable price. This is not usually a problem for the areas near the line of rail where the domestic market is concentrated. But for the outlying provinces the *transport situation* constitutes an important constraint. Table 7.7 gives transport cost as a ratio of consumer price assuming a distance of 100 miles between producer and market. (In fact 100 miles is not a great distance in Zambia, as can be seen from Map 7.2.) The obvious conclusion from Table 7.7 is that the cost of transport ensures that many crops must be grown close to their final markets.

TABLE 7.6

Value of Zambia's main imports of foodstuffs
(K'000)

Commodity	1965	1966	1967
Wheat and wheaten flour	1,434	2,320	2,419
Beef and offals	991	2,017	2,320
Sugar, raw and refined	2,478	1,600	1,995
Soft vegetable oils, groundnuts, cotton-seed, sunflower	1,001	1,678	1,517
Milk powders and condensed milk	694	919	1,533
Sorghum and malted barley	777	984	640
Pork, bacon and ham	226	655	581
Rice and pre-cooked rice grain	280	442	558
Tea	427	540	323
Mutton and lamb	261	304	268
Butter	315	476	263
Coffee	229	256	245
Apples	152	195	228
Potatoes	150	242	213
Beans	142	182	185
Onions	127	91	175

Source: Annual Statements of External Trade, 1965, 1966, 1967, Central Statistical Office, Lusaka.

TABLE 7.7

Transport rates per 100 miles as a percentage
of producer price for selected food commodities

Commodity	Producer price (K)	Transport rate for 100 miles as a percentage of producer price
Maize	2.90/200 lbs bag	28
Rice (unhulled)	8.00/200 lbs bag	10
Rice (hulled)	14.00/200 lbs bag	6
Sorghum	4.70/200 lbs bag	17
Groundnuts	10.20/180 lbs bag	7
Potatoes	1.50/37.5 lbs bag	10
Onions	1.50/30 lbs packet	8
Beans	10.50/200 lbs bag	8
Bananas	2.20/200 lbs bag	37
Citrus	1.00/30 lbs packet	12
Sugar	10.00/200 lbs bag	8

Note: Producer prices are in general the prices paid to producers by the Grain Marketing Board at its depots in 1967–8. These prices are well below import parity. Transport rates have been worked out on the basis of 8 ngwee per ton/mile, that is, about the average long-distance rate charged by Smith Youngson Ltd.

The Zambian roads system is far from ideal in this connection.

Improvement of main roads to make them suitable for heavy traffic, and construction or improvement of feeder roads from farm to market would naturally lower transport costs in the long run. It has been calculated, however, that even the paving of main gravel roads would not reduce costs of transportation by more than 10 to 15 per cent.[16] For products with a low value in relation to weight this would not change the basic conclusion suggested by Table 7.7. Neither would that conclusion become invalid if we could assume backload rates even as low as 50 per cent of ordinary rates.

Policy implications

The major principle guiding Zambian agricultural policies is *self-sufficiency*. This principle has certain advantages over the principle of comparative advantage. The major objection to comparative advantage as a policy guideline is that this principle is not followed in the rest of the world. Additionally, if comparative advantage leads to an increase in foreign trade, the domestic economy is subject to the fluctuations inherent in world markets. On the other hand, the disadvantage of self-sufficiency is that it sets a limit to the expansion of output—namely the size of the home market.

The principle of self-sufficiency implies *import substitution*. We have already observed that in regard to many food commodities there is a good case for import substitution in Zambia. This is, however, not true for *all* commodities.

Import substitution seems to be an obvious strategy where goods could be domestically produced at prices below import parity. But where production costs would be above import parity (and hence tariffs would have to be raised and consumer prices increased), import substitution is no longer such an obviously wise policy. In that case it should be undertaken only if the following conditions apply: first, that alternative policies such as expanding primary product exports or starting to export manufactured goods are not feasible; second, that external effects such as attraction of other domestic production, increased employment, and breaching of other bottlenecks through the expenditure of the foreign exchange thus saved clearly outweigh the loss of welfare implied by rising consumer prices. Self-sufficiency may indeed be an important political aim. From the economic point of view,

[16] See, for example, NEDECO *Report on Transport*, Lusaka, 1964, p. 27.

however, it is not regarded as an end in itself but only as a means of stimulating development.

Of course, domestic production at a price above import parity may be defended with the 'infant agriculture' argument which implies that in the course of developing home production the producer price might be expected to fall. Where the initial excess over import parity is not substantial (such as in the case of pigs where it would probably be between 5 and 10 per cent) this argument can be more easily accepted than where the difference is substantial (such as in the case of sugar).[17]

Most of the commodities in Table 7.6 could be grown in Zambia against producer prices which would compare favourably with import parity. In the case of wheat, however, there are supposedly adverse climatic conditions. Unless research reveals that with irrigation these could be profitably overcome, Zambia should not strive for self-sufficiency in wheat but rather concentrate more on certain export crops.[18] As for tea, even Zambia's best conditions are only marginal. Besides, there are some economies of scale involved in tea production since a processing factory is required close to the production areas. It seems that Zambia's scarce agricultural management resources could at present be put to better use than running a tea plantation.

For the commodities which can be profitably produced in Zambia the next policy question is: where? Of course the answer to this is not only dependent on considerations regarding the market but on production conditions in the various parts of the country. It is, moreover, essential that there be some sort of production surplus everywhere, in each province as well as in each district. The Zambian philosophy of *humanism* stipulates that development be spread all over the country instead of being confined to the areas near the line of rail. 'Humanism in Zambia is a decision in favour of rural areas,'[19] President Kaunda has said. Therefore production policies can be determined by production and market conditions only within the limit, set by humanism, that there should be development everywhere.

---

[17] Currently the domestic production price is more than 50 per cent above import parity. But it should be noted that present world prices are very depressed.

[18] See below pp. 219 ff.

[19] Dr. K. D. Kaunda, 'Zambia towards Economic Independence', address at Mulungushi, April 1968, in B. de Gaay Fortman (ed.), *After Mulungushi; The Economics of Zambian Humanism*, East African Publishing House, Nairobi, 1969, p. 42.

Table 7.7 gives an indication of the importance of distance to the market for location policies. In general, crops with a low value in relation to weight should preferably be grown as near to their market as production conditions will allow. However, some crops can be profitably produced some distance from their markets. *Bananas*, for example, can be grown in the Luapula Valley at a producer price which is a quarter of the usual consumer price on the line of rail. This means that despite their low unit value they can be profitably produced at a fairly long distance from the market. Other crops, such as *rice*, require specific production conditions. This implies that rice production too can take place at a considerable distance from the line of rail market, as in Luapula and Barotse Provinces. It can be further concluded from Table 7.7 that the establishment of a huller close to the production area would notably reduce transportation costs. The same observation may be made with regard to *cotton*. The cost of transporting cotton can constitute a significant proportion of the producer price— about 10 per cent in the case of a 100-mile journey to the market—but it can be reduced by as much as 60 per cent if there is a local ginnery.

For *coffee*, *tobacco*, and to a lesser extent *beef*, *goats*, and *sheep*, transport costs constitute a smaller proportion of the producer price. This implies that these commodities can be produced anywhere in the rural areas where their production is feasible. *Coffee* could probably be profitably grown in Northern Province and perhaps also in North-Western. Economies of scale of a coffee factory are insignificant. *Tobacco*—particularly Virginia—is grown in Central, Southern, and Eastern Provinces.[20] *Cattle* can be raised in practically every area that is tsetse-free. Commercial production policies should perhaps first concentrate on traditional cattle-raisers such as the Ngoni, the Lozi, the Ila, and the Tonga.

For *pigs*, *poultry*, and *eggs*, transport costs are not very large, but here cost of transport of inputs is important, implying that production for the line of rail market is not economical in the more distant provinces. The same is largely true for *vegetables*. At present, however, the shortage in supply on the line of rail is so great—and hence prices so high—that in the short term production of these commodities is profitable anywhere.

Home production of *sugar* is more expensive than imports. The 8 per cent price increase for 100 miles transport mentioned in Table 7.7

[20] See below, p. 221.

assumes processing has taken place in a factory close to the production area. Production has started in Southern Province at Nakambala Sugar Estate. Import tariffs protect the home industry, which provides work for about 2,700 men.

Table 7.7 clearly shows the significance of distance to market for *sorghum*. This crop is mainly grown in Southern Province, i.e. near the line of rail. It may be inferred from Table 7.6 that there is still ample room for import substitution. This applies especially to high-quality sorghum which is used for brewing opaque beer.

Apart from the export market, *groundnuts* can be grown for the domestic oil market. Demand for groundnut cake for animal feeding could also create local markets in the provinces. At present the constraint is not in the market—profitability of groundnut production compares well with that of other crops—but in the extreme labour intensity of stripping and shelling.

Where transport costs are so high that production for the line of rail market is not profitable, production might still be undertaken to satisfy local markets. But these would certainly not absorb large enough quantities to set in motion a significant income-generation process. As far as the home market is concerned, the unused potential for the outlying provinces is mainly in *rice* with a high income elasticity of demand and ample room for import substitution, and *beef*, with large opportunities for import substitution and income elasticity of demand at about unity. But the production of these commodities may well not be enough to initiate self-generating development. The biggest market is for *maize* which can be grown practically everywhere in the country.[21] But transport cost is a very high proportion of the producer price for maize: 28 per cent for the relatively small distance of 100 miles. In the case of maize there seems to be a clear conflict between the economics of the market and the requirement implied in Zambian humanism, of spreading development to the rural areas. This makes a more detailed discussion of Zambia's maize policies necessary.

Maize. Before Independence in 1964 Zambia imported maize from the South. Since maize is Zambia's staple crop, it was clear that priority should be given to self-sufficiency in this crop. Table 7.8 demonstrates the progress of commercial maize production in Zambia.

Quite understandably in view of its low value in relation to weight, the policy is to direct maize production towards local markets, i.e. to

[21] Maize is difficult to grow where rainfall exceeds 45 inches per annum.

TABLE 7.8

Progress of commercial maize production in Zambia
(in thousands of 200 lbs bags)

Harvest year

Province	1964	1965	1966	1967	1968	1969 (estimate)
Barotse	1	1	2	4	20	30
Central	1,176	1,889	2,330	2,320	1,575	1,110
Eastern	90	80	151	89	117	50
Luapula	2	7	14	18	23	50
Northern	23	33	26	69	95	120
North-Western	2	4	7	12	20	30
Southern	963	898	1,704	1,700	876	1,192
Western	3	4	11	20	32	20
Totals	2,260	2,916	4,245	4,232	2,758	2,602

Source: Ministry of Agriculture statistics, Lusaka.

make each outlying province self-sufficient in maize and let the line of rail areas produce for the line of rail market. Since marketing has been centralized, prices too are determined centrally. For each market, first pre-planting producer prices are announced in September, and 'confirmed prices' in March or April of the following year. The new prices announced may be 25 ngwee above or below the previous price.

The announced prices aim at equalizing demand and supply in the market concerned. They are limited, however, by two ceilings: import and export parity. Where demand exceeds supply, producer price is determined by the price of mealie meal imported from the line of rail. Where supply exceeds demand producer price is reduced as much as possible to the price at the line of rail depots—which is determined by the price that can be got on the only profitable export market, the Congo —minus the cost of transport to the line of rail. Prices in district centres are based on prices in the provincial centre where a roller mill is or will be established, minus the cost of transport to this processing facility.

The result of present pricing policy can be seen in Table 7.9. The difference between Eastern Province producer price and the price on the line of rail is striking. Because the Eastern Province has for long been more than self-sufficient in maize, its producer price is as low as is politically possible. Table 7.8 shows that the relatively low maize price has produced some results in Eastern Province. Actually the province still produces a surplus—in 1968 its own demand for roller meal and beer brewing was estimated at 25,000 bags—which the

TABLE 7.9

Pre-planting producer prices for maize
(1968–9 crop year)

Collecting point		Price K/200 lbs bag	Collecting point	Price K/200 lbs bag
Southern Province	Line		*North-Western*	
Central Province	of	3.20	*Province*	
Western Province	rail		Kabompo	4.80
			Solwezi	3.60
Northern Province			Mwinilunga	4.20
Kasama		3.70	Kasempa	4.00
Mbala		3.70	Balovale	4.75
Mporokoso		2.59	Chizera	4.15
Luwingu		2.71		
Mpika		2.35	*Barotse Province*	
Chinsali		2.43	Mongu	5.05
Isoka		2.60	Mankoya	3.80
			Sananga	4.10
			Sesheke	4.60
			Lukulu	3.95
			Kalabo	4.30
Luapula Province				
Mansa		3.90	*Eastern Province*	
Kawambwa		3.40	Main road depots	2.40
Samfya		3.70	Village markets	2.20

Source: Ministry of Agriculture, Lusaka.

government has to subsidize because the price seems to have reached the politically attainable minimum. A second striking point in Table 7.9 is the price difference between provincial and district centres, again based on costs of transport. If a farmer lives far from the district centre he gets a much lower price for his produce.[22]

In fact, Table 7.9 gives a clear picture of the market constraint in a sparsely populated country such as Zambia. Because maize is the staple food in Zambia and is also easy to grow, its production can give the impetus to commercial agriculture in the outlying provinces. But as soon as the extension policy begins to be successful, i.e. when a province has reached self-sufficiency, it has to be reduced and producers are penalized for the distance between their farms and the already prosperous line of rail. The more remote a farmer's production area the heavier he is penalized in the price he gets for his maize. In each country the rural areas have to provide the food for the non-agricultural workers.

[22] Except in Eastern Province.

Unfortunately, economic considerations determine that in Zambia the bulk of this food has to be produced relatively close to the area where the non-agricultural workers are concentrated.

Should Zambia with its philosophy of Humanism accept the economic rationale of the present price policy for maize? This is a matter of alternatives. Fortunately there are food commodities which can be more profitably produced in the outlying provinces than maize and for which the limits of the market will not soon be reached—notably beef and rice. In fact in many rural areas it is presently much more profitable to feed maize to cattle than to sell it to marketing organizations.

Marketing

Marketing is performed by various types of organization in Zambia: government-directed statutory boards, co-operative societies, and private enterprises. It is not possible in this chapter to comment on all these organizations and their performance.[23] Most commentators agree that they should be better co-ordinated—an end that may soon be achieved by the establishment of a National Agricultural Marketing Board.

Marketing problems do not so much arise on the line of rail where commercial farmers can themselves arrange for transport to centralized collecting depots on the main line of communication. But in the outlying provinces where overhead costs of primary marketing could not be borne by the individual farmer, the problem is acute. The principal dilemma is then the choice between a centralized and a decentralized organization.

The co-operative system of marketing which arose in Eastern Province, for example, has proved very successful.[24] In theory the co-operative approach ensures participation of the individual farmer in the marketing of his produce. This tends to make production more

---

[23] The interested reader is referred to the chapter on marketing in S. M. Makings, *Problems of African Agricultural Development*, Lusaka, 1964 (mimeo); 'The Place and Function of the Grain Marketing Board in the National Economy', in *Monthly Economic Bulletin of the Ministry of Agriculture*, Government Printer, Lusaka, December 1966; and J. Donkin, 'Marketing Organizations of Zambia', in *Monthly Economic Bulletin of the Ministry of Agriculture*, August 1967.

[24] Of course, a co-operative structure gives rise to problems too. See *Report of the Committee appointed to Review the Co-operative Structure in the Eastern Province of Northern Rhodesia*, Lusaka, July 1964.

flexible with regard to the opportunities of the market than a more centralized approach would do. It also promotes the farmers' understanding of marketing problems. The situation which arose in Luapula Province in 1967 when farmers refused to bring their produce to the established markets and forced the Agricultural Rural Marketing Board (ARMB) to collect goods from the farm gate would probably not have arisen if the producers themselves had been involved in the organization of marketing.

In fact, there are large rural areas in Zambia where co-operative marketing organizations could not provide farmers with the essential marketing services. Here the ARMB performs a useful function. In 1968 it operated 88 markets (depots where the farmer could bring his produce and at the same time collect requisites for planting his new crop) in North-Western Province, 109 markets in Barotse Province, and 111 markets in Luapula Province. These markets were operated by mobile buying teams. The optimum density of operation is that no producer should be more than five miles from his nearest market. Of course, such services are very expensive to run. This often means that the price ARMB can offer is much lower than the price farmers could get by marketing their goods themselves. In Barotse Province, for example, the present price of maize at Mongu is K 5.05 per bag, whereas in the villages it can be as high as K 6.60. In Mankoya District 1,575 bags of maize were sold to ARMB in 1967 but it was estimated that sales to private traders totalled as much as 8,500 bags.[25] In Northern Province it may be more profitable for farmers to grow millet and sorghum for the villages than maize for the Northern Province Co-operative Marketing Union (NPCMU). For ARMB and the unions the unfortunate result of this is that they buy—and hence sell—less than they could, which means that overhead cost per unit handled is disproportionately high.

Industry

Zambia's home market for industrial products is large in relation to its population, size and stage of development. In 1966 the country imported manufactures valued at K 255.2 m. while domestic production amounted to K 60.2 m. This market is principally

---

[25] This was also due to the fact that the ARMB team arrived in the area too late.

the result of Zambia's copper mining industry. Not only do the mines use manufactures as inputs, but the income generated by copper production stimulates demand for intermediate products, especially those associated with construction and consumer goods.[26]

TABLE 7.10
Growth of manufacturing production in Zambia

Year	GDP factor cost (K m.)	Manufacturing factor cost (K m.)	Growth rate of manufacturing as compared with previous year (%)	Manufacturing as a %age of GDP
1964	464.9	28.2	—	6.1
1965	548.7	40.0	41.8	7.3
1966	644.5	60.2	50.5	9.3
1967	733.4	78.9	31.1	10.8

Source: Monthly Digest of Statistics, Central Statistical Office, Lusaka, January 1969.

A market of Zambia's size offers opportunities for domestic production of manufactures. Indeed, as Table 7.10 shows, such opportunities are increasingly exploited. Since Independence the nominal value of manufacturing production has grown at an average rate of about 40 per cent per annum, which implies a real growth rate of about 30 per cent. However, in comparison with other countries with comparable levels of population and income per head, Zambia is still seriously under-industrialized in most manufacturing sectors.[27]

Import substitution is not as easy in the industrial sector as in agriculture because of larger economies of scale and the greater input of technical skills. Zambia, however, is still in the 'easy' stages of import substitution, i.e. the establishment of industries for which economies of scale are insignificant and no important technical skills are required. Ewing has described this category in the following words:

Nearly all African countries, whatever their size or level of development, have installed or are in the process of installing the following industries: flour milling, beer and beverages, clothing, boots and shoes, sawn wood and joinery, including wooden furniture, plastic manufactures, soap, liquid air, paint, metal products for construction, household utensils, repair of motor vehicles,

[26] See below, pp. 260 ff.
[27] For a comparison see A. Young, 'Patterns of Development in Zambian Manufacturing Industry since Independence', *Eastern Africa Economic Review,* Vol. 1, No. 2, December 1969, and above pp. 5–6.

and, where appropriate, repair of railway equipment or small ships. These are typical import-substitution industries, largely consumer goods and to a limited extent simple intermediate goods.[28]

In Zambia the limits of the 'easy' stage of import substitution have not yet been reached, as the continuing increase in manufacturing production over the past four years indicates. Table 7.11 gives some idea of the relationship between domestic production and imports for various manufactures.

TABLE 7.11
Domestic manufacturing production as compared to imports of manufactures in 1965 and 1966

	Domestic production (Factor cost)		Imports	
	1965	1966	1965	1966
Food	6.5	7.9	12.2	14.4
Beverages and tobaccos	5.9	12.3	3.5	4.7
Textiles and wearing apparel	3.8	4.5	31.7	29.1
Sawmills, joinery, etc.	2.3	3.5	4.4	5.5
Paper products, printing, and publishing	2.0	2.5	6.2	7.9
Rubber products	0.8	0.9	4.8	5.7
Chemicals and petroleum products	2.7	3.4	37.6	36.5
Non-metallic mineral products	6.1	6.2	5.3	7.3
Foundries and metal products	5.7	8.0	24.5	27.0
Machinery	1.2	1.3	26.2	37.0
Electrical equipment	0.4	1.1	16.2	21.7
Transport equipment	2.5	8.3	34.3	50.0
Other manufacturing industries	0.1	0.3	7.5	8.4
Totals	40.0	60.2	214.4	255.2

Source: *Census of Production, 1965 and 1966*, Central Statistical Office, Lusaka, May 1968.

In 1966 import substitution led to an absolute decrease of imports of only one category of goods—wearing apparel.[29] There seems to be considerable scope for expansion of Zambian textile production. The opening of Kafue Textiles mill, in which the government-owned Industrial Development Corporation holds a 50 per cent interest, is an important step towards meeting domestic demand. It will produce

[28] A. F. Ewing, *Industry in Africa*, Oxford University Press, London, 1968, p. 22.

[29] The fall in imports of chemicals and petroleum products was not so much due to import substitution as to petrol rationing introduced as a result of Rhodesian UDI.

cloth which can be used by the Zambian clothing industry. Another important aspect of this enterprise is that it requires 18 million pounds of seed cotton annually, which is more than Zambia's present production of cotton. Thus the Kafue Textiles mill has increased the home market for cotton considerably. The same kind of development may take place as a result of the home production of grain bags by Kabwe Industrial Fabrics Ltd., a wholly INDECO-owned enterprise. At present the Kabwe mill uses imported jute as an input but it may switch to local fibres such as kenaf—which can be grown in Zambia—as soon as large amounts become available.

TABLE 7.12

Value of principal imports of prepared foodstuffs

(K '000)

Commodity	1965	1966	1967
Infant food	419	597	840
Biscuits	439	426	547
Tinned fruit	176	175	271
Jams, etc.	133	139	142

Source: *Annual Statements of External Trade, 1965, 1966, 1967,* Central Statistical Office, Lusaka.

The main possibilities for import substitution in food production have already been discussed. Table 7.12 shows the four principal imported prepared foods. The size of the home market seems to be fairly limited. A pineapple canning industry will probably be set up in Mwinilunga district where pineapples are traditionally grown.

The problem with many of the commodities for which import substitution is easy is that the value added domestically is relatively small. Zambian production of beer and beverages, for example, is based on imported materials and bottles. Transport equipment is assembled, rather than manufactured locally. The shoe industry uses imported raw materials. Besides, these industries do not usually attract other industries through backward or forward linkages. Thus, their establishment may be a rather incidental development; it does not accelerate the rate of change of the structure of the economy.

Industries for which the value added domestically is large and which could easily attract other industries through forward and backward integration or because of other external effects usually involve considerable economies of scale. This is true, for example, of an integrated iron and steel plant, most chemical products, transport equipment and components, machinery and machine tools, electronic equipment, and to a lesser extent also of an integrated pulp and paper mill, glass production, and cement.

A project in the more difficult sector of import substitution is the ammonium nitrate plant which is being constructed at Kafue. This factory will produce 26,000 tons of ammonium nitrate per annum, of which 7,000 tons will be used for the production of explosives at Mufulira and the rest for the production of fertilizer. The price of this product (for which a minimum production of about 50,000 tons is necessary to acquire reasonable economies of scale) will be considerably above import parity. The factory will create employment for 600 people, requiring an investment of K 30,000 per worker.

In the case of the ammonium nitrate plant it can be observed that the project is likely to be annually capital-absorbing. The increased price of explosives will reduce the profits of the mining companies and hence government revenue. This money could have been used for more profitable development projects. If domestic production raises the prices of products, it should certainly not be undertaken before a careful comparison has been made with alternative investment projects.

Another venture which is controversial because of Zambia's market constraint is the proposed iron and steel mill. Zambia's steel consumption per head is about 25 kg., which is considerably below South Africa's 120 kg. and Rhodesia's 90 kg. per head.[30] However, it compares well with Egypt's 12 kg. per head, and Egypt is an established producer of iron and steel. But, of course, it is not just steel consumption per head but total domestic consumption which is relevant. With its small population of four million, Zambia's steel consumption totals approximately 100,000 metric tons a year.[31] In fact, production for the domestic market would have to be smaller because the range of imported steel products is fairly wide and these could not all be produced. Since an integrated iron and steel works would have to produce an estimated minimum annual output of about 500,000 tons in order to equal import parity,[32] Zambia seems to have an effective market constraint.

INDECO's investigation department is still working on an iron and

[30]   cf. F. A. K. L¨th, 'The Establishment of Steel Industries in the African Countries', Afrika, No. 2, 1968, p. 47.

[31]   This figure is based on the Annual Statement of External Trade, 1967. The reader should be warned that the figures given on p. 165 of the UN publication on World Trade in Steel and Steel Demand in Developing Countries, New York, 1968, are completely unreliable.

[32]   cf. Lüth, op. cit., p. 48 and Ewing, op. cit., p. 14.

steel project. The original suggestion was for an iron and steel works near Lusaka based on local coal and ore from the Sanje deposits, producing mainly reinforcing bars and sections for the domestic market. INDECO's annual report for 1967 states:

> Preliminary conclusions ... were that capital costs and operating costs of such a works would be considerably higher than was estimated in the report prepared for INDECO in 1965, and *production costs of reinforcing bars and sections would be greatly above current import prices*. Evaluation of the new findings continued in 1968.[33] (my italics)

These preliminary conclusions are not surprising. In Liberia the Atkins study estimated that production of 160,000 tons of steel products per annum at Buchanan would raise the price per ton to the equivalent of about K 25 above import parity price, including transport costs.[34] It seems reasonable to assume that the Zambian producer price would be not less than K 25 above the current average price. Besides, backward linkages would not be significant, since Zambia's supply of coal is, at least for some time to come, insufficient to meet domestic demand.

An integrated iron and steel plant is a highly capital-intensive enterprise. In Liberia investment per worker was estimated at about K 60,000. Although external economies may be important—these are difficult to measure, however—it seems clear that the Zambian market does not yet make an iron and steel works an attractive investment. We should, however, note that the question has an important political aspect. At present Zambia imports its steel supplies mainly from Rhodesia and South Africa. Table 7.5 shows a rate of K 18 per short ton transported from Johannesburg or Beira. But for political reasons the country wants to diminish its dependence on the South for imports or transport of imports. The alternative supply route of Dar es Salaam would increase the current price by at least K 17 per ton. Besides, it is highly doubtful whether this route could bear an extra 100,000 tons in the short run. Such considerations may, of course, make the creation of a national steel industry less unattractive.

In general, however, it does not seem to be wise to spend investment funds on industrial projects for which the Zambian market is essentially too small as long as there continue to be good investment opportunities

---

[33] *Eighth Annual Report (1967) of the Industrial Development Corporation of Zambia Ltd.*, Lusaka, p. 18.

[34] *The Liberia Steel Project, an Engineering-Economic Study*, February 1968, report for the United Nations by the firm of W. S. Atkins and Partners.

in agriculture and the production of simple intermediate and consumer goods. Another possibility to which we now turn is production for a larger market, i.e. for export.

EXPORT MARKETS

Naturally, constraints on export markets are quite different from those on the home market. Demand is there, but the question is whether the goods can be produced at a profitable producer's price, taking into account the cost of transport to the main markets. The situation is made more complicated by the possibility of fluctuations in prices on the international market. Let us briefly consider these factors in relation to the main commodities which Zambia could produce for export. Table 7.13 lists Zambia's present principal exports.

TABLE 7.13

Value of Zambia's principal export commodities in 1967
(K '000)

Copper	431,888
Maize	8,749
Zinc	8,066
Cobalt	5,621
Tobacco	3,698
Lead	2,696
Shelled groundnuts	660
Timber	599
Manganese concentrates	516
Precious and semi-precious stones	441
Cotton lint	371
Copper anodes	314
Silver	202

Source: Annual Statement of External Trade, 1967, Central Statistical Office, Lusaka.

Copper

Zambia is a major producer of copper. Its share in world mine production of copper excluding the Communist countries has fallen slightly from about 15 per cent in 1963 to 14 per cent in 1968. In 1967 the country exported copper worth K 432 million, which represents 92 per cent of the total value of its exports.

Obviously, Zambia's economy is highly dependent on the world copper market. The present situation on the world market would seem to favour an expansion of production. Average production costs of copper in Zambia, including the cost of transportation to the major markets, are about K 468 per ton. In 1968 and the first half of 1970 the world price oscillated between K 750 and K 1,300. The question is, of course, whether the price can remain so high.

In the Bottelier report[35] a projection was made of world demand and supply of refined copper and blister in the non-Communist countries for the years 1968–75. As can be seen from Table 7.14, Bottelier's projection gives market equilibrium for 1968 and slightly increasing oversupply for the years thereafter. It now seems that, whereas his projections of supply were fairly correct, he underestimated world demand for copper in 1968 and 1969; firstly, because China has bought more copper than was expected; secondly, because more restocking took place after the end of the strike in the non-ferrous metals industry in the US than was foreseen; and finally, because economic growth in major markets (particularly the US, Japan, the UK, Italy, and Canada) was faster than had been assumed. It may well be, therefore, that Bottelier's prediction of oversupply will not prove correct in the immediate future. As far as supply is concerned, it seems probable that the expected increase in Peru's production from 180,000 to 400,000 tons will reach the world market later than had been foreseen, since the political troubles between that country and the US have discouraged investment.

Zambia has reasonable prospects of increasing her copper production. The situation on the world market should indeed encourage her to do so. From 1959–68 world demand has increased at an average annual rate of 4.7 per cent. During the next five years other major producers such as the US, Chile, Peru, Canada, and Australia are planning to expand their production by appreciably more than 4.7 per cent per annum. Zambia could very well plan an annual production increase of about 5 per cent. In this respect the constraint is not so much in the market as in government policy and legislation.

Agriculture

Maize

Table 7.13 shows maize as Zambia's second largest foreign exchange earner in 1967. However, in 1968 and 1969 maize production was

[35] P. P. C. Bottelier, *Problems of Investment, Production, Trade and Pricing in*

TABLE 7.14

A projection of supply and demand for refined copper in the non-Communist countries, 1968–75

('000 metric tons)

	1967	1968	1969	1970	1971	1972	1973	1974	1975
Total demand for refined copper (incl. blister)	5,006	5,336	5,564	5,829	6,127	6,425	6,691	7,055	7,380
Total supply of refined copper (incl. blister)	4,782	5,336	6,121	6,498	6,956	7,284			
Supply minus demand	−224	0	557	669	829	859			

Source: P.P.C. Bottelier, *Problems of Investment, Production, Trade and Pricing in Mineral Commodities—a Case Study of Copper*, New Holland, Amsterdam, 1968.

much lower than in 1967—see Table 7.8—mainly because of a bad
season (due to low yields rather than small acreages planted). In 1969
Zambia will probably again be importing maize (reportedly about
1 million bags). Certainly the country should continue to aim at some
production surplus in maize but it seems doubtful whether this
commodity with its high weight/value ratio could ever become a really
important export crop.

Zambia's only profitable export market for maize is the Congo
(Kinshasa). (Export to Japan and China has taken place at a loss.) In
1968 firm enquiries had been received from Congo for 2.5 million bags,
which Zambia could not deliver in that year, a considerable increase
from the 0.85 million bags delivered in 1967. The 1968 demand was
made up from 1.0 million bags in Kasai Province and 1.5 million in
Katanga. It is expected that Kasai will have reached self-sufficiency in
maize in one or two years. The Katanga market may remain open for
Zambian produce for a little longer, but in the long run it seems highly
doubtful whether there will be any profitable export markets for maize.

Tobacco

As far as physical conditions are concerned, tobacco could become
Zambia's main export crop. Present production consists mainly of
Virginia. Out of a total production of 10.7 million pounds in 1967,
8.7 million pounds were exported at a value of K 3.5 million. In
1968, 13.8 million pounds were sold in Zambia at a total value of K 4.2
million. But this production increase was accompanied by a fall in
average price per pound: from 43.85 ngwee in 1967 to 30.54 ngwee in
1968. In fact, 1967 prices were quite exceptional because of the shortage
on the world market resulting from Rhodesian UDI. It was not
surprising that Zambia's larger 1968 crop had to be sold at a lower price.
Again, the 1968 crop was reported to be of lower quality than in the
year before. In May 1969 the average price was up again to over 36
ngwee.

It is hard to generalize about the profitability of Zambia's Virginia
tobacco. It is estimated that a moderate profit for the European farmers
growing this crop would require an average price per pound of 36–38
ngwee. There are, however, considerable variations in both prices and

Mineral Commodities—a Case Study of Copper. Report prepared for the
Institute for Study of Less Developed Areas (ISMOG), Amsterdam, 1968.

yields. In 1968 prices varied from 12 to 60 ngwee per pound and yields from 500 to 1,800 pounds per acre.

Prospects on the world market for Virginia do not look discouraging; the market is certainly not in surplus at present. The big question mark is, of course, Rhodesia, which is reported to have about 300 million pounds in stock. But even if Rhodesia were to enter the market again without any restrictions, this would bring the big buyers to this part of the world and might hence facilitate the marketing of Zambia's crops.

Zambia is planning to increase her production of Virginia to 82 million pounds by 1980. The problem here is that Virginia tobacco is presently almost exclusively grown by Europeans, mostly expatriate farmers. It is true that INDECO's Mukonchi Tobacco Scheme and the so-called 'one-acre schemes' are likely to increase production by Zambians, but for many years to come the major part of supply will still come from European farmers. With the instability of the European farming community, this implies a great uncertainty in planning.[36]

Burley and Turkish tobacco are grown almost exclusively by Zambian farmers. In 1968 the value of the Burley crop was K 106,000 and that of Turkish K 50,000. The production of both crops is quite heavily subsidized. For Burley the government pays about 20 ngwee per pound whilst the average price realized for this crop was 12.23 ngwee in 1967 and 16.96 ngwee in 1968. With regard to Turkish it appears to be very difficult to sell Zambia's small crop at all. It is said that if the country could produce over 5 million pounds per annum, selling the Turkish crop would not present such a problem, but an increase on this scale seems risky, with a world market already in surplus. Although both Burley and Turkish are easier to grow, the policy implication from the world market situation seems to be that Zambians should be trained to grow the highly sophisticated Virginia crop rather than concentrate on Burley and Turkish.

Shelled groundnuts

Production of confectionery groundnuts in the Eastern Province is oriented towards the world market, where top grades can fetch over K 280 per long ton c.i.f. Europe, which amounts to over K 13.00 per bag to the Zambian producer. With a producer price of about K 10.00

---

[36] See below, pp. 275 ff.

shelled groundnuts are a profitable export commodity. As was noted already with regard to groundnut production for the domestic oil market, the constraint is not so much in the market—Zambia's Chalimbana nut is reported to be of a very good quality—but in the extreme labour-intensity of stripping and shelling.

Other commodities

Other commodities could become available for export after the possibilities of import substitution have been exhausted. In 1967 Zambia exported cotton lint valued at K 371,000, mainly to South Africa. At present production is purely for domestic demand (the Kafue Textiles mill). It is estimated that in 1969 14 million pounds of seed cotton will be processed, which is 4 million pounds less than is needed for domestic textiles production. But after two or three years there may be an exportable surplus of cotton lint. Similarly, with regard to meat: it is conceivable that pork, for example, will be exported to Congo after local production has increased sufficiently.

Industry

In Zambia's present stage of development she could not easily become a major exporter of manufactures. Only if Zambia had obvious advantages such as the use of local inputs (resource-oriented industries) could exports become feasible, although even then tariffs in most countries are sufficiently high to keep Zambian manufactures out of the market. For this reason cigarettes, for example, of which Zambia exported a value of K 6,918 in 1967, could not easily become a major export commodity.

Wire rope and electric wire and cable could possibly be exported to East Africa. In the Western developed countries the tariff on manufactured copper is over 10 per cent. Since there is no duty on unwrought copper this amounts to an effective tariff of over 50 per cent on added value. Hence Zambia will have to continue exporting unwrought copper rather than copper manufactures.

Zambian teak is used for timber products. The major market is for local mining timbers. Zambezi Sawmills in Barotse Province used to export railway sleepers and parquet flooring blocks to Rhodesia and South Africa, but this market has been almost completely lost. It is reported that export sales probes are now being made into Malawi, Botswana, and certain overseas countries.

Services

The main services which Zambia provides for non-residents are air transport and tourism.

Through Zambia Airways, which operates a thrice-weekly flight to Europe, Zambia is able to exploit the international air transport market. As is well known, prospects on this market are favourable. Because of economies of scale it may, however, appear to be even more profitable to get a share of international airline profits by merging with East African Airways.

After copper, tourism is intended to become Zambia's second largest foreign exchange earner. The number of visitors in 1968 totalled 97,000, but only 7 per cent of these were described as real tourists. Revenue from tourism for 1968 was estimated at K 2.5 million. The target for 1970 was 150,000 visitors spending K 12 million. Although this would seem to be a quite moderate aim in comparison with Kenya's K 29.4 million earnings from tourism in 1967, it is doubtful whether it can be achieved, particularly in view of the fact that Uganda, a neighbour of Kenya's and substantially nearer Europe, seeks to expand earnings from tourism to only K 6 million by 1971. While she lacks a rival to Kenya's seaboard, Zambia has considerable tourist attractions—the Victoria Falls and the Luangwa Game Park foremost among them. But there has been little investment in the industry as yet and facilities are therefore inadequate. Since there is a considerable lag between supply and demand in tourism—tourists must be assured of a comfortable holiday before they will risk the outlay involved—it will be some time before the latent demand becomes effective.

POSSIBILITIES FOR ECONOMIC INTEGRATION AND CO-OPERATION

In a region such as Central Africa, it is inevitable that one of the most important constraints on economic integration is transport. The gradual removal of this constraint, consequent upon the recasting of Zambia's political role, will be dealt with substantially in Chapter 12.

Where the transport constraint has been eliminated, markets can be enlarged through the removal of tariff barriers. The higher degree of specialization in production which is likely to result from this could either be effected through the operation of market forces or be arranged through negotiations on the location of new industries which would serve the whole integrated market.

With Angola and Mozambique there has never been much trade. But in future the situation could change. An advantage of trade relations with these two countries would be that their present stage of development is similar to Zambia's. Besides, from a purely economic-geographical point of view the Benguela Railway through Angola is a very attractive link with the West African coast. The idea of a new railroad directly connecting the Zambian Copperbelt with the Benguela Railway in Angola—thus bypassing the section running through the Congo—definitely has a certain appeal. Not only would this be the shortest connection with the west coast (and the present state of the Suez Canal makes the west coast even more attractive), but it would also open up for development Zambia's backward North-Western Province by providing it with readier access to domestic and foreign markets. Now that copper taxation is on a more equitable basis, this transport link could render profitable exploitation of the large low-grade copper ore deposits in Lumwana near Mwinilunga and it could also boost commercial maize production in the North-Western Province along the new line of rail. (The present line of rail areas could then change to more sophisticated crops.) However, in view of the present political situation in Angola it is better not to dream too much about what could happen *if* that new rail route came into existence. Zambia seems to be firmly committed to the Zambia-East Africa rail link which will need Zambian traffic in order to operate at a profit. But it is well to be aware that when Angola and Mozambique have gained independence, mutually advantageous transport links and trade relations could be established. This is one reason why Zambia should not tie herself too closely to East Africa.

Thus, although new transport routes and improvement of existing routes will facilitate Zambia's communications with practically all her neighbours, promotion of trade relations can at present be considered only with regard to the Congo and East Africa. But it is only with regard to East Africa that the possibility of *economic integration* is under discussion.

The East African Common Market

The Treaty for East African Co-operation which was signed in June 1967 by the heads of state of Kenya, Tanzania, and Uganda has established an East African Economic Community of which the East African Common Market is an essential part.[37] The Treaty provides for free trade among the East African countries in goods of East African origin (i.e. goods of which the value of imported materials does not exceed 70 per cent of their ex-factory value).

TABLE 7.15

Composition and shares of inter-country trade in East Africa, 1966
(K '000)

	Exports	Imports	Balance	%
Unprocessed food and raw materials				
Kenya	6,300	5,240	+1,060	
Uganda	3,580	4,850	−1,270	
Tanzania	2,872	2,662	+210	
Total	12,752	12,752		14
Processed food				
Kenya	6,836	2,980	+3,856	
Uganda	2,714	3,082	−368	
Tanzania	642	4,130	−3,488	
Total	10,192	10,192		12
Drink and tobacco manufactures				
Kenya	2,250	504	+1,746	
Uganda	476	916	−440	
Tanzania	92	1,398	−1,306	
Total	2,818	2,818		3
Other manufactures				
Kenya	42,416	13,522	+28,894	
Uganda	14,104	24,074	−9,970	
Tanzania	5,690	24,614	−18,924	
Total	62,210	62,210		71
All items				
Kenya	57,802	22,246	+35,556	
Uganda	20,874	32,922	−12,048	
Tanzania	9,296	32,804	−23,508	
Grand Total	87,972	87,972		100

Source: P. Robson, *Economic Integration in Africa*, Allen and Unwin, London, 1967, p. 122.

Free trade in East Africa has a long history. From 1923 onwards there were no tariffs on trade between the three countries. Like Southern Rhodesia in the Federation, the Kenyan white settler economy derived

[37] *Treaty for East African Co-operation*, Government Printer on behalf of the East African Common Services Organization, Nairobi, 6 June 1967.

the main benefits from the East African customs union. Since the independence of all partners it has required tremendous efforts to keep them together in one economic unit. The Treaty is an attempt to stabilize the relationship by adjusting market mechanisms in order to improve distributive justice in a situation of unequal stages of development. Table 7.15 shows the result of the operation of market forces with regard to trade flows.

On basic agricultural products which, as Table 7.16 indicates, are of basic importance to all three East African countries, quantitative restrictions may be imposed. However, the imbalance in trade flows was mainly the result of trade in manufactures which constituted almost 71 per cent of all intra-regional trade. In 1966 Kenya had a surplus on this trade of almost K 29 million. The Treaty has now provided that countries which cannot as yet offset their imports of manufactures from another Community member by at least 80 per cent of exports to the other member may impose a *transfer tax* on imports from that other country. It is true that the rate of transfer tax cannot exceed 50 per cent of the common external tariff, but since the external tariff is quite high transfer taxes can work as effective restrictions on inter-country trade.

Is it in Zambia's interest to join the EACM as a full member? At present Zambia is a market for East Africa rather than East Africa for Zambia, as Table 7.17 demonstrates. However, the situation is not so unfavourable as the table would seem to indicate, since over K 8 million of Zambia's imports consist of petrol and diesel oil from the Tanzanian oil refinery. The rest of Zambia's imports are made up of food commodities and livestock (over K 1 million), chemicals (about K 0.5 million), and manufactures (about K 1.75 million). Manufactures are imported mainly from Kenya and consist of such items as leather and footwear, cardboard and paper products, glass, textiles, furniture, pottery, and plastic manufactures. These are, of course, exactly the type of goods which Zambia would like to produce herself and, in fact, has begun producing.

The East African countries are in a better economic and geographical position for adding value to imported inputs than Zambia. Certainly, Zambia will be protected by the transfer tax system, but although the rates can be fairly high it is doubtful whether this protection will be effective. Zambian wage rates far exceed those in East Africa (in 1967 the average annual income for African employees was K 666).[38]

---

[38] cf. Knight's discussion of this subject, pp. 106–11.

TABLE 7.16

Main economic indicators for Zambia, East Africa, and Congo, 1967

Country	Population ('000,000)	Employment ('000)	GDP factor cost	GDP/ Cap (K)	Subsistence agriculture as a % of GDP	Cash agriculture as a % of GDP	Mining and quarrying as a % of GDP	Manufacturing as a % of GDP	Imports (K m.)
(a) Zambia	4.0	347.0	733.4	183.4	5.4	2.9	32.1	10.8	306.4
(b) Kenya	10.0	597.0	799.2	79.9	23.5	11.1	0.4	11.1	213.0[1]
(c) Tanzania	12.2	336.0	579.0[2]	47.5	25.0	28.6	2.6	4.9	68.0[1]
(d) Uganda	7.9	250.0[2]	520.0[2]	65.8	27.0	31.3	2.4	7.8	41.3[1]
EACM =b+c+d	30.1	1,183.0	1,898.2[2]	63.1	24.8	21.4	1.6	8.4	322.33
Congo (Kinshasa)	16.4	796.8	502.6	30.7	10.3	11.8	11.2	7.0	187.9

[1] Excluding intra-regional imports from East Africa.
[2] Estimate.

Sources: Summaries of economic data—latest year 1967; Kenya, Tanzania; Uganda, Economic Commission for Africa, Addis Ababa, 1968; Zambia, *Monthly Digest of Statistics*, Central Statistical Office, Lusaka, April 1969; Congo, *Rapport Annuel 1967*, Banque Nationale du Congo, Kinshasa, 1969.

TABLE 7.17
*Zambia's trade with the East African
countries and Congo (Kinshasa), 1967*
(K'000)

Country	Exports (excluding re-exports)	Imports	Balance
(a) Congo (Kinshasa)	3,778	236	+3,542
(b) Kenya	393	2,911	−1,518
(c) Tanzania	280	9,003	−8,723
(d) Uganda	28	10	+18
(e) E A C M=b+c+d	701	11,924	−11,223

Source: *Annual Statement of External Trade, 1967*, Central Statistical Office, Lusaka, 1968.

Moreover, the working of the transfer tax system is to be reviewed in 1972, and in 1982 it is to cease altogether.

The greatest objection to Zambian membership of the EACM, however, concerns the *external tariff*. The East African tariff is much higher than Zambia's. Membership of the EACM would imply an estimated price rise of imported articles in Zambia of about 5–6 per cent in 1970.[39] This would lead to further wage rises so that the price Zambia would have to pay for joining the EACM would almost certainly have to be a considerable devaluation of the kwacha. It is hard to see why Zambia should increase her tariffs for the benefit of East African producers.

An additional disadvantage of the East African tariff is that it is levied on c.i.f. value of imports as against the Zambian f.o.b. system. Hence a change to the East African system would give an artificial preference to goods landed at Dar es Salaam over those coming via Beira, Lobito, or Matadi. The level of the East African tariff and its system of valuation of imports may seriously impede promotion of trade relations with the Congo and future relations with other neighbours which achieve independence.

Can Zambia attract enough foreign investment outside the EACM? In fact, we may well ask whether foreign investment would come to Zambia if she joined the EACM. Investors will choose a Zambian location from which to serve the EACM only if certain agreements are reached on the location of industries. Such agreements could probably also be made if Zambia were not a full member of the Market. It

[39] Recent experience in the Netherlands reveals that producers use such an occasion to increase prices by more than twice the necessary rate.

certainly seems advisable that Zambia should enter negotiations with the East African countries on the location of new industries which involve considerable economies of scale. Unfortunately, co-operation with regard to the location of new industries has until now been disappointing. Overcapacity is not an unfamiliar phenomenon in East Africa. During 1965 Kenya failed to implement the industry-sharing agreements made in Kampala in 1964. Tanzania has or is going to have excess capacity in, among other things, aluminium piece goods and textile production. Textiles are, in fact, produced in all three East African countries. Uganda is planning a nitrogenous fertilizer factory which, along the lines of the Kampala agreement, would be intended to serve the whole East African market. Kenya, however, started construction of a fertilizer plant at Mombasa in 1967. This plant will supply all Kenya's requirements. Tanzania, too, has started construction of a fertilizer plant (ammonium sulphate, triple superphosphate, and granular compounds).

Apart from production of textiles and fertilizers, Zambia would be greatly interested in a large market for its proposed iron and steel works. As we have seen already,[40] the Zambian market is far too small for production of iron and steel products at import parity price. At a conference of the Economic Commission for Africa on harmonization of industrial development programmes in East Africa, held in Lusaka in 1965, it was proposed that there would be three integrated works, each of about half a million tons annual capacity, at Que Que (Rhodesia), Tororo (Uganda), and Lusaka together with a large re-rolling mill (250,000 tons capacity) at Dar es Salaam and smaller re-rolling works of about 50,000 tons annual capacity at Addis Ababa and in Madagascar. These targets were in line with the estimated market in 1980.

Present developments indicate that no country is ready to accept an iron and steel production allocation smaller than its own domestic market. Uganda's planned integrated iron and steel factory using local iron ore reserves will need more than the existing three-nation East African market to be viable. Tanzania has, however, begun construction of its rolling mill and Kenya has announced plans for a steel rod and bar mill at Mombasa. It is true that initial capacities are small (30,000 tons in Dar es Salaam and 36,000 tons in Mombasa) but these developments definitely imply that other countries cannot make plans based on the Tanzanian and Kenyan markets.

[40] See above, pp. 216–18.

Although complete integration does not seem to be in Zambia's interest, increased co-operation and promotion of trade relations with the EACM is a reasonable goal. However, in view of recent experience Zambia should not be too optimistic with regard to the possibilities for enlarging her markets. Arguments stressing the importance of comparative advantage and the loss in allocative efficiency through trade diversion do not have much appeal in developing countries.

The Democratic Republic of Congo

At present the Congo is hardly regarded as a trading partner for Zambia. It is not difficult to explain this attitude: the Congo has a completely different system of administration, with French as its official language; and its political instability used to be an even greater obstacle to close relations. Nevertheless, it is unfortunate that Zambia, which spends a vast sum of money on consultants' reports, has never seriously investigated the possibilities for economic co-operation with the Congo.

Table 7.17 shows Zambia's positive trade balance with Congo in 1967. Zambia's exports, however, consisted almost exclusively of maize. From 1958 to 1966 the Congo's agricultural production has decreased considerably. (The value of agricultural exports fell from K 114 million or 41 per cent of total exports in 1958 to K 54 million or 16 per cent of total exports in 1966.) Since 1962 the Congo has begun to import rice and maize. As mentioned previously, it is expected that Kasai Province will soon become self-sufficient in maize again and will eventually produce enough to supply Katanga. However, other crops might, in the long run, be relatively more profitable for Kasai. Zambia should investigate the position. She could herself become an importer of Congolese tea, cocoa, and—at least for some time to come—coffee. Palm oil is already imported from Congo. Rubber, for the Zambian tyre factory, could become an important import from the Congo. In ten years or so, Zambia could possibly begin to export meat to the Congo.

Negotiations on the location of new industries would be easier with the Congo than the three East African countries. Unfortunately the Congo too has decided to set up an iron and steel works (in the Kinshasa area, with an annual capacity of 300,000 tons). But there may be other possibilities, such as fertilizer production.

There may also be possibilities of co-operation in copper production.

When new mines are opened in the pedicle, the Congo will need extra smelter capacity. It is possible that extensions to Zambia's smelters would be more economical than building a new smelter in the pedicle. In the short run the best possibilities for co-operation are, however, in manufacturing of mining equipment and servicing of existing equipment.

Gradually increasing economic integration between Katanga and the Zambian Copperbelt could be mutually advantageous. Both areas need more competition in the retail trade in general and in the supply of food commodities in particular.

Finally, a few remarks should be made with regard to Zambia's transport link with the Congo. At present the route to the Congolese port of Matadi is difficult—by rail to Port Francqui, from there by boat to Kinshasa and then by rail again to Matadi—and expensive. The cost of transporting one ton of goods from Matadi to Lusaka is over K 50, which is higher than the cost for any of the other routes (see Table 7.5). Even when the proposed railway line between Port Francqui and Kinshasa has been built this figure will still be around K 40. This is much more than the K 25 per ton which the Zambia-East Africa rail link might charge for transport from Lusaka to the coast. Nevertheless, Zambia should keep an eye on the Congo route. If she were to reallocate all her imports and exports which are presently transported through the South, except coke and coal, Zambia would need extra harbour capacity for the handling of about 1 million tons of Zambian goods. In 1970 Dar es Salaam harbour will be able to handle 600,000 tons of Zambian goods (exports and imports together) which is only 100,000 tons more than in 1969. Matadi harbour, on the other hand, worked in 1967 at only two-thirds of its 1958 capacity. This harbour would probably be able to handle more than 500,000 tons for Zambia.

Thus, it is not at all impossible that Zambia will have to make use of the Congo route. The best solution to the harbour constraint would, however, be to connect the Zambia-East Africa rail link with the excellent harbour of Mtwara at the East African coast, south of Dar es Salaam. Mtwara is a natural harbour which would be capable of extensive development at much lower cost than Dar es Salaam.[41]

[41] For a fuller discussion, see below, pp. 346–52 and 360–62.

8

The Foreign Exchange Constraint

STEPHEN GOODMAN[1]

INTRODUCTION

FOREIGN exchange is an especially important resource in economic development, because with it can be bought both the raw materials of production and inputs of the productive process that may be lacking locally. The lack of sufficient foreign exchange to finance necessary imports of capital goods, intermediate products, consumption goods, or resources may act as a binding constraint on the level of economic activity and the rate of growth in the economy as these necessary imports can only with difficulty be replaced by local substitutes. The presence of surplus foreign exchange, that is, foreign exchange in excess of the requirements necessary to pay for imported goods and services not easily produced by the domestic economy, can, by substituting for indigenous inputs, eliminate other gaps or bottlenecks and thereby permit a higher level of economic activity.

If the substitution possibilities between the various inputs in the production process are infinite, then no import will represent a constraint or gap in required resources. The output of the economy will simply be determined by the total supply of all factors suitably measured, that is, the production function will be of the form:

$$Y = f\left(\sum L_1, L_2, \ldots, L_n, K_1, K_2, \ldots, K_n, R_1, R_2, \ldots, R_n\right)$$

where Y is the output of the economy, $L_1, L_2, \ldots, L_n$ are labour inputs of various types, $K_1, K_2, \ldots, K_n$ are capital inputs of various types, and $R_1, R_2, \ldots, R_n$ are resource inputs of various types. In such an economy there can be no foreign exchange constraint as distinct from a resource shortage in general.

[1] Formerly Lecturer in Economics, University of Zambia; currently at Yale Growth Centre.

If the possibilities of substitution between inputs in the production process are zero, that is, if production corresponds to the assumptions of input-output analysis, then in most circumstances only one input will represent the single constraint or bottleneck in the economy at the level of output, all other inputs being free goods. The output of the economy will simply be determined by the supply of the bottleneck input or combination of inputs. The production function will be of the form:

$$Y = f(\min(L_1, L_2, \ldots, L_n, K_1, K_2, \ldots, K_n, R_1, R_2, \ldots, R_n)$$

In such an economy additional foreign exchange will only be useful if foreign exchange is the input in limited supply or if foreign exchange can substitute for or serve the same purpose as the input in limited supply.

In many less developed economies it is assumed that foreign exchange and domestic savings are the inputs in scarce supply. The fact that foreign exchange can be substituted for domestic savings has led to the formulation of a two-gap model which emphasizes that, over a certain range of foreign exchange availability, foreign exchange can be employed successfully to fill both the foreign exchange gap and the foreign exchange and savings gap simultaneously.

In most economies the possibilities for substitution between inputs in the production process are not likely to be either infinite or zero. Rather, depending on the inputs and the direction of substitution, substitution will usually be possible but at increasing cost, that is, the production function will be of the usual form:

$$Y = f(K_1, K_2, \ldots, K_n, L_1, L_2, \ldots, L_n, R_1, R_2, \ldots, R_n)$$

In most less developed economies the resources that are usually in relatively scarce supply include foreign exchange, domestic savings, skilled labour, and organizational entrepreneurship.[2] It is necessary for these economies to attempt the very difficult, although not impossible, substitution of other abundant inputs, particularly unskilled labour, for the resources in scarce supply, or to rely on outside assistance.

Zambia, however, was fortunate, as will be indicated in the next section, in that foreign exchange has not been in scarce supply and

[2] The term 'organizational entrepreneurship' is used in reference to the ability to organize, manage, and motivate complex organizations with delegated authority. This is an ability quite distinct from the petty entrepreneurship that is in abundant supply in most less developed economies.

is not likely, given present trends and resource levels, to be in relatively scarce supply until the 1970s. The Zambian economy has, therefore, been able to attempt the more unusual but probably less difficult substitution of foreign exchange for skilled labour and organizational entrepreneurship—two resources that have been in relatively scarce supply. Zambia has also attempted to employ its available foreign exchange to alleviate two sectoral non-resource bottlenecks: limited construction capacity and limited politically acceptable transport capacity.

To alleviate the shortage of skilled indigenous labour the Zambian economy makes use of approximately 30,000 expatriate workers, primarily skilled.[3] Although this substitution in the production process of foreign exchange in the form of expatriate labour for unavailable skilled indigenous labour is technologically possible it is relatively expensive, both economically and socially. An expatriate manager or chief engineer earns about K 8,000 per annum, intermediate management personnel about K 6,000, and senior foremen and foremen about K 4,000–K 5,000, in addition to fringe benefits of approximately K 2,000 per annum. The foreign exchange cost of a senior foreman earning K 5,000 and receiving fringe benefits of K 2,000 will, given present expenditure patterns, be approximately K 3,800 compared with a total cost of only about K 2,400 and a foreign exchange cost of only about K 775 for a Zambian equivalent.[4]

The foreign exchange cost of alleviating the resource gap in indigenous skilled labour is, therefore, at least K 3,000 per worker at senior foreman level or above. Although foreign exchange may substitute in the production process for indigenous skilled labour it requires an expenditure of approximately K 3,000 in foreign exchange to substitute for one unit of labour. In practice, this estimate of the foreign exchange cost of replacing one unit of indigenous skilled labour is probably too low, as indirect foreign exchange costs, such as the

---

3 Data on manpower are taken from the *Manpower Report*, Government Printer, Lusaka, 1966, adjusted by more recent data taken from the *Monthly Digest of Statistics*, Central Statistical Office, Lusaka.

4 A senior foreman's total remuneration of approximately K 7,000 will have direct foreign exchange costs in the form of remittances, gratuities, fares, travel, and overseas education costs of about 30 per cent or K 2,100. Out of the remaining income after tax, about 40 per cent or K 1,400 is spent on consuming imports. The Zambian will spend about 38 per cent of his income after tax on imports.

foreign exchange cost of a pronounced demonstration effect, and the foreign exchange costs of employing expatriate labour in the production of domestic output have been ignored. The marginal cost is probably even higher than the average cost, given the additional inducements required to attract the necessary manpower. The social cost of employing expatriates is probably still higher.

Despite these high costs the Zambian economy, in recognition of the almost total lack of skilled indigenous labour relative to other resource availabilities, has chosen to substitute foreign exchange for unavailable indigenous labour in the production process. This substitution probably amounted to approximately K 100 m. in 1968.

In addition to substituting foreign exchange for unavailable indigenous skilled labour the economy has also attempted to substitute foreign exchange for unavailable indigenous organizational entrepreneurship. Taking a relatively permissive attitude towards foreign investors possessing organizational entrepreneurship, at least prior to the Mulungushi Reforms, few restrictions were placed on profit repatriation or overseas payments of expatriate-controlled firms. Expatriate firms were permitted to remit substantial amounts of foreign exchange in return for the organizational ability and small amounts of capital they supplied to the economy. This permissive attitude toward foreign firms who provided organizational entrepreneurship in return for foreign exchange represented a substantial substitution in the production process of available foreign exchange for unavailable or scarce indigenous organizational entrepreneurship. This substitution took place not only in the private sector but also in the public sector where the government made frequent use of management and consultancy agreements through which organizational entrepreneurship was provided to the economy for a consideration that was usually remitted overseas.

As in the case of skilled labour, however, the substitution in the production process of foreign firms and contracted management, that is, foreign exchange for unavailable indigenous organizational entrepreneurship, was costly in terms of foreign exchange. The foreign exchange remittances of private firms were approximately K 75 m. per annum in the pre-reform period, although it certainly was not the case that these remittances represented payments solely for the provision of organizational entrepreneurship. The foreign exchange remittances of contracted management are difficult to estimate. Fees range from $\frac{1}{2}$ per cent of sales to 25 per cent of profit, or in many cases the fees are fixed with a few firms receiving compensation on the same basis. It is impossible given the existing material to make any realistic estimate of the foreign exchange cost of substituting foreign firms and contracted management for unavailable indigenous organizational entrepreneurship in the production process, but the cost was probably substantial.

In addition to employing foreign exchange to fill gaps in resource availabilities the economy has also employed foreign exchange in an effort to alleviate the transport and construction bottlenecks. To reduce dependence on the existing inadequate rail transport system through Rhodesia, foreign exchange has been employed to finance the foreign exchange components of a new oil pipeline, newly constructed or paved roads, an airlift, and a substantial number of new rail and road vehicles. To reduce dependence on the inadequate existing supply of contractors and construction personnel and equipment, substantial foreign exchange remittances of contracting firms have been permitted. In general the economy has with increasing success but at a substantial cost used the available foreign exchange both as substitute for other inputs in the production process and to alleviate non-resource bottlenecks.

BALANCE OF PAYMENTS ON CURRENT ACCOUNT

Zambia has maintained a balance of payments surplus on current account including invisibles and transfers in every year since Independence. This surplus, which is a consequence of the very large trade surplus essentially generated through copper exports, has enabled the economy to substitute foreign exchange for other scarce inputs in the production process. It is not likely, however, that the balance of payments position will remain as favourable in the future and it is possible that by 1972 foreign exchange itself may be a scarce resource if continued substitution takes place (Tables 8.1 and 8.2).

Exports

As has been indicated, Zambia's favourable foreign exchange position is essentially a consequence of substantial foreign exchange earnings from copper exports. Approximately 90 per cent of Zambia's exports

TABLE 8.1

Zambian balance of payments on current account—goods

	1961	1962	1963	1964	1965	1966	1967
Exports							
Total K m.	239.4	239.2	258.0	330.3	351.1	431.4	467.3
Copper							
'ooo long tons	601	585	633	751	753	660	663
value K m.	220.2	217.6	235.6	296.8	343.2	460.6	434.0
Other minerals							
value K m.	7.3	9.3	14.1	16.1	17.4	17.7	16.9
Tobacco & maize							
value K m.	5.0	5.4	3.6	5.7	6.8	6.3	12.4
Imports							
Total K m.	n.a.	n.a.	n.a.	142.9	208.9	250.5	308.0
Trade surplus							
Total K m.	n.a.	n.a.	n.a.	187.4	142.2	180.9	159.3

Projections 1968-72

	1968	1969	1970	1971	1972
Exports					
Total K m.	516.0	540.5	555.4	570.0	575.4
Copper					
'ooo long tons	690	735	780	800	820
value K m.	483.0	514.5	530.4	544.0	549.4
Other minerals					
value K m.	15.0	14.0	14.0	14.0	14.0
Tobacco & maize					
value K m.	8.0	6.0	5.0	5.0	5.0
Imports					
Total K m.	399.9	459.5	491.6	512.8	524.5
Trade surplus					
Total K m.	116.1	81.0	63.8	57.2	50.9

Source: Data for 1961–7: *Monthly Digest of Statistics,* Central Statistical Office, Lusaka.

by value are refined copper. The balance of payments position, therefore, is very sensitive to movements in copper prices. In the early 1950s copper prices, in conjunction with other commodity prices, reached unprecedently high levels. Following the Korean war and the collapse of the commodity boom in 1955, prices settled at what was thought to be their approximate long-run equilibrium price of about K 500 per long ton c.i.f. The price remained relatively steady in that range until the new boom that followed in the wake of increased American military participation in Vietnam and the general worldwide economic expansion of the 1963–8 period.

TABLE 8.2

Zambian balance of payments on current account—invisibles

	1964	1965	1966	1967
Net payment for services value K m.	−46.1	−31.6	−60.6	−69.9
Net investment remittances value K m.	−69.1	−45.5	−58.0	−50.6
Net transfers value K m.	3.4	−3.5	−9.6	−0.6
Total invisibles value K m.	−111.8	−80.6	−128.2	−121.1
Trade surplus value K m.	187.4	142.2	180.9	159.3
Balance on current account value K m.	75.6	61.6	52.7	38.2

Projections 1968–72

	1968	1969	1970	1971	1972
Net payment for services value K m.	−66.5	−68.9	−69.0	−69.0	−69.0
Net investment remittances value K m.	−46.3	−51.5	−46.5	−43.6	−43.6
Net transfers value K m.	−9.7	−8.8	−7.8	−4.8	−4.5
Total invisibles value K m.	−122.5	−129.2	−123.3	−117.4	−117.4
Trade surplus value K m.	116.1	81.0	63.8	57.2	50.9
Balance on current account value K m.	−6.4	−48.2	−59.5	−60.2	−66.2

Source: Data for 1964–7: *Monthly Digest of Statistics*, Central Statistical Office, Lusaka.

The Zambian mining companies, even more so than their principal competitors, the Chilean mining firms, have been very sensitive to the threat that high and unstable prices may pose in the form of substitution by consumers of other metals for copper. Therefore, in early 1964 when the price of copper rose significantly on the London Metal Exchange, the Zambian producers introduced a system of fixed producer prices substantially below the market prices. The system of producer prices had a substantial negative effect on foreign exchange earnings in 1965 that was not offset by the benefit of long-run stable prices, because in April 1966, following further substantial increases in the LME price and in the Chilean producer price, the Zambian mining firms switched from a fixed producer price to the LME three-month forward price. More recently contracts have been made on the basis of the cash price rather than the forward price, but the difference between the two prices is not generally significant.

In 1967 the expectation was that copper prices would return to what was considered an equilibrium level, in normal circumstances a little less than K 700 per ton c.i.f. The continuing conflict in Vietnam, the hostilities in the Middle East, a prolonged copper strike in the United States, and the threat of a strike in Chile had the consequence, however, that copper prices rose sharply at the end of the year and the average price for 1967 remained significantly above K 800. In 1968 and 1969 copper prices remained firm at a price rising from K 800 per long ton c.i.f. to over K 1,200 in June 1969 because of continued Vietnam war demand and heavy stock replenishment.

The future trend in copper prices is difficult to predict. If no extraordinary demand develops as a result of intensified hostilities or expectations of intensified hostilities, if the growth rate in world economic activity does not accelerate, if no prolonged strikes or production cutting disasters occur in any major producing country, and if present output expansion plans of the major producers are for the most part realized, it does not seem likely that copper prices in the medium future will rise significantly above K 1,000 per ton. If the cold war does not end, if the world economy does not enter a period of serious recession or depression, and if no unexpected increases in output occur, it does not seem likely that the copper price in the medium future will fall below K 750 per ton. The range of K 1,000–750 per long ton, therefore, seems a reasonable, if not necessarily certain, prediction as to the level of prices in the 1970–72 period, with the tendency being for the price to decline within this range through the period.

The difficulties of planning for economic development in the presence of such an uncertain variable as the copper price are many. The level of economic activity and therefore government revenue, and the level of induced investment, are all a function of the gross injection into the economy, that is, a function of the flow of export receipts and autonomous investment, particularly the flow of export receipts. If copper prices decline below expected levels the development effort must be reduced at great social and economic cost, as the Ghanaian experience has demonstrated in the case of cocoa revenue. If copper prices rise above expected levels added impetus is given to the development effort. The danger, however, is that the added impetus of high copper prices will give rise to inflation and structural imbalance that will continue to have a detrimental effect on the development of the economy, even after the export boom has ceased.

Foreign exchange earnings from copper exports in Zambia have not been as favourable as the high copper prices might indicate. After a steady climb in copper output throughout the 1950s which accelerated with the opening of two new mines in the early 1960s, copper output fell sharply in 1966. The reduction in output below the record 1965 levels was primarily a consequence of the transport, fuel, and labour difficulties which followed in the wake of Rhodesia's Unilateral Declaration of Independence, and the policy of selective economic sanctions. In spite of these difficulties substantial increases in output have been registered since 1966, although it is unlikely that output will again reach the 1965 level until 1969–70. The development of two new mines by the RST group, the development of one new mine by the Anglo American Corporation group and the introduction of the TORCO process that will permit the refining of low-grade oxide ores under financial arrangements which will guarantee substantial exports to the Japanese market, make an output of 760,000 long tons in 1972 a likely possibility.

Although copper is by far Zambia's most important export, the country also exports a small amount of other minerals, particularly zinc, lead, cobalt, and manganese, and some agricultural products, particularly maize and tobacco. Zinc and lead are, however, in growing surplus on world markets, and there has been a steady decline in the average price of these metals, particularly since 1966, which has endangered the economic viability of the Zambian producer. Output has remained relatively stable in the post-Independence period but there is some danger that production will be discontinued if the price falls significantly lower. Manganese and cobalt, which are essentially by-products of copper mining, have had mixed performance in the post-Independence period: cobalt exports have increased, while manganese exports have declined. Taking minerals other than copper as a group, foreign exchange earnings increased dramatically to a peak in 1966, but will be sustained at that level only with difficulty.

Tobacco has traditionally been Zambia's most important agricultural export. However, the exodus of expatriate cultivators, the principal producers of Virginian flue-cured tobacco, the shortage of agricultural labour, and the relatively favourable maize prices, have led to a very substantial decline in output. Although prices rose significantly in 1966–7 in response to the international boycott of Rhodesian tobacco the price has since declined and is likely to decline further as more of the Rhodesian crop becomes available. Maize, the staple food, was in substantial surplus in 1965–6 and, therefore, it was sometimes necessary to export at unfavourable prices. It is expected, however, that in the immediate future Congo (Kinshasa) should be able to absorb almost a million bags per annum at relatively favourable prices (almost K 3 per bag). The foreign exchange earnings from agricultural exports are likely to remain relatively constant, therefore, at a level somewhat below their 1967 peak.

Imports

The level of imports in any economy is a function primarily of the level of expenditure and the import coefficient or propensities associated with that expenditure. The import coefficients are essentially determined by the structure of the economy and its institutional practices. In Zambia the economy has, because of the favourable foreign exchange position, generally been open. This openness, combined with the complex consumption requirements of an advanced modern sector and expatriate consumers, and the general lack of indigenous secondary development, has the consequence that the average import coefficients are generally very high (Table 8.3).

TABLE 8.3
Estimates of Zambian import coefficients

	A ONDP estimate	B Author's estimate	Average of A and B
Private consumption	0.40	0.37	0.39
Government consumption	0.40	0.25	0.33
Investment	0.60	0.41	0.51
Changes in stock	0.35	0.69	0.52
Exports	0.08	0.14	0.11

Estimates of Zambian imports[1]
(K m.)

	1968	1969	1970	1971	1972
Private consumption	167.7	187.2	202.8	214.5	222.3
Government consumption	62.7	72.6	79.2	82.5	85.8
Investment	112.7	137.7	143.3	147.9	147.9
Changes in stock	0.0	2.6	5.2	5.2	5.2
Exports	56.8	59.4	61.1	62.7	63.3
Total imports	399.9	459.5	491.6	512.8	524.5

[1] Based on use of average estimate.

In the medium future it is not likely that the average import coefficients will decline. It is almost certainly the case that given indigenous supply inelasticities the marginal import coefficients are significantly greater than the average coefficients. Expansion in the economy should, therefore, significantly increase the import coefficients. The tendency for the import coefficients to increase is probably further accentuated by a relatively more rapid increase in prices in Zambia than in the world as a whole. Although the prices of imports landed in Zambia have risen substantially because of higher transport costs and profit margins, it is not likely that the price of imports will continue to increase as rapidly as the price of Zambian-produced substitutes.

The effect on the level of imports of first the deterioration in transport following UDI and then the subsequent slow improvement in transport is difficult to assess. It is likely that the poor state of the transport system has kept the import coefficients lower than they might otherwise have been, but this effect may have been neutralized by the increased stock-carrying requirements, particularly of imports, that is a consequence of the transport situation. It appears that with improvement in transport the average import coefficients for most expenditures may increase but the required level of stocks and the import coefficient for stocks may decline.

The level of expenditure, particularly investment expenditure with its high import coefficient, has risen substantially in Zambia throughout the pre-Independence and Independence period and is likely to continue to increase through 1972. This rapid increase in the level of expenditure, coupled with high import coefficients, has had the consequence that the level of imports has risen dramatically, and it is likely to continue to increase rapidly in the foreseeable future.

Government investment expenditures, after overcoming administrative bottlenecks, probably reached their targeted level of K 161 m. in 1968. Even assuming restraint in the rate of increases in development expenditures it is reasonable to expect government investment to reach at least K 190 m. in 1969 and K 210 m. in 1970, particularly when consideration is given to existing commitments. The level of private investment is difficult to estimate. The Mulungushi Reforms and recent developments in the mining industry may create a spurt of investment that will taper off slightly in the later period. The level of government consumption is likely to continue to increase despite efforts to reduce such expenditure. The level of public consumption will follow the increase in national income, although probable increases in taxation and reductions in the excessive profits of resident expatriates, coupled with increased wage restraint, will lead to a tapering off in the growth rate of private consumption after 1969. Changes in stock after adjusting to improved transport conditions should increase slightly with the growth in the economy.

The overall picture is one of a substantial increase in the level of imports as the economy grows and a steady erosion in the trade surplus. The projections are, of course, highly speculative and very sensitive to a great number of economic and social variables, but, given present trends and reasonable expectations, by 1972 the trade surplus should be almost completely eliminated.

Direction of Trade

Before considering other elements in the current account of the balance of payments it is useful and interesting to note the historical direction of Zambian trade and the very substantial changes that have occurred since Independence and Rhodesian UDI (Table 8.4).

In the case of exports the pattern has remained relatively constant except for the very substantial increase of exports to Japan, a process that is likely to continue and accelerate in the future. In 1967 Japan was Zambia's second largest customer. The United Kingdom, however, was still Zambia's most important customer, with West Germany being the third largest consumer, followed by South Africa.

In the case of imports there has been a very substantial change in the pattern of trade. In consideration of the United Nations policy of selective economic sanctions against Rhodesia, Zambia's imports from Rhodesia have declined dramatically. Although in 1967 Rhodesia was still Zambia's fourth largest supplier, its share of the Zambian market had declined from approximately 40 per cent to about 10 per cent. The chief beneficiary of this drop in Rhodesian trade has been South Africa. South Africa, therefore, has both retained its market share and acquired a substantial portion of Rhodesia's market share. Since UDI, South Africa has been Zambia's most important supplier, particularly for consumer goods. The growing requirements for construction and transport equipment have also led to a substantial increase in the market share of the United States, with the consequence that in 1967 the United States was Zambia's third largest supplier.

TABLE 8.4

Direction of exports and imports
Exports (in K m.)

	1964	1965	1966	1967
United Kingdom	109.0	143.1	160.2	128.3
EEC	104.4	113.0	167.6	125.1
EFTA (excluding UK)	9.8	15.8	27.4	27.4
Other Europe	6.4	7.4	13.9	11.4
South Africa	26.2	24.8	28.0	25.4
Rhodesia	13.8	10.9	5.0	2.0
East Africa	0.8	0.9	1.2	1.0
United States	8.9	1.6	0.1	23.9
Japan	37.1	46.2	69.5	95.8
Middle East	0.1	0.1	0.1	0.5
Soviet Bloc	6.0	8.7	10.0	6.6
Total	355.5	380.3	493.5	470.0

Imports (in K m.)

	1964	1965	1966	1967
United Kingdom	26.8	42.0	54.4	62.9
EEC	8.8	15.5	20.1	37.5
EFTA (excluding UK)	2.5	4.0	5.7	7.7
Other Europe	0.1	0.1	0.7	2.4
South Africa	32.4	41.4	58.5	72.1
Rhodesia	61.7	71.0	46.4	32.2
East Africa	0.7	1.1	2.2	11.9
United States	8.0	13.0	27.1	32.9
Japan	3.2	7.6	8.8	18.6
Middle East	3.8	2.0	4.1	3.2
Soviet Bloc	0.1	0.3	0.4	2.0
Total	156.4	210.7	246.1	306.3

Source: Monthly Digest of Statistics, Central Statistical Office, Lusaka.

Invisibles

In addition to merchandise or trade transactions the balance of payments on current account includes invisible transactions, that is, non-trade transactions that give rise to or use up current income.

Service Transactions

The most important group of invisible transactions are the service transactions. Service transactions that are import equivalent, that is, use up foreign exchange, include transport of imports to, and exports from, the borders of Zambia, travel of residents overseas, education of residents overseas, diplomatic expenditures of Zambian missions, insurance premiums, and related items. The foreign exchange cost of these services has increased steadily throughout the post-Independence period and is likely to continue to increase through the 1970s. Transport charges move with the volume of imports and exports and although improvements in transport along alternative routes may reverse part of the sharp increase in transport costs following UDI, the overall freight bill should increase slightly because of increases in the volume of trade. Travel expenditures will probably continue to decline gradually as less reliance is placed on expatriates while other service expenditures, with the possible exception of education and insurance, where some import substitution can take place, should increase. The expansion of the national airline and the creation of a national shipping line should not significantly reduce the cost of services as little value added will be indigenously provided in either activity.

Service transactions that are export equivalent include transport charges on exports to the Zambian border, diplomatic expenditures of foreign governments, and travel costs of tourists in Zambia. These sources of foreign exchange should continue their gradual increase, although the development of new tourist facilities in 1969 and 1970 may accelerate the rate of increase in tourist income. Overall, the net foreign exchange cost of services should rise gradually through 1972 (Table 8.2).

Returns on Capital and Management

The second largest group of invisible transactions in the Zambian balance of payments are the foreign remittances and receipts of government and others that represent payments for or returns on capital and management. This item is particularly important in Zambia as it is more easily controlled by government policy than is the service component of the invisibles and it accounts for much of the deterioration in the current account surplus from the substantial surplus on merchandise account. Government remittances and receipts have been relatively insignificant in foreign exchange terms. Although the asset position of the Zambian government is likely to deteriorate after 1968 as increasing government deficits on total account lead to increased overseas borrowing, government interest payments should not be substantial until at least after 1972.

Private firms, however, prior to the Mulungushi Reforms, had made substantial remittances and it is likely that these payments would have continued at their high level through 1972. The reduction in this very heavy drain on Zambia's available foreign exchange is one of the objectives of the Mulungushi policy. Under the Mulungushi provisions, the profit remittances of firms will be limited to no more than 50 per cent of their after-tax profits or 30 per cent of their equity capital, whichever is smaller. The effect on future levels of investment remittances should be substantial. Using the mining companies as an example, profit remittances prior to the Reforms were approximately 80 per cent of after-tax profits; under the Mulungushi provisions these remittances will be reduced to no more than 50 per cent of profits, a reduction of approximately 36 per cent. It is difficult to know the exact magnitude of the Reforms' total effect on investment remittances, although a 35 per cent reduction in the remittances of corporations below the level they would otherwise have attained seems a reasonable estimate for the immediate future. The decline in mining company profits that will be a consequence of rising costs and a slightly declining price after 1969 will also reduce the flow of future remittances. In the medium run, because of the Mulungushi Reforms and the decline in mining profits, it is likely that the net foreign exchange cost of expatriate capital and management will decline, despite the deterioration in the government asset position.

Transfers

The last substantial group of invisible transactions includes government transfers and personal remittances. Transfers by the government of Zambia have been relatively small, consisting primarily of assistance to the government of Tanzania and pension and other benefit payments due to former civil servants. Aid received by the government of Zambia, primarily from the UK, has also been insignificant, with the exception of a K 27 m. grant to alleviate the consequences of UDI. Transfers by the Zambian government will probably decline slightly through 1972 as the transport crisis eases and the number of new expatriate retirements declines. The flow of overseas aid should increase, however. In this regard, the UK government has committed itself to providing further relief to offset some of the costs of UDI, once Britain's internal economic position improves. Personal transfers have declined slightly in the post-Independence period and are likely to continue to decline as the number of expatriates is reduced. Overall, the level of net transfers is likely to decrease through 1972 but should remain negative.

Considering all invisibles as a group, the net foreign exchange cost is likely to remain relatively constant as the increased cost of services is offset by the reduction in investment remittances and transfers. Overall the net foreign exchange cost of invisibles should remain constant at something over K 110 m.

Considering the current account of the balance of payments as a whole, the very large surplus or positive balance that was generated annually in the immediate post-Independence period will probably be eliminated and reversed, primarily because of the very substantial increase in the level of imports. It is possible that the current account of the Zambian balance of payments will be in deficit by 1972 with the deficit growing substantially through 1974.

BALANCE OF PAYMENTS
ON CAPITAL ACCOUNT

Exactly offsetting the balance of payments on current account is the balance of payments on capital account, as any surplus or deficit that has been generated in a particular year must be financed. The consequent sterility of the capital account as an analytical tool has promoted various attempts to identify the autonomous transactions and induced or balancing transactions. In the case of Zambia, the immature development of the internal money market has the consequence that few financial transactions are autonomous, and it is probably more useful, therefore, to consider the entire capital account as balancing with the allocation of increases in assets or liabilities being determined by interest and institutional considerations.

Reserves

As has been indicated, Zambia has generated large surpluses in the balance of payments on current account in the post-Independence period, despite the substantial substitution of foreign exchange for other scarce inputs in the production process. Because of these surpluses Zambian firms, banks, and the government have acquired sizeable reserves of foreign exchange (Table 8.5). These extensive reserves will permit Zambia to continue its past policies at least through 1972, despite the substantial projected current account deficits. However, the cost to Zambia's reserves of financing these deficits will be quite considerable, assuming that large-scale international borrowing is not undertaken. By 1972 Zambia's foreign exchange reserves, including the IMF credit *tranche* position, should be no more than adequate to cover transaction requirements.

TABLE 8.5

International liquidity[1]

	1964	1965	1966	1967	1968[3]
Total reserves[2] $ m.	n.a.	212.4	229.1	197.5	223.1
Bank of Zambia $ m.					
Gold and gold *tranche*	n.a.	6.8	9.0	12.0	12.2
Foreign exchange	n.a.	73.5	83.6	84.3	107.0
Government $ m.	57.2	118.8	118.0	83.1	98.7
Commercial banks $ m.	n.a.	13.3	18.5	18.1	5.2
IMF credit *tranche* $ m.	n.a.	50.0	50.0	50.0	50.0

[1] Excludes foreign exchange holdings of mining firms.
[2] Excludes IMF credit *tranche* position.
[3] As of September 1968 for the Bank of Zambia, as of April 1968 for others.

Source: International Monetary Fund, *Financial Statistics.*

The composition of Zambia's reserves are similar to that of many former British colonies. Almost half of Zambia's reserves are in the form of government and public agency holdings with the Crown Agents and the Bank of England Number Two Account. Although these holdings are managed by the Bank of Zambia, this commitment to sterling proved relatively costly at the time of British devaluation. Holding of dollar assets and gold are relatively insignificant. Dollar assets probably do not account for more than 10 per cent of reserves, while the holdings of non-IMF gold probably do not exceed 3 per cent of reserves. The advantage of using the familiar London money market, the high British bank rate, the value of having reserves in a currency that is employed in the majority of trade relations, and the British government guarantees on future devaluations, have prompted the Zambians to continue maintaining their reserve holdings in sterling, despite the devaluation experience. The composition of reserves among maturities is relatively balanced with the portfolio containing both short- and long-term assets. The high level of reserves relative to anticipated requirements has permitted the Bank of Zambia and the government to invest in higher-yield, less-liquid assets than might otherwise have been the case.

INTERNATIONAL MONETARY INSTITUTIONS

Zambia became a member of the International Monetary Fund on 23 September 1965. Its quota in the Fund has been fixed at 50 million dollars, of which 3.2 million dollars have been paid in gold. Zambia has chosen to accept the special transitional arrangements of Article 14 of the Fund's Articles of Agreement, although in practice Zambia has maintained a liberal and non-discriminatory exchange and import policy except for remittances to and imports from Rhodesia. Zambia has not made use of its drawing rights at the Fund, and in fact, because of the substantial reserves it has acquired, has been obligated to enter into repurchase arrangements.

Zambia is also a member of the World Bank. Despite some earlier differences that were a consequence of the Bank's unwillingness to finance the Zambia-Tanzania rail link because it was thought to be uneconomic, relations between the Bank and the government of Zambia have recently been relatively friendly. The Bank has negotiated several medium- and long-term loans that have provided the government with supplementary foreign exchange. The proceeds of these loans have been used to finance road improvements, educational developments, and a dairy and cattle ranch scheme.

FOREIGN EXCHANGE AS A FUTURE RESTRAINT

As has been indicated, foreign exchange has not itself been a constraint on Zambian development in the immediate post-Independence period. In practice, the economy has, at a substantial foreign exchange cost, substituted foreign exchange for other inputs in the production process. As has also been indicated, however, given present trends and the present institutional and economic structure of the economy, it is likely that by 1971–2 the balance of payments on current account will be in relatively substantial deficit, and by 1974 the large foreign exchange reserves will have been depleted. Assuming, therefore, that corrective action is not undertaken, it is likely that by 1974 foreign exchange will represent a real and effective constraint on Zambian development.

Reverse Substitution

A possible solution to the impending foreign exchange difficulty is to reduce or end the practice of substituting foreign exchange for other inputs in the production process. It has been estimated that the foreign exchange cost of substituting expatriate skilled labour for unavailable indigenous skilled labour is almost K 100 m. per annum. It is expected that this cost will decrease as the number of expatriates is reduced. The foreign exchange cost, however, of the large number of expatriates remaining in 1972, given present plans, is quite considerable, and is probably almost as large as the balance of payments deficit on current account. Although the removal of all expatriates by 1972 would probably eliminate the exchange imbalance, it would also probably have a disastrous effect on the level of exports and the level of economic activity in general. Acceleration of the government's Zambianization programme would, however, be a sound policy alternative on economic grounds.

As in the case of skilled labour, the use of expatriate organizational entrepreneurship poses a substantial foreign burden on the economy. Institutional reforms, such as Mulungushi's new economic policy, serve a useful purpose in this regard by limiting the foreign exchange drain, but the development of indigenous organizational entrepreneurship must be accelerated as a more fundamental solution.

Expenditure Restraint

More fundamental than reverse substitution as a policy alternative capable of reducing or eliminating the foreign exchange deficit is expenditure restraint. The superiority of expenditure restraint is particularly apparent when consideration is given to the fact that although the consumption patterns of Zambians and non-Zambians may differ, they do not differ significantly in their import propensity. The replacement of expatriate labour by Zambian labour and of expatriate entrepreneurs by indigenous entrepreneurs, although reducing the level of remittance, will have only limited consequences for the balance of payments unless private consumption can be restricted: that is, unless the disposable income of the Zambian replacements would be on a significantly lower scale.

Foreign exchange difficulties essentially arise because a nation is choosing to consume and invest more than its existing resources can generate and the nation can borrow. Zambia is fortunate in that its resource endowment is relatively favourable, but not so favourable as to permit both further rapid increases in public and private consumption, and investment. The economic reality which Zambia must face is that, given the present structure of the economy, it is impossible to attain the projected levels of expenditure without incurring very serious foreign exchange difficulties. Either private consumption, and, therefore, disposable income, must be reduced below projected levels, government consumption must be reduced, or the level of investment must decline, if balance of payments difficulties are to be avoided.

Overseas borrowing may postpone the required reduction of projected expenditure levels as may a favourable copper price shift; an unfavourable shift may accelerate the required reduction, but the basic policy dilemma must eventually be faced. The projected levels of expenditure, given the structure of the economy and likely trends, cannot be attained and then maintained. This policy dilemma may be formulated for 1972 in the form:

0.39 (reduction in private consumption)+0.33 (reduction in government consumption)+0.51 (reduction in investment)≈K 70 million.

IMPORT SUBSTITUTION-
EXPORT PROMOTION

An alternative solution to the foreign exchange dilemma is to alter the import coefficients through a policy of import substitution, or to increase the supply of foreign exchange available to finance imports through a programme of export promotion. Most less-developed economies have chosen both courses.

A fairly extensive programme of import substitution is being undertaken by the government of Zambia as part of the development effort associated with the First National Development Plan. Projects have been started that will reduce Zambia's import requirements for sugar, textiles, clay products, fertilizer, fibre bags, tyres and tubes, copper cable, explosives, distilled spirits, pharmaceuticals, meat, milk, other agricultural products, coal, and electric power. In addition, the private sector, with government assistance in the form of protective tariffs, income tax relief, duty rebates, and a preferential buying policy, has established a large number of import substituting enterprises, particularly for mass-consumption goods. This programme of import substitution is essentially directed at redressing some of the imbalance that is a consequence of Zambia's earlier participation in customs unions.

The Zambian market is small, however, in terms of both the number of consumers and total purchasing power. The range of commodities for which import substitution is feasible is limited. It is not likely, therefore, that the import-substituting investments that are feasible will have a significant negative effect on the size of the import coefficients, particularly when consideration is given to the high import content of most import-substituting projects, especially those in industry. Although inefficient import-substituting enterprises may be established, the foreign exchange gain, that is, the product of such enterprises, is small.

INSTITUTIONAL CHANGE

Institutional changes such as the Mulungushi Reforms have important consequences for Zambia's balance of payments as well as for the economy as a whole. At various times consideration has been given by the government of Zambia to at least two additional institutional changes with potentially important economic and foreign exchange consequences: membership in the East African Community and devaluation of the kwacha.

Zambia has formally applied for membership of the East African Community and preliminary negotiations have begun among the relevant parties. Although the motivation for membership in the Community was probably more strategic than economic, that is, more motivated by a desire for increased influence in the administration of Zambia's access routes than by a desire for increased exports, the economic consequences will still remain. Assuming Zambia joins the East African Community under trade arrangements similar to those now existing between the three East African countries, it is likely that Zambia's relatively unfavourable location and higher cost structure will place her in trade deficit with her partners, as is already the case (Table 8.4). Although Zambia would be permitted to impose transfer taxes which should be sufficient to protect those import-substituting industries that she has been able to attract, some of her other purchases would be diverted to higher-cost partners. It is unlikely, given Zambia's cost structure and her location on the market perimeter and away from ocean trade routes, that she will be able to attract any offsetting major industries producing for the larger Community market. Zambia's most likely exports, copper products, probably have a comparative advantage in the East African market in any case and therefore do not require a customs union.

On the whole the likely effects of Community membership on the balance of payments on current account will be limited at least in the medium future to a slight increase in the total cost of Zambian imports. In the long run, if the Zambian cost structure can be improved, Zambia may be able to undertake exports of electrical equipment, light capital goods, and consumer durables, and thereby improve her foreign exchange position.

Devaluation of the kwacha, given Zambia's relative insignificance in world trade, would probably leave the foreign currency price of Zambia's exports and imports unchanged. The relative local cost of exports will decrease, and there will be an increase in mining company profits with a consequent increase in output or government revenue. If higher taxes are not placed on the additional profits of the mining firms, Zambia's foreign exchange position will probably remain unchanged in the short run as the decrease in private consumption imports that will be a consequence of the decline in real income will be offset by the increase in profit remittances. In the long run, however, an impetus may be given to output increases.

If higher taxes are placed on the mining company profits after devaluation, Zambia's foreign exchange position may be significantly improved. The improvement in Zambia's foreign exchange position that is a consequence of devaluation essentially takes place because devaluation has, by lowering real domestic income, lowered the level of expenditure for private consumption. It would be just as effective and more direct to institute policies which would limit expenditure rather than attempting a devaluation and generating unnecessary instability and uncertainty. Restriction of expenditure, particularly for private consumption, to levels significantly below those projected is therefore a more desirable policy alternative.

Part II

CONSTRAINTS ON INDIVIDUAL INDUSTRIES

9

Mining and the Factors Constraining Economic Development

NORMAN KESSEL[1]

INTRODUCTION

THOUGH there is sharp controversy in development economics as how best to launch development, ranging all the way from subsistence agriculture first (René Dumont), through textiles first (Arthur Lewis), to heavy industry first (P. Mahalanobis), there is nevertheless a clear unanimity as to the contribution of mining to the process. The controversy thus only becomes pertinent in cases where underdeveloped countries are lacking in mineral wealth.

Mining contributes to development through its various effects, which may be categorized as direct, fiscal, and indirect. Direct effects can be considered as the backward and forward linkages which the industry has with the rest of the economy, where the former represent purchases of inputs required by the mines from local suppliers; and the latter, the use of the new mining output as an input for other local industries—in other words the consequences arising from direct contact of the mineral enterprise with the rest of the host economy. Even if the mineral sector fails to become integrated in the host economy, as is argued by economists who support the 'enclave theory',[2]

---

[1] A Research Fellow at the University of Leeds, England.

[2] e.g. C. F. Rollins, 'Mineral Development and Economic Growth', *Social Research*, 1956, *passim;* H. W. Singer, 'The Distribution of Gains between Investing and Borrowing Countries', *American Economic Review*, May 1950, though Singer in J. H. Adler (ed.), *Capital Movements and Economic Development*, London, 1967, p. 69, admits to having modified his argument in the light of the work by Albert Hirschman, *The Strategy of Economic Development*, Yale University Press, New Haven, Connecticut, 1966.

it nevertheless contributes substantially to fiscal revenue (this being greatly facilitated by the general profitability of mining and the relative ease of levying taxes on large corporations), so that its proportional contribution to government revenue account is usually larger than its share in net national income.[3] Finally, there are the indirect effects which are represented by the new economic activity in the form of the expansion of the domestic market, the generation of incomes, and investment funds in the case of retained earnings. To the extent that operating and investment costs, taxes, and dividends are payable to domestic factors of production and to the extent that the output is exported, mining also provides foreign exchange with which to import capital goods for development in other sectors of the economy. The enterprise enlarges the exchange economy by providing wage opportunities for those in its employ as well as in the satellite industries around it, and this, *inter alia*, benefits the economy by providing opportunities for acquiring skills and learning the discipline involved in modern industrial economies. It also stimulates the development of the infrastructure by providing economies of scale, especially in transport and power, the effect of which is to cheapen these inputs for complementary industries as well.

In general these indirect socio-economic effects are associated with the qualitative transformation induced by the mining activity on the way of life, skill, general level of education, inventiveness, store of technology, aptitudes, and new demands in the host country, whilst the direct and fiscal effects provide the quantitative benefits that are the means and motive force for these changes. It is thus these quantitative effects that demand consideration in economic terms.

THE IMPACT OF MINING

As a starting point one could establish the benchmark where investment in the mineral export industry would provide no quantitative direct or fiscal benefits; this would be the case where all equipment, supplies, and labour were imported, and the entire product exported at internal accounting prices so that there was no profit left for taxation

---

[3] In 1966 the copper industry of Zambia contributed 47 per cent to net domestic product and provided 64 per cent of government revenue.

or distribution to local shareholders. Chandler Morse[4] considers such a situation not altogether unrealistic, especially in the case of petroleum extraction, where expenditure in the host country is often limited to unskilled labour in minute quantities.[5] At the other end of the scale one could postulate the case where all the costs incurred in extracting (and refining) the mineral are expended in the host country. This is usually the case in developed countries which have sufficient local industries to cater for the requirements of the mining industry's needs for stores, raw materials, and capital equipment such that none of this need be imported, and where the industry itself is owned by resident nationals.

It is between these extremities on the scale of what Reynolds[6] has termed 'domestic retained value' that the direct and fiscal effects of mining in underdeveloped countries will usually lie. It is not so much the fate of underdeveloped countries as much as their distinguishing characteristic that these quantitative and fiscal effects fall between the third and seventh decile, whereas in more developed countries they tend to fall above the ninth.[7]

PURCHASED INPUTS

Despite structural changes occasioned by the rapid diversification in the Zambian economy in the last two years, if one examines the most recent input-output table (which is for 1966) one finds that a total

---

4 'International Investment in Raw Materials' in Marion Clawson (ed.), *Natural Resources and International Development*, The Johns Hopkins Press, Baltimore, 1964, p. 381.

5 C. F. Rollins (ibid. p. 259) estimates that less than 5 per cent of the sales revenue from Middle East petroleum is expended on wages. R. E. Baldwin, *Economic Development and Export Growth*, University of California Press, Berkeley, 1966, p. 61, gives the figures of 3.3 per cent and 2.6 per cent for Venezuelan and Saudi Arabian producers.

6 C. W. Reynolds, 'Development Problems of an Export Economy—the Case of Chile and Copper', in M. Mamalakis and C. W. Reynolds, *Essays on the Chilean Economy*, Homewood, Illinois, 1965.

7 H. B. Chenery and P. G. Clarke, *Interindustry Economics*, John Wiley, New York, 1967, Chapter 8, part C, on the similarities in input coefficients for countries with similar industrial structures. See, too, A. C. Krogh's privately constructed input-output table for the South African economy (*South African Journal of Economics*, 1961), which indicates that the gold mining industry

of K 103,984,000 was expended by the mines on goods and services in order to produce K 464,412,000 worth of minerals.

TABLE 9.1

Non-labour inputs purchased by the Zambian metal mining industry, 1966
(*K'000*)

		Locally produced	Import content of local production
(1)	Metal mining	5,866	399
(2)	Other mining and quarrying	1,564	199
(3)	Saw mills and joineries	1,566	450
(4)	Chemicals and petroleum	900	388
(5)	Cement and cement products	560	110
(6)	Foundries and metal products	10,726	4,374
(7)	Machinery	1,260	678
(8)	Transport equipment	514	181
(9)	Construction	15,962	3,318
(10)	Electricity and water	13,934	6,646
(11)	Distribution	7,324	600
(12)	Banking and insurance	3,760	386
(13)	Railway transport	1,354	305
(14)	Posts and communications	680	172
(15)	Business services	2,422	94
(16)	Unspecified	2,276	1,318
(17)	Other	1,818	600
	Total	72,506	20,218
	Direct imports	31,478	
	Total non-labour inputs	103,984	

Note: The import content of local production has been calculated as a weighted average. Owing to the aggregation of the Zambian economy into only 38 producing and consuming sectors in the input-output table from which Table 9.1 has been derived (consolidation into 17 sectors has not affected this further), it is likely that the import content of local production purchased by the mines is *understated*, as, being highly capital-intensive, the mines would require more sophisticated inputs than those used in other sectors. (See Tibor Barna, 'Classification and Aggregation in Input-Output Analysis' in Tibor Barna (ed.), *The Structural Interdependence of the Economy*, Allen and Unwin, London, 1956.)

Source: National Accounts 1964–1966 and *Input–Output Table 1966*, Central Statistical Office, Lusaka, 1968.

imported only K 9.72 million worth of goods for a total output of R 505 million in 1956–7. (The figures produced by Krogh are at a slight variance with those supplied by the Transvaal and Orange Free State Chamber of Mines and ignore profits remitted to overseas shareholders.)

Of the total of K 103,984,000 spent on goods and services, K 31,478,000 or approximately 30 per cent was imported, leaving K 72,506,000 to be met from domestic production. Now, of the K 72,506,000 supplied from the 17 producing sectors represented in Table 9.1, K 57,592,000 (or nearly 80 per cent) was produced by only 6 of the 17 sectors (sectors nos. 1, 6, 9, 10, 11, and 12) with 3 of these sectors (nos. 6, 9, and 10) supplying 56 per cent of all the domestically produced non-labour inputs purchased by the mines. Whilst this does not indicate the full extent of inter-industry dependence (as the demand for foundry and metal products by the mines will, for instance, cause the foundry and metal products sector itself to purchase goods from other sectors), it nevertheless does reveal the low degree to which mining is integrated with other sectors of the economy, and in particular, the extent to which this integration is largely limited to only a few producing sectors. Through successive approximations or iterations, one can further calculate the import content of the locally produced goods and services of K 72,506,000 purchased by the mines. As a weighted average for the first round, this is K 20,218,000, which reduces the domestic content of local production to K 52,288,000 and increases from K 31,478,000 to K 51,696,000 the import content of goods and services purchased by the mines.[8]

Thus with the gross output of the mining sector at K 464,412,000 (1966) and industrial interdependence at K 72,506,000 (with this latter figure containing imports worth K 20,218,000), it is clear that the general characteristics of underdeveloped countries are exhibited in the absence of substantial and complex inter-industry connections,[9] with most domestic payments being for wages and salaries (K 80,670,000), and financial payments to government for income tax, export tax, and royalties (K 163,000,000). Expressed as percentages of output, these figures are 15 per cent for inter-industry transactions (only 11 per cent if the import content of domestic purchases is excluded), 18 per cent for wages and salaries, and 35 per cent for financial payments to government. This illustrates how constrained the spread or multiplier effects of mining activity are, and how important it is to reduce the import dependence of the industry through a policy

---

[8] It is important to note that further iterations would successively decrease the local content and increase the import content of the domestically produced goods and services.

[9] B. Van Arkadie and C. Frank, *Economic Accounting and Development Planning*, Oxford University Press, Nairobi, 1966, p. 111.

of import substitution. This has in fact been occurring very rapidly, especially since the dissolution of the Federation, with further stimuli coming after Independence and again after Rhodesian UDI, so that the combined index of manufacturing production (1961=100) has more than doubled, rising from 106.5 (1963) to 220.0 (1967).

IMPORTED INPUTS

The first input-output table for the Zambian economy was the modified table prepared for the Seers Report[10] for 1961 which showed imports of K 41.4 m. out of a total of K 68.0 m. expended on materials and stores[11] and on the basis of certain recommendations projected that imports by the mining industry would be K 46.2 m. out of a total consumption of materials and stores of K 78.6 m. in 1965. Expressed as percentages, the imported component of materials and stores is 68.0 for 1961 and 59.0 for the 1965 projection, whereas the actual percentage for 1966 indicates that the industry only imported 30 per cent of its goods and service requirements, though this is increased to 49 per cent when the import content of local production is included.[12] Though this is a substantial increase, it is still only 11 per cent of the gross output of the mines, so that most of the linkage effects of the industry with the host economy are firstly through payments to prime factors: and secondly and more substantially through financial payments to government. As these latter payments are determined either entirely or partially by the copper price, they are highly sensitive to world market prices. Furthermore, much of the local expenditure of the mining industry is related to investment,[13] so this too is subject to cyclical changes.

Among the more important examples of import substitution that have taken place recently are the development of Zambian coal deposits: output rose from nil in 1965 to 116,000 tons in 1966 and 416,000 tons

---

[10] UN/ECA/FAO, *Report of the Economic Survey Mission on the Economic Development of Zambia*, Falcon Press, Ndola, 1964, Appendix A.

[11] Electricity and transport are not treated as imports, and no import content is assumed for them.

[12] R. E. Baldwin, op. cit., p. 37, estimated that only between 15 per cent and 20 per cent by value of the industry's operational requirements for stores were produced locally in 1960.

[13] See Table 9.1, item 9.

in 1967. Though this coal is not as suited for smelter operations as coal from Wankie, it has led to a reduction of K 1,080,000 in imports. Since 1964 ammonium nitrate for use in explosives has been prepared in Zambia, and in 1967 arrangements were concluded whereby Kobe Steel Ltd. will manufacture ammonium nitrate at Kafue for the production of fertilizers and explosives which will assist in the production of the blasting agent which is already being processed at Kafironda. Possibly the major advance in this direction is the intention to build the Kafue hydro-electric scheme, which, aside from its national importance, will produce the primary input used by the mines which has the largest import content.[14] In other respects the mines attempt to purchase as many of their requirements from domestic producers as possible, but this is limited to relatively simple inputs such as timber, foundry products, e.g. ball mill liners and ball mills, limestone, cement, oxygen, clothing, nuts, bolts and washers, and brick and cement products. In addition they also make considerable use of local service industry, light engineering and repair workshops, printing etc., though they have only recently started to make use of Zambian sub-contractors. Following a request by the President, the value of these contracts increased from K 48,000 for the period July-December 1967 to K 249,000 for January-June 1968,[15] with most of the work relating to general transport, land clearing, building, decorating, carpentry, supply of sand, crushed stone and brick, painting, township clearing, refuse removal, road construction, burglar proofing, glazing, sign writing, and grave digging, with 32 contracts awarded to private contractors and the remainder going to co-operatives.

From Table 9.2 (showing the disaggregated import bill of the mining industry) it can be seen that K 15,898,000, or more than 50 per cent, is represented by manufactured equipment in one form or another (sectors nos. 10, 11, 12, and 13). Closer examination will reveal these to be goods emanating from highly technical capital-goods-producing industries in advanced economies. A further K 6,836,000, or 21 per cent, is composed of chemicals and petroleum products (sector no. 7) for which only limited import substitution possibilities in the form of explosive processing can be considered economic in the near future. Many of the remaining items are either

[14] See Table 9.1, item 10.
[15] Ministry of Labour, *The Progress of Zambianization in the Mining Industry*, Government Printer, Lusaka, 1968, p. 6.

TABLE 9.2

Imports by the mining industry, 1966 (c.i.f. Zambian borders)

(*K'000*)

(1)	Farming, forestry and fishing	90
(2)	Metal mining	60
(3)	Other mining and quarrying	2,006
(4)	Textiles and wearing apparel	366
(5)	Sawmills and joineries	76
(6)	Paper and paper products	440
(7)	Chemicals and petroleum products	6,836
(8)	Bricks and clay products	1,156
(9)	Cement and cement products	92
(10)	Foundries and metal products	4,458
(11)	Electrical equipment	6,110
(12)	Transport equipment	3,630
(13)	Other manufactures	1,700
(14)	Electricity and water	1,180
(15)	Other transport	488
(16)	Unspecified	1,352
	Total imports	31,478

Source: *National Accounts 1964–1966* and *Input–Output Table 1966*, Central Statistical Office, Lusaka, 1968.

required in quantities too small for economies of scale in domestic production or are impossible to produce here because of their natural resource content, as in the case of refractory bricks in sector 8 and some of the mineral and quarry products in sector 3. In fact very few, if any, of the items imported are or could be produced in Zambia in the near future, with the exception of coal, some of the chemicals used in explosives, and electricity.[16]

All these imports are essential to the continued existence of the industry, so any change aimed at reducing them could only be effected through using more labour-intensive techniques, i.e. labour/capital substitution. On account of the non-linear production function this would reduce output and increase costs.[17] It would also have the effect of reducing profits, and to that extent be at the expense of profits and

[16] Electricity imports from Le Marinel were substantially reduced as from December 1966, when a second transmission line from Kariba came into commercial operation, from which date the Le Marinel connection was retained on a standby basis only.

[17] At the labour/output ratio prevailing in the early 1950s, the wage costs would be almost trebled at the 1968 wage and output levels.

taxation. Because there would be no compensating relief in royalty and export taxation this would act as a deterrent to further investment. On the other hand, the bigger labour force would increase the domestic consumer market, and also stimulate production of the implements required by the labour-intensive techniques. However, it is precisely on account of the higher supply cost of labour that the mines have substituted capital for labour, and as income generated by local payments depends on the multiplier as well as the multiplicand, it may very well be that there is greater redistribution of income through government expenditure of taxation than there would be through goods and factor payments.

ZAMBIANIZATION

Local payments by the mines are also being increased by the Zambianization of expatriate employment, and the expatriate wage bill, aside from being smaller than the African wage bill in 1966 for the first time in history, actually showed a decrease from K 44,842,000 to K 42,176,000. The figures below show past and projected Zambianization in the mines for the period December 1964 to December 1972.

TABLE 9.3
Progress of Zambianization

	Total no. of expatriates	Total no. of Zambians in field of expatriate employment
Actual		
December 1964	7,621	704
March 1966	6,592	1,138
September 1966	6,358	1,884
October 1967	5,671	2,617
June 1968	5,024	3,671
Forecast		
December 1969	4,444	4,102
December 1970	3,774	4,661
December 1971	3,551	5,195
December 1972	3,168	5,587

Source: Ministry of Labour, *The Progress of Zambianization in the Mining Industry*, Government Printer, Lusaka, December 1968, p. 9.

Aside from the welfare consideration of wage payments accruing to Zambian nationals, the Zambianized positions will involve Zambians in greater job responsibility and curtail the considerable outflow of personal savings that are currently being repatriated by non-Zambian miners.[18] Incomes of Zambians will probably be spent to a greater extent on items of local production in addition to saving foreign exchange.[19]

FORWARD LINKAGE

Until now all copper produced in Zambia has not led to forward linkages in that it has all been exported in blister or refined copper form and has not been used as an input for domestic industries. Recently the Industrial Development Corporation in conjunction with the mining groups has formed a metal fabricating company to produce electrical wire and cable with a projected output of K 6,000,000 and employment for 80 personnel. It also has plans for developing an export market, though this will have to be limited to the relatively small domestic markets of neighbouring countries on account of the familiar features of escalating tariffs around the larger markets of developed countries.[20] The absence of such a fabricating industry should therefore be viewed as a factor that has constrained the development forces of mining activity to the value added in the extraction, smelting, and refining stages, aside from the opportunity cost in income, employment, and foreign exchange entailed in having to import fabricated copper requirements.

[18] Expatriate employees incumbent at Independence are permitted to repatriate 30 per cent of their earnings, whilst later recruits are permitted 50 per cent. These figures take on added significance in view of the high salaries of expatriates, who between 1945–63 received almost twice the wage bill of Africans despite being outnumbered approximately 7:1.

[19] The import content of all personal consumption for Zambia (1966) is estimated at 23 per cent personal expenditure, and was as high as 33 per cent for the Federation according to the *National Account and Balance of Payment of Northern Rhodesia, Nyasaland and Southern Rhodesia 1954–1963*, Central Statistical Office, Salisbury, 1964, Table 10, p. 7 and Table 39b, p. 34. These figures would of course be higher still for the highly-paid Copperbelt workers. cf. A. G. Irvine, *The Balance of Payments of Rhodesia and Nyasaland 1945–1954*, Oxford University Press, London, 1959, pp. 604 ff.

[20] See H. G. Johnson, *Economic Policies Towards Less Developed Countries*, Allen and Unwin, London, 1967, pp. 90 ff. and B. Balassa, 'Tariff Protection in Industrial Countries—an Evaluation', *Journal of Political Economy*, 1965.

CONCLUSION

Even when the Zambianization programme is completed and when all the import substitution and forward linkage schemes become fully productive, it will still be likely that most of the domestic expenditures by the mines will be financial rather than goods and factor payments. Since these are linked more to profits and price rather than output and income they will make the economy very sensitive to world copper market conditions. Already the increases in domestic expenditures by the mines since Independence have been most marked in financial payments to government, and if the experiences of Chile[21] and other mineral-producing countries are anything to go by, further increases in economic integration of the industry in the economy are likely to be at the financial rather than the goods and factor level. The temporary restriction limiting the repatriation of dividends to 30 per cent of capital, provided that this is less than 50 per cent of profits, may have acted as a form of enforced re-investment in sophisticated cost-reducing techniques that reduced goods and factor integration, so that income-generating effects came to depend even more on the ability of the government to utilize the revenue so derived in productive activities.

Mining generally acts as a fountain-head for, rather than an engine of, growth in that it provides financial revenue rather than sustaining a high demand for domestically-produced goods and services in the host country. It requires a sensible all-round policy that will maximize local goods and factor payments without restraining the growth of the industry, for it is from the latter that the government derives its revenue for the execution of national development objectives. Perhaps the most serious drawback of mining is that whereas income generated by local payments tends to be relatively stable, it is smaller than the financial payments that are related to less predictable world market conditions and which often encourage otherwise injudicious policies designed to enlarge the former component of mine expenditure. Certainly measures that raise mining costs, thereby reducing profits and hence government taxation and possible re-investment without increasing goods and factor integration, do constrain the spread effects of mining activity, and it is in this category that some of the trade diversionary policies of

21 C. W. Reynolds, 'Development Problems of an Export Economy—the Case of Chile and Copper', op.cit., *passim.*

the government lie. Mining also requires a sensible utilization of government revenue, and to the extent that it is not exclusively expended on providing infrastructural facilities for the mines, it enables the government to finance schemes for developing other areas of the economy. During Federation not only did Zambia lose between K 160,000,000 and K 200,000,000 (which was between 40 and 50 per cent of all government revenue) but 'expenditure designed specifically to foster African rural development was surprisingly modest'[22]—not to mention the location of mine-oriented industries in Rhodesia that would otherwise have been located in Zambia. It has only been since Independence, when for the first time Zambia has control over its own economy, that it has been able to harness the growth forces of mining activity and channel these into broad development objectives. But whilst domestic payment by the mines is increasing and the government is embarking on a policy of investing in directly productive activities and social overhead capital, this revenue is not being raised in the most efficient manner nor is it being maximized in the long run. As emphasized in Chapter 6, the former royalty and export tax system, being determined solely by price and output and not at all by profitability, acted as a distinct disincentive to exploiting the lower-grade ores. This not only represented an opportunity loss of current income, employment, and taxation, but with the constantly increasing costs of production, their economic value may have been lost forever. The government could, if it pursued a policy of encouraging the production of lower-grade ores, increase the level of mining activity and at the same time prolong the life of the mines in a manner consistent with maximizing production using techniques that allow for the greatest spread effects. To this end the single most constraining factor is the absence of a comprehensive mining code that will permit the attainment of these objectives.

---

[22] R. E. Baldwin, op.cit., p. 186. See too R. Hall, *Zambia*, Pall Mall, London, 1965, p. 286: 'In Zambia a variety of areas and institutions related to a small proportion of the population has more or less monopolized private enterprise expenditure, and until recently government expenditure has been concentrated on the same areas'.

10

Constraints in Agriculture

R. A. J. ROBERTS AND CHARLES ELLIOTT[1]

INTRODUCTION

THE importance of agriculture in the Zambian economy can hardly be overemphasized. The dominant position of the copper industry modifies only the nature rather than the measure of that importance. While it is true that, unlike the countries of East Africa, Zambia is not dependent upon the agricultural sector to generate foreign exchange, the central fact is that any strategy of development that leaves unchanged the standard of life of the rural population will be judged as misconceived. Indeed, Zambian humanism, like 'Ujamaa', derives much of its inspiration from and gives much emphasis to the quality of life in the villages. Philosophically and politically, then, agricultural development has a unique importance. But from the point of view of the structural adaptation of the economy, the continuing reliance upon imports to meet the rapidly growing demand for food, the unabated drift of labour from the rural areas to the towns, and the failure of the agricultural sector to generate its own investment finance, all indicate both the serious problems that the process of agricultural modernization is raising, and the high priority that must be accorded their solution.

It is misleading, however, to conceive of the agricultural sector as a homogeneous productive unit. At the risk of oversimplifying the spectral character of the sector, as one group shades into the next, we have distinguished between three groups of farmers—large-scale commercial

[1] R. A. J. Roberts is Field Officer of the Universities of Nottingham and Zambia Agricultural Labour Productivity Investigation. Charles Elliott, formerly Reader and Head of Department of Economics in the University of Zambia, is now Assistant Secretary of the Committee on Society, Development, and Peace of the World Council of Churches and the Pontifical Commission Justice and Peace.

farmers (almost exclusively European), emergent farmers who sell more than 50 per cent of their crop, and subsistence farmers. Paradoxically, it is important to emphasize both the artificiality of this distinction and the fact that each group is, in an important sense, non-competitive with the other groups. Although recent organizational changes in credit and marketing have disguised the separation of the European farming community from the African, the large-scale farmers do not effectively need to compete for factors of production or markets with African producers. Equally, since subsistence farmers do not enter substantially the cash economy, they do not compete with emergent farmers for inputs: indeed typically their only inputs are their own labour, seed hoarded from the previous season, and ash or occasionally cattle manure.

To quantify these groups is almost impossible. In 1968 there were about 700 registered European farmers, who probably accounted for over 95 per cent of the large-scale non-state production. In terms of maize, non-Africans (i.e. Europeans and a very few Indians) produced over 60 per cent of the total crop, and although there have been fluctuations in that proportion, the share of the total maize crop produced by non-Africans has lain between 50 per cent and 70 per cent throughout the 1960s. Europeans produce all the milk and all the Virginia flue-cured tobacco, much of the cotton, and most of the better-quality beef and pork. Vegetables, eggs, and fowls have come increasingly from co-operatives situated close to the urban areas, while Turkish tobacco and pineapples have been the objects of major extension efforts in specific areas.

It is impossible to tell how many emergent farmers there are—or even how rapidly this crucial class is growing. An estimate based on the sale of maize would put the number of emergent farmers at around 30,000—or around 5 per cent of the rural population. But the emergent farmers are geographically concentrated along the line of rail, in the Eastern Province (a fairly narrow band following the Great East and Mundazi-Chipata roads), and, to a lesser extent, Luapula and Northern Provinces. This access to transport is no accident, and it is roughly true to say that the progressiveness of agricultural technique varies inversely with distance from the railway or an established first-class road: or to put it another way, the nearer one approaches good transport facilities, the higher the probability of finding large-scale farmers and the lower the probability of finding subsistence farmers.

In the pages that follow, we shall describe the principal bottlenecks restricting the development of each of the main groups of farmers: but, as an essential preliminary, we must assess the climatic and ecological environment within which all three groups have to operate.

PHYSICAL ENVIRONMENT

The physical environment within which agriculture is practised in Zambia must itself be recognized as one of the principal constraints on production. To the casual observer Zambia might appear to offer a hospitable environment for progressive agriculture. Frost is rare and in many parts of the country unknown; rainfall is reasonably predictable and confined to four months of the year; land and water are in plentiful supply; most cattle and crop diseases are remediable and easily recognized; and pests, particularly locusts and tsetse, are under control if not totally exterminated. But that gives a misleading impression. First, crude average rainfall figures disguise more than they reveal. Precipitation is intense, local, and, over the four-month 'rains' period (December to March), irregular, with the result that during the rains all but the most hardy crops are liable to extensive damage which is often exploited by pests and diseases acting on lacerated tissues. With precipitation rates of over an inch per hour by no means infrequent, sheet erosion is common and overgrazed land is soon marked by rapidly extending gullies. Conversely, long hot dry spells, particularly early in the season, can kill a newly planted crop: replanting is then hazardous since the season is already well advanced. The very local nature of heavy rainstorms implies that some farms will be suffering from drought while others close by are water-logged. In 1968 two farms in the Lusaka area had rainfalls differing by 28 inches, with the drier farm receiving only 8 inches. The farms were five miles apart.

Nor is the soil structure of most of Zambia very encouraging. The quantity of Class I soils, i.e. soils which will grow maize crops successively, is tiny in relation to the whole area of Zambia, and Class I and Class II soils together still represent less than 10 per cent of the whole surface. Typically, therefore, the soil needs careful husbanding and particularly the application of very substantial quantities of nitrogenous fertilizers, since all Zambian soils are deficient in nitrogen, and the technical problems of the introduction of legumes into pastures have still not been adequately solved. The nature of the soil, therefore, militates against an easy transformation of shifting cultivators to settled husbandmen.

As we have already hinted, the second major feature of the physical environment in which agriculture is conducted is the substantial transport costs incurred by most farmers off the line of rail, stemming from the original pattern of settlement and colonization of the country. Although in recent years the government has introduced a number of transport subsidies, both of inputs and of produce, the fact remains that the enhanced costs of inputs and reduced value of products erodes the margins of farmers off the line of rail to an extent that greatly reduces the incentive effect of any given price. Chapter 7 has already demonstrated this effect and shown how the high bulk/low value crops are particularly vulnerable to long hauls.

From the map on p. 202 it is obvious that distance from a processing plant or the final consumer has the same effect on the profits of the producer as a fall in the price of the product. This observation can lead to two different and conflicting conclusions. The first is that only high-value crops should be grown at great distances from the line of rail. The second is that transport should be subsidized in order to increase returns to rural producers. Both arguments will be examined in turn.

The former implies that under a completely rational location policy, the bulk/value ratio of crops would decline as distance from the main consuming or processing centres increased. Maize, for instance, would be grown near the line of rail; cattle would be produced in the next zone; and tobacco, exotic fruit, and vegetables would be produced furthest away. Such a locational policy would go far in equalizing the ratio of transport charges to net income for all producers. This argument may look appealing from the point of view of transport; from nearly every other point of view it is seriously deficient. It ignores interdependence of agricultural production. Maize is a stock feed and the grazing of stock on maize stover produces a costless and moderately effective fertilizer. Similarly the production of leguminous crops on maize land is a most beneficial rotation, but most legumes, e.g. beans and groundnuts, have a much lower bulk/value ratio than maize. Lastly, the distribution of farming skills in Zambia is the opposite of that required by the locational policy above. Those with the greatest technical skill and accumulation of capital are situated along the line of rail and in the Central and Southern Provinces. It would be a gross misallocation of resources and quite inequitable to permit those farmers to grow only maize.

A variant of this argument lays emphasis on the establishment of local processing plants as a means of reducing the bulk/value ratio of crops that have to be transported great distances; or, alternatively in a limited number of cases, of eliminating the need for transport altogether. The spinning of cotton, expressing of vegetable oils and sawing of timber are examples of the former; the grinding of mealie meal and the local slaughter and storage of cattle are examples of the latter. There is much in this suggestion, but an important question is that of the economic viability of the local processing unit, and the comparison between the economies of scale of a large unit which incurs large transport costs and a small local unit which does not. A further problem is that the financial costs of the two operations are easy to compare, but since they ignore the social and possibly the opportunity costs, they do not take full account of the factors involved. The *social (opportunity) cost* of manufacturing in Lusaka is the loss of employment in the rural areas. The opportunity cost of transporting bulky ground-nuts to Lusaka is the alternative use to which the transport could be put,[2] or the waste of valuable by-products that could be utilized by farmers.

The other possible conclusion is that since transport costs so closely affect the net returns to farmers, transport should be subsidized so that farmers pay less than the full cost of the service, thus reducing the impact of these costs on net revenue. There are serious objections to permanent subsidies. A traditional objection is that they obscure the real distribution costs. Both to the individual farmer and the industry as a whole, they make the marketing and distribution of the crop appear cheaper than they really are. It is therefore impossible to ascertain the true social costs and benefits of given crop and resource distributions. Implicit in this argument is the further belief that subsidies distort the distribution of crops by making it possible and profitable to grow crops with a high bulk/value factor at great distances from centres of consumption. A social cost is thus involved, since resources are misallocated, both in terms of productive use (i.e. growing maize instead of tobacco or cotton) and in terms of geographical distribution (i.e. producing crops at Mbala instead of Monze).[3] Now it must be admitted immediately that, *within its context,* this

---

[2] If the transport market were perfect and fully flexible, these opportunity costs would be reflected in the price charged for transporting groundnuts. But although there is flexibility and local divergences, price formation is seldom so sophisticated as to take account of opportunity costs.

[3] The likelihood of misallocation is increased if subsidies are direct (as in UK) rather than indirect in the form of non-chargeable overheads (as in Zambia).

argument is valid. But that context is nineteenth-century Europe and not twentieth-century Africa. It not only ignores the technical inter-dependencies described above, but also, and no less important, the political and social forces demanding the development of the rural areas on the base that already exists—predominantly low value/high bulk crops such as maize and sorghum. It would be no more practicable for the Zambian government to withhold subsidies to encourage high value crops in distant areas, than it would be to charge farmers for the extension service. Both could be defended on narrow classical grounds but both would be inconsistent in both the short run and the long run with rapid socio-economic advance in the rural areas.

There are basically two types of transport subsidy in Zambian agriculture—direct and indirect. A direct subsidy is paid only on inputs, principally fertilizer, to the more distant provinces. This naturally has the effect of making it more profitable to apply fertilizer and can therefore be regarded in the less progressive provinces as an expenditure on agricultural extension. As we shall stress below, one of the greatest disincentives to the use of modern techniques is the financial risk involved. The severity of the risk is a function of the initial outlay, with the result that reducing that outlay by transport subsidy on inputs is an attempt to moderate the risk for farmers. It might be objected that a more economic method of achieving the same end—i.e. of popularizing the use of fertilizer—would be to pay a subsidy only to the technically marginal farmers—i.e. to those farmers who are on the verge of adopting modern techniques. There is much in this argument, but the administrative difficulty of screening farmers makes it impracticable.

An indirect subsidy is paid when the services of the former Agricultural Rural Marketing Board, and its successor, the National Marketing Board, are given to farmers at below cost.

The extent to which systems of land tenure are a real constraint on agricultural output is a moot point. Most European farmers have either freehold or 999-year leases on what was formerly Crown land, and are therefore free from the alleged insecurity that less permanent types of tenure are said to bestow. The only class of farmer who could be said to suffer from the present system of land tenure is the emergent farmer, gradually selling a higher proportion of his crop. It has been argued that since these farmers do not have security of tenure they have no incentive to invest in permanent improvements in their land, e.g. fencing, drainage, irrigation, and building. However, there is increasing evidence that villagers are adapting to this situation and headmen in the more advanced areas connive at payment for improvements by incoming land-holders.

LARGE-SCALE COMMERCIAL FARMERS

Policy problems

There are two distinct problems facing policy-makers in the large-scale agricultural sector. The first is the growth of output; the second is the composition of output. The first is self-explanatory; the latter needs a word of explanation. In very broad terms, the most efficient perspective plan for Zambian agriculture would entail using the managerial skills, technical competence, and capital of the European farmers to produce pioneer and export crops—cotton, tobacco, fruit. 'Easy' crops for home consumption—beef, maize, vegetables, poultry— should be produced by Zambians on small or moderate-sized holdings, preferably (and in the case of most of the maize, essentially) near the line of rail. There are many reasons—geographic, agronomic, economic —why this division of labour cannot be implemented quickly and easily, but the vitally necessary restructuring of the sector, implying a much wider range of products and rapid growth of output in all but maize, can most efficiently begin with the large-scale commercial sector. In the discussion of constraints that follows we shall refer to both types of change in the sector. Since many constraints are common to both, we make no attempt to consider growth and restructuring as two separate policy objectives.[4]

Confidence

There can be little doubt that the most powerful constraint acting on the expatriate commercial sector is that of confidence. This is made up of three components: confidence in the industry, confidence in the political stability of the country, and confidence in the economic milieu in which the industry is conducted. Of these we shall consider at length only the first.

---

[4] In fact, of course, restructuring is the result of different rates of growth of each commodity *post-facto*.

By confidence in the industry we mean assurance that the price policies followed by the government will ensure a 'reasonable return' to the 'average' farmer. This was indeed the basis of maize pricing during Federation. By annual negotiation with the Ministry of (European) Agriculture, the European farmers were assured that the price of maize took account of the rising costs and the falling real value of constant money margins. Increases in efficiency were therefore pure gain. Although the inherent absurdity of combining this policy with that of limiting total (i.e. African and European) maize production to the size of the home market eventually brought to an end the automaticity of the protection of the real margins of the technologically stagnant, it did so only as the Federation began to show signs of breaking up.

The Zambian government has taken the view that maize exports, except to the Congo and, to a very much more limited extent, Angola and Mozambique, are unprofitable and uncompetitive as a result of high transport costs (approximately 70n per 100 miles per bag). Therefore production must be limited to the home market and the Congo.[5] The European farmers fear that this necessarily implies, in the long run, that the dreaded spectre of competition with African producers —a recurrent theme in European farming circles since the late 1920s— will become a reality. The following table shows how the maize production of African farmers has in fact increased. Although it is difficult to extrapolate from such an irregular series, Table 10.1 suggests that African-grown maize could meet all domestic requirements by the end of the 1970s.

The European farmers' fear that they will be competed out of maize production by African farmers is justified only if two implicit assumptions are correct. First, it must be the case that African producers' costs per unit of production are lower than those of European producers. This implies that the former use less inputs and/or do not pay the full cost of those inputs, or that they are more efficient managers. Both of the first two implications have been true in the past, and in some areas and for some kinds of farmers still are. But as mechanization spreads, as the cost of stumping rises (making more intensive use of existing land desirable and therefore increasing the input of fertilizer

[5] Congo (Kinshasa) is reliably reported to be willing to buy up to 2.9 m. bags of Zambian maize per year for six years at a price that would be (just) profitable to Zambia. Internal consumption is 2.5 m. bags and is rising. There is therefore ample scope for higher domestic production.

TABLE 10.1

Total maize deliveries to GMB in the year
ended 30 April
(in '000 standard bags)

Year	Non-African	African	Total
1954	600	467	1,067
1955	664	658	1,322
1956	606	433	1,039
1957	900	746	1,646
1958	1,174	883	2,057
1959	544	36	580
1960	1,021	516	1,537
1961	945	738	1,683
1962	1,298	955	2,253
1963	1,288	839	2,127
1964	655	354	1,009
1965	1,342	797	2,139
1966	2,129	675	2,804
1967	2,582	1,581	4,163
1968	2,552	1,579	4,131

Source: Grain Marketing Board, as quoted in Ministry of Agriculture *Monthly Economic Bulletin*, April 1968.

or decreasing the yield) and as budgetary shortfalls reduce generalized subsidies to African farmers, so the costs of production of such farmers are likely to rise to a level where they approach those of the European farmers. When to this is added the great disadvantage with respect to location and transport costs suffered by the majority of African farmers already amply discussed in Chapter 7, it is evident that the cost advantage of small-scale producers is not as great as is often supposed— except perhaps for producers relying exclusively on family labour. However, the contribution of these to total marketed output is small.

Secondly, the Europeans' fear implies that the long-run supply elasticity of African producers is greater than unity for upward price changes and less than unity for downward price changes. In other words, for African maize production to become a real threat to European producers, it would have to be the case that a rise in the GMB price greatly increased the African-grown crop while a fall in the price had little effect on output. In fact, of course, the data suggest the reverse— namely that African producers are moderately responsive to upward changes in price but highly responsive (negatively) to falls in price. Any downward adjustment of price is therefore more likely to increase the share of the European producer, at the same time as it reduces his profit per acre—and probably his total income from maize.

The European farmer would argue that, except in the longest run (a time period in which he is not usually interested) what matters is not his share of the domestic market but profit per acre. In the period 1965–8 costs rose from K 32 to K 42 per acre. As the introduction of SR52 maize was virtually complete by 1964, this increase in costs was not readily offset by gains in yield. To this extent, the European farmers feel that since Independence the pricing policy has been loaded against them. If by this they mean that profit margins have come under pressure, they are right. But from this it does not follow either that a decent living cannot be earned from maize or that for reasons we have already seen, in the medium term at least, the price is likely to be so low as to drive them out of production.

But the price of maize is not the only cause of concern. Beef prices were held constant from 1964 to 1967 and over this period many European producers came to the conclusion that intensive grass management and full supplementary feeding were not profitable, especially in light of the erosion of the quality bonus since Federation. Accordingly crude ranching methods continued to be used on most European farms and the total stock of beef cattle declined from 194,000 in 1962 to 136,000 in 1966 while cattle sold for slaughter fell from 30,000 in 1963 to 19,000 in 1966.[6] A significant fall in the off-take of the total herd is disguised by the fact that many herds were eliminated as farmers left the industry. This trend was reversed in 1968 by a substantial (38 per cent) increase in the average price paid by the Cold Storage Board for beef cattle, and although the prime object of the higher price was allegedly to encourage the traditional cattle-owner to sell, the most noticeable short-run effect was in fact to reverse the run-down of the European herd and increase the take-off.

One effect of the huge rise in beef prices has almost certainly been that the dairy herd has continued to contract. Milk prices have not risen substantially since Independence while costs, especially of labour and food-stuffs, have risen sharply. Even efficient producers situated near urban centres have therefore found their margins contracting dangerously and many have responded by selling off dairy stock as beef cattle and going over to beef production. The modest recovery of milk production in 1966 was not maintained in 1967 and, with milk's strongly rising domestic demand (partly resulting from a subsidized consumer price in areas of social need), the shortfall of domestic production can be expected to increase.

[6] 1667 showed very small recoveries in stock and sales.

But it is in tobacco where the disappointment over prices has been the most acute. The poor prices received by producers in 1966-8 resulted from a combination of factors which included dissatisfaction with the Lusaka sales floor and the new auctioning system employed there, a swing in demand towards lower grades of tobacco, and difficulties attending the outward transport of the leaf which made buyers reluctant to pay premium prices for good-quality leaf. More than any other crop produced in Zambia, tobacco is labour-intensive and demands a high level of managerial skill. Rapidly rising labour costs, the introduction of minimum housing requirements (valued at over K 450 per worker), and increasing labour unrest meant that the transfer earnings of the management involved tended to exceed the profits of the crop. Hence the production of Virginia flue-cured fell from 24 m. lbs in 1964 to 10.9 m. in 1967. Although the government has done much to encourage the production of tobacco, especially by the inauguration of a tenant farmer scheme, the large-scale producers are reluctant to invest heavily in a crop that is so dependent upon the two most difficult productive factors in the Zambian economy—semi-skilled labour and extra-territorial transport.

As a result of the decline in confidence in the industry, there has been a marked change in the pattern of large-scale commercial farming since Independence. The following table shows how the area under principal crops has experienced a marked swing away from the labour- and management-intensive crops towards the 'easy' crop of maize.

TABLE 10.2
Indices of area planted

Crops	1961	1962	1963	1964	1965	1966	1967
Tobacco	65.27	66.51	82.64	100.0	70.82	76.24	44.3
Maize	114.42	109.38	84.44	100.0	138.33	192.14	165.21
Other crops	135.14	120.95	105.40	100.0	61.35	75.00	n.a.
All crops	113.64	106.59	91.25	100.0	102.05	120.87	114.52

Source: Agricultural and Pastoral Production Statistics (for Commercial Farms only) 1966–67, Central Statistical Office, Lusaka, May 1967–8.

Together with this has gone a substantial rise in the productivity of land under maize—a two-fold increase 1961-6—and a fall for many other crops, especially tobacco.

With maize prices mainly strong,[7] the increase in the proportion of output accounted for by maize has been marked—52 per cent in

[7] See above pp. 209–10.

1961, 50 per cent in 1964, 68 per cent in 1966.

Similarly the investment pattern reflects conditions of uncertainty. The following table shows how the trend of three major components has been downward since 1962.

TABLE 10.3

Indices of sales to commercial farmers of vehicles, 1961–7
(1964: 100)

Farm machinery	1961	1962	1963	1964	1965	1966	1967
Tractors	102.40	101.05	98.74	100.0	87.64	84.27	84.53
Trucks and vanettes	—	104.91	104.91	100.0	90.39	99.25	102.00
Cars/station wagons	—	101.84	102.30	100.0	69.77	82.64	69.01

Source: Agricultural and Pastoral Production Statistics (for Commercial Farms only) 1966–67, Central Statistical Office, Lusaka, May 1967–8.

However, investment in labour-saving machinery—e.g. harvesters, electric milking machines, and tower silos—has tended to increase. The point here is precisely that those items are substitutes for labour and thus allow a farmer to handle the same acreage with a smaller work force. Output per man in the sector has thus risen from K 504 in 1961 to K 780 in 1966 (market prices).

One additional effect of the decline in confidence has, of course, been a drop in the number of farmers actually operating. Although not an entirely accurate guide, membership of the Commercial Farmers' Bureau dropped from 1,200 in 1964 to 550 in 1969.[8] A further reason for this drop in numbers has been the high transfer earnings for Europeans with managerial or mechanical skill. The additional attraction of geographical mobility forfeited by ownership of land has an appeal inversely related to confidence in the political stability of the country.

Credit

Given this poor performance in investment when investment and seasonal funds were plentiful for most commercial farmers, it may seem contrary to argue that one of the most important constraints on the industry since the Mulungushi Reforms has been the shortage of capital —both working and fixed.

The sector has traditionally been a substantial borrower, primarily

---

[8] The 1964 figure probably exaggerates the number of real farmers. One thousand may be a better estimate.

but not exclusively on a crop-season basis. The Land Bank was, until 1966, the principal source of funds for the sector: its loans had grown in the Federal era from K 1 m. in 1954 to K 11 m. by 1966. The commercial banks were also heavily involved: from their point of view seasonal loans were an ideal investment. In 1966, the banks lent K 1.5 m. to the sector. It is hard to overemphasize the crucial role this finance played in the operations of most farmers. With average direct costs in 1966 of K 35 per acre of maize, the working capital required for European-grown maize alone was over K 6 m. A relatively modest farm of, say, 500 acres with 200 acres under maize and the rest ranchland would require a working capital of around K 8,000. Given the history of the sector and particularly the Federal government's attempts to lure immigrants without great resources of capital, the dependence of most farmers upon the Land Bank or the commercial banks for working capital was extreme. Although many made substantial profits in the mid-60s which, unlike in Federal days, were not reinvested in the industry, bank lending to the industry remained critical. [9] When this source of finance was abruptly turned off in 1968, the commercial farmers were left in an extremely exposed situation. Technically, the Credit Organization of Zambia became the sole supplier of credit to the industry, but administrative problems within the organization meant that a proportion of loan applications were dealt with too late to allow planting for the 1968/9 season.

Clearly it is still too early to ascertain whether the shortage of seasonal credit will become a permanent feature of large-scale farming in Zambia. It is already obvious, however, that unless realistic steps are taken to ensure an adequate, properly administered flow of credit to the sector, production will be further distorted (from capital-intensive to capital-cheap crops), and will almost certainly fall. If it becomes necessary to reduce the total flow of credit to the sector—in order, for instance, to increase the availability of capital to small-scale farmers—the premium on proper organization and administration is even greater. Crop plans can be revised in July but not in December.

Technology

There can be little doubt that, given the size of the sector, the Northern Rhodesian commercial farmer was one of the best served in the world

---

[9] It seems that many commercial farmers were remitting large sums abroad

in terms of research and extension input. After Independence the research effort was maintained until 1967 when the Agricultural Research Council—a Federal creation—was abolished. Thereafter a number of agricultural scientists of considerable renown left the country and the emphasis on research was both reduced and redirected. With the combination of European and African farming under one ministry after Independence it was inevitable that the former should lose its privileged claim on scarce extension resources. Decisions in both fields were perhaps unavoidable, but their implications are serious.

For as long as Zambia maintains a pool of experienced farmers who have had the benefit, albeit privileged and inequitable, of the Federal research and extension system, the technical level of large-scale farming, *under existing regimens and techniques*, will remain relatively high. But as this pool contracts,[10] and, more important, as the need increases to diversify from well-known crops into new ones—e.g. cotton, fruit, tea, coffee, large-scale vegetables—so the level of technical competence is likely to decline, with all that that implies for input-output ratios.

Labour

Labour cannot be said to be a constraint in the sense of being in short supply. Unskilled farm labour is in almost totally elastic supply. However, the sector shares, perhaps to a greater degree than any other, in the general shortage of skilled labour. In general, as can be seen from Table 10.4, agricultural wages are lower, skill for skill, than in other occupations, and in non-monetary terms the sector competes poorly with urban-based occupations. The tendency to use labour more efficiently and more productively, illustrated in Table 10.5, springs from two basic causes.

First, largely as a result of the Minimum Wage Orders, wages have risen rapidly in the sector, from K 120 p.a. in 1960 to K 190 in 1966. This is illustrated in Table 10.4. Further, minimum housing requirements, which came into force in 1968, effectively meant a

after Independence, in many cases with the object of buying land elsewhere.

10 The rate of emigration of large-scale farmers with high technical competence is largely, of course, determined by the confidence factor already discussed. Further the extent to which some new techniques—e.g. spray weed control—can be applied depends upon the availability of seasonal finance.

TABLE 10.4

Average annual earnings of employees by industrial sector

(K p.a.)

Sector	1960	1961	1962	1963	1964	1965	1966
Agriculture, forestry, fishing	120	120	128	132	176	172	190
Mining and quarrying	570	578	592	596	732	826	934
Manufacturing	236	274	284	346	406	486	478
Construction	236	240	254	276	286	322	332
Electricity, water, sanitary services	210	248	260	254	320	388	456
Commerce	232	268	300	314	388	464	488
Transport and communications	292	345	388	426	482	486	688
Services (excluding domestic)	256	284	300	328	392	458	526
Domestic services	162	170	180	186	196	216	248

Source: Monthly Digest of Statistics, Central Statistical Office, Lusaka, 1967.

TABLE 10.5

Index of physical and value labour productivity, 1961–6[1]

	1961	1962	1963	1964	1965	1966
Physical (crops only)	72	75	58	100	122	303
Value (crops and livestock at market prices)	85	79	79	100	116	145

[1] Comparable figures are not available for 1967.

Sources: Indices of Production: *Census of Agricultural and Pastoral Production,* 1966.

Employment: *Monthly Digest of Statistics,* Central Statistical Office, Lusaka.

capital charge of K 450 per man employed, thus providing a powerful stimulus to mechanization.

Second, and probably more important, has been the problem of labour discipline. Particularly with highly time-sensitive crops such as tobacco, the risk inherent in labour unrest is so acute as to drive the farmer out of that crop and into less time-sensitive and labour-intensive crops.

For both these reasons, then, the *quality* of labour constraint has tended to discourage the degree of restructuring that the sector, and the economy as a whole, so urgently needs. The tendency has inevitably been to abandon labour- and technique-intensive crops such as tobacco and vegetables and to expand the production of commodities that can be easily mechanized and/or require modest inputs of unskilled labour—maize, cotton, beef.

EMERGENT FARMERS

By emergent farmers we mean those who sell between 50 and 100 per cent of their crop and who practise some or all of the improved technology characteristic of commercial farmers but whose scale of operation is, by definition, too small to be ranked with that of commercial farmers. These farmers have, therefore, overcome many of the constraints on subsistence producers without yet encountering those of the large-scale producers. In many ways they are the most interesting group in Zambian agriculture, since on them depends the long-run future of the industry.

Motive power

There can be little doubt that the principal constraint facing these producers is that of motive power. In general they have sufficient skill to grow maize or groundnuts in considerable quantities—say up to 100 acres—and since they provide their own seed and apply only limited fertilizer, on which credit is usually readily available, working capital is not a real problem. But fixed capital, in the form of motive power, is the most obvious constraint, since that alone determines how much a man can plough and, no less important, how much he can weed during those two crucial months, December and January. This has been appreciated for some time in Zambia, but the wrong conclusions have been drawn. The Seers Report, for instance, saw the motive power constraint as the prime justification for a massive farm mechanization—'tractorization'—programme.

Mechanization in this context means, basically, the use of tractors for cultivation. The need for this arises from the limited area of land that can be cultivated by hand, hoe or ox-plough in readiness for the optimal time of seeding. The physical opportunity for this mechanization is great. To a large, but not precisely known, extent, tractors would enable settlement to penetrate the margin of tsetse-infested areas and thus to cultivate land which the fly denies the ox. Mechanization may also raise output significantly in the same oxen-ploughed lands, and in further large, but imprecisely known, areas of bush and veld fallow.

It may be objected that mechanization is inappropriate in circumstances where unemployment is chronic and heavy underemployment is the general rule. Despite the general surplus of labour in Zambia, however, there is evidence of inadequate labour in the fields at the time of cultivation, and but for this, more crops could be sown, and certain highly profitable crop rotations made practicable. Mechanization could therefore lead to more output and higher net income per unit of labour of the present rural labour force. This is feasible not merely through sowing larger areas and reducing the area of unproductive fallow; other practices necessary to increase production quickly become associated with mechanization. For instance, to the extent that tractors replace oxen, the quality of beef production can be improved and its quantity increased.

Despite these potential benefits, attempts to mechanize agriculture in Africa have not always been successful . . .[11]

This policy was enthusiastically adopted by subsequent ministers and it was not until the President's strictures on ill thought out mechanization programmes in his Mulungushi speech that this enthusiasm was tempered with restraint. In the meantime the value of the import of tractors and spares doubled between 1964 and 1967. The resultant waste is impossible to quantify, but it is nearly true that it would be difficult to find a village in the more advanced areas of the country without a tractor rendered useless by lack of servicing and/or spares. This vast scrap heap represents no more than a burden of irredeemable—but often dishonoured—debt around the necks of the more advanced farmers who, by definition, were the first to plunge into this innovation. More mischievous still, it justifies scepticism of and disillusionment with advanced techniques—not only mechanization but the use of improved seeds, better cultural practices and a higher standard of management. Identified with mechanization, these essential improvements were jeopardized by the wholesale mechanical failures of the tractors.

Immediately it must be recognized that the problem is not simple. Ox cultivation is suitable on the lighter soils in areas where there is no risk of tsetse infestation. But trained oxen are no longer easy—or cheap—to acquire and the rise in beef prices has accelerated their disappearance. Semi-tractors or Western-type market garden implements have not proved tough enough to withstand Zambian conditions and anyway lack the enormous prestige effect of a four-wheel tractor. Further, they cannot be used as rural taxis—a most important source of revenue for many tractor owners in the winter.[12] Tractor pools look a

---

[11] Seers Report, op. cit., p. 62.

[12] One of the authors knows of a tractor-taxi service that plies between Mumbwa and the Copperbelt—to the operator's great profit.

sensible solution on paper—high use-intensity, adequate maintenance, lower cost per acre for the individual, and easy transformation into co-operative ownership and operation—but the administrative and technical problems have so far proved formidable. One case was discovered, certainly extreme, where full costs exceeded K 100 per operating hour. Further, as with all such schemes, very few individuals can have their operations performed in accordance with the ideal time-profile; and with a crop as time-sensitive as maize this is a serious disadvantage. It may well be the case, therefore, that individual tractor ownership is the long-run solution, but a solution that is only viable when a vastly improved maintenance service is readily available in the field. Certainly in the short run Zambia can no longer afford either the finance or the foreign exchange implied in the policies of 'mechanization by saturation' that were in vogue 1964–7. In the short run, mechanization can best be promoted by loans to individual contractors. Such contractors should be mechanically competent and financially strong enough to undertake loans on a proper commercial basis.

Capital

As far as *financial* capital is concerned a strong case can be made for the opinion that emergent farmers have been constrained by the quality of credit available rather than by the quantity.[13] Since 1964 Zambian farmers have usually had easy access to credit, particularly for seasonal loans of fertilizer and tractor hire. In fact, so great has been the desire of credit officers, at the district level, to make their area stand out as a successful development district, that farming loans have been seemingly forced on people who have had no desire to receive them. The other recipients of loans suffered because no proper study was given to the individual loanee, with the consequent drawing up of unrealistic farming programmes involving inputs far beyond the management capacity of the farmer. Loan repayment facilities, usually arranged by stop order on the produce sold, is only effective when a loanee produces a saleable surplus. In the case of many marginally emergent farmers no such surplus has been consistently produced; when it has, it has been sold privately in order to bypass the stop order system. Thus the govern-

---

13 By 'quality of credit' we mean the administration of individual loans—this includes the prior assessment of the loanee's farm production capacity, the production programme, and the loan servicing arrangements.

ment farm credit system, itself subject to pressures to achieve the maximum in the minimum time and judged solely on loans granted, has forced emergent farmers into the situation where they have been unable to use credit effectively and have thus had a poor introduction to improved farming techniques. To this extent, the credit programme may be regarded as having hindered the permanent acceptance of the improved techniques necessary to bring about an increase in agricultural production.

The two biggest farm machinery supply firms operate a credit system for emergent as well as commercial farmers. These loans, of necessity, have been on normal business lines, with character security being used in some cases. Because of the small extent of these private credit operations, individual attention has been given to each loan with the result that the loanees have been able to service their loans and make satisfactory profits.

Land

On the supply side, brief mention may be made of further constraints operating on this class of farmer. The first is land. We have already suggested that, despite the theoretical legal and traditional position, actual practice has been accommodated to the need for an improving farmer to be recompensed for his investments. In areas most heavily settled by emergent farmers, therefore, land tenure is not often a practical difficulty. But the availability of additional land can be. The normal process of enlarging holdings is by clearing contiguous land. Clearly this process can continue only while uncleared land is vacant between farms, and there inevitably comes a time when an expanding farmer finds there is no free land adjacent to his holding. This position has already been reached in parts of the Southern, Central, and Eastern Provinces. Fragmentation is the inevitable result if enlargement is to continue from the same homestead. The farmer is thus faced with a choice. He can cease to enlarge his holding; he can clear land some distance from his present holding; or he can move out of the area altogether and start clearing new land in a less densely settled area. This last alternative is unattractive since it ignores tribal and kin bonds as well as the possibility of capital loss implicit in abandoning cleared land if no 'purchaser' can be found. An ambitious farmer is unlikely to find the first alternative more acceptable, especially if he realizes that he has spare capacity within his farming unit—e.g. a tractor owner will only be making optimal use of his resources when he has 100–200 acres under the plough. Fragmented holdings are therefore becoming more common in the three advanced provinces, with all the inefficiencies they entail. In some areas, especially in the old reserves in the Southern Province, there is no unused land available, with the result that expansion of the existing enterprise is not possible. However, it does not necessarily follow that land is then a real constraint on output. Since yields are usually low—i.e. less than 12 bags of maize per acre—output can be increased by more intensive farming methods: more fertilizer, better weed and pest control, more regular spacing, and the use of hybrid seed. Only when diminishing returns to those factors set in can land be said to be a real constraint.

Labour

These techniques, however, demand a greater input of labour, and that brings us to consider the availability of this factor to the emergent farmer. By definition, the latter is still dependent upon his family for the bulk of his labour supply. It may be supplemented, however, by hired labour and occasional exchange of labour service with neighbours. Although in theory labour can readily be hired—since the supply of labour is highly elastic—in practice farmers are often reluctant to become dependent upon employees and tend to view them as a marginal reserve for use when family labour is temporarily inadequate. Cases of semi-permanent employment appear rare despite the fact that marginal returns to labour are high.[14] Where labour is a non-substitutable input, therefore, it can set a limit to production. The most obvious case is that of the hoe-cultivators who sell a high proportion of their crop. Their output is limited by their labour and much the same is true of those who are dependent on hired tractors for ploughing and who subsequently plant and weed by hand. The labour supply problem has its principal effect, however, in limiting the range of crops a farmer is prepared to produce. The more labour-intensive crops—tobacco, cotton, and groundnuts—decrease in attraction, *ceteris paribus*, in proportion as they threaten or seem to threaten, the success of staple food crops—maize and sorghum. In so far as peak labour requirements coincide in December and January, only farmers with the most plentiful labour supply can countenance diversifying into these crops.

---

[14] E. S. Clayton, 'Labour Use and Farm Planning in Kenya', *Empire Journal of Experimental Agriculture*, Vol. 28, No. 110, 1960.

Extension

The emergent sector, compared with the subsistence sector, receives much attention from the Extension Service. However, the actual contact men of the Extension Service, the crop demonstrators and animal husbandry officers, are not of a sufficiently high calibre to make much difference to farming decisions. Frequently these extension officers learn from the more successful emergent farmers, rather than the other way round. At the same time the typical farmer is not a good farm manager and much productive capacity is wasted because of poor management decisions.

Marketing

The final constraint is that of marketing which, with the effect of transport on farmers' returns, has been discussed in Chapter 7. These considerations apply particularly to emergent farmers in the Eastern Province, who, in 1968, refused to sell their maize because the charges made by the Eastern Province Co-operative Marketing Association were considered to leave too small a net margin. Of the charges made by EPCMA the greatest was for transport, but the administrative efficiency of the association was so low that other charges climbed to insupportable heights. Yet the association's difficulties are typical. Collecting grain from a huge and ill-developed area, storing it, grading it, and transporting it is no inconsiderable feat. Since EPCMA handles beans, cotton, and groundnuts as well, the administrative task of keeping accurate accounts for all its members is immense. With the shortage and cost of manpower it is no surprise that the EPCMA virtually broke down in 1968.

Elsewhere farmers are dependent upon the National Marketing Board, in which the former Grain Marketing Board and African Rural Marketing Board were combined in 1969. In general the provincial organization of the board is considerably stronger than EPCMA, but the charges levied by the board are still substantial. Nonetheless there is in the board's pricing structure an element of subsidy, in so far as the large line of rail producers pay a disproportionately high share of the cost of the board's services.

Livestock

As far as livestock are concerned the distinction between emergent and subsistence farmers tends to break down, in so far as neither group produces cattle on a commercial basis. The only significant differentiation is the sign of the supply elasticity. The numbers of Zambian cattle owners who respond positively to changes in price are small and largely limited to the Southern and Central Provinces. In considering the constraints on cattle production, therefore, we can distinguish between constraints on *supply* and constraints on *sales*.

Supply

Constraints on supply are threefold. First and most important is the very low rate of reproduction, stemming largely from low standards of management. A recent survey of cattle owners and caretakers in Barotse Province revealed that, contrary to the claims of Gluckman, the Lozis are largely ignorant of elementary facts of breeding such as length of oestral cycle, gestation period, and optimal growing rates. Such practices as castration, dehorning, and deworming are rarely followed except in the immediate environment of the Veterinary Department, and supplementary feeding in winter is quite unknown.

Second, mortality among cattle and particularly calves is high. To some extent this is attributable to the common practice of milking cows with calf at heel and thus reducing the milk available to the calf. In adult cattle, disease and predators take a very heavy toll.

Third, wherever tsetse are prevalent, cattle cannot be kept by villagers. The tsetse-free areas of Zambia are limited to a corridor 150–200 miles wide up the line of rail, the Zambesi flood plain, the northern parts of Northern Province, and parts of the Eastern Province.

Sales

Constraints on sales are three. First, among many cattle-owning tribes, it is customary for many members of a kin group to have a share in a given animal. The sociological explanation of this is complex, and includes notions of familial ties, witchcraft, and religious bonds. Economically, the result is that it is seldom possible to obtain universal approval of a sale since one or more 'owners' are absent. This is especially the case where urban migration is important. It would be considered highly improper to sell a beast without the consent of all the owners unless there was an emergency, or particularly important social occasion, or the beast was about to die.

Second, a large but indeterminate number of cattle are killed in the villages, thus reducing the volume of commercial sales. Cattle may be slaughtered in the villages for ceremonial occasions—in which there is no cash transaction—or because the beast is about to die or because the owner(s) need cash. In the latter cases, the meat is sold locally at 20n–25n per lb—a rate which often gives the owner a higher return than he would obtain from selling the beast on the hoof to a butcher or the Cold Storage Board.

Third, and most important, cattle are not sold because they represent a store of value and a source of prestige. This argument is well known. Cattle are sold if money is urgently required and no other resources are available. The most frequent needs are clothing, medicines, food in times of crop failure and, until recently, school expenses. Writing of the Lozis in the Mongu area, Jo Lutke-Entrup had this to say:

Only for necessary things like food needs or school expenses do they seem to be prepared to sell cattle. If this is accepted as true and if the increasing effect of incentives is lacking and if price reductions or taxes are impracticable for any reasons there is not much hope of increasing the cattle-take-off considerably in the near future. School expenses certainly had and still have a positive effect on cattle sales. It is said that before school expenses were almost entirely covered by the Government, and when boarding school fees were about £18/ year, this amount could only be submitted by the parents after having sold a head of cattle. Very often the informants referred to school expenditure when asked about the reason for selling cattle. It is a delusion to expect a higher sale rate after having reduced the cash needs of the people. Almost the same applies to price incentives; if the cattle owner can cover more cash needs by a smaller number of sales due to higher prices and if his cash needs do not increase, he is likely not to react in the expected way but to sell the same amount or even less. This negative supply elasticity is demonstrated by the answers to questions about reaction to price changes: only five out of 121 said that they would react positively on a short-term price increase (the question was: 'If the CSB from now on pays £5 more per head for the next two months, would you sell cattle during this time ?'). To find out the reaction on a long-term price increase, the following question has been asked: 'If the CSB from now on pays £10 more per head, will you sell more, less, or the same number as before ?' Eleven informants said that they would sell more, 46 said that they would sell less, and 65 said that they would sell the same number as before.[15]

One final point needs emphasis. Cattle are more than a source of meat and milk. There can be little doubt that they have contributed substantially to the progress of African farming in the Southern, Eastern, and parts of Central Province, since they provide both a

[15] *Preliminary Report on Socio-Economic Survey of Barotse Cattle Industry,* (mimeo), 1967, Ministry of Agriculture, Lusaka.

source of fertilizer and motive power. To this extent, their absence in the tsetse areas represents the lack of two of the most crucial inputs in small-scale farming.

SUBSISTENCE FARMERS

The generally accepted definition of a subsistence farmer is one who sells less than half, by value, of his total production. His needs for food, fuel, and some fibre are supplied directly by his own labour. Within the subsistence sector of the economy the predominant feature of the control of production and distribution is that it is social. The economic activities of the people are embedded in the social structure of their society so that it is difficult to isolate an economic system from the all-embracing social control of the society. Thus the constraints on agricultural production by the subsistence sector are largely social and cultural in nature. Social factors are those involving the pattern of life and customs of the people; cultural factors are those involving their values and aspirations. As subsistence farmers form the bulk of the population of Zambia, it is in this sector that small, general improvements in input can bring about great increases in total production. Nevertheless, it is widely recognized that overcoming the constraints on this sector is necessarily a slow process.

Social environment

By and large the subsistence farmer lives far from the line of rail and therefore from transport and markets. Thus the constraint of transport cost, discussed above, operates more fully on the subsistence sector than on other sectors. Equally, the lack of the demonstration effect of town and shops results in a lowered demand for cash. Items such as clothing, not normally obtainable by subsistence farming, are commonly provided by wage-earning relatives. The social ties between those in paid employment and their village-dwelling relatives, though gradually weakening, are still strong enough to make the transfer of goods and money from urban areas to the villages a significant factor in the economic life of villagers, in that it reduces still further the incentive to produce a saleable surplus in their farming operations.

Education, used in the broad sense to include agricultural extension, has had little positive influence on the development of agriculture in this sector. The education purveyed has been of the European type, teaching European ways, values, and technology. But European farming methods are so far removed from what seems possible to the subsistence farmer that he feels it futile for him to take any steps at all in the direction of improving his input to bring about an increase in production. The Extension Service, the educational wing of the Ministry of Rural Development, is unable to reach every farmer in the country. Thus, like its predecessors in colonial and Federation times, it operates a 'reinforcement of success' policy which ensures that the production and development gap between the subsistence and emergent sectors is widening.

Investment

Investment of private *money* in farming input is practically non-existent in the subsistence sector. What investment there is takes place in the few areas where it is possible to hire privately owned tractors to plough the land. The aim of this type of investment is to reduce the work load rather than to increase production, the area ploughed by the tractor being no larger than that formerly dug by hand. Practically all subsistence farmers have some capital in the form of cash. Their reluctance to invest this in farming input stems from three main sources. Firstly, they use their cash savings as a form of contingency insurance. Traditional society had built-in safeguards in case of disaster. These safeguards, based on collective responsibility in the village, still exist, but the additional safeguard of the individual's cash reserve shows the extent to which economic factors have changed without a corresponding change in social modes. Secondly, subsistence farmers are, in the main, ignorant of the costs and returns associated with, for example, the use of improved seed or fertilizer. Coupled with this is the fact that in many areas of the country such input is difficult, if not impossible, to buy locally. Thirdly, and this factor also stems partly from ignorance, the subsistence farmer would regard investment in farming as risky and therefore in conflict with the first motive above.

Investment of government loan money in subsistence agriculture has increased greatly in recent years. It is well known that the repayment record for this type of loan has been extremely poor, being, at the time of writing, something less than 10 per cent. Basically the cause of this low rate has been poor administration, resulting both in the granting of loans to farmers who have proved unable to service them and in lack of action against defaulters. Both of these factors point to the fact that loans have been given and obtained without due attention to their purpose, which is to increase production and money income, the value of the increased production being greater than the amount of the loan. The short-term result of the government loan programme to subsistence farmers has indeed been to increase and diversify production. The achievement of a surplus of maize in the Northern Province is a case in point. But this has been achieved at tremendous cost to the government, even if some of the amount involved is written off as having been a politically necessary fruit of Independence. The long-term effects of the loan programme are even more serious than this large wastage of money. Subsistence farmers are developing a 'loan complex', in that obtaining a government loan is regarded as a necessary precondition for the use of modern inputs. This is restricting the development, in the subsistence sector, of attitudes that would favour investment of farmers' own money in the purchase of farming inputs.

This raises the general issue of the nature of what may be called the loan elasticity of supply in the subsistence sector. Although research continues, initial impressions are that diminishing returns set in very early and returns become negative long before casual observation would suggest that saturation has been reached. If this is so, the era of financial austerity heralded by the 1969 budget speech may have very little effect on output in the subsistence sector. The possibility is that it will actually increase it.

Labour and Management

Studies elsewhere in Africa and a study in Zambia, as yet unpublished, suggest that the available labour in the subsistence sector is working at, or close to, maximum capacity. Idleness, so often apparently observed amongst subsistence farmers, is in reality the fulfilling of the social obligations of village life during periods of low work demand in the farming programme. The volume of available labour is further reduced by the migration of the young and able to the urban-industrial sector. But more important as a constraint is the lack of managerial ability and technical knowledge. This results in much of the labour input being used inefficiently at a time when labour has a high opportunity cost. For instance, in the Eastern Province a simple change in the method of planting groundnuts could save up to 40 per cent of the time required for harvesting. Naturally, the lack of managerial ability shows up most when a farmer uses a new technology. Fertilizer, for instance, is applied haphazardly in the wrong quantities at the wrong times. Phosphatic fertilizer is often used as a side-dressing applied when the maize is already four feet high. Farmers then complain that it is ineffective.

Part of the reason for the lack of managerial ability is that the farmer is not governed entirely by the profit motive. He is obliged to make economic decisions on resource allocation within a social framework that does not allow economic factors to act unfettered.[16]

Effects of Urban Elitism

Another constraint on the incentive to produce a saleable surplus is a result of Independence. Firstly, villagers have been promised great benefits by politicians. Inevitably most of these benefits have not materialized. But the original promises have developed in the villagers the dangerous attitude to development that they are to be recipients only; that material benefits will come to them eventually by political machination in Lusaka rather than by their own efforts in the rural areas. Secondly, the concept of individual wealth causing social difficulty within a village has often been quoted as being a constraint of agricultural production. However, there is evidence that this concept has altered in recent years to include the élites in urban areas rather than the relatively rich within the village who make an effort to produce a saleable surplus. Independence has brought the European trappings of wealth—fine houses, modern cars—to a large number of Africans and thus, as is well known in other countries too, created new élites. Subsistence farmers are painfully aware of the difference between their own standard of living and that of these new economic and political élites. Brought up in the socialist traditions of the village, where excessive wealth on the part of any one individual was once frowned upon, they feel that it is up to the wealthy urban Africans to share with the poor before the poor need do anything to help themselves.

Cultural change

By definition, the subsistence farming sector has yet to make much of an impact on the cash economy of the country. The farmers handle

---

16 For further analysis of this point, see C. M. Elliott, 'Agriculture and Economic Development in Africa', in E. L. Jones and Stuart Woolf, *Agricultural Growth and Economic Development*, Heinemann, London, 1969.

cash, certainly, but a great deal of it is hoarded, or merely exchanged within the village 'beer economy'. The economic development necessary to bring about their fuller participation in the cash economy of Zambia is dependent on changes in farming technology, in cultural factors, and in the social structure of the village. These changes cannot take place in isolation;[17] they must complement one another. Improvements in technology depend, *inter alia*, on receptivity to education (hence the importance so far appreciated but not implemented of producing education of a suitable type) and on attitude to investment. Cultural changes are therefore necessary in order to produce new sets of values and aspirations. Finally, none of these changes can be lastingly effective if changes are not made in the social framework of the sector. The subsistence farming sector is backward, but it is not stagnant. Development is taking place and some of the constraints mentioned above, particularly as regards marketing infrastructure, are being overcome. Continuing progress in development depends on striking a balance between economic and technological development on the one hand and cultural and social changes on the other.

CONCLUSION

We have shown that rapid progress in the agricultural sector is politically and economically crucial, and have described the areas in which that progress is likely to be most difficult. If the recent history of agricultural policy in Zambia is unhappy, with many failures, inconsistencies, and hesitations, some consolation can be found in the fact that this is by no means unusual. There is scarcely a developing country in the world where agricultural policy has been wholly or even mainly successful. In Zambia's case, the natural complexity of the agronomic problems has been compounded by the range of agricultural skills which policy must mobilize and it would perhaps be a fair criticism that policy has too often failed to distinguish between these different groups. Although it is often impossible to have one policy for one group and an inconsistent one for another, in credit, marketing, and pricing we have shown

---

17 Labour migration of Lozis under the WENELA scheme resulted in economic change in the form of money inflow into the then Barotseland. But this economic change was unaccompanied by the other necessary types of change. Thus no real development resulted.

how policies that may have been appropriate for one group have been inappropriate and even destructive for another. It therefore becomes even more important to select the key group and consistently adopt policies that will evoke the required responses from that group, and make good deficiencies created by contrary responses from other groups by state action, including direct participation where this is appropriate.

A final obvious point is worth emphasizing. We have stressed the counter-productive effect of ill-considered policies, even when they result in the transfer of resources from the urban-industrial sector to the rural sector. That emphasis should not disguise the fact that the absorptive capacity of the rural sector has increased substantially since Independence as a result of a relatively high level of infrastructural investment. Yet the flow of resources to the rural sector actually fell in 1969 and it is a strange commentary on government priorities that one of the biggest cut-backs in budgetary allocations in the deflationary budget of that year fell on the Ministry of Rural Development. This raises the question of official determination to revolutionize rural life. Despite enthusiastic utterances, a revolutionary zeal has not yet appeared when scarce resources are distributed. In the allocation of manpower, in the petty politicking over departmental jurisdictions, in the gingerly approach to school syllabus reform, in the reluctance to improve radically the farmers' terms of trade *vis-à-vis* the urban sector, and in the increasing social distance between the rural and urban populations, one senses a lack of resolve, perhaps of necessary fanaticism, to solve almost insoluble problems. Agricultural revolutions do not happen: they are created.

11

The Development of the Manufacturing Sector

MICHAEL FABER[1]

INTRODUCTION

TABLE 11.1 shows the growth of the manufacturing sector in the economy as a whole in Northern Rhodesia from 1954 to 1963 and in Zambia from 1963 to 1967. In real terms, the volume of manufactured output grew at an average rate of about 11 per cent during the earlier period while Northern Rhodesia was a part of the Central African Federation; once Independence had been obtained, and the new nation of Zambia had been born, the rate of increase doubled to about 22 per cent.

TABLE 11.1
Growth of the manufacturing sector

	1954	1963	1967
Contribution of manufacturing to GDP (K m.)	9.2	24.2	78.9
Manufacturing as a proportion of GDP	3.3%	6.1%	10.8%

	1954–63	1963–7
Average annual rate of growth of volume of manufacturing output	11%	22%

Sources: National Accounts of Northern Rhodesia, 1954–63; Monthly Digest of Statistics, Central Statistical Office, Lusaka.

This chapter will take the following form: first we shall look at the factors which accounted for the great acceleration in the increase of manufacturing output from 1964 onwards. We shall then consider what form that increase took and how it was achieved. In the following section we shall discuss the development of a coherent industrial policy, and we shall then make a brief summary of the implementation

[1] Senior Lecturer at the Institute of Development Studies, University of Essex, England, formerly Under-Secretary, Ministry of Commerce and Industry, Republic of Zambia.

of some of the longer-term government projects. Next we shall discuss what constraints operated to prevent manufacturing output growing at an even faster pace. Finally we will offer an assessment of the immediate, intermediate, and long-term prospects for the manufacturing sector in Zambia.

Industrial expansion of the kind we are considering may take four forms. The most normal, and least noticeable, comprises an increase of output by existing firms of the same products that they had previously been making. Alternatively new firms may enter the industry to make these same products. A third form takes place when existing firms diversify into entirely new products. Or fourthly, new firms may be established to manufacture entirely new products. As would be expected, all four of these forms of expansion took place during the years we are surveying, but it is to the manufacture of new products, usually by new firms, that most attention will be paid. This form of expansion is the most difficult to achieve and represents the real frontier of progress.

In the discussion that follows, it will often be useful to make certain broad distinctions. The first such distinction is between major projects, say those involving an initial outlay of more than K 1 m., and smaller projects. A second distinction can be drawn between those projects resulting from direct government initiative or sponsorship, and those which evolved more or less spontaneously as a result of initiatives by the private sector. A third distinction, providing it is not imposed too rigidly, may be made between the two-year period 1964–5 and the subsequent two years 1966–7.

On this basis we can say that the expansion in the 1964–5 period took place mainly amongst smaller firms in response to market conditions. The major projects that were started in this period (cigarettes, soaps and edible oils, radios, clay pipes, sugar) in a few cases had a minority INDECO interest but were mainly not started as a result of government initiative. The 1966–7 period was characterized by a slowing down of the rate of expansion owing to the difficulties created by the Rhodesian UDI and its aftermath, followed by a recovery. The increase in the activity of smaller firms continued, the larger projects initiated mainly by the private sector in the earlier period progressively came on stream and, most markedly of all, a series of major new manufacturing projects were negotiated and commenced directly as the result of government initiative, and often with a government majority shareholding right from the start. The year 1968 then has to be treated separately as the year of the Mulungushi Declaration.

THE CAUSES OF THE RISE
IN MANUFACTURING OUTPUT

In 1964 four factors conjoined to create a situation extremely favourable to the expansion of manufacturing production. Two of these stemmed directly from the dissolution of the Federation at the end of 1963. With the end of the Federation, the system of interterritorial transfers of revenue also came to an end; and the Northern Rhodesian government recovered both the right to formulate its own industrial policy and the power to impose tariffs upon imports from Rhodesia. A third factor was the return of buoyancy to the world demand for copper, and the fourth was the recovery of the main mineral rights in the country from the British South African Company at Independence. In 1965, three further factors, all more or less favourable, became evident. One was the formulation of a new and more active government industrial policy manifested by a change in the role and chairmanship of INDECO. Another was the continued rise in the copper price, although the full effect of this was not felt until the Zambian producing companies changed their pricing policy in 1966. And the last was the UDI in Rhodesia which both added urgency to the programme of import substitution and also added to the effective degree of protection that local manufacturers obtained as import licensing, introduced as part of the sanctions effort, progressively prevented the purchase of Rhodesian goods.

During the ten years of Federation, it has been estimated that the net transfer of public revenues from Northern Rhodesia to the other two territories totalled K 194 m., in the sense that revenue collected from Northern Rhodesia exceeded expenditure within (or for the benefit of) Northern Rhodesia by that amount. Consequently the demise of the Federal arrangements for interterritorial transfers might have been expected by itself to have benefited the Zambian treasury by an average of K 19.4 m. a year. But the steady increase in the price of copper and therefore of the taxable income of the copper companies, which was a main source of Federal government revenues, in fact meant that the saving (or extra income) accruing to Zambia as a result of the cessation of the transfer arrangements was substantially greater than this.

The reversion of the mineral rights enjoyed by the BSA Company to the Zambian government at the moment of Independence put an end to a grievance that had been harboured for almost forty years. By the agreement reached, the BSA Company was paid K 4 m. by the Zambian government and a further K 4 m. by the British government, both sums being paid in a manner that allowed them to be treated as free of tax. The extra revenue received by the Zambian government as a result of the agreement can be estimated as follows. Prior to Independence, by an earlier agreement reached in 1950, the BSA Company paid over 20 per cent of the gross royalty income to the Northern Rhodesia government and paid the normal company rate of tax, which was 8s. in the £1 on their revenue from the remaining 80 per cent, administrative costs required for collection of the royalties being negligible. The government was therefore effectively receiving 52 per cent of the royalty income with the remaining 48 per cent net of local taxes being kept by the company. What the Zambian government therefore acquired for its outlay of K 4 m. was the acknowledged right to the remaining 48 per cent of the mineral royalties. How much was that worth? The total mineral royalties received in 1965 were over K 70 m., so that the extra revenue received as a result of the agreement in that year alone will have been of the order of K 34 m.

The benefit through income tax as a result of the higher copper prices is somewhat more difficult to estimate, partly because expenses tend to rise with revenue and partly because the receipts by government are somewhat lagged as income taxes were determined (and technically collectable) retrospectively. But a K 420 a ton increase in the LME copper price which is what occurred between early 1964 and early 1968 (from about K 480 a ton to about K 900 a ton) would leave the companies after payment of additional royalties with an extra K 358 a ton. Out of this the export tax of K 120 a ton (40 per cent of the amount by which the LME price exceeded K 600) would be paid over direct to the Zambian government. Assuming other costs of the companies, transport and wages in particular, to have risen by approximately K 80 a ton during the period, the extra taxable income that they would be left with would be of the order of K 160 a ton. At the now higher standard mining company tax rate of 45 ngwee in the kwacha, the government would expect to receive a further K 72 a ton in company income tax. We therefore reach a position where, as a result of an assumed increase in the LME price of K 420 a ton, an additional K 80 a ton is assumed to be taken up by increased production expenses, an additional K 56 a ton is payable in royalties, a new impost of K 120 a ton is payable as export tax, the additional income tax (chargeable a year later) is K 74 a ton, and the producing companies are left with an additional K 90 a ton for company profits. What is important here from our point of view is not the extra K 90 a ton that is available for shareholders, but the extra K 250 a ton that goes into public revenues.

To estimate even roughly what the total effect of this was on actual government revenue in any one year, we must take into account the reduced production caused by fuel and transport difficulties (which itself contributed to the higher LME price), and also avoid double-counting a part of K 34 m. additional benefit derived in 1965 from the acquisition of the mineral rights (which figure itself incorporates some of the rise in price). For the conclusion that we will want to draw, no exact figure can or need be derived. But even assuming an enforced production cut of 25 per cent of capacity output the additional government revenue as a result of the price increase would be of the order of K 120 m.

Now let us put these three factors—the cessation of the inter-territorial transfers, the recovery of the mineral rights, and the increase in the price of copper—together. Together they account over a period of scarcely more than three years for an increase of government revenue of about K 170 m. But this figure has to be seen in proportion. In 1963 total central government spending in Northern Rhodesia (including both Federal and territorial governments on both capital and recurrent account) amounted to less than K 60 m. The factors that we have cited taken alone, even without the higher revenue from customs duties and other side-effects, explain how it was possible for the Zambian government in the four years between 1964 and 1967 to quadruple its total spending, and to multiply eightfold its spending upon capital account, and to do so—up to that point—without either incurring a budget deficit or running down foreign exchange reserves. We need therefore look no further for the cause of the post-Independence boom which played so large a part in creating the conditions which spurred the rapid growth of the manufacturing sector. The boom was caused primarily by the rapidly increasing level of government expenditure, which was in turn made possible by the break-up of the Federation, the cessation of the system of interterritorial transfers of revenue, the recovery of the mineral rights, and the buoyant world demand at greatly increased prices for Zambia's copper. Other contributory causes there were, but they were secondary.

Amongst the other contributory causes was the greatly increased sum in African wages paid out by the copper companies as the power of the old European Mine Workers Union was broken, the industrial colour bar abolished, Zambianization programmes introduced, and all-round general wage increases awarded. Other industries too tended to increase their wages, particularly African wages. The government's own wage and salary scales were sharply increased, as were the minimum statutory wage rates set by government boards. The proportion of household expenditures directed towards the purchase of locally produced goods is higher amongst African households than it is among expatriate households,[2] so that the shift in the national income distribution towards African wages and salaries accentuated the demand for local manufactured products. Similarly, government capital formation (a large part of which is construction) also results in a higher direct demand for local manufactures than either government recurrent expenditure or, for that matter, private sector capital formation. Thus the fact that government investment increased as a proportion of overall investment, and in relation to government recurrent expenditure, again accentuates the demand for locally manufactured goods.

Given therefore both the 1964–7 boom and the *form* which the boom took, we are in a position to appreciate one phenomenon of the period that persisted so generally that it came almost to be accepted as a matter of normality. This was a demand for locally manufactured goods that grew so rapidly that the sale of any locally made commodity of reasonable standard was hardly ever a problem. In other words we can ignore any deficiency in demand as a constraint during this period. Almost equally exceptional—and again a consequence of one aspect of the copper boom—was the plenitude of local funds available to finance expansion plans, at least until mid-1967. Initially these funds were made available on relatively easy conditions to foreign-controlled as well as locally-controlled firms. It was not until 1967 that the supply of funds started to become tighter; and it was not until the Mulungushi Declaration in 1968 that the terms on which they were made available to other than Zambian-owned firms became thoroughly restrictive.

The new flood of demand unleashed by the government's greatly increased investment expenditure and by the increased employment at generally higher wages for Zambian labour most affected two parts of the manufacturing sector. These may be crudely described as 'components for the building industry' and 'African household goods'. The former category would cover such items as cement, bricks, tiles,

---

[2] But see pp. 114–17 for a quantitative discussion of the effects of increases in wages on the domestic market.

worked timber, metal doors and windows, flooring blocks, cut glass, conduits, porcelain and metal sinks and bowls, asbestos and metal roofing, light fittings, etc. The latter would particularly include such items as clothing of all sorts, processed foodstuffs, cigarettes, beer, blankets, bicycles, and furniture of all kinds.

THE COMPOSITION OF THE RISE IN MANUFACTURING OUTPUT

The most rapid response to the new circumstances came from the clothing industry. The industry already existed in embryo, and thus a base existed for rapid expansion. Besides that, the skills employed are comparatively easy to learn and the clothing industry had traditionally served as the bridge across which the Indian merchant passes to become an industrialist. The clothing industry was helped by other special circumstances stemming from tariff and import licensing arrangements. Tariff levels inherited from the Federal structure of tariffs were already high, since these had been introduced to protect the Rhodesian clothing industry. Once these were imposed against Rhodesia also, the Zambian industry was already comparatively well protected. But when, at the end of 1965, the old four-column tariff embodying imperial and commonwealth preferences was replaced by a single-column tariff, for most clothing items the tariff was consolidated around the column B rather than the lower column C or D rates. In part this may have been a result of a miscalculation of the amount of duty intended. But there were probably other influences at work as well. The higher duty to the extent that it had to be paid (for the local industry was not able to meet all local demand) was likely to constitute a tax payment by those whose incomes had grown quickly but might still be below the level tapped by income tax. More importantly, it was known that a textile mill was being planned for the future and that the price of the cloth from the mill was likely to be somewhat higher than the cheapest available imported cloth. Rather than raise the clothing tariff subsequently when local clothiers would be compelled to make use of local cloth, it was thought preferable to set the tariffs initially at a high level in the hope that with a plenitude of new firms there would be some genuine price competition. When they were introduced early in 1966, sanctions against Rhodesia also helped the home clothing industry, for clothing from Rhodesia was amongst the first items for which importation from

Rhodesia was refused. And later, when it was government policy to route specific imports through Dar es Salaam, the selection of footwear and clothing as one such item once again helped the local industry, this time by cutting out much of the competition from South African suppliers, for it was known that Tanzanian dockers would not handle South African goods.

While the provision of shirts, vests, dresses, pants, undergarments, socks, and other such clothing was taken care of by a host of mainly small firms, only one major footwear factory was set up, and that by the Bata Shoe Company which was already established in Southern Rhodesia and which had had experience in other independent African countries.

Although tariffs against Rhodesian goods were not applied until mid-1964, the clear prospect of the Federation's dissolution had induced certain other international firms to make moves towards establishing manufacturing facilities in Zambia even before the actual dissolution of the Federation had been formalized. Amongst such firms producing consumer goods were the cigarette manufacturers (BAT and Rothmans), Lever Brothers, and Supersonic Radios.

The response of firms supplying the building industry was much slower. In part this may have been because the building boom took slightly longer to materialize. It was one thing for local businessmen to be told by the new politicians and the equally new planners that there was going to be a tremendous expansion in investment: it was quite another to feel the impact of this on sales, and obviously many business-men preferred to wait for the proof of the predictions before investing in facilities to expand output. But there appears to have been another reason as well. In the clothing and consumer goods industries, many of the firms seemed to be either small enough to be genuinely locally based or else large enough to be genuinely international. In the building industry the firms tended to be of an intermediate size and in most cases came under the direct control of associated companies in Southern Rhodesia. Since these parent or associated companies in Rhodesia were not at that time producing at capacity it must have appeared advantageous to supply the burgeoning Zambian market from these under-worked Rhodesian firms rather than to move up plant—at least until forced to do so—to manufacture in Zambia itself. Even when South African or Rhodesian firms made undertakings to the government that they would commence manufacturing within Zambia, it was normal for them to ask in exchange for an undertaking that they could continue to import from South African or Rhodesian associates until the local plant was in production. Table 11.2 shows for the first four years following Independence in what segments of the manufacturing sector the growth in output took place.

TABLE 11.2

Index of manufacturing production

	Food-stuffs	Bever-ages & tobacco	Tex-tiles & cloth-ing	Non-metallic mineral products	Metals & metal products	Others	Total
Weights:	15	18	3	11	14	17	78
1963	100	100	100	100	100	100	100
1964	109	120	154	151	99	112	117
1965	121	145	207	219	148	148	152
1966	136	190	201	246	165	99	162
1967	159	229	212	298	164	209	208
1968[1]	180	227	229	357	158	254	226

[1] Average for first nine months of 1968 only.

Source: Monthly Digest of Statistics, Central Statistical Office, Lusaka, April 1969.

THE DEVELOPMENT OF POLICY

We turn back now from those favourable factors which accounted for booming market conditions and the availability of finance to those factors which manifested the government's re-assumed ability to formulate industrial policy. The first statement, *An Outline of Government's Industrial Policy,* was put out in 1964 and was as reassuring as it was unexciting. It contained little more than the offer of reasonable degrees of protection where this could be shown to be necessary and desirable and the proffer of loan finance from INDECO towards the initial cost of establishing approved industries. INDECO was at that time controlled by non-government shareholders, its chairman was the Governor of the Bank of Zambia, its role was a conservative one, and the extent of its success in encouraging new industrial enterprises is perhaps best indicated by the fact that its share capital was never fully called up.

During 1964, and more particularly during 1965, it became evident that the existing industrial policy was neither aggressive enough nor socialistic enough to coincide with the Cabinet's mood—or indeed the advice of some of the government's new economic advisers. The new policy that emerged had two main features. It was decided that new manufacturing industries to be established would be divided into (1) those which would be entirely owned and controlled by the state, (2) those upon which the state would embark in partnership with private sector companies, and (3) (by implication the remainder) those that would be left entirely to private enterprise. This new policy was the subject of a Cabinet decision and of a later declaration in the National Assembly. But though it certainly influenced the trend of manufacturing development, its divisions were not strictly adhered to, and it had become largely irrelevant by the time it was superseded by the 1968 Mulungushi Declaration.

The second and probably the more influential of the changes that took place in 1965 concerns the role and direction of the Industrial Development Corporation. The government bought out the other private sector shareholders, a new combined chairman/managing director of great energy was appointed, and the tasks of the corporation were expanded most particularly to include the identification of justifiable projects, the active seeking-out of partners with whom to implement them and, where such partners could not be found, the establishment itself of project teams and then new corporations to implement the projects. The effect of this more dynamic policy can be gauged from Table 11.3 which indicates the growth of INDECO'S assets and profits from 1964 to 1967. It should be realized, however, that from 1966 onwards these were not restricted to solely manufacturing enterprises, since they included a road transport company, a pipeline company, several hotels, certain agricultural projects, and two whole-saling corporations, even before the Mulungushi takeovers.

TABLE 11.3

Industrial Development Corporation of Zambia Ltd.:
growth indicators

Year ended 31 December	1964	1965	1966	1967
Investments in industrial securities (K m.)	1.0	2.7	6.9	10.5
Loans advanced (K m.)	1.1	1.7	1.4	3.4
Investment income (K'000)	143	249	445	619
Surplus on current account (K'000)	+45	+81	+269	+414
Total assets (K'000)	2,176	4,902	8,870	16,278
Paid up capital (K'000)	2,030	3,138	7,057	13,364

Source: *Statistical Year Book, 1968*, Central Statistical Office, Lusaka.

To understand why the government's policy evolved in the way it did, particularly towards greater state participation in what Western terms would have been considered traditionally private sector enterprises, it is necessary to go back to before 1964. The Ministry of Commerce and Industry (like most of those concerned with economic affairs) had been a Federal ministry centred on Salisbury pursuing a markedly conservative Western-oriented policy. When the Federation broke up, the new Northern Rhodesian ministry started off as scarcely more than a rather despised department of the Ministry of Finance cast out to look for their own scattered and shabby offices, and on the whole staffed by officials that Finance found it did not want plus two or three officials who came up from Salisbury and were the only ones who knew what the technical work of the ministry was about. 'You will find we are treated as a bit of slum', was how one of the officials put the matter at the time. The ministry also experienced no less than four different ministers during the first two years of its existence, not including a period when the Minister of Finance acted as Minister of Commerce and Industry as well, and an almost equal number of permanent secretaries. It was not until the triumvirate of Mr. Justin Chimba, a strong political minister, Mr. Goodwin Mutale as Permanent Secretary, and Mr. Andrew Sardanis as Chairman and Managing Director of INDECO became firmly established that industrial policy started to become articulate. And much of the incisiveness of action in industrial matters following 1965 is clearly owed to the success with which these three worked together.

The successive shocks to which the Central African area has been subject during this whole period (the Congo disturbances, the break-up of the Federation, the Rhodesian rebellion) have without doubt discouraged external investment and made it more expensive to attract in terms of the return that would have to be in prospect. And even peaceful changes, such as the introduction of African government and the attainment of Independence, tended to add to the nervousness of private investors. In these circumstances and when it is remembered that the economy was growing by more than 20 per cent a year, there were certain to be many industrial opportunities, viable as commercial propositions and thoroughly desirable on economic grounds, that were simply not taken up. Besides that, the policy of the Zambian government, quite naturally, was to favour further Zambianization and Zambian ownership in business and to progress towards African Socialism. Since very few Zambians had either the necessary capital or

TABLE 11.4

INDECO's subsidiary and main associate companies, December 1968

Company	Business	Eventual capital (K)	INDECO voting %	Fixed assets (eventual value) (K)	Eventual employment
Country Hotels	Rural hotels & game lodges	2,000,000	100	2,000,000	225
Indeco Milling	Rural maize roller mills	500,000	100	300,000	120
Indeco Properties	Staff housing	6,000	100	900,000	13
Kabwe Industrial Fabrics	Grain bag & hessian manufacture	1,600,000	100	2,000,000	570
Kafue Estate	Residential & industrial township	200,000	100	12,000,000	100
Mukonchi Tobacco	Virginia tobacco farming	300,000	100	190,000	270
Mwaiseni Properties	Commercial development	40,000	100	1,200,000	—
Progressive Development	Factory leasing	4	100	100,000	—
Rucom Industries	Food canning & rural industries	500,000	100	160,000	22
Zambia Steel & Building Supplies	Wholesale of steel & building materials	1,000,000	100	1,000,000	800
Anros Industries	Metal windows & doorframes	200,000	100	600,000	540
Consumer Buying Corporation of Zambia	Department stores	3,250,000	52	4,000,000	2,000
Crushed Stone Sales	Quarry sales	200,000	51	450,000	380
Lakes Fisheries of Zambia	Fish catching & marketing	1,000,000	51	2,500,000	165
Metal Fabricators of Zambia	Fabricator of copper & aluminium	1,200,000	85	2,000,000	80
Mining Timbers	Timber for mines	80,000	51	550,000	195
Monarch (Zambia)	Metal windows, etc.	300,000	51	350,000	360
Mwaiseni Stores	Retail selling	300,000	51	270,000	300

Table 11.4 (Continued)

Company	Business	Eventual capital (K)	INDECO voting %	Fixed assets (eventual value) (K)	Eventual employment
National Breweries	Opaque beer	n.a.	51	7,000,000	600
Nitrogen Chemicals of Zambia	Ammonium nitrate manufacture	8,000,000	83	16,000,000	600
Northern Breweries	Lager beer, stout, & ale	5,600,000	51	10,000,000	1,200
Smith & Youngson	Freight transport	100,000	51	3,500,000	1,100
Tazama Pipelines	Oil transportation	500,000	67	32,000,000	200
Transport Holdings of Zambia	Freight & passenger transport	2,000,000	51	6,500,000	3,120
Zambesi Sawmills	Sleepers & parquet blocks	500,000	51	470,000	1,160
Zambia Clay Industries	Salt-glazed pipes and face bricks	600,000	56	780,000	140
Zambia Hotel Properties	Major hotels	2,080,000	80	4,500,000	550
Z.O.K.	Trading stores	500	51	1,500,000	220
African Farming Equipment	Supplier of agricultural equipment	85,000	29	300,000	200
Chilanga Cement	Cement manufacture & sales	8,000,000	45	16,000,000	800
Duncan, Gilbey & Matheson (Zambia)	Distillery & bottling plant	300,000	33	250,000	25
Dunlop Zambia	Tyres and tubes	2,200,000	23	4,000,000	435
Kafironda	Explosives for mines	1,900,000	33	5,550,000	500
Kafue Textiles of Zambia	Spinning, weaving, dyeing, & finishing	2,000,000	50	3,500,000	960
Nkwazi Manufacturing	Fishing nets & twine	125,000	5	135,000	93
Scaw-Tow Foundries	Castings & grinding balls	850,000	2	863,000	600
Miller & Wixley	Pharmaceuticals, cosmetics, and technical instruments	100,000	40	200,000	64
Zambia Sugar	Sugar estate, factory, & refinery	4,240,000	12	14,000,000	2,500
Zambia-Tanzania Road Services	International road transport	3,000,000	35	10,000,000	2,000

Note: n.a. = not available.

Sources: INDECO *Annual Report,* 1967; *Enterprise,* First Quarter, 1969.

the required expertise to start up any large manufacturing enterprise, both the economic conditions and the government's political and social policies indicated a move towards far greater state initiative and participation in the manufacturing sector.

In discussing the 1964–5 period we have placed the main emphasis on extremely favourable market conditions as being the main cause of the expansion by private firms of their manufacturing activities. These same favourable conditions persisted through 1966–7 and into 1968, and may be said to have been accompanied by a growing confidence in the stability of the Zambian government. The new factor that distinguished the 1966–7 period was the successful conclusion of a series of agreements that would lead to the establishment of several major new industries, some of which would be controlled from the outset by the government (usually through INDECO), while in others the state would have a major equity holding. The most important of these new industries were the nitrogenous chemicals plant (to manufacture feedstock for both the fertilizer and the explosives factories) and the textile mill, both of which were to be situated in an entirely new industrial and residential complex at Kafue. The Nitrogen Chemicals Company was to be controlled from the outset by the government; in the textile mill, the government would initially hold 50 per cent of the equity but would have the right to assume majority control at a later date. Other new industries in which the government would have majority control from the outset were the copper-fabricating project and the hessian and grainbag plant. New projects that were finalized to start with substantial government minority interests included the tyre and tube factory, an explosives factory, and a drugs and nutritional foods plant. The proposals relating to the fertilizer granulating, mixing, and bagging plant were not finalized during this period, but it seemed likely that this plant too would be controlled by the government.

Table 11.4 lists the subsidiary and main associated companies of INDECO, and indicates the nature of their business, the eventual capital issued, INDECO'S proportionate holding of the voting rights, an estimate of the eventual fixed asset value, and the approximate employment that the projects, when completed, will provide.

The policies embodied in the Mulungushi Declaration were framed, as regards the manufacturing sector, not mainly to increase investment but to associate Zambians more with the running of local businesses. This was to be achieved in two main ways, first by the government itself moving to take a 51 per cent interest in twenty-six named companies, and second by severely curtailing the local financing facilities and by preventing the issue of trade licences in certain areas to firms that were not 100 per cent Zambian.[3] There were also restrictions imposed on the proportions of capital and of profits that could be paid in any one year to overseas shareholders. The twenty-six firms in question and their lines of business are indicated in Table 11.5. By the end of September 1968 all twenty-six of them had agreed to terms upon which they would transfer 51 per cent of their equity to the government, and it was already apparent in what way rationalization of firms in certain lines of business would proceed.

The initial effect of Mulungushi was naturally to increase the feeling of nervousness within the business community and to lead to some falling off of investment in stocks, particularly by Indian traders. This was in itself no bad thing, for the economy was already at the time over-heated and imports in particular were rising too quickly. But the Mulungushi Declaration did abide by one important principle. There was no change in the position of any firm which already had an investment agreement with the government (or INDECO). Bearing this in mind we may estimate that the long-term effects of Mulungushi are likely to be as follows: (1) some permanent loss of confidence by foreign investors, leading to a lower level of absolute foreign investment by private interests and a higher required rate of return for those foreign investments that do occur; (2) a likelihood that in future all substantial foreign investments will from the outset involve a signed agreement with the government and a determinate amount of government equity participation; (3) a greater financing problem for foreign-controlled firms operating locally even for those which may wish to expand; (4) greater facility for 100-per-cent Zambian firms to obtain their financing requirements for expansion, always provided that their plans are credit-worthy; (5) some tendency for firms, at the margin, to change hands from non-Zambians to Zambians; (6) a greater total availability of local finance, at least in the medium run, as a result of the limitations on dividends that can be sent abroad. There is reason to suppose that the copper companies would be willing to channel a part

---

[3] The more severe financing restrictions were relaxed following the President's declaration of 11 August 1969. Local financing provisions were thereafter to be allowed to local firms provided a simple majority of the shareholding was held by Zambians.

of these additional funds into economic activities outside mining. The net consequence of all these effects is of course hard to judge. That there will be greater participation by Zambians seems certain. But the result on the potential rate of growth of the sector is indeterminate. Perhaps it would be fairest to say that if there is any dampening effect, it appears likely to be slight.

TABLE 11.5

The 'Mulungushi' companies, i.e. those which were invited to offer 51 per cent of their shareholding to the government

A. *Window and door frame manufacturers*
      Anros Industries
      Monarch (Zambia) Ltd.
      Crittal Hope (Zambia) Ltd.

B. *Building material merchants*
      Anglo African Glass Company Ltd.
      P. G. Timbers
      Baldwins Ltd.
      Steel Supplies of Zambia Ltd.
      Zamtimbia Ltd.
      May and Hassell (Zambia) Ltd.
      Johnson and Fletcher

C. *Crushed stone suppliers*
      Nicholas Quarries
      Gerry's Quarries
      Greystone Quarry
      Crushed Stone Sales Ltd.[1]

D. *Breweries*
      Northern Breweries Ltd.
      Heinrich's Syndicate Ltd.

E. *Road transporters*
      Smith & Youngson Ltd.
      Central African Road Services Ltd.

F. *Wholesale and retail distribution*
      C.B.C. Stores
      O.K. Bazaars
      Standard Trading
      Solanki Brothers Ltd.
      Mwaiseni Stores Ltd.

G. *Timber extractors*
      Zambesi Sawmills Ltd.
      Mining Timbers Ltd.

H. *Fish refrigeration and distribution*
      Irvin and Johnson

I. *Newspaper publishers*
   Zambia Newspapers Ltd.

[1] This company was a wholly-owned subsidiary of the other quarrying companies listed.

Source: 'Zambia's Economic Revolution', address by H.E. The President, Dr. K. D. Kaunda, at Mulungushi, April 1968.

CASE STUDIES IN IMPLEMENTATION

In line with the higher level of demand, import route capacities, manpower availability, and other physical limitations within Zambia, it would be theoretically possible to attempt to establish a maximum attainable rate of manufacturing growth for any series of years, and then to measure actual performance against this maximum, and to ask what the shortfall had been and what accounted for it. In such a planned model, a cluster of new industries would be so phased that each would become viable by selling its output to the other—or to the larger domestic market that the existence of the others would create. In practice such an exercise would be frivolous—or at least misleading— because it would bear no relation to what was administratively possible in the Zambia of 1964 and 1965. If we are to talk about constraints realistically, it seems preferable therefore to do two rather more mundane things: one is to review individual projects or segments of the sector and to ask whether there was any unnecessary delay in their progress, and the other is to assess the importance of various circumstances or factors that certainly did act as constraints and caused cancellations or delays.

Five of the major projects which the government and/or INDECO were discussing with outside private interests during 1964–5 involved (1) sugar; (2) salt-glazed pipes; (3) cement; (4) tyres and tubes; and (5) a steel mill. A brief description of what happened on the implementation of these five projects may be instructive. At the time of the break-up of the Federation there was a large sugar refinery at Ndola, owned by Tate & Lyle, the throughput of which was insufficient to make it profitable. The sugar raws for this refinery were brought up from Southern Rhodesia. The growing and milling of sugar within Zambia itself was an obvious objective of government policy, and the decision of the Tate & Lyle organization to establish an estate and mill near Mazabuka was both an obvious backward integration of their operations and a sensible protection of their existing investment since, if they did not undertake these earlier processes, it was clear that the government would make an agreement with some other enterprise to do so. Bearing in mind the complexity of the negotiations which had to cover the controlled importation of raws, the permitted retail price for refined sugar, the government's participation in the new company, and the provisions that would be made for small growers and co-operatives to sell their cane to the mill, an agreed exchange of letters was achieved reasonably quickly. The same judgement can be made with regard to the less complicated establishment of a factory at Kitwe to manufacture salt-glazed pipe and face bricks.

The expansion of cement production, however, gave rise to difficulties. The only cement plant in the country, Chilanga Cement, was effectively controlled by Portland Cement companies in Rhodesia which during 1964 and 1965 were operating well below capacity. The Chilanga Cement Company was, in the view of Zambia's planners, somewhat laggard in embarking at that stage upon any expansion plan, and preliminary discussions had already been started with outside firms with a possible view to establishing a completely new and separate cement plant on the Copperbelt. When the Chilanga company did announce its plans in December 1964, the Minister of Commerce and Industry of the day promptly complained that he had not been consulted and did not approve of the plans which would have left control of the company in the hands of Southern Rhodesian shareholders. There followed a period of negotiations at the conclusion of which the Zambian government acquired sufficient equity in the company (on deferred-payment terms) to ensure that its own holding plus that of the Commonwealth Development Corporation were sufficient to constitute a majority holding of the equity. Upon this basis a new expansion plan, involving an additional kiln at Chilanga and an entire new plant on the Copperbelt, was approved and the Chilanga company maintained its monopoly position as the country's sole producer (and licensed importer) of cement. Since Zambia had to import cement from 1965 all the way through to 1969—a quantity totalling over half a million tons in all—it is clear that the expansion of output was achieved far later than would have been desirable. On the other hand, no action taken *since* Independence could have speeded up the increased production by more than a few months; and the final arrangement reached as a result of earlier differences may be considered a satisfactory one from the Zambian government's viewpoint.

A preliminary plan for the Dunlop Company to manufacture bicycle tyres and tubes within Zambia (to supplement the larger tyre production of their factory in Bulawayo) existed before the Federal dissolution. And on the understanding that this plan would be proceeded with, Dunlop tyres and tubes were admitted into Zambia from Bulawayo at lower rates of duty than would otherwise have been applied. But for almost three years the Dunlop Company took no firm steps to start constructing a factory on the Ndola site for which they had long held an option. Indeed it was not until the Zambian government had initiated discussions with a rival (the Pirelli Company) that the Dunlop Company manifested its willingness to enter into a firm commitment to commence work on a factory that would manufacture both car and bicycle tyres and tubes. From this experience it is tempting to frame a general principle. When a foreign manufacturer holds a majority share of a local market, he is likely to express his willingness to commence manufacturing locally but is apt to delay actually doing so until he feels that his position in that local market is threatened by the plans of a serious competitor.

The story of the steel mill is in every sense a cautionary tale. An agreement for the construction of a steel mill to be based upon local scrap supplemented by imported billets was signed with the John Howard organization at the end of 1964. The scheme had not been prepared locally or by consultants employed by the government but was 'sold' to the government as a turnkey project by what may be described as high pressure salesmanship. At the time that the contract was signed, the project had not been properly appraised and it was known to be opposed by some of the government's own leading economists. It was indeed a thoroughly poor scheme from Zambia's viewpoint, and it must be considered fortunate that some of the assumptions upon which the project was thought to be based turned out to be mistaken so that, by agreement, the operation of the contract was quietly held in suspension. Subsequently a decision was taken in principle to establish an integrated iron and steel industry based upon local iron ore and coal; but the detailed planning of this far more rational project was quite properly deferred pending the completion of far more extensive geological and economic appraisals.

Is there a conclusion that can be drawn from these assorted recitations, and from experience gained on other projects? There are two. The first is that the economic losses involved in finalizing a project too quickly are likely to be larger and more enduring than those suffered through the risk of a small delay. The second is that it is worth going to considerable time, trouble, and expense to get two competing groups interested in performing a project, for the cost of the project, the time taken to complete it, and the efficiency with which it operates thereafter are all likely to be improved. There are few things more difficult for government negotiators than to be sitting across the table from company representatives who know that the government regards the project as urgent but that there are no other interests competing for it. And when ministers at the same time issue press statements stating that the government is firmly committed to the project and that a contract will shortly be signed, the price of the project nearly always rises and the frustration of the negotiators is correspondingly increased.

CONSTRAINTS ON FURTHER GROWTH OF MANUFACTURE

Although the longer-term effects of Zambia's sanctions effort against Rhodesia were to create more opportunities for local industry, the more immediate effect of the post-UDI crisis was to cause a slowing down of the rate of Zambia's expansion. This is clearly reflected in the statistics. The rate of growth of the manufacturing sector fell from 31 per cent in 1965 to 16 per cent in 1966, before recovering again to 27 per cent in 1967. There were a variety of reasons accounting for industry's difficulties. Fuel shortages were particularly severe in the early part of 1966. Throughout 1966 and 1967 there were difficulties in obtaining regular and prompt delivery of both machinery and materials across the Rhodesia Railways system, and for considerable periods no loadings upon the railways were made at all at the ports while the backlog of goods in intermediate stations was cleared. The Zambian authorities attempted to divert some imports to Lobito Bay and the Benguela Line, to Dar es Salaam for carriage by road, to Beira for transportation through Malawi, and even to Mtwara. But all these routes proved subject to delays and disruptions, and upon most of them the freight charges were heavier than they had been through Rhodesia.

A further course of difficulty stemmed from the far stricter immigration requirements that were imposed by the government after UDI. These not only made permanent recruitment particularly from Rhodesia or South Africa very much more difficult; they also on occasion held up the arrival of professional or technical staff urgently required to commission or repair inoperative plant. The recruitment of foremen and skilled artisans, especially by local businesses without international connections, had proved a serious problem for many firms which UDI, with its effect of forcing expatriates to show more overtly where their loyalties lay, made worse. As a consequence, small local firms had frequently to resort to trying to attract staff away from other local companies, so that salary levels and costs rose without the supply of this type of scarce manpower becoming any greater.

The labour regulations in force for much of this period prohibited firms from laying off workers without government permission and this probably also had a slightly depressing effect upon output. Though introduced only a month after UDI, they were only indirectly related to it in the sense that they reflected a fear that the economic effects of Rhodesia's actions might lead to a sudden increase in urban unemployment. Manufacturers at the time argued that the strictness of the regulations made it difficult to maintain industrial discipline and thus led to a lowering of both productivity and production. As regards productivity, statistics do lend some support to this argument.

The shortages caused by transport difficulties and other effects of UDI created the possibility of profiteering, and for this reason price control was introduced. The regulations on the whole allowed for genuine cost increases by the suppliers to be passed on, but margins had to remain the same in absolute terms and therefore as a proportion of final price they were reduced. In a basically inflationary situation, where the supply and transport costs of many items were rising rapidly, price control could not keep prices stable but it probably prevented them from rising quite as fast as they otherwise would have done. To manufacturers, price control was a cause of nervousness and complaint. Indeed, it was quite often cited by manufacturers themselves as a disincentive to increased production especially of new products, but the extent to which it really did act as a deterrent is open to doubt.

Another consequence of sanctions policy which did have some constraining effect upon expansion in Zambia concerned the foreign exchange regulations. Two of Zambia's larger manufacturers, Stewart & Lloyds and BAT, were eager to expand their local facilities, but in order to do so had to remove the equity control of their local companies from Rhodesia and transfer it to other sources outside. This in turn required a payment to be made to the Rhodesian associated company which, even if the payment was made from non-Zambian sources and was credited to the Rhodesian company only momentarily, the Zambian exchange control authorities were not prepared to allow. A similar impasse prevailed for a time with regard to certain Central African Power Corporation funds, which, if they were released by exchange control, the Commonwealth Development Corporation was prepared to use in part to help form a local Industrial Finance Corporation. This latter corporation which had been planned for some time still had not been launched by the end of 1968.

The conduct of the trade unions which were generally not strong in manufacturing plants does not appear during this period to have inhibited expansion in the manufacturing sector. There were naturally a number of stoppages but no markedly serious strikes. It is also plausible to suppose that the close links between trade union and UNIP officials and the knowledge that the weight of government support was now behind the Zambian worker may have contributed to those conditions in which individual productivity sometimes declined. With the number of jobs available expanding fast, wage levels rising rapidly, and promotions frequent, it is hardly surprising that labour problems were comparatively subdued.

PROSPECTS

We may now turn to the future and assess the prospects on the basis of what we have understood about the past. The immediate prospects for the continued rapid growth of the index for manufacturing production are extremely good. What we may call small private-sector activities have not yet caught up with the new permanent level of home demand. Moreover, several major undertakings will commence production in 1969 and contribute their first full year's production in 1970. Amongst the projects in this position are likely to be the second cement factory and the tyre factory at Ndola, the explosives factory (stages one and two) at Kafironda, the nitrogen chemicals factory and the textile factory at Kafue, and the hessian and fibre bag factory at Kabwe. Other factories, such as the fertilizer mixing and bagging plant, may be finished a year or so later. The prospects up to and including 1970 are therefore extremely good just on the basis of plans that have already been approved and projects that have already been started. Bearing in mind the increased demand for existing commodities that the employment generated by this expansion will create amongst urban workers, and the extent to which a cluster of factories provides markets for each other, it seems entirely safe to predict that the manufacturing sector (perhaps alone amongst all the productive sectors) will comfortably exceed the real output targets set for it in the First National Development Plan.

In the early 1970s we may expect this frantic rate of expansion to decline, though it will be somewhat revived by two more very large projects that are likely to come into production about the middle of the decade. These are (1) the oil refinery that will be located at the end of the pipeline at Ndola, and (2) the integrated iron and steel mill which will form part of the industrial complex at what will be, by that time, the proud city of Kafue. Each of these basic industries are of the type that attract smaller secondary industries either to supply them with components or to elaborate their products, and it would be sensible to imagine that the establishment of plants of these kinds would comprise an important component in the manufacturing growth of the second half of the next decade.

But we must now turn back to consider those two factors that nobody had to worry about much in the first few years of Zambia's industrial development, namely market demand and the availability of finance. The factors that accounted for the extremely rapid growth of demand in the years 1964 to 1968, and the relatively ample provisions of finance, have been analysed sufficiently carefully for it to be clear that these unique conditions will not be repeated. By 1969 government expenditure had reached a level where the rate of increase required to be drastically reduced, and expenditure itself levelled off—indeed, rather belatedly so. If there is a large fall in the copper price from current levels (K 600 per ton in June 1969) there may even have to be a drop in the real value of government spending, which is likely to be absorbed by the capital account, however unfortunate that may be in terms of economic policy. The balance of payments position will in that event also be more acute.

In these circumstances we would not expect that demand for manufactured products would actually be reduced; what would happen would be merely a slow-down in the expansion of such demand. One way of putting this would be to say that the exceptional revenue increase caused by the break-up of the Federation, the take-over of the mineral rights, and the exceptionally high copper price will have been absorbed (or possibly more than absorbed) in the adjusted level of normal government spending, and that the exceptional cluster of manufacturing opportunities created by the ability to impose duties on Rhodesian imports and by the higher level of local expenditure will also have been absorbed. Thereafter progress on the marketing side (as the easy import-substitution activities are taken up), on the financing side (as money becomes very much scarcer and the balance of payments goes into deficit), and on the production side will be much more of a slog. Zambia's position will in a sense have become much more typical of other less developed countries who find that in order to finance the development government requires credit creation is necessary, and that in order to create new markets for local manufacturers (or even to protect the existing ones) higher and higher tariffs are called for. These steps in turn put up the cost of living, give rise to labour discontent and further wage demands, imperil the stability of the currency, and ultimately force a devaluation or series of devaluations. In short, by then, Zambia will have run into the familiar harsh, structural problems. But by then, too, the manufacturing sector will be six or seven times as large as it was at the break-up of the Federation. That will be some considerable achievement to look back upon.

12

The Transport Sector

R. M. BOSTOCK[1]

INTRODUCTION

Since Zambia is an export economy which is landlocked, problems of transport assume crucial importance in the country's development programme. Not only has the transport system to ensure the export annually of some 700,000 tons of copper, the country's main export mineral, but it has also to cater to the needs of imports of more than 2½ million tons of a variety of goods, ranging from foodstuffs to machinery and equipment. Any disruption or dislocation in the transport system is therefore likely to jeopardize the growth of the economy. Before UDI the bulk of the external trade of Zambia was carried out through the two nearest ports to Zambia, namely Lourenço Marques and Beira in Mozambique, at a distance approximately of 1,600 miles by rail from the Copperbelt. The complexity of the transport problem was heightened by the sanctions policy against Rhodesia which necessitated the establishment of alternative transport routes to the East African ports, and also the search for new sources of supply. In fact, transport problems stemming from the objective of swiftly decreasing dependence on Rhodesia dominated the economic scene in 1966. Attainment of this objective had far-reaching repercussions on the economy, since it implied the reordering of the priorities implicit in the First National Development Plan. The aim of diverting at any rate the export traffic away from Rhodesian routes has made considerable progress during the last two years. This is reflected in the fact that the traditional railway routes through Rhodesia accounted for only about one-third of the total tonnage of copper exported in 1968.[2]

This lengthy extract from the Bank of Zambia's *Annual Report* is incorporated as a preamble to this chapter because it illustrates the increasing awareness of the relationship between the transport sector and economic development which has arisen in Zambia since the illegal

[1] R. M. Bostock, of Maxwell Stamp (Africa) Ltd., was formerly Lecturer in Economics, University of York, England. This chapter is submitted by the author in his personal capacity, and was completed in 1969.
[2] Bank of Zambia, *Report and Statement of Accounts for the Year ended December 31, 1968*, p. 22.

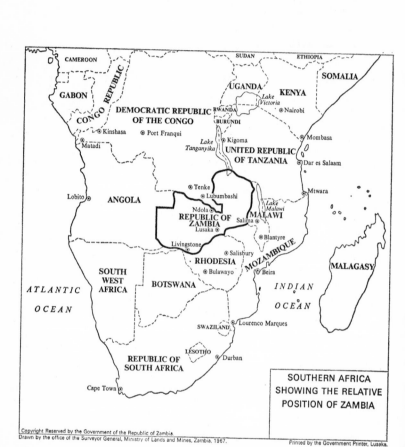

SOUTHERN AFRICA
SHOWING THE RELATIVE
POSITION OF ZAMBIA

Map 12.1

seizure of independence by Rhodesia in November 1965. The 1968 *Economic Report*[3] prepared by the Finance Division, Office of the Vice President, declares that 'economic development in Zambia has undoubtedly been adversely affected by the lack of adequate transportation routes to and from the sea'. The stresses and strains imposed by UDI and the process of disengagement from the Southern Rhodesian economy have been the root cause of the transport crises with which Zambia has been faced during the five years 1965–9. Not only has there been strain on the available administrative and managerial capacity, but there has also been a massive reallocation of resources which has led to a re-ordering of the priorities implicit in the First National Development Plan.

Despite the categorical statements quoted, the experience of the last five years has highlighted the need for long-term planning, not only to anticipate the problems surrounding the diversification away from dependence upon Rhodesia Railways, but also to minimize the cost of such a policy to the economy as a whole. Despite possible inadequacies in the long-term overall planning effort, several extremely significant developments have taken place within the transport sector:

1. the development of new transport routes to meet Zambia's traffic requirements, in particular the Great North Road to Dar es Salaam;
2. the division of Rhodesia Railways and the Central African Airways Corporation;
3. the construction of the oil pipeline from Dar es Salaam to Ndola;
4. the establishment of the joint Zambia and Tanzania government-controlled Zambia-Tanzania Road Services Ltd. to move goods between the Zambian line of rail and the Tanzanian port of Dar es Salaam;
5. the establishment of a joint government/private enterprise company to air-freight goods mainly from Ndola to Dar es Salaam (Zambia Air Cargoes Ltd.);
6. the detailed investigation of the Zambia-East Africa rail link;
7. the invitation by President Kaunda to the two major passenger and/or freight companies to invite the government to participate to the extent of 51 per cent of their equity.

---

[3] Finance Division, Office of the Vice President, *Economic Report, 1968,* Government Printer, Lusaka, p. 166.

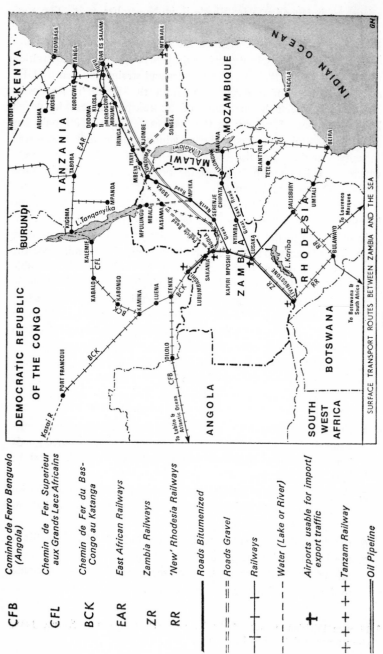

SURFACE TRANSPORT ROUTES BETWEEN ZAMBIA AND THE SEA

Map 12.2

CFB   Cominho de Ferro Benguela (Angola)

CFL   Chemin de Fer Superieur aux Grands Lacs Africains

BCK   Chemin de Fer du Bas-Congo au Katanga

EAR   East African Railways

ZR   Zambia Railways

RR   'New' Rhodesia Railways

━━━━━   Roads Bitumenized

= = = = =   Roads Gravel

┼┼┼┼   Railways

– – – –   Water (Lake or River)

✚   Airports usable for import/ export traffic

+ + + +   Tanzam Railway

━━━━   Oil Pipeline

In short, it can be seen that Zambia, since the day of her political Independence in October 1964, has been faced with making substantial transport decisions of a permanent nature, with far-reaching long-term repercussions on the economy. In the course of this chapter several of these new developments will be considered further.

A cursory glance at a map (see Map 12.2) will immediately highlight the major transport routes servicing the needs of Zambia. The mere fact that the country is landlocked emphasizes the importance of transport, and Zambia's dependence on it, and it is in the nature of a truism to say that transport will always pose acute problems for the country. The two areas in which it promotes the development of the economy are, firstly, the extent to which the inherited system has been, or is, an inducement to economic development, as opposed to a means of ensuring adequate administrative control; and secondly, the effect on the economy of the structural change in the transport sector which has occurred as a result of the illegal declaration of independence by the Smith regime in November 1965. In other words, it is conceptually useful to identify and analyse first the transport 'bottlenecks' in so far as the present system supports current levels of development, and second the effect of new projects within the transport sector on the level and growth of economic activity. At the same time, the transport sector meets the internal requirements of the economy and the demands made for moving goods into and out of the country.

The full significance of these developments within the transport field cannot be fully appreciated without a brief consideration of the development of the transport sector in general, and railways in particular. The starting point is that transport has been a constraint to the economic development of Zambia, as indicated in the opening quotation. The significance of this can only be understood after an attempt has been made to establish some of the costs of diversification. The main aspects to be considered are the effect on the economy of diverting export/import traffic away from the pre-1964 'traditional' routes; the period covered in the analysis is between 1964 to 1967. During this period, all petrol, oils, and lubricant products were diverted to new routes and an oil pipeline was in the course of construction; there was a substantial drop in the importation of Wankie coal from Rhodesia; and 50 per cent of all copper exports were despatched from the Zambian Copperbelt on new routes. The cost of this diversion together with an assessment of the 'new' transport routes and various organizational aspects of transport are considered in this chapter. Finally, the chapter ends with an indication of some of the many criteria which must be considered in any long-term transport planning.

Table 12.1 shows that the relative importance of the transport and communications sector to GDP has increased from 4.4 per cent in 1964 to 6.5 per cent in 1967. It will be seen that within the sector as a whole railway transport has declined in importance as road transport has increased. This is the structural change in the sector which has come about as a result of the government's policy to reduce Zambia's dependence on the railway through Rhodesia, following UDI.

TABLE 12.1

Gross domestic product by industry
at current price
(K m.)

	Factor cost			
	1964	*1965*	*1966*	*1967*
GDP	464.9	548.7	644.5	733.4
Agriculture	53.3	54.8	60.5	64.4
Mining	220.8	208.9	240.1	235.5
Manufacturing	28.2	40.0	60.2	78.9
Construction	20.0	39.4	54.0	63.3
Transport and communication	20.6	32.4	32.4	47.9
Railway transport	n.a.	19.4	14.7	18.1
Road transport	n.a.	8.5	13.0	19.3
Other transport	n.a.	1.6	1.3	6.7
Posts and telecom.	n.a.	2.9	3.4	3.8
Other sectors	122.0	173.4	197.3	243.4

Source: Statistical Year Book, 1968, Central Statistical Office, Lusaka.

The National Income figures do not adequately reflect the importance of the sector in terms of total economic activity, the geographical distribution of which is dependent on transport in some form or other. Since the bulk of all economic activity takes place within the line of rail area, it is therefore hardly surprising to find that the only major long-distance bitumen road runs parallel to the railway. This position will change once the Great East and Great North Roads have been bitumenized. It is probably fair to say that within the line of rail economy, transport in the normal course of events is not a constraint on general economic activity. However, the situation within the remaining part of Zambia is very different, and the slow development of the rural areas, although caused by many other factors, is undoubtedly due in part to high transportation costs or even the lack of transport facilities. This factor is clearly of significance, especially when crops with a low unit value are being transported.

Unfortunately space precludes a detailed discussion of these matters since the emphasis in this chapter is on external transport links between Zambia and the sea.

DEVELOPMENT OF THE TRANSPORT SYSTEM BEFORE UDI

A study of the history of Central Africa will bring out the background and policies which over the years have shaped Zambia's dependence on transport routes through Rhodesia to Mozambique and South Africa. In other words, the heritage of Zambia has meant that her economy in general, and her transport sector in particular, have until recently been an integral part of the economy of Southern Africa. However, since UDI, significant changes have occurred in the structure of the transport sector. The government has diverted a large volume of traffic away from the traditional route (via Southern Rhodesia) to new routes. The effect on the economy of this substantial change in the structure of the sector has been considerable.

From 1953 to 1963 Zambia, then Northern Rhodesia, formed part of the Federation of Rhodesia and Nyasaland; during this period there was complete free movement of all commodities between the three constituent members comprising the Federation. Moreover, the Federation constituted a customs union and several Federal-owned common services in the fields of power and transport were established. [4] One of these common services, Rhodesia Railways, serviced both Northern and Southern Rhodesia, traversing both countries and linking them with the ports in Mozambique and South Africa via contiguous railways. [5] As will be shown in greater detail, the historical

---

4 The Rhodesia Railways; Central African Airways; Central African Power Corporation.

5 The southern contiguous railways to the Rhodesia Railways are CFM (Caminhos de Ferro de Moçambique) with its access to Beira and Lourenço Marques, and SAR (South African Railways) with its access to Durban. In addition, the northern routes which until UDI were virtually unavailable to Zambian traffic were BCK (La Compagnie du Chemin de Fer du Bas-

development of the Rhodesia Railways is tied up with the attempts of the Railways themselves, the Federal government, and the Southern Rhodesian government to ensure that all the highly lucrative copper traffic originating from the Zambian Copperbelt be moved over the whole length of Rhodesia Railways. These agreements, which will be discussed later on, virtually precluded the development of alternative routes and in particular the use of the rail route to Lobito, or the use of road transport. The break-up of this monopoly position only came when alternative routes were developed following UDI.[6] Up to this time, the Inter-Governmental Agreement of 1963,[7] which was signed by both the governments of Northern and Southern Rhodesia at the time of the dissolution of the Federation, ensured that if either of the two countries diverted traffic to an alternative route, the government of that country would have to pay the Rhodesia Railways compensation equal to the revenue it would otherwise have

TABLE 12.2

Distribution of Rhodesia Railways track

(miles)

	Zambia	Southern Rhodesia	Botswana	Total
Main lines	495	1,122	399	2,016
Branch lines	160	530	—	690
Total	655	1,652	399	2,706
Percentage	24.2	61.1	14.7	100.0

Source: Rhodesia Railways, *Report and Accounts, June 30, 1966.*

Congo au Katanga) with its access via the CFB (Caminho de Ferro de Benguela) to Lobito (Angola), via the CFL (La Compagnie des Chemins de Fer du Congo Supérieur aux Grands Lacs Africains) to Kalemie and then via EARH (East African Railways and Harbours) from Kigoma to the Tanzanian port of Dar es Salaam, and finally via CFML (La Compagnie du Chemin de Fer, Matadi–Léopoldville) to Matadi (see Maps 12.1 and 12.2).

[6] Several problems connected with the running of the joint railway system occurred following UDI, and on 1 July 1967, the former unitary system was divided from an operational point of view and Zambia Railways was established.

[7] 'Agreement between the Government of Southern Rhodesia and the Government of Northern Rhodesia Relating to the Rhodesia Railways', dated 10 December 1963.

earned. Since UDI, therefore, and in particular during the last four years, considerable efforts have been directed to up-grading and bitumenizing the Great North Road so that large amounts of traffic could be moved between the Zambian line of rail and the Tanzanian port of Dar es Salaam. In addition, the Great East Road which links Lusaka with the railhead at Salima in Malawi has been bitumenized.

Until 1 July 1967, Zambia Railways was an integral part of the former unitary Rhodesia Railways which operated in both Southern and Northern Rhodesia. The origin of the former unitary Rhodesia Railways undertaking lies in the rapid development of rail communications in the early part of the domination of Central Africa by the British South Africa Company (BSA), which enjoyed a monopoly of rail and mineral concessions. Within Central Africa, virtually all the railway development, except for branch lines[8] and the 1955 South East rail link (Bannockburn to Malvernia), was completed by 1909. The main railway activity of Central Africa started soon after the BSA had been given its charter and its power to administer the area in 1889. The railway line which ran from Livingstone in the south through Lusaka and Broken Hill (Kabwe) to the Congo border in the north was the hub of European economic life. The important dates as far as railway development is concerned are as follows:

1. 1897: line built from Mafeking through Bechuanaland (Botswana) reached Bulawayo, and in 1898 Salisbury was linked with Beira via Umtali. In 1902 Salisbury and Bulawayo were linked.

2. 1904: a line from Bulawayo reached Victoria Falls (via Wankie to tap the coal field there) and the line was extended northwards through what was then Northern Rhodesia.

3. 1906: the railway reached Broken Hill (Kabwe) and in 1909 reached the Congo border at Sakania where it now links up, through the Chemin de Fer du Bas-Congo au Katanga (BCK), with the Benguela Railway in Angola to Lobito.

In these early days of railway development the mineral wealth of what is known today as the Copperbelt was virtually untapped and in fact the Broken Hill/Congo border link-up was financed by Tanganyika Concessions Ltd.,[9] with the agreement of the BSA, as an

---

[8] The main Zambian branch lines were commissioned as follows: Ndola to Luanshya, 22 January 1929; Ndola to Nkala/Kitwe, July 1930; Nkana to Nchanga, 20 June 1931; Chambishi to Mufulira, 1 April 1932.

[9] The Rhodesian-Katanga Junction Railway and Mineral Company was formed.

outlet for Katangese minerals. In other words, it was the lead and zinc deposits at Broken Hill which first sparked off railway development in what is now Zambia. The BSA seemed to be more motivated by the prospects of increased mineral royalty than by transportation receipts. Thus it could possibly be argued that the company's dual financial interest accelerated the development of the railway system beyond what would have taken place if the mines and railroads had represented separate financial interests. 'The Company was able to capture the external economies of the railway industry on the mining industry and vice versa.'[10] The extension of the railway from Broken Hill to the Congo border in 1909 certainly did not involve these joint interests; the rapidly developing Katanga copper mines wished to connect with the Rhodesia system mainly to obtain coke from the Wankie Colliery deposits in Southern Rhodesia. They also needed a rail link to the sea for their copper until the Benguela line[11] to Lobito Bay in Angola was completed. After the British government, in 1922, had taken over the administration of the Rhodesias from the BSA, the Rhodesia Railways Ltd.[12] became the working company responsible for the entire system and the unification was complete when the

[10] R. E. Baldwin, *Economic Development and Export Growth: a Study of Northern Rhodesia, 1920–1960*, University of California Press, Berkeley, 1966, p. 172.

[11] The Benguela Railway was eventually opened in 1931 and was constructed by Tanganyika Concessions Ltd., which acquired about 15 per cent of the Union Minière du Haut Katanga. Tanganyika Concessions also owned 90 per cent of the Benguela Railway with the balance belonging to the Portuguese government of Angola.

[12] In 1927 the rail system in the Rhodesias was known as the Beira and Mashonaland and Rhodesia Railways (BMR) and was composed of various sections of line owned by six different companies who were the Rhodesia Railways Ltd. (1899), the Mashonaland Railway Co. Ltd. (1897), the Beira Railway Co. Ltd. (1892), the Beira Junction Railway Co. Ltd. (1895), the Blinkwater Railway Co. Ltd., and the Rhodesia-Katanga Junction Railway Co. Ltd. (1908). In 1927 Rhodesia Railways supplanted the Mashonaland Railway Co. Ltd. as the working company responsible for the combined working and gave its name to the entire system. The construction of the railway system had been financed in sections as and when required for the extensions and branch lines. Although the above companies were legally separate entities, they were physically one unit since all sections were under the same management (see Frank Austin, *The Rhodesia Railways, a Short History*, Rhodesia Railways Public Relations Office, Bulawayo, December 1966).

Rhodesian-Katanga Junction Railway was purchased from Tanganyika Concessions Ltd., in 1929. In 1936, the Rhodesia Railways Ltd. acquired all the assets of the Mashonaland Railway Company and therefore became owners of the whole railway system in Rhodesia and Zambia and of the Vryburg-Bulawayo section.

With the development of the copper mining industry in Northern Rhodesia, an opportunity was created for Rhodesia Railways to secure valuable traffic, provided, of course, that this traffic was not diverted northwards through Lobito (the Benguela Railway opened in 1931). As a result of the potential use of alternative routes, the history of Rhodesia Railways revolves around ensuring a flow of traffic from the Copperbelt to Beira (and Lourenço Marques). The first agreement which the Railways entered into was a twenty-year agreement in 1936 with the Zambian copper companies, by which the latter undertook to ship all their copper via Rhodesia Railways in return for extremely low rates on the copper (about £3 per ton) and an even lower fixed rate on coal from Wankie Colliery (owned by Anglo American Corporation), which was needed for power and ore processing. This agreement formed a precedent for the future and in many ways determined the future role of the Railways. To assure the continuation of two-way traffic (coal/copper), the mining companies agreed not to develop hydro-electric power as a substitute for coal.

During the late twenties, the Railways enjoyed a comfortable income arising from the extensive construction activity both on the Copperbelt and in the Congo. However, this picture changed with the collapse of the copper market in the thirties and no dividends were paid from 1931 to 1938.[13] It was due to a lack of capital in the thirties and the inability to raise any capital during the war that the Southern Rhodesian government eventually, in 1947, purchased Rhodesia Railways. The government was able to raise a K 60 m. (£30 m.) loan, K 6.6 m. (£3. 3 m.) of which was earmarked for the acquisition of the shareholding of Rhodesia Railways. The company remained a joint stock company incorporated in the UK until 1949, when the Rhodesia Railways Act created a statutory Railway Corporation.[14] With this act, a Higher

---

13 See Rhodesia Railways Ltd., *Report for the Financial Year ended September 30, 1947*. This annual report contains a useful summary of the railways, covering the period 1938 to 1947.

14 The Rhodesia Railways operated all the railways in Southern Rhodesia and Zambia with the exception of the Shabani branch. In 1949, the Portuguese

Authority was established which included the Governor of Northern Rhodesia. This gave the colonial government, for the first time, some say in the policy of the railway which ran through its territory and which depended for its viability on the traffic provided by the copper mines located within its boundaries. The net effect of the legislation was that Northern Rhodesia became residually responsible for meeting 20 per cent of the deficiency if in any year the Railways' receipts were insufficient to meet the charges on its revenue—including interest, sinking fund, and other loan charges. Bechuanaland was responsible for meeting 5 per cent of any deficit, whilst Southern Rhodesia met the remaining 75 per cent.

A fundamental change took place in the Railways when the Federation of Rhodesia and Nyasaland was established, when it was deemed that the Railways would become an exclusive Federal responsibility. This in effect meant that the Federal Minister of Transport and Communications constituted the Higher Authority for the Railways and the Federal government assumed all the obligations of the territorial governments for meeting any deficiency on the Railways' revenue account. During its existence, the Federal government loaned to the Railways sums raised on the market totalling in all K 44.5 m. (£22.25 m.). In addition, other loans were raised for the Railways—$10 m. from the Foreign Operations Administration of the USA in 1954, and $19 m. from the International Bank for Reconstruction and Development (IBRD) in 1958. However, before the Federal government had taken over the Railways, and after the Railways had been established as a statutory corporation, the government of Northern Rhodesia had raised on the market a loan of K 15.46 m. (£7.73 m.) and a further sum of K 4 m. (£2 m.) was lent from the government's own resources. In addition, the Federal government was able to raise an IBRD loan of $14 m. which was made available to the Railways to assist them in financing the construction of the new railway line from Bannockburn to the Mozambique border in Southern Rhodesia, as part of the Lourenço Marques link. For its part, the Southern Rhodesian government advanced a sum of K 10 m. (£5 m.) to Rhodesia Railways in 1953. Finally, a large amount of money over the years was loaned to the Railways by the two principal Railway Staff Pension Funds. Indeed these loans became an annual feature of railway finance and by 1965

government exercised its right to expropriate the Beira Railway Company Ltd., that is the section from Beira to Umtali.

had totalled over K 28 m. (£14 m.). The total loan indebtedness at the time of the Federal dissolution was around K 180 m. (£90 m.).

On financial grounds alone, therefore, the Federal government had strong reasons for ensuring that all traffic was directed via Rhodesia Railways to protect its investment in the system. In addition to these direct financial incentives, there were other considerations—especially since Rhodesia Railways ran through the Federal area and traffic on it thus generated income and employment in that area. The first major agreement was signed in 1950, before the Federation was established. The Beira Convention was entered into by the UK government in 1950, on its own behalf and on behalf of the government of Southern Rhodesia, and the government of Portugal. The terms of this Convention were, *inter alia*, that in return for a Portuguese undertaking to develop the port of Beira and the Beira Railways, it was agreed that these latter should be used as far as possible to their full working capacity. The Convention guaranteed running rights on the Rhodesia Railways and the Caminhos de Ferro de Moçambique line, and in addition contained agreements on traffic rights and rates. However, despite these arrangements to encourage the flow of traffic on the Mozambique routes, and to prevent rail competition from the route to Lobito, the latter route was able to get its share of copper exports. This led in 1956 to the 'Tripartite' Agreement between Rhodesia Railways, the Benguela Railway, and the BCK[15] which permitted the railing, via BCK-Benguela, of a certain proportion of exported copper, subject to a ceiling of 20 per cent of the tonnage available for export.[16] The agreement, *inter alia*, provided for an equalization of rates on copper exports as between the Copperbelt and Beira/Lourenço Marques,

[15] 'Tripartite Agreement between the Companhia du Caminho de Ferro de Benguela (CFB), Compagnie du Chemin de Fer du Bas-Congo au Katanga (BCK) and Rhodesia Railways', dated 7 November 1956, superseded the 1936 Agreement and the 1939 'Agreement between Union Minière du Haut Katanga and Rhodesia Railways', in which UMHK were required to despatch not less than 20 per cent of their copper output via Beira and also to obtain not less than 30 per cent (minimum 1,500 tons monthly) of their coke requirements from Wankie in return for rating inducements.

[16] Article 5 states: 'In the case of copper no greater tonnage shall be accepted by the contracting parties for export via Lobito than 10% of the present railings by the Zambian Copper Mines to Beira and Lourenço Marques plus 50% of any additional tonnage which would be available for railing to Beira and Lourenço Marques in the future subject to no higher tonnage than 20% of the total tonnage available for export overseas.'

and the Copperbelt and Lobito. The through-rate on copper for the three ports was established at K 29.70 per ton. The 'Tripartite' Agreement was directed to prevent competition on railway tariff rates between the Lobito and the Southern routes, and was limited to a prescribed proportion of total output of the quantity of copper from Northern Rhodesia which could be routed through Southern Rhodesia. Despite this, railings via Lobito continued and in 1959 reached 90,255 tons. Although this was less than 20 per cent of the total tonnage available for export overseas, it did nevertheless represent a substantial loss of potential revenue to Rhodesia Railways. As a result of this, Rhodesia Railways broke the provisions of the 'Tripartite' Agreement by offering large discounts to the Northern Rhodesia mining companies to route all their copper traffic via Rhodesia Railways. These so-called 'Rebate' Agreements[17] ensured that the mining companies agreed not normally to consign more than 36,000 tons of copper via Lobito in return for a special low rate of K 19.05 per ton on the Beira/Lourenço Marques route in respect of copper which would otherwise have been railed to Lobito under the 'Tripartite' Agreement. In 1962, the 'regular' rate was raised to K 30.67 per ton and the special rate to K 20.96. These 'Rebate' Agreements achieved their purpose and by 1962 Northern Rhodesian copper via Lobito was virtually nil (see Table 12.3). These agreements appear to have been taken quite unilaterally by Rhodesia Railways and show that during the Federal era the interests of the unitary railway system, in which admittedly the then Northern Rhodesian government had acquired a considerable financial stake, were not necessarily in accord with the best interests of the territory.

When the Federation was dissolved in 1963, it was decided that the Railways should continue to operate the rail system north and south of the Zambesi as the same body corporate as had existed before Federation, but constituted as a body corporate for Northern and Southern Rhodesia jointly. The Higher Authority was reconstituted and under the terms of the Inter-Governmental Agreement of 10 December 1963, it was stated that regarding 'the ownership of the Railways, and subject to the provisions of this agreement, the financial responsibility for them will be with the two governments in equal share'. In other

---

[17] The 'Rebate' Agreements between Rhodesia Railways and Roan Selection Trust and Anglo American Corporation were entered into in 1960.

TABLE 12.3

Shipments of copper from the Congo and Zambia via principal
export routes, 1953–63

('000 tons)

	1953	1954	1955	1956	1957	1958	1959	1960	1961	1962	1963
Beira/Lourenço Marques											
Ex Congo	65.54	84.58	75.78	84.07	79.34	76.42	90.11	129.19	124.85	75.39	89.71
Ex Zambia	381.56	412.25	380.95	390.45	409.92	349.58	493.36	544.44	586.63	579.45	608.60
Total	447.09	496.83	456.74	474.52	489.27	426.00	583.47	673.63	711.48	654.84	698.31
Lobito											
Ex Congo	37.69	46.33	48.73	52.42	52.29	53.10	61.91	125.67	196.41	241.69	168.75
Ex Zambia	—	—	—	—	34.33	52.05	90.26	69.60	22.85	0.22	0.01
Total	37.69	46.33	48.73	52.42	86.62	105.14	152.16	195.27	219.26	241.91	168.76
Matadi											
Ex Congo	112.40	106.13	99.48	110.78	92.37	92.97	114.45	63.65	—	0.07	13.79
Ex Zambia	—	—	—	—	—	—	—	—	—	—	—
Total	112.40	106.13	99.48	110.78	92.37	92.97	114.45	63.65	—	0.07	13.79

Source: Edwin T. Haefele and Eleanor B. Steinberg, *Government Controls on Transport: an African Case*, Brookings Institution, Washington, 1965, p. 7.

words, this agreement, together with the Dissolution Order in Council, made sure that Northern Rhodesia achieved an equal measure of ownership and control of the Railways *vis-à-vis* Southern Rhodesia and an equal financial responsibility for meeting their liabilities, should the latter become necessary.[18] The agreement also covered the free movement of rolling stock and locomotives, and the construction of new lines to which reference has already been made. The net effect of all this was that the still-dependent government undertook with Southern Rhodesia alone the heavy future refinancing and other obligations entailed by the loan capital structure of the Railways.

Although the new arrangements for the Railways came into effect on 1 January 1964, the now self-governing Northern Rhodesia government's equal voice in control of the railway administration proved to be more apparent than real. This was partly due to the fact that the executive machinery of the Railways was concentrated in Southern Rhodesia, and the Secretariat operated from the offices of the Ministry of Transport and Power in Salisbury. The Higher Authority did not in fact meet until a few days before UDI in November 1965.

When Zambia achieved her Independence in October 1964, she assumed, in terms of the Zambia Order in Council, the existing rights and obligations of the former colonial government, including those incurred under the Inter-Governmental Agreement of 1963 and other such 'inherited' contractual obligations in relation to the Railways.

During the period between Zambian Independence and the illegal assumption of independence by the government of Southern Rhodesia (November 1965), serious difficulties began to develop in the operation of the unitary system; the effect of these on the accounts of Rhodesia

[18] In contrast to the joint ownership as stipulated in the Inter-Governmental Agreement, the allocation of immovable assets by book value was roughly: Bechuanaland 4 per cent, Rhodesia 66 per cent, and Zambia 30 per cent. The Chairman of Rhodesia Railways stated in Lusaka on 12 May 1965, that 'this apparent unbalance in assets, compared with the financial responsibilities assumed by the two governments, is explained in the growth and development pattern of the countries served by the Railways for some 70 years'. The Chairman continued, 'As a unitary system, the alignment of railway routes and the siting of railway installations were influenced primarily by over-all economic factors and considerations of sound railway operating practice'. (From an address presented to a meeting of businessmen in Lusaka sponsored by the Lusaka Chamber of Commerce and the Junior Chamber of Commerce International on 12 May 1965.)

TABLE 12.4

Rhodesia Railways: summary of net revenue and appropriation accounts, 1960–67 (30 June)
(K m.)

	1960	1961	1962	1963	1964	1965	1966	1967[1]
Surplus on working account	12.5	12.5	6.6	7.2	14.1	12.8	8.4	(10.1)
Plus: Net surplus of investments	1.1	1.6	1.8	1.3	1.2	1.3	1.6	0.6
	13.6	14.1	8.4	8.4	15.3	14.1	10.0	(9.5)
Less: appropriations[2]	1.1	1.5	0.3	0.2	2.5	1.4	0.7	n.a.
	12.5	12.6	8.1	8.3	12.8	12.6	9.2	n.a.
Interest & expenses on loans	7.3	7.4	7.3	7.3	7.3	7.3	7.2	7.1
Contributions to sinking fund	1.8	1.8	1.9	2.4	2.6	2.7	2.7	2.7
	9.1	9.2	9.3	9.8	10.0	10.1	10.0	9.8
Appropriations to (from) rates & wages stabilization account	3.4	3.4	(1.2)	(1.5)	2.7	2.5	(0.7)	n.a.
	12.5	12.6	8.1	8.3	12.7	12.6	9.2	n.a.

[1] Forecast based on July–December 1966 results.
[2] Loss on Messina Beit Bridge, disposal of unit assets, obsolete stores written off, provision for accrued leave pay, etc.

Note: Errors due to rounding.

Source: Rhodesia Railways *Annual Reports.*

Railways are shown in Table 12.4. However, UDI created an entirely new situation and a myriad of legal questions were immediately raised. Of particular importance was the status of the Higher Authority which could not be convened because the lawful government of Southern Rhodesia could not be determined. The Higher Authority was charged with such matters as capital expenditure, raising of loans, etc., and since it could not now meet, the Railways were likely to enter a potentially critical financial situation. In addition, various policy decisions were taken which were to lead to a complete disruption of the unitary railway system. Some of the events[19] which took place after UDI were as follows:

1. In December 1965, the Rhodesian 'illegal' government directed the Railways that no petroleum products carried by Rhodesia Railways were to leave Rhodesia for Zambia. The former was subsequently amended to allow petroleum products to be carried to Zambia under export licence. In effect, by this action, the Rhodesians were denying Zambia transit traffic rights for POL which originated outside Rhodesia.

2. In April 1966, payments made by the Railways in Zambia to the Rhodesia Railways account in Bulawayo were blocked. This led to the southern contiguous railways demanding payment for railage in advance of shipment. The net effect was that the Railways in Zambia were deprived of the bulk of their accustomed receipts from imports. Furthermore, on 25 May 1966, Zambia's copper companies declared *force majeure* on their contracts with buyers, thereby relieving themselves of liability for damage because of conditions beyond their control. The payments crisis continued with the Bank of Zambia refusing applications for foreign exchange needed to pay railage on goods going over Rhodesia Railways. This was subsequently eased and on 22 July the government announced the resumption of copper shipments via Rhodesia Railways.

3. In May and June 1966 controls were introduced to limit the movement of locomotives and rolling stock across the border on a one-for-one basis, which effectively stabilized the existing distribution of rolling stock between the two countries. The effect of this was, essentially, to create two railway systems.

The net result of these interruptions, and the need to reduce trade with the rebel regime while at the same time maintaining the import/export levels of vital commodities, led Zambia to develop alternative routes and encourage the greater use of the three main surface routes—through Congo (Kinshasa), Tanzania, and Malawi.

The diversion of traffic from Rhodesia Railways led to various accusations being made by the Rhodesian regime that Zambia was in breach of the Inter-Governmental Agreement. The net effect of this

---

[19] See Richard L. Sklar, 'Zambia's Response to UDI', *Mawazo 1*, June 1968, No. 3.

build-up was that the unitary railway system was operationally divided on 1 July 1967.[20]

Some of the main conclusions which emerge from this brief survey are:

1. Mineral exploitation after the completion of the Livingstone/ Congo border railway had little effect in stimulating additional railroad development. For example, with the development of the Copperbelt in the 1920s, the only effect on the Railways system was the construction of a few short branch lines, since the main line already traversed the area. At the same time, the best agricultural land happened to be close to the line of rail, and this fact did not act as a stimulus to further railway development. In other words, the railway system over the years consolidated the line of rail economy, with the result that the effect on the economy as a whole has been more than a little concentrated. Furthermore, it could be argued that the rather 'simple' railway system, cutting the country in half as it does, has been the cause of the very marked dual economy.

2. Zambia until 1966–7 has been completely dependent on the unitary Rhodesia Railways system for its links with African ports. The mining industry has been the major customer of the Railways, and the Railways in turn have made significant purchases of other Zambian productive inputs. At the same time a great deal of the 'politics' surrounding the development of the Railways has centred around ensuring that the copper traffic is moved on the Rhodesia Railways system. As a result the administrative authorities in Zambia have never been in a position, until recently, to direct effectively railway policy to meet the needs of the country.

3. The Railways have, until recently, been protected from competitive road transport. Table 12.5 shows that during the calendar year 1965, 97 per cent of all imports entered Zambia on Rhodesia Railways via Livingstone. A similar dependence on Rhodesia Railways will be found for exports. Of course, with regard to imports, Rhodesia was the most important supplier to the

---

20 The Zambia Railways Act, 1967, established a body corporate, the Zambia Railways Board, with power to operate and maintain transport services for the carriage of persons and goods in the Republic. At the same time, the Transport Services (Railways and Airways) (Transitional) Act, 1967, was passed in Rhodesia to establish 'a body concerned with the provision, operation, and maintenance of rail transport and other related services within and for Rhodesia and Botswana with effect from 1 July 1967'.

Zambian market in any case, with more than 30 per cent of total imports. The dominance of the Railways was secured by an agreement between the Long Distance Road Transport Operators' Association and Rhodesia Railways.[21] This agreement reduced the extent of competition by the association's undertaking to limit its licensed capacity on the principal road routes of the territories concerned and not to charge less on these routes than the corresponding rail rates for certain specified traffic. In return for this the Railways agreed not to reduce their rates for this traffic to compete with the association, where the latter had agreed to limit its licensed capacity.

4. No attempt has been made to document the presence or absence of subsidization of Rhodesian traffic by Zambian traffic. The rate structure of the former unitary railway system offered favourable rates for export products, for imported goods needed for their development and for local traffic. The actual rate structure of Rhodesia Railways was based on the recommendations of the Harragin Commission which set out in a most concise statement the philosophy of pricing on the railways of Central Africa:

TABLE 12.5
Imports into Zambia, 1965
('000 short tons)

Imported via Rhodesia Railways		
General goods	713.2	
POL/bitumen	179.5	
Coal/coke	1,369.9	
		2,262.6
Imported via road from Rhodesia		
CARS	20.6	
Smith and Youngson	10.0	
Clan	11.0	
Imported by rail via Congo		41.6
Lobito	15.1	
Congo	13.9	
		29.0
Total		2,333.2

Source: Unpublished data.

[21] Co-ordination Agreement between Rhodesia Railways and United Transport Overseas Services Ltd. and all its associated and subsidiary companies in

... the broad principles of railway rating should be such as to secure no lower revenue from any particular traffic than the direct cost of carrying it and ... the burden of overhead costs should be distributed over the total traffic of the system in accordance with the ability of each traffic to pay.[22]

In other words, the rating structure was a collective system based on the principle of 'charging what the traffic will bear'. The Harragin Report points out that the

commodities are classified on a basis in which value is the dominant factor, but in which regard may also be had to other factors, such as risk, packing, cost of handling, the volume in which the goods normally move, and weight in proportion to bulk.[23]

It further states that:

this system can be used to assist certain classes of traffic which for one reason or another are unable to make their full contribution towards expenses. Consequently it assumes that there are other classes of traffic which can make more than a full contribution according to their ability to pay, always provided in the ultimate end, the revenue collectively so derived is adequate to meet the expenses of the undertaking as a whole. Clearly, however, such a system assumes conditions of monopoly, or near monopoly, if it is to be successfully carried out.[24]

This condition of monopoly[25] was afforded to Rhodesia Railways by the 1963 agreement with the Long Distance Transport Operators. In other words, an accurate application of these principles should result in a system of rates geared, on a commodity-by-commodity basis, to the price elasticity of demand for transport sources. It is an accepted practice of most railways that direct costs are identified for each type of commodity carried, and that these are allocated on a ton mileage basis as a basic part of the rate. Indirect and overhead costs are then recovered by discriminatory rate fixing—charging

Southern and Northern Rhodesia, Clan Transport Co. (Private) Ltd., Smith and Youngson Ltd. (collectively as founder-members of the Long Distance Road Transport Operators' Association, and individually), effective from 1 March 1963.

[22] Federation of Rhodesia and Nyasaland, *Report of the Commission of Inquiry into the Rating Structure of the Rhodesia Railways*, 31 March 1959, p. 9.

[23] ibid., para. 29.

[24] ibid., para. 30.

[25] In addition to the absence of alternative carriers, this kind of rating structure is also dependent on other factors such as the cost characteristics of the railway; quantity, value, and elasticities of demand of the commodities carried; and the railways financial/capital structure.

relatively higher rates on goods with inelastic demands (supplies) and for which freight costs are relatively small in proportion to value. This method therefore means that some commodities are, in a sense, subsidizing the movement of other commodities. While it is reasonable to expect this sort of subsidization within a country, the case is not so clear for rail systems which serve a number of countries. Clearly, with the establishment of Zambia Railways the whole question of the tariff structure has to be reconsidered. The implication of this type of marginal cost pricing in terms of utilization of existing facilities has to be reassessed in terms of the economic development of the country, railway operating efficiencies, the effect on the size of the railway investment, and the effect on investment in other sectors of the economy.[26]

Although emphasis in this chapter is on Zambia's transport requirements for international trade, the importance of other modes of transport, particularly roads, in fulfilling the internal requirements of the economy must not be overlooked. The cursory way in which this is considered is in no way meant to understate the significance of roads.

The Zambian road network has been gradually built up over the past fifty to sixty years to meet the ever-growing needs of the administrative and economic activities of the country. Historically, road development has been concentrated along the line of rail, parallelling the railway line, from Livingstone in the south to the Copperbelt in the north, and traversing land with promising agricultural prospects. The road network spread with the progress of administrative control over outlying areas, and a quick glance at a road map will show the way in which the line of rail acts as an artery from the point of view of transport. The NEDECO report[27] points out that as a result of road development:

> It may be said that the existing main roads give more or less adequate service by their location and geographical distribution, though not necessarily by their structural and geometric standards, and meet the current requirements of the more populated areas and of the economically developed or promising regions of the country.

These areas and regions are reasonably well connected with the centres of administration and trade. Road densities vary considerably across

---

[26] See Edwin T. Haefele and Eleanor B. Steinberg, *Government Controls on Transport: an African Case*, Brookings Institution, Washington, 1965.

[27] Netherlands Engineering Consultants, *A Survey of Transportation in Zambia*, November 1964.

the country, and as would be expected the densities are far greater in the fast developing centres along the line of rail. The report further states that investments in roads should follow economic principles in order to ensure the greatest possible development. Despite the established pattern that most inhabited parts of the country are serviced with roads connecting that area with the line of rail, intra-rural roads are not adequate and in many cases simply non-existent. It was as a result of this that recommendations were made for the establishment of a feeder road programme to meet specifically local development requirements.

As a result of UDI, considerable emphasis has been placed on the development of the Great North Road and the Great East Road, to provide greater capacity. The former route, in particular, has been the main means of moving goods between Zambia and the Tanzanian port of Dar es Salaam. This will be considered further later.

Road transport is the backbone of the internal transport network for the movement of freight and passengers. To a certain extent the internal transport needs can be treated in isolation to the external requirements, although at the margin there is a substantial amount of inter-dependence. The major companies which have been operating within Zambia are Smith and Youngson and Central African Road Services.[28] The latter has had an exclusive concession[29] since 1 January 1965 to operate passenger buses along certain roads, including most of those connecting the Copperbelt municipalities and townships, the main trunk routes (Livingstone-Lusaka-Kapiri Mposhi-Ndola, Kapiri Mposhi–Tunduma, Kapiri Mposhi–Kasama–Mbala–Tunduma, Mufulira–Mansa–Luwingu–Kasama, Lusaka–Chipata–Lundazi, etc.), and those within the boundaries of most of the municipalities, townships, and mine townships.

---

[28] Following the Mulungushi Declaration in April 1968, both Central African Road Services Ltd. (CARS) and Smith and Youngson Ltd. were invited to offer at least 51 per cent of their shares for purchase by government. As a result of this, CARS was renamed Transport Holdings of Zambia Ltd., and besides operating the passenger road transport service in Zambia, it has a substantial freight business. Smith and Youngson, on the other hand, deals exclusively in freight and orginally concentrated mainly on the Great North Road

[29] Due to expire in 1975. The concession is covered by Sections 190 and 265 of the Roads and Road Traffic Ord. It was originally granted to Thatcher, Hobson, & Co. Ltd. and was subsequently transferred to CARS.

In 1968, 73 buses out of a total of 222 were running in various towns on local routes, 80 buses were on the main trunk routes and on the Copperbelt inter-township runs, and the remaining 69 buses were kept in reserve. Of the total of 220 buses in operational use, the large bulk are employed on intra-provincial runs and not inter-province. The Central Statistics Office has estimated that, taking the entire fleet of buses and taxis into consideration, 'one bus is available to every 13,000 people and the ratio of taxis to total population works out to be 1:14,000.'[30]

Water transport in Zambia is, as yet, of no importance. It is of a mainly local nature as there are no through-going water arteries at present in the country. This may seem a strange situation given the Zambesi and Kafue Rivers, but Zambia's rivers are essentially 'upper' rivers which in effect means that they tend to have rocky beds, steep slopes, and high current velocities. These conditions make navigation very difficult and as a result the rivers are not suitable as through-going waterways. The Zambesi River is navigable between Senanga and Balovale and is not much used due in part to the low population densities. Lake Bangweulu is an important focus for local communications, whilst Zambia's only port is situated at Mpulungu on the southern shores of Lake Tanganyika. This port is connected with the other lake ports and in recent years has had a significant throughput of freight following the government's decision to develop the route to Dar es Salaam via Kigoma.

The airways provide a useful means of transporting persons from one administrative centre to another. Zambia Airways was founded on 1 January 1968, when the former unitary Central African Airways in which Zambia had a 45 per cent interest was dissolved.

THE SEARCH FOR NEW ROUTES

During the time of the Federation of Rhodesia and Nyasaland there was free movement of all commodities between the three constituent members of the Federation, a common tariff operated and the member countries benefited from various common services including the Rhodesia Railways and Central African Airways. In short the economies

---

[30] *Report on Passenger Road Transport in Zambia*, Official Statistics 68, Central Statistical Office, Lusaka, 7 July 1968, p. 6.

of the two Rhodesias developed together and all Zambian traffic, as is shown in Tables 12.6 and 12.7, was routed southwards. The pattern developed despite the rail connection via the Benguela Railway to the port of Lobito in Angola. At the time of UDI alternative routes, other than those mentioned to the east coast, via Malawi or Tanzania, were non-existent—the road link to Tanzania at the time was an earth road of indifferent quality and while there was a road/rail link through Malawi this was of limited value. The condition of these road links precluded road transport operators from competing with the established routes on grounds of price alone. At the same time, Federal government policies, in particular the restrictive licensing of road transport and the granting of monopolies to specific operators, kept the control of road/ rail competition firmly in the hands of the government, which was thus to the benefit of the railways.

Technically, in addition to the southern rail route, and the contiguous BCK/Benguela railway line via the Congo to Lobito, there were a number of other routes available for the movement of Zambia's import and export traffic (see Map 12.2):
1. via the Congo to Port Francqui/*Matadi*;
2. via the Congo on BCK/CFL to Kalemie/Kigoma on EARH to *Dar es Salaam*;
3. via Kasama/Mpulungu/Kigoma on EARH to *Dar es Salaam*;
4. via Kasama/Mpanda on EARH to *Dar es Salaam*;
5. via the Great North Road to *Dar es Salaam* or *Mtwara*;
6. via the Great East Road to Salima (Malawi)/*Beira*.

Since none of these routes on grounds of capacity, distance, cost, or availability posed any threat to the Southern Rail route during the Federal period, no restrictive measures other than those mentioned earlier were necessary to secure the use by traffic of the Rhodesia Railways route.

Prior to the end of the Federation in December 1963, therefore, the flow of Northern Rhodesia's import/export traffic had been determined by the country's recent economic development originating from the south, by the large government investment in the railways, and by the desire to protect that investment with beneficial side-effects on incomes and employment within the Federal area. Although this policy was undoubtedly beneficial to the Federation, it was not necessarily so to Northern Rhodesia whose revenue supplied or financed the capital required for rail development throughout the two Rhodesias. Whilst no specific analysis has been made of the operation of the former unitary system, it must be emphasized that Northern Rhodesia would almost certainly have gained by competition for traffic between the Lobito route and the Southern route railways (Rhodesia Railways). On the former route Northern Rhodesia would probably have had capacity available without any additional investment by herself.

Traffic statistics for Zambia are not available prior to 1964, but Tables 12.6 and 12.7 give data for 1963–4 to 1966–7 inclusive.[31] These tables show that between 1963–4 and 1965–6, the total tonnage moved into and out of Zambia increased by 17 per cent, whereas there was a 14 per cent drop in volume in 1966–7.

	Total traffic ('000 tons)	Index (1963/4=100)
1963–4	3,038.2	100
1964–5	3,274.7	108
1965–6	3,545.2	117
1966–7	3,034.3	100

The increase in the earlier period was due to a substantial rise in import traffic which followed, and was a result of, Independence and the subsequent very large increase in both public and private sector expenditure. This increase in expenditure, particularly in the private sector, put severe strain on the Rhodesia Railways system which in 1965 was probably working to capacity without substantial further capital investment.

The problems of the railway system, discussed earlier, were further aggravated by the illegal declaration of UDI by the Smith regime, and the effect of this declaration was the more dramatic since Zambia was so entirely dependent on the then unitary Rhodesia Railways network for the movement of traffic into and out of her territory. The realization of Smith's stranglehold on Zambia as supplier of essential imports— for example coal and POL as well as many consumer and industrial goods—and through the control of import and export routes, gave immediate impetus to the creation of major alternative transport routes as well as alternative sources of supply. It was not, however, uniquely the Rhodesian declaration of UDI which led to Zambia's policy to divert trade and traffic, as plans for this existed prior to

---

[31] No definitive transport statistics are available for the movement of external trade. There is significant difference between the data presented in Tables 12.6 and 12.7 and that given in the 1968 *Economic Report* prepared by the Finance Division, Office of the Vice President.

TABLE 12.6

Traffic into Zambia (imports)[1]

('000 tons)

	Year ending 30 June			
	1964	1965	1966	1967
BY ROUTE				
To Zambia				
From Beira	42.8	70.3	94.2	151.8
From Lourenço Marques	197.5	195.0	110.2	77.2
From Lobito	4.6	10.2	53.4	126.0
From South African ports	17.0	23.4	34.0	24.5
From South African inland stations	152.7	162.9	238.8	310.5
From Congo	3.7	6.8	34.4	39.5
From Rhodesia	1,371.4	1,527.5	1,819.8[2]	969.4[2]
From Dar es Salaam and North (POL)	—	—	101.6[3]	244.5[3]
From Dar es Salaam (General goods)	—	—	—	20.0[3]
Total	1,789.7	1,996.1	2,486.5	1,963.4
To Congo—coal	226.0	298.0	n.a.[2]	n.a.[2]
Total System	2,015.7	2,294.1	2,486.5	1,963.4

[1] Excludes traffic entering Zambia by road from Rhodesia.
[2] Congolese coke/coal included in Rhodesian traffic.
[3] Approximate.
[4] POL imports for calendar years 1966 and 1967 as follows:

	Calendar years	
	1966	1967
Airlifts		
— British ex E. Africa	20.7	—
— Canada ex Congo	4.1	—
— ZAC ex E. Africa	13.6	16.7
— Miscellaneous	13.1	2.8
	51.5	19.5
Ex Tanzania		
— Via Isoka	76.3	72.8
— Direct tankers/freight	3.5	68.6
— Kigoma/Mpulungu	17.1	27.2
— Kigoma/Albertville	1.8	—
— ZTRS	5.3	19.7
	104.0	188.3

(Continued on page 350)

(*Continued from page 349*)

	Calendar years	
	1966	*1967*
Ex Congo		
— Kinshasa/Port Francqui	15.4	5.1
— Lobito Bay	1.7	0.5
	17.1	5.6
Ex Malawi		
— Beira/Salima (drums)	16.4	15.2
— Beira/Salima (bulk)	16.6	38.6
	33.0	53.8
Total	205.6	267.2

	Year ending 30 June			
	1964	*1965*	*1966*	*1967*
BY COMMODITY				
General Goods				
— Beira	40.5	67.0	94.2	151.8
— Lourenço Marques	56.3	70.2	103.3	77.2
— Lobito	4.6	10.2	38.3	87.7
— Rhodesia	446.0	566.0	317.8	174.5
— S.A. inland stations	148.7	159.5	235.3	307.2
— S.A. ports	17.0	23.4	34.0	18.3
— Congo	3.7	6.8	34.4	39.5
— Dar es Salaam	—	—	—	20.0
	716.8	903.1	857.4	876.2
POL				
— Beira	2.3	3.3	—	—
— Lourenço Marques	141.2	124.8	6.9	—
— Rhodesia	—	34.0	86.9	—
— Dar es Salaam North[4]	—	—	101.6[4]	244.5[4]
	143.5	162.1	195.4	244.5
Coke/coal				
— Rhodesia	925.4	927.5	1,415.1[2]	794.9[2]
— Lobito	—	—	15.1	38.3
— South Africa	4.0	3.4	3.5	9.6
	929.4	930.9	1,433.7	842.8
Total	1,789.7	1,996.1	2,486.5	1,963.4

[1] Congolese coke/coal included in Rhodesian traffic.
[2] See above for POL imports for calendar years 1966 and 1967.

TABLE 12.7
Traffic out of Zambia (exports)[1]
('000 tons)

	Year ending 30 June			
	1964	1965	966	1967
BY ROUTE				
Ex Zambia				
To Beira	363.3	362.4	441.2	218.9
To Lourenço Marques	399.6	393.9	251.3	184.8
To Lobito	—	—	33.1	158.2
To South Africa	100.2	106.2	95.8	89.6
To Congo	6.4	9.5	50.8	80.4
To Rhodesia	n.a.	n.a.	24.2	10.8
To Dar es Salaam[4]	—	—	9.0	161.9
To Beira via Malawi	—	—	4.1	35.9
To Rhodesia by road	—	—	—	3.5
Total	869.5[2]	871.9[2]	909.5	943.9
Ex Congo				
Copper	85.0	53.3	80.0[3]	56.0[3]
Zinc	32.0	55.4	69.2[3]	71.0[3]
Zinc concentrates	36.0			
Total	153.0	108.7	149.2[3]	127.0[3]
Total System	1,022.5[2]	980.6[2]	1,058.7	1,070.9

[1] Excluding road transport between Rhodesia and Zambia.
[2] Excludes tonnages destined to Rhodesia.
[3] Approximate.
[4] Details of copper routes as follows:

	1965–6	1966–7
Via Great North Road		
ZTRS	0.3	86.2
CARS	4.8	42.2
Via Mpanda	—	3.3
Via Mpulungu	—	0.3
Via air	3.9	29.9
	9.0	161.9

(Continued on page 352)

(*Continued from page 351*)

	Year ending 30 June			
	1964	1965	1966	1967
BY COMMODITY				
Copper — Beira	321.2	332.6	406.0	146.8
— Lourenço Marques	362.9	356.0	216.4	103.9
— Lobito	—	—	33.1	158.2
— South Africa	25.4	28.8	30.0	26.9
— Rhodesia	—	—	3.3	0.1
— Dar es Salaam	—	—	9.0	161.9
— Beira (Malawi and road)	—	—	4.1	39.4
	709.5	717.3	701.9	637.2
Lead	18.2	15.0	20.6	22.3
Zinc	53.2	51.5	51.8	43.9
Manganese	32.2	31.0	31.6	25.2
Cobalt	3.3	1.4	1.7	1.4
Other minerals	3.1	2.7	31.1	13.8
General goods	50.0	53.0	70.8	200.1
	869.5	871.9	909.5	943.9

Independence. UDI was a catalyst and its effect can only be seen over time in terms of the development of alternative routes and the diversion of traffic away from the former unitary system (see Tables 12.6 and 12.7).

Traffic levels

One of the major problems with which Zambia has been faced so far as traffic movement is concerned is that the crucial traffic direction is the inward one. In other words, as the tonnage hauled into Zambia is roughly double that going out, the outward traffic can, to a large extent, be ignored. That is not to suggest that export traffic does not pose any problems. But by and large copper freight is a relatively straightforward commodity to handle, given its weight/volume ratio and its profitability. Table 12.6 shows that general goods were in 1967 still mainly imported into Zambia via the Rhodesia Railways system.

Imports—petrol, oils and lubricants (POL)

In 1964–5 a total of 162,100 tons of POL products were railed into Zambia from Rhodesia. One of the immediate effects of UDI[32] was

---

[32] On 18 December 1965, Rhodesia formally placed an embargo on the export of petroleum fuels from Rhodesia by preventing the Railways from carrying these products out of Rhodesia into Zambia.

the suspension of those supplies of POL to Zambia which in 1965–6 originated from the Rhodesian oil refinery at Feruka on the Mozambique border.[33] As a result of this oil sanctions policy, a massive improvised air, road, lake, and rail lift of POL products was set up, and during 1966 a total of 205,600 tons, and in 1967, 267,200 tons, of POL was brought into Zambia. The relative importance of the various routes during this period is shown below:

	Calendar years (%)	
	1966	*1967*
Ex airlifts	25.0	7.3
Ex Tanzania (via GNR)	50.5	70.4
Ex Congo — Matadi	7.6	1.9
— Lobito	0.8	0.2
Ex Malawi	16.1	20.1
	100.0	100.0

Despite the interruptions in supply routes, Zambia was able to find alternative routes for importing a 50-per-cent increase in domestic consumption. By the end of 1967 an enormous fleet of large-capacity road tankers was in operation. It comprised some 500 vehicles, with a payload of about 30 tons each, operating between Dar es Salaam and Zambia and betwen Salima, the Malawi railhead of Malawi Railways, and Zambia.

The cost of utilizing the alternative routes has been substantial. Part of it was passed on to the consumer in the form of a K 0.10 surcharge on a gallon of petrol, but the large share was borne by government. The additional transport costs created by the alternative routes varied considerably. Probably one of the most expensive routes was the Great North Road from Dar es Salaam at K 0.32 per gallon of bulk diesel (to Ndola) with the Matadi/Port Francqui/Ndola route costing K 0.26 per gallon for diesel imported in drums and the Beira/Salima/Lusaka route costing about the same. The former Rhodesia Railways rate was K 0.08 per gallon for diesel and K 0.12 per gallon for petrol. The overall increase in costs of importing POL on the

---

[33] While in 1963–4 all POL imports entered Zambia through the ports of Beira and Lourenço Marques as refined products, Rhodesia supplied the Zambian market from early 1965 after completion of the Lourenço Marques/Feruka oil pipeline and the Feruka Refinery.

alternative routes probably amounted to about 170 per cent, and the annual subsidy, which the government met, was around K 600,000 per month or about K 7.5 m. per year, with the consumers having to face an additional surcharge amounting to some K 200,000 per month or K 2.4 m. per year. It would seem, therefore, that in 1966 the direct annual additional cost of POL was around K 10 m. In 1967 this figure was probably increased further to, say, K 12 m. With the opening of the oil pipeline from Dar es Salaam to Ndola in 1968, the transport costs of importing POL into Zambia was reduced substantially.

Imports—coal and coke

Until 1966 Zambia's substantial coal/coke requirements of about 1 million tons per annum, used principally for the smelting of copper (at the rate of 65,000 tons per month), and the fueling of the railways, were met from Wankie Colliery which is some 40 miles south of the Victoria Falls, in Rhodesia. Prior to UDI, the government had under investigation the development of the local coal resources situated in the Gwembe valley. With UDI and the consequent difficulties experienced in the movement of traffic and supply of coal from the south over the jointly-owned Rhodesia Railways system, it became necessary to move the coal by road to the Zambian Railways railhead at Livingstone. At the same time, the exploration and development programme for local resources was accelerated with the result that mining operations started at the Nkandabwe coalfield in the middle of 1966. The effect of this can be seen in the traffic figures (see Table 12.6), with the 1967 coal tonnages down some 44 per cent on the previous year.

Traditionally, coal has been carried on Rhodesia Railways at direct cost, and as such Wankie coal has been relatively inexpensive, with a landed cost Kitwe of about K 5.45 per ton (pre-UDI). The current cost of Wankie coal is around K 7.82 per ton (landed Kitwe), which represents an increase of 43.5 per cent, accounted for by higher transport costs. The cost of local coal, landed Kitwe, is K 10.00 per ton ex-Batoka siding, plus K 2.16 transport. In terms of Wankie equivalent, this amounts to K 14.65 per ton, an increase of 168.8 per cent on the original Wankie coal.

With the installation of the coal-washing plant at Maamba Mine, the increased cost of local coal in terms of Wankie equivalent will be lower. In the calendar years 1966 and 1967, Zambian coal production from the Gwembe valley amounted to 114,000 tons and 404,000 tons respectively. An additional cost has arisen following the introduction of local coal on the Zambian market. In particular the copper companies have incurred losses in production due to the lower calorific value of local Maamba coal. Because of the high ash content in coal from the latter and the effect of this coal and silica on the brick lining of the furnaces which were designed for Wankie coal, the furnaces have to be shut down more frequently.

Imports—general goods

Unlike POL products and coal and coke imports, the diversion of general goods away from the former unitary Rhodesia Railways system has been less marked and less successful (see Table 12.8). In fact, over the four years under review, the percentage of

TABLE 12.8
Diversion of general goods
(% of total imports entering by specified routes)

	1963–4	1964–5	1965–6	1966–7
From Mozambique ports	13.5	15.2	23.0	26.1
From S.A. ports	2.4	2.6	4.0	2.1
From Rhodesia	62.2	62.7	37.1	19.9
From S. Africa	20.7	17.7	27.4	35.1
Total entering by Rhodesia Railways	98.8	98.2	91.5	83.2
From Lobito	0.6	1.1	4.5	10.0
From Congo	0.5	0.7	4.0	4.5
Total entering from West Coast ports	1.1	1.8	8.5	14.5
From Dar es Salaam	—	—	—	2.3
Total	100.0	100.0	100.0	100.0

Source: Table 12.6.

general goods being imported through the Mozambique ports has increased. At the same time, the amount of general goods travelling on the Rhodesia Railways system and entering Zambia at Livingstone has fallen from 99 per cent to 83 per cent of total requirements. This fall has been due to a reduction in the relative importance of Rhodesia as a source for imports. With the exception of the Lobito route, the 'new routes' developed since UDI have been of little significance. However, this pattern changed in 1969, following the completion of the oil pipeline from Dar es Salaam to Ndola, and the more efficient utilization of the Great North Road. Recent figures for Zambia-Tanzania Road Services show that, in 1967–8, general goods imported on the road could have amounted to 80,000 tons, a fourfold increase on the previous year.

TABLE 12.9
Total traffic carried by ZTRS, 1967–9
(*tons*)

		1967–8 July–January	1968–9 July–January
Imports —	POL	18,694	16,371
—	General goods	45,131	57,793
Exports —	Copper	72,496	89,406
Total		136,321	163,570

Source: ZTRS data.

Despite this increase, and further capacity made available by the use of POL carriers for general goods, the bulk of general goods will in all probability continue to be imported from the south on a significant scale until a long-term solution to the Zambian transport problem has been found and implemented.

Up to 1966–7 therefore, the problem of transporting general goods on routes other than from the south had scarcely begun to be tackled. As is discussed below, the diversion of copper export traffic had been partially achieved by the end of 1966–7 and could technically have been achieved completely without too much difficulty by this time. However, tonnages of copper travelling over the Southern Rhodesia Railways route had to remain there because, basically, if they had been entirely removed and diverted to the 'new routes' this would have led to a much more severe increase in the rates charged for general goods imported via, and from, the south. Because of the slow development of the northern routes for general goods during this period, the Zambian government was reluctant to restrict imports via the southern rail route, or imports of South African origin. The diversion of general goods traffic to the northern routes, partially rail via the Congo to Lobito, partially road via East Africa, was certainly the most critical problem facing Zambia's transport planners at the end of 1966–7, and it still remains critical. Moreover, since the capacity available for general goods movement was limited, the new Rhodesia Railways Authority was in a position to raise rates on imports of general goods to compensate themselves for the loss of copper exports. On the completion of the oil pipeline, spare capacity was available for greater utilization of the Great North Road for carrying tonnages of general goods.

During the period since UDI, the government has introduced a system of import licensing which has provided a mechanism to direct traffic into Zambia via specific routes. These measures were aimed at diverting imports from the ports of Beira and Lourenço Marques to the Tanzanian ports of Dar es Salaam and Tanga. Overall, this policy was not significant in terms of tonnages until, probably, 1968–9.

The additional costs incurred by directing traffic away from Rhodesia Railways are difficult to establish. On division of the unitary Rhodesia Railways system, the 'taper' (which meant that the railway user benefited from a reducing marginal transport cost) was abolished. Before 1 July 1967, a quoted through rate was applicable to all goods imported through Beira or Lourenço Marques, whilst for exports the local goods rates from Lusaka to the Portuguese East African border were used with a quoted rate from the border to Beira. On Division Date, the taper was broken at the Victoria Falls Bridge. The effect of this on general goods was to increase the transport costs between 5.6 per cent and 28.8 per cent, from 5.6 per cent for fertilizers to 28.8 per cent for machinery and mining appliances.[34] The average increase was around 20 per cent, amounting to an additional K 3 m. transport costs for general goods in 1966–7.[35]

Exports—copper

Copper accounts for between 70 per cent and 80 per cent of Zambia's total exports, measured in tonnage terms, and for a higher proportion of payments to transporters for the transport of export commodities.[36] Prior to UDI all copper was exported via the south and the circumstances surrounding this movement have already been described.

During 1966–7, Table 12.10 shows that only 44 per cent of all Zambia's copper was exported through Rhodesia, with 39 per cent

34 For further details see Rhodesia Railways, *Official Tariff Books* No. 30, dated 1 September 1963 and No. 31, dated 1 March 1968. The increases refer to Beira/Ndola.

35 Assuming an average haul on Rhodesia Railways of 836 miles, and average receipts per net ton/mile of 1.27 ngwee (1.526d) (see Rhodesia Railways, *Report and Accounts, June 30, 1965*).

36 Zambian copper accounted for 25 per cent of total revenue for Rhodesia Railways in 1964–5, but only 7 per cent of the total tonnage of goods hauled on the system (see Rhodesia Railways, *Annual Reports*).

being despatched through the Mozambique ports. At the same time, Zambia was able to send more than 50 per cent of her copper on the northern routes to Lobito or Dar es Salaam.

TABLE 12.10

Distribution of copper exports by route
(%)

	1963–4	1964–5	1965–6	1966–7
To Mozambique ports	96.4	96.0	88.7	39.3
To South Africa	3.6	4.0	4.3	4.2
To Rhodesia (road)	—	—	0.5	—
	100.0	100.0	93.5	43.5
To Beira (Malawi/road)	—	—	0.6	6.2
	—	—	94.1	49.7
To Lobito	—	—	4.7	24.8
To Dar es Salaam	—	—	1.3	25.4
Total	100.0	100.0	100.0	100.0

Source: Table 12.7.

The export routes developed since UDI have had a very significant impact on costs. An analysis of these for 1966–7 is given in Table 12.11.

Assuming the costs of transporting copper from the Zambian Copperbelt to the African ports given in Table 12.11, the average cost per ton was K 44.60. In 1964–5, when all the copper was sent by Rhodesia Railways, the average rate was K 30.34[37] per ton. The increase in freight charge is therefore 47 per cent, representing an additional K 9 m. on 637,200 tons per year. However, it will be noted that the copper rate has increased substantially on Rhodesia Railways. This has been in part due to the abolition of the through-export rate which was operative prior to the division of Rhodesia Railways on 1 July 1967, and in part a special surcharge which the new

[37] The standard rate from Ndola to the Mozambique ports was K 32.67 per short ton. When the tonnage of copper available for export overseas exceeded 633,000 tons per annum, the standard rate applied to 80 per cent of the total and the remaining 20 per cent was carried at an incentive rate of K 20.96 per ton. Up until December 1965 when all copper was exported via the eastern ports, the average rail rate from Ndola was K 30.34 per short ton. The marginal railway rate used to be K 20.96 per ton on Rhodesia Railways, and so at this margin the costs in 1966–7 were 113 per cent higher.

TABLE 12.11

Transport costs for copper, 1966–7

	'000 tons carried	%	Average costs per ton of transport to African ports (K)
To Dar es Salaam			
— ZTRS	86.2	13.5	40.00
— CARS	42.2	6.6	40.00
— via Mpanda	3.3	0.5	40.00
— via Mpulungu	0.3	—	40.00
— via air	29.9	4.7	107.14
	161.9	25.4	52.40
To Lobito	158.2	24.8	41.07
To Beira via Malawi	39.4	6.2	51.60
By road through Rhodesia	0.1	—	—
By rail through Rhodesia	277.6	43.5	41.07
Total	637.2	100.0	44.60

Source: Unpublished data.

Rhodesian Railways Authority first introduced at the same date. At the same time, the special provisions concerning the incentive rate, covered in the 'Tripartite' Agreement, fell away. The net effect of these changes was that the ZTRS rate for moving goods from Dar es Salaam on the Great North Road was lower than the revised Rhodesia Railways tariff.

In addition to these extra costs for transport, two further direct costs must be considered. Firstly, the port handling and freight charges turned out to be higher at the northern ports. The costs probably increased from about K 11.00 per ton to K 13.50 per ton— an increase of 22.7 per cent per ton. Secondly, the copper companies were faced with additional financing charges following the lengthening of the pipeline stock. The increased costs from the latter are difficult to calculate. The length of the present transit time has increased substantially from the 1964–5 average of 13 days from the Copperbelt to Beira/Lourenço Marques. For example the route via Salima in Malawi to Beira took a minimum of 45 days because of the various transshipment points.

The *Copperbelt of Zambia Mining Industry Year Book* for 1968 indicates that the average costs of transport per short ton of copper f.o.r. mine station to c.i.f. United Kingdom and Continental ports increased by 43.4 per cent for the Copperbelt copper as a whole between 1958 and 1959 and by 36.0 per cent between 1963 and 1967.[38] The K. 16.00 increase in transport costs which occurred during this latter period represented 6.3 per cent of the total increase in the Zambian cost structure of K 252 per short ton. These costs exclude any increase in financing costs.

This analysis has not attempted to quantify the full costs resulting from the transport position which has arisen since UDI. Many additional costs must clearly be quantified—changes in production following disruptions of supplies caused by the transport system, the cost of utilizing local coal from the Gwembe valley, the cost of stockpiling copper concentrates. Indeed, the real cost of diversification away from Rhodesia has in all probability been much more substantial than the estimated K 16.00 per ton increase between 1963 and 1967. A large proportion of the balancing item, K 85, must be directly attributable to transport.

Alternative routes

The routes alternative to the south lie through either the Congo, East Africa, or Malawi (see Map 12.2). During the period 1965–9 numerous studies have been undertaken to assess the ultimate capacities of these various routes, given certain investment criteria. The routes through East Africa are entirely through independent African countries, whilst the Congo and Malawi routes involve the crossing of either Portuguese colonial Angola or Mozambique, so that whilst they are alternative in the sense that they bypass Rhodesia and South Africa, similar problems arise, or will arise, to those being faced presently on the southern rail route.

Congo—rail route to Lobito

This is the logical, simplest, and cheapest route for Zambia as an alternative to the southern rail route. However, it runs through one country which has been peculiarly susceptible to political disturbances affecting the operation of the railway, and through Angola, a Portuguese colony which is also subject to disturbances. Although 25 per cent of Zambian copper exports and 10 per cent of imported general goods used the Lobito run in 1966–7, further substantial diversion is

---

[38] *Copperbelt of Zambia Mining Industry Year Book, 1968*, Copper Industry Service Bureau, Kitwe, Table 11, p. 43.

probably inhibited by considerations of security, despite the good development potential which it has.

Ndola is virtually equidistant from Lobito and the Mozambique ports of Beira and Lourenço Marques.[39] Moreover, the Lobito route has a 3 ft. 6 in. gauge which enables traffic to move between the various railway systems without any trans-loading. The Lobito route comprises the Benguela Railway (CFB) from Lobito to the Congo border near Dilolo, and the BCK from Dilolo to Sakania on the Zambian border. As was mentioned earlier, the Congo exported some 127,000 tons of copper and zinc, and imported probably 250,000 tons of coal, through Zambia and Rhodesia in 1966–7. Therefore in discussing the capacity available to Zambia on this route, the effect of diverting this Congolese traffic away from Rhodesia Railways must also be taken into account. However, given a relatively small investment programme, it would technically be feasible to build up the capacity of the Lobito route so that it could carry the diverted Congolese traffic in addition to a large proportion of the Zambian traffic. Estimates of the investment requirements vary considerably but would appear to be in the region of at least K 70 m. (excluding rolling stock, etc.). The expenditure would be directed towards overcoming the bottlenecks which have limited the capacity on the BCK because of the low level of operating efficiency, and on the Benguela Railway due to line capacity limitations on the escarpment section (Cubal Variant).[40] The former bottleneck has been in the past caused by the current technical level of operating personnel and the state of locomotives and rolling stock. In order to overcome these problems and to allow an orderly build-up of Zambian traffic on the Lobito route, an agreement was drawn up in Lubumbashi in July 1966, on the basis of which Zambia Railways would make available rolling stock, personnel, and locomotives to enable capacity for Zambian goods to be increased.

Congo—Port Francqui/Matadi

This is a long and expensive route. To date it has carried negligible quantities of Zambian traffic, and it is unlikely to carry more in the

[39] Ndola is some 1,680 miles from Lobito, 1,457 miles from Beira, 1,452 miles from Lourenço Marques, and 1,188 miles from Dar es Salaam on the Great North Road.

[40] It has been announced that Tanganyika Concessions will be building the Cubal Variant at a cost of K 17 m. See *African Development*, May 1969.

future because it is primarily a route developed, for nationalistic reasons, to carry Katangese traffic. Its use and expansion would be prohibitively expensive and unlikely to be undertaken by Zambia in the face of cheaper and more politically acceptable alternatives. The limiting section on this 1,894-mile route is the water transport between Port Francqui and Kinshasa. To a large extent this could be overcome if the suggested trans-Congo Railway (tentative cost: K 172 m.) from Luluabourg to Banana is built.

Congo—Kalemie/Kigoma

This third alternative via the Congo is the rail route via BCK and CFL (La Compagnie des Chemins de Fer du Congo Supérieur aux Grands Lacs Africains) to Kalemie, thence by barge across Lake Tanganyika to Kigoma and by rail on the East African Railways (EAR) to the port of Dar es Salaam. This route is long as it involves trans-shipment, and is expensive due to high ton/mile rail rates on the CFL. Since this route is an alternative to the more reliable Kigoma/ Mpulungu or Mpanda routes, it is not really significant except possibly for moving small tonnages of Zambian goods.

Tanzania

The alternative routes on which Zambia has concentrated since UDI lie through Tanzania and the Tanzanian ports of Dar es Salaam, Tanga, and Mtwara. There are five basic routes, only one or two of which are likely to be subject to sustained development. All the others can be viewed as 'temporarily useful routes', but do not justify the necessary large investments involved in substantially raising their capacity. The major routes are:

Great North Road — Zambia/Dar es Salaam
    ,,   ,,   ,, —   ,, /Tanga
    ,,   ,,   ,, —   ,, /Mtwara
Mpulungu/Kigoma/EAR/Dar es Salaam
Mpanda/Dar es Salaam.

Although the Great North Road connects Zambia with the three Tanzanian ports, as from 30 June 1967, no traffic had been routed through the port of Tanga—despite the fact that something like 5,000 tons/month capacity in both directions was available. As at this time, no traffic has used Tanga since spare capacity has been available at Dar es Salaam. Mtwara port has a magnificent natural harbour with unlimited potential for development, but the road between Iyayi and Mtwara would require something like K 30 m. spent on its reconstruction. The only alternative to the road would be an airlift, and some K 2 m. has been spent on developing an airstrip for use by the Zambian Air Cargoes fleet of Hercules aircraft. The road route to Mtwara has been used during the past two years by small private contractors operating on short-term contracts to a prime contractor, Central African Road Services. However, since high payload vehicles cannot be used, the overall cost of movement is probably some 50 per cent higher than on the direct run to Dar es Salaam. Given the concentration on the latter, and the substantial investments in the up-grading of this direct route made by both governments, there seems little prospect at present that Mtwara will be substantially used.

An investment of probably K 60 m. has been made in up-grading the Great North Road in Zambia and Tanzania to the status of a first-class tarred road. The Zambian section of the road was completed by 1970, with the Tanzanian section following by the end of 1971. The Tanzanian Second Five-Year Plan has indicated that: 'The construction of the TanZam highway overshadows all other developments in the (transport) sector, particularly during the first three years of the Plan.'[41] An allocation of K 39.4 m. has been made in the plan, but a great deal of the road has been financed by USAID and IBRD. With the completion of the up-grading of the road, there will be a steady diversion of increasing quantities of Zambian traffic on to the route.

Although in the interim the immediate possibilities for increasing traffic over the Great North Road are limited by the present condition of the road, the chief limitation is the available port capacity at Dar es Salaam. The Harbours Corporation has recently secured an IBRD loan for the expansion of the deep-water berth facilities from three to eight berths at an estimated cost of K 13.5 m. It is planned that the first three new berths will be completed in 1970–71. The final two berths are likely to be container berths. On completion of these developments, it is anticipated that the port will be able to handle 850,000 tons of Zambian traffic per annum.

The two remaining routes via Mpulungu/Kigoma and Mpanda/EARH are little used in comparison with the direct road route to

41 The United Republic of Tanzania, *Tanzania Second Five-Year Plan for Economic and Social Development*, Volume II, 'The Programmes', p. 80.

Dar es Salaam. The second route has not been significantly used because of its relatively high-cost circuitous route. The Mpulungu/Kigoma route was being used for some POL products and a little copper. The current rated capacity is around 5,000 tons per month in each direction and recent estimates have suggested that in order to handle an additional 250,000 tons per annum on a basis competitive with the Great North Road, it would require an investment of up to K 16 m.

Malawi—Salima/Beira

This is the only route through Malawi and consists of a road to Salima and rail from there to Beira via Malawi Railways. At present the capacity is around 10,000 tons per month in each direction. However, with the completion of the bitumenizing of the Great East Road in 1969, the capacity on this run could be increased substantially. Furthermore, with the commissioning of the rail link between Malawi Railways and the port of Nacala, Zambia will technically have access to another east coast port. Even with the completion of the up-grading of the Great East Road, the Beira/Malawi Railway is also a constraint, although the capacity could be increased with additional motive power. Despite this, this route has been slow due partly to trans-shipment at Salima.

Air routes

Although technically traffic could be flown out of Zambia, the enormous cost of the various operations which have been undertaken has been such as to discourage further investments in this field. Having said this, the three airfields which could be significant are Mtwara, Dar es Salaam, and Nairobi. Large-scale air freight is still in the future, and when introduced on a competitive basis, could be of great significance.

Summary

Political and security reasons have precluded the development of Zambia's most logical alternative route to Rhodesia Railways, that via the Congo and Angola to the port of Lobito. These factors have led to a concentration of attention on the development and use of road routes through Tanzania. Of these routes, the direct road route to Dar es Salaam is being developed as the major outlet. Broad indications only are given below of the magnitude of investment required for each major route:

	Investment	Total throughput in both directions
Lobito route, say	K 70–K 80 m.	1,770,000 tons
Mtwara (road) „	K 30 m.	500,000 „
Dar es Salaam „		
— Great North Road	K 60 m.	600,000 „
— Port	K 14 m.	850,000 „
Mpulungu/Kigoma	K 16 m.	370,000 „
Malawi	K 25 m.	360,000 „

Operators

Following on the government's decision to divert traffic away from Rhodesia Railways, several organizations were established to expedite this policy.

As was indicated, an airlift was established between Zambia and the Congo/East Africa immediately on UDI for the carriage of vital POL imports. In the early months of 1966 it was operated by the British, American, and Canadian Air Forces and civil operators. During 1966, this airlift brought into Zambia some 20,700 tons of POL (see Table 12.6). Subsequent to this airlift, Roan Selection Trust Ltd. purchased two Hercules aircraft, each with a 20-ton payload, for operation, initially, between Zambia and Dar es Salaam. The Zambian government purchased a further three aircraft. These latter were operated on a pool basis with the RST aircraft by RST's subsidiary company, Zambia Air Cargoes Ltd. With all aircraft operational, the monthly movement between Dar es Salaam and Zambia was about 3,000 tons in each direction. Two aircraft were destroyed early in 1968, and it was subsequently announced that the operation would cease as from March 1969 since the enormous costs made the whole operation only marginally viable.

From 1966–7 there have been some 1,000 vehicles using the Great North Road. Zambia-Tanzania Road Services was established in May 1966 under emergency conditions to carry goods between Dar es Salaam and Zambia. The K 3 m. company, jointly owned in three shares by the Tanzanian government, Zambian government, and the Italian Intersomer Company, operates 440 trucks with a rated monthly tonnage capacity of 13,500 tons. The 767 sub-contractors provided an additional

5,500 tons per month of capacity. The latter group largely disappeared with the opening of the oil pipeline in September 1968.[42] The overall ZTRS operation has had substantial interruptions, especially during the rainy season of 1967–8. During these periods the ZTRS fleet was only managing one round trip per vehicle per month and as such the costs per vehicle/mile were substantially higher than the original estimates of K 0.50 per mile on the basis of which the company was established.

Following the oil embargo, the Rhodesian Feruka Refinery was shut down and Rhodesia Railways became unavailable for the shipment of POL products. As has been mentioned, early in 1966 a substantial proportion of total demand was being met by various emergency routes. These events led Zambia to consider the economics of an oil pipeline. A jointly owned company, Tazama Pipelines Ltd., established by the government of Tanzania (33 per cent) and of Zambia (67 per cent) was set up to build the K 32 m. oil pipeline. The current capacity of the 1,058 mile pipeline is around 500,000 tons.

THE ZAMBIA-EAST AFRICA RAIL LINK (ZEARL)

During the 1960s a great deal of discussion centred on the possibilities of connecting the Rhodesia Railways system with the East African railway system. Over the years, the possibility of building a railway has been the subject of many reports. Although during the German regime in Tanganyika several railway surveys for extensions south of the central line had been carried out, it was only during the period 1925–33, when the territory was under British mandate, that active steps were actually taken to survey possible alignments connecting the Kenya-Tanganyika systems and extending southwards to the then Northern Rhodesian border with a view ultimately to linking with the Rhodesian system. Tanganyika Railways, East African Railways and

---

[42] The Industrial Development Corporation of Zambia Ltd. publication *Enterprise*, 2nd Quarter, 1969, states that 'under the new arrangements, the contractors who used to bring in oil on behalf of Zambia's Petroleum Finance Board until the opening of the Tazama Pipeline last September (1968) will become sub-contractors to Zam-Tan. They will provide an extra 7,500 tons of capacity a month in each direction. Since Zam-Tan itself can carry 13,000 tons a month both ways, total capacity on the route will be about 20,000 tons of copper going out and 20,000 tons of general goods coming in.' (p. 9).

Harbours, and the British government all did reports in the period prior to 1960. In 1952 for example, the EARH concluded that from an engineering viewpoint there were no apparent difficulties in building the proposed 1,150-mile railway, despite the fairly substantial construction costs. More recently, EARH reviewed their report in 1963; Lonrho Ltd. prepared a report in 1964 recommending alternatives to certain sections of the previously proposed routes; and the World Bank sent a mission in 1963 in answer to a request made by the Northern Rhodesian government for preliminary advice on the rail link. The most detailed analysis, however, was undertaken by a British-Canadian team in 1966.

The World Bank Mission suggested improved roads as an alternative to the railroad project. They stated that:

> Urgent need for investments in other parts of Northern Rhodesia and Tanganyika and in other sectors of the economy raises doubts about the feasibility of concentrating such a large amount of money (K 117 million) on one single project at this time.[43]

The World Bank Mission failed to anticipate the 1965 Rhodesian crisis and as such concluded that:

> As far as traffic between the Copperbelt and the Ocean is concerned, no major addition to existing facilities is likely to be required for ten or twenty years because existing railway lines to Beira, Lourenço Marques, and Lobito are operated efficiently and cheaply, have ample spare capacity and will be able to expand capacity with small investments.

The World Bank argument has therefore been overtaken by events. Moreover, it was apparent that they failed to identify and isolate the increased capacity requirements needed by Rhodesia Railways as a result of a substantial growth in traffic in 1964 and 1965. To a large extent, this had arisen from the increased demand in Zambia for imports. Despite the differences in approach, a comparison of the three most recent studies is given in Table 12.12. Here it will be seen that the Anglo-Canadian survey estimated an increase of more than 100 per cent on the previous study. This in part was due to the assumption that all Zambian traffic other than POL products, coal and coke requirements, and a certain small amount of general goods would be made available to ZEARL. Furthermore, the 1966 study took the project up to a final design stage and as such was much more detailed than the earlier studies.

43 Ministry of Transport and Works, *World Bank Mission's Report on the North East Rail Link*, 1963.

TABLE 12.12
Cost comparisons for ZEARL
(*K m.*)

	World Bank estimates 1963	EAR estimates 1964	Anglo-Canadian 1966
Cost of line construction	80.7	74.8 }	137.8
			19.6[4]
Contingencies	16.2	—	17.4
Rolling stock	6.0	10.7	53.0
Interest during construction	14.0[3]	17.1[2]	17.8[1]
Working capital	—	—	7.0
Total	116.9	102.6	252.6

[1] At 6%.
[2] At 7%.
[3] Not specified.
[4] The cost of converting the EARH central line to 3 ft. 6 in. gauge.

The Anglo-Canadian study was based on the projected traffic levels given in Table 12.13. It will be noted that both POL traffic and coal/coke imports, which accounted for some 60 per cent of total traffic into Zambia in 1964–5, were excluded from the traffic available to ZEARL. On the basis that it would be possible to charge the same rate for moving a ton of freight to or from the sea whether it be via Beira and Rhodesia Railways or by the rather shorter route offered by ZEARL, then given the assumed traffic levels (see Table 12.13), the operating revenue would amount to K 44.8 m. in 1971[44] and K 72.4 m. in 1981. Operating costs were based on the 1965 Rhodesia Railways rate of 1.14d per ton mile and on an estimate of 0.83d per ton mile.

[44] The study which was finished in 1966 assumed that ZEARL could be completed within four years from the beginning of mobilization. In 1967 it was announced that the People's Republic of China had offered to build and finance the link. As a follow-up to this an engineering survey and design of the proposed ZEARL was undertaken in 1968–9 by a Chinese team and is scheduled for completion in 1969–70 when a final design of the link will be started. The Tanzania-Zambia Railway Authority (TAZARA) has been established by the governments of Tanzania and Zambia to ensure the smooth implementation and early completion of the project. The Tanzanian government has made a provision of K 30.5 m. to cover the costs of the project during the Second Five-Year Plan period, 1969–1974 (see *Tanzania Second Five-Year Plan* and *Annual Economic Surveys* for 1965–6, 1966–7, and 1967–8). (Construction began in 1970—*ed. note*.)

TABLE 12.13

Traffic assumptions for ZEARL
('000,000 tons)

			1971	1981
Outward				
Ex Zambia	—	copper	0.929	1.254
	—	lead/zinc	0.101	0.101
	—	miscellaneous	0.050	0.100
			1.080	1.455
Ex Congo	—	copper	0.056	0.056
	—	zinc	0.067	0.067
			0.123	0.123
Ex Tanzania			0.136	0.398
Total			1.339	1.976
Inward				
To Zambia	—	general goods	1.150[1]	2.140[1]
To Tanzania			0.070	0.165
			1.220	2.305
Total			1.220	2.305
Total System			2.559	4.281

[1] Assumes that 300,000 tons in 1971 and 400,000 tons in 1981 of general goods will continue to enter Zambia via the south.

The latter assumption was based on the anticipated overall operating pattern of ZEARL. It was assumed that the through-running trains carrying end-to-end traffic, with few local trains, and a wholly bulk cargo outward movement, would enable ZEARL to undertake an ideal railway operation. Therefore, on the basis of the revised operating cost, it was estimated that the operating surplus in 1971 would be K 22.8 m. and in 1981 K 37.0 m., giving a gross operating return of 9 per cent on the K 252 m. capital employed in 1971, and 13 per cent on the estimated K 284 m. capital employed in 1981.

The study concluded that the railway is a feasible and economic proposition. The engineering and economic feasibility studies did not include a full-scale cost/benefit analysis of the proposed link in terms of assessing the social and developmental benefits. However, due to the rather unpromising nature of a great deal of the country (particularly in northern Zambia) through which ZEARL would run, the benefits, though real, would probably not go far towards justifying the construction of the link if the financial returns to be expected were small. The study therefore concluded that: 'The economic case for the link, however, can stand on its own financial feet'. The only really significant transport-induced developments which could come about are the exploitation of the Ruhuhu-Songea iron-ore/coal deposits and the agricultural potential of the Kilombero Valley, Usangu Plain, and the Southern Highlands areas of south-west Tanzania. However, with regard to the latter, it is difficult to determine whether these agricultural developments would be likely to be rail-induced, or whether they are rail-dependent in the sense that costs of road transport would prohibit them. From Tanzania's point of view, the significance of Zambian traffic arising from ZEARL is substantial. Such benefits on a lesser scale have already started to accrue following the Zambian policy of diversifying transport routes, and the establishment of various joint ventures—ZTRS, ZAC, Tazama, etc.

At the same time as the Anglo-Canadian survey team was considering ZEARL, Stanford Research Institute undertook a route selection and feasibility analysis of the TanZam Highway. Their overall conclusion seems to have been that the cost of improving and maintaining the Great North Road to carry the diverted Zambian traffic would be such that copper traffic which was formerly shipped via Rhodesia Railways would not be able to bear the combined costs of maintenance and truck operation. It was suggested that the total road transport cost could be in the order of K 32.40 per ton, and that this exceeded the then current Rhodesia Railways rate of K 25.70 per ton. They estimated the cost of the road, constructed to take all copper traffic, would be around K 124 m. SRI therefore argued in terms of providing road improvements designed to meet normal and development traffic rather than using the Great North Road as an alternative for moving all Zambia's traffic requirements. This covered only traffic that would use the highway regardless of its improvement and traffic that would grow out of normal development of current activities stimulated by improved road conditions. In other words, their conclusions in no way conflicted with the traffic projections assumed for ZEARL. In effect, the two groups were of the same opinion with regard to the feasibility of transpoiting Zambia's copper traffic.

The economic case for constructing a railway link between East Africa and Zambia stands or falls in the last analysis upon the decision as to whether or not it should carry the copper traffic. Indeed, the whole pattern of transport development within Central Africa has revolved around this central point and, as a result, has not necessarily been in the long-term interests of Zambia. Besides the actual calculation of profitability, the argument for or against the rail link must necessarily hinge on the effect that a new link might have on existing railways. The rail link can therefore be seen either as a separate entity which does not in any way interfere with the current level of traffic on the existing railways, or it can be debited with the notional loss incurred by Rhodesia Railways as a result of its failure to carry the full amount of the increased freight.

To a large extent, much of the argument used in both the EAR report and that of the World Bank has been superseded by events. Whilst the EAR report assumed that in 1970, when it was estimated that the line would be in operation, it would carry 200,000 tons of copper, 100,000 tons of general imports, and 50,000 tons of POL imports, the World Bank report disregarded copper traffic entirely. The Bank argued that the existing facilities were efficient and of low cost and that the marginal costs of additional traffic on them would be low. This argument was disproved by the Anglo-Canadian study which indicated that Rhodesia Railways was operating at nearly full capacity in 1965 and that in order to meet the projected traffic demands on the unitary system, a K 153 m. programme of electrification and double tracking would have to be undertaken during the period up to 1981. Zambia, as a former joint owner of the Railways, would in the normal course of events have had to find, together with Rhodesia, the capital required for such an investment. It has been estimated that even if all Zambian traffic used routes other than Rhodesia Railways, the growth in Rhodesian traffic alone would more than compensate for Zambia's withdrawal. In other words, on the basis of the revenue traffic up to 1971 on the former unitary system, Rhodesian traffic alone is equal in 1971 to the 1964–5 total, including Zambia and Congo. Therefore, if Zambian traffic was to be diverted at the same rate as Rhodesian traffic increased, the revenue traffic in Rhodesia could be kept at least constant until 1971 and would therefore grow quite rapidly on the basis of Rhodesian traffic alone. It was thus assumed that the avoidable investment in Rhodesia Railways, given Zambian traffic diversion, amounted to some K 73 m.

CONCLUSIONS

The prominent feature which has determined the pattern of the transport sector and its development over the past fifty years or so has been mineral development—originally the lead and zinc deposits around Kabwe (Broken Hill), and, more recently, copper. The historical concentration of the railway, and until recently the primary road system within the line of rail economy, has been a substantial obstacle to economic development within the rest of the economy. However, as an export-oriented economy, it has been essential to establish an efficient and cheap system to transport export products to the ports for subsequent shipment. Historically Zambia, a land-locked country, has been dependent upon transit through other countries for access to the sea, and has been intimately bound up with Southern Rhodesia, with the result that the main transport links with the outside world have been through that country. In addition, many of her imports have originated there and in South Africa. In recent years, and particularly since UDI, it has been the policy of the Zambian government to remove substantially this dependence by seeking both alternative supply routes and sources of supply. The rate at which Zambia has been in a position to divert trade away from Rhodesia Railways has clearly been dependent on the availability of these alternative transport routes, on the additional transport costs, and on overall transport management and planning. These factors in turn have affected the level of general development in the economy, particularly in an economy which is so dependent on extensive transport to move its three million tons of goods into and out of the country. The effect of this substantial change in the structure of the transport sector on the economy as a whole has been marked, as was indicated in the Bank of Zambia quotation given at the beginning of this chapter.

The main conclusions which emerge are summarized below:

1. As a result of Zambia's policy of diverting traffic away from the Rhodesia railway system on to alternative routes, between 1964–5 and 1966–7 the total traffic entering or leaving Zambia (including Congolese goods) decreased from 3.3 m. tons to 3.0 m. tons, or by nearly 10 per cent over the two-year period. At the same time, the total amount of traffic entering Zambia via the Victoria Falls Bridge at Livingstone fell by a third, from 3.2 m. tons to 2.2 m. tons, due to the complete diversion of POL products away from Rhodesia Railways and to 50 per cent of the copper exports using the northern routes to either Lobito or Dar es Salaam. The use of alternative routes for the importation of general goods was not marked by 1966–7. As dependence on the Rhodesia Railways system was reduced, the importance of the

two main alternative routes—via Lobito and via Dar es Salaam—was increased. By 1966–7, nearly half a million tons of goods, mainly POL and copper, were being moved through Dar es Salaam; and the increased utilization of Lobito by Zambia was from 26,500 tons in 1964–5 to 404,100 tons in 1966–7, which represented 0.8 per cent and 13.3 per cent of total tonnages respectively.

2. The costs of this traffic diversion have been substantial. These additional costs can be broken down into recurrent costs and capital. An indication has already been given as to the magnitude of some of these annual increases—POL K 12 m., coal/coke K 6 m., general goods K 3 m., and copper K 11 m. It would appear that the direct costs of diverting traffic away from the Rhodesia Railways system are in the region of K 35 m. per annum. This figure is hypothetical in the sense that the increase is based on the simple assertion that all the traffic requirements, including coal, in 1966–7 were met by the former unitary Rhodesia Railways. To calculate an overall figure for the real cost of changes in the transport sector, a large number of additional factors would have to be quantified—the cost of shortages of goods, the cost of financing pipeline stock and holding larger inventories, the costs involved in diverting resources into contingency projects, the costs resulting in higher costs in the mining industry, and the projected losses on Zambia Railways. Of particular significance is the mining industry in so far as transport has been a cause of the overall increase in production costs which has arisen over the period since 1963. In addition to the added transport costs, the mining industry has had to incur considerable extra costs following the use of local coal with its lower calorific value and high ash content. The loss of production, although difficult to calculate, has probably been substantial. To a certain extent, this problem will be alleviated with the commissioning of the new K 2.15 m. washing plant at Maamba Mine. Despite these problems and the low level of production in 1966, 1967, and 1968 as compared with 1965, the value of copper production has increased during this period due to the high copper LME prices. In a sense, therefore, the full effect of the additional costs incurred by the mining sector has been cushioned. The additional transport costs have also had a significant effect on the remainder of the economy. In the period 1964–5 to 1966–7, these costs have had a sub-

stantial effect on the inflationary tendencies which have been a characteristic of the Zambian economy in recent years. During the period from June 1965 to December 1967, money supply more than doubled. There is no doubt that the rapid credit expansion arose in part from the financial requirements necessitated by UDI. In particular, a considerable amount of credit during this period was extended to the mining sector because of its increasing credit requirements for financing the large stockpiles of concentrates and the longer haulage implicit in the new export routes. Against the background of rapid expansion in money supply, the trend of consumer prices has also been upward. The Bank of Zambia report for 1967[45] indicated quite specifically that the price increases reflected the impact of UDI on the economy:

Firstly, the new trade routes for imports as also the diversion of imports away from Rhodesia to new suppliers increased the cost of imported goods. Secondly, because of delivery delays resulting from longer pipelines, temporary shortages in the supply of certain commodities manifested themselves. Thirdly, traders and merchants perhaps also tended to build up larger inventories in view of uncertainties in supplies, thereby increasing the marketing costs.

Despite the significant progress which has been made in overcoming the transport and supply problems, the overall effect of the short-term impact has been substantial. In particular, the credit restrictions introduced in 1968-9 were in part introduced to counter the effects of the transport sector on the economy as a whole.[46]

3. Besides the additional annual recurrent costs which have to be borne by the Zambian economy, substantial investments have also been incurred. These have arisen from the need to develop the alternative routes already discussed. Certain of these expenditures have already been authorized—K 32 m. on the oil pipeline connecting Dar es Salaam and Ndola, K 25 m. on bitumenizing the Great North Road from Kapiri Mposhi to Tunduma, K 22 m. on bitumenizing the Great East Road from Lusaka to Chipata, and the expenditures incurred in setting up Zambia-Tanzania Road Services, Zambia Air Cargoes, and the Tanzania-Zambia Railway Authority. In determining the long-term transport

---

[45] Bank of Zambia, *Report and Statement of Accounts for the year ending December 31, 1967*, pp. 27–31.

[46] Bank of Zambia, *1968 Report*. Also Mulungushi Declaration of April 1968.

strategy for Zambia a great deal must hinge on the emphasis given to the development of one outlet to the coast as an alternative to the Rhodesia Railways system, as opposed to following a policy of 'keeping all options open' with the simultaneous development of several routes to meet Zambia's traffic requirements.

An important determinant for policy purposes is the overall political constraint within which any transport strategy has to be worked out. However, conflicts can arise between economic criteria and political necessities, with the resulting high costs being borne by the economy as a whole. In the Zambian context, at the time of UDI the country was faced with a situation in which there was no particular route which could accommodate Zambian traffic on a scale which would be significant without a substantial capital outlay. The only possible exception to this was the Lobito route which technically had spare capacity available. A broad indication of the order of magnitude of the investment requirements could be as follows:

	Investment (Zambia's share)	Increased throughput (tons)
Rhodesia Railways	K 77 m.	1.0–2.0 m.
Lobito route	K 70 m.[1]	2.0 m.
ZEARL	K 127 m.	2.6–4.3 m.
Dar es Salaam		
— Great North Road	K 60 m.	0.6 m.
— Port of Dar es Salaam	K 14 m.	0.9 m.
Mpulungu/Kigoma	K 16 m.	0.4 m.
Great East Road	K 25 m.	0.4 m.

[1] Large portion of this would presumably be paid by BCK/CFL.

Even if UDI had not occurred, considerable finance would have had to be raised, given the capacity problem on the Rhodesia Railways system. In terms of concentrating the transport investment on a single alternative, the development of the Lobito route and the construction of ZEARL are the two alternatives open. As a result of Zambia's geographical situation, substantial security problems arise which could preclude the development of the Lobito route even if a rail connection were to be built from the Copperbelt through Solwezi and Mwinilungu to join the Benguela Railway near Dilolo.

However, the time perspective of the whole political development of Southern Africa is of crucial importance. On the assumption that

ZEARL is completed, Zambian traffic, excluding POL and coke/coal, will be virtually tied to this route in order to ensure its profitability and to enable the proposed railway to meet its capital repayment commitments, spread over many years. As an alternative to this strategy, an 'options open' policy might involve using several transport routes which would include placing traffic on the Great North Road to Dar es Salaam and Great East Road to Salima for onward shipment to Beira or Nacala, the use of the Lobito route, and with the balance of the traffic being shipped to Beira and Lourenço Marques.

Such a policy would clearly have a degree of flexibility on the assumption that any two of the routes developed could handle all Zambia's traffic if the occasion arose. Such an assumption could only be made if capacity on the Lobito route were increased or else substantial reliance were to be placed on Rhodesia Railways. Again the short-term security constraints are significant. In constructing the railway connecting the Zambian railway system with the port of Dar es Salaam, a notable move will have been made in developing the economic and other links with the East African economy. This could be of long-term significance to the economy of Zambia in its orientation away from the Central/Southern African economic structure with which it has been historically associated.

The transport problems of Zambia are complex. The cost to the Zambian economy of reorienting its economic links away from the south and towards East Africa has been and will continue to be high, particularly in the short term. Investment decisions within the transport sector have to be taken after full evaluations of all existing and potential alternatives have been considered, in order to ensure maximum benefits at minimum costs. In determining strategy, an overt decision on the allocation of scarce resources between the various sectors within the economy has to be made.

13

The Construction Sector

CALLUM CHRISTIE[1]

INTRODUCTION

CONSTRUCTION output in Zambia is important in relation to total output, employment, and capital formation, as indeed it is in most countries. In the world as a whole, construction represents 5 per cent of GDP with the proportion tending to be higher in the rich countries (about 6 per cent) than in the poor (just over 3 per cent).[2] In Zambia, the proportion has varied between 4 per cent and 10 per cent since 1954, with the highest occurring in the period 1956–8. At the end of the 1950s and in the early 1960s there was a considerable slump in construction activity and by 1963 the proportion of construction to total GDP was only 4 per cent. Since then, construction investment by both the public and private sectors has raised the proportion to 8.6 per cent of GDP in 1967.[3] As is the case with most countries, in Zambia investment in construction has varied within fairly narrow bounds as a proportion of total gross domestic fixed capital formation. Between 1954 and 1967 it varied between 53 per cent and 66 per cent of total GFCF.

In the period 1954 to 1967, employment in construction has varied enormously, more so than output. It has been as high as 24 per cent (in 1956) and as low as 10 per cent (in 1963) of the economically active population. This is a very high proportion in relation to other countries where construction employs between 3 per cent and 10 per cent of the economically active population. It is due not to the greater labour intensity of construction activity in Zambia but to the very high capital

---

[1] Planning Division, Ministry of Finance, Republic of Zambia.

[2] International statistics in this section are obtained from the UN publication, *Industrialization of Building*, reference H/C. 6/70/Add. 1, 1967.

[3] *National Income and Accounts, 1954–64, 1964–66*, Central Statistical Office, Lusaka; *Monthly Digest of Statistics*, Central Statistical Office, Lusaka, December 1968.

intensity of the mining industry which contributes over 40 per cent to GDP with only 17 per cent of the registered labour force. In 1956, employment in the construction industry amounted to 69,000 and fell to 25,000 in 1963 after declining rapidly after 1958. Since 1964 employment has risen rapidly and reached 64,000 in 1966. The most recent figures indicate that the employment continued to rise, but more slowly, in 1967 to around 70,000 and then began to fall after mid-1968 as a result of the reduction in private sector demand and a slackening of activity on public sector investments as well.

The input structure of the construction industry is typical of other African countries. In most of them, half of the cost of the materials used in construction is direct foreign exchange expenditure. In Zambia's case, imports represent 40 per cent of the construction industry's requirements of plant and materials, and if the intermediate import content of Zambia-produced building materials is included, the proportion of imports in the industry's requirements of materials rises to 59 per cent.

The input of materials amounts to around 60 per cent of the value of total construction output in Zambia, which is fairly typical of the less developed countries but higher than the average for the developed countries where it averages between 40 per cent and 45 per cent of total construction output. In fact, the shares of materials input and value added is the reverse in less developed countries of what it is in the more developed, probably because of the relatively higher materials costs and lower labour costs of the former.

THE PRE-INDEPENDENCE BACKGROUND OF THE CONSTRUCTION SECTOR

In 1964, the construction industry was more British than Zambian. The principal contractors, and nearly all the architects, engineers, and quantity surveyors in government service and private practice in Zambia were British born and trained or trained in South Africa in the British tradition. The shapes and standards of construction materials, components and machines, design concepts of building, civil engineering works, and even of whole towns were either identical to those in Britain and South Africa or else directly derived from them.

Some statistics will illustrate the expatriate dominance of the construction sector. In 1964, only one of the 200 largest contracting firms in Zambia was actually Zambian-owned. Of 256 general contracting firms registered with the Public Works Department, only 26 were owned by Zambians and all but one of them were registered in the lowest category, i.e. as firms qualified to execute contracts up to a value of K 10,000. Out of 135 architects and quantity surveyors working in government and private practice only two were Zambians (both town planning officers trained in Britain), and out of 277 civil engineers only one was a Zambian.

At the lower level of works supervisors and fully apprenticed artisans the domination of expatriates was also fairly complete. In 1956 Europeans comprised 5.5 per cent of the labour force in the construction industry; in 1963 the proportion had risen to 6.8 per cent since the local artisans were paid off more rapidly than the expatriates during the five-year decline of the industry mentioned earlier.

The settler government of the Central African Federation encouraged immigration by artisans which in turn encouraged employers to restrict opportunities at middle management level to expatriates. Until 1959, the Apprenticeship Regulations required that all applicants for apprentice training should have a minimum of two years secondary education to be acceptable for apprenticeship. This effectively excluded Africans since at that time there were only two secondary schools for African boys in the whole of Northern Rhodesia. After 1959, this regulation was waived, but Africans were in fact still excluded from apprenticeship training which was provided on a limited scale within the industry to the sons of expatriates on an 'old boy' basis. The colour-bar practices of the construction industry also discouraged African entrants of high quality. Even Africans with City and Guild certificates from the Technical College in Lusaka preferred to look for jobs outside construction.

Mention has already been made of the high import dependence of the construction industry. In 1964, this import dependence was largely directed to Southern Africa. Forty-nine per cent of imported building materials in that year came from Rhodesia and South Africa. Moreover the Zambian building materials industry was heavily dependent on Southern Africa for its intermediate imports of materials. Typical was the manufacture of metal door and window frames where 56 per cent of the cost of production (excluding profits but including depreciation) was accounted for by the costs of sheet steel sections and fittings obtained from South Africa.

The dependence of the building materials manufacturers on Rhodesia and South Africa went beyond this reliance on imported intermediate products. In most cases, Zambian manufacturers were only the last link in a manufacturing and distributive chain that went back to Rhodesia and South Africa and, in some cases, to the UK as well. Production and pricing and other important management decisions were, therefore, made in the context of company strategy, dictated mainly by the overall (mainly South African, Rhodesian, and British) interests of those companies rather than by the purely Zambian ones.

The same dependence on external decision-making and control was evident in the spheres of building materials, merchandizing, and large-scale contracting. All the large building material merchants had parent companies in Rhodesia or South Africa and the six largest contractors were offshoots of either British or South African companies.

THE CONSTRUCTION INDUSTRY
AFTER INDEPENDENCE

The implications for the construction sector of government policies

Since 1964, government policies have greatly influenced the behaviour of, and level of activity in, the construction sector and at the same time have been affected by the response of the sector to these policies.

For example, the government's determination to press ahead as speedily as possible with economic and social development greatly increased the public sector's demands for construction work. Equally the construction industry's apparently cynical response to this, which was to raise its profit margins as high as possible, fostered the determination of the government to put an end to expatriate domination of this sector as quickly as it could and made the sector one of the foremost targets for the economic reforms that have taken place since Independence.

Three policies may be distinguished as the foundations of government actions since Independence and all have had their effect on and been affected by the consequent behaviour of the construction sector.

Rapid economic and social development and the availability of construction capacity

The first policy that may be defined is the rapid promotion of economic and social development, particularly in the fields of education, health, agriculture, and industry. Capital formation in building and works on behalf of central and local government and public corporations increased from K 16 m. in 1963, to K 19.0 m. in 1964, to K 39.1 m. in 1965, K 50.8 m. in 1966, and may have been as high as K 76.6 m. in 1967 and K 115.9 m. in 1968.[4]

In contrast to Federal and territorial government capital expenditures which were heavily concentrated on the Copperbelt and line of rail, a much larger proportion of the Zambian government's expenditures on buildings and works have been in the rural areas hitherto starved of development capital. In the fifteen-year period prior to Independence only about 25 per cent of public sector capital expenditures was devoted to the rural areas and only a very small proportion of that was spent on rural development proper. Since Independence, the proportion of capital expenditures spent in the rural areas has risen to around 40 per cent with a much higher proportion being spent on economic and social programmes than in the pre-Independence days.

The construction industry took advantage of the increase in the government's demands for buildings and civil engineering works by increasing its profits enormously. In 1964, net profits in the construction industry amounted to 9.0 per cent of total turnover; in 1965 they rose to 15.1 per cent and in these two years, the amount allowed for depreciation rose from 1.2 per cent of turnover to 4.5 per cent. Thus gross profits—in this case, probably a more reliable indicator of profitability than net—rose from 10.2 per cent of total turnover in 1964, to 19.6 per cent in 1965. In other words gross profit margins nearly doubled between 1964 and 1965.

Distributors of building materials also took advantage of the government-induced prosperity in the construction sector to increase their prices. For example, the price of timber rose by 9.8 per cent in 1965, whereas the average price rise in each of the previous four years was slightly under 1.2 per cent. The price of pipes and guttering also went up by over 9 per cent whereas in each of the previous four years the annual increase was just 2 per cent. These materials are almost entirely of foreign origin and their prices could hardly have been affected either

---

[4] Figures for 1964–6 from *National Accounts, 1964–66*, Central Statistical Office, Lusaka. For 1967, 1968, the figures are estimates derived from the government's capital expenditure figures for 1967 and 1968, on the assumption that the proportion of construction is the same in these two years as in 1966.

by Zambia's domestic wage inflation or by the effects of Rhodesia's UDI which did not affect the supply situation until 1966.

It is likely, therefore, that building material suppliers increased their profit margins considerably, but it is impossible to be sure since they are only shown as part of the distribution sector. As a whole, that sector has earned exorbitant profits since 1964, net profits averaging 37.5 per cent of value added in the period 1964–6.

As a result of these increases in profit margins prices of construction work rose by 14 per cent in 1965 and by a further 15 per cent in 1966; in the latter year the price rise was due more to rising wage rates—the wages and salaries bill in construction rose by 46 per cent compared with an increase in total output of 26 per cent and of 28.7 per cent in net profits.

Part of the cause of the increased prices of construction goods was the adoption of more than minimum cost techniques by contractors in order to meet the government's desire to shorten the construction period of certain of its projects regarded as strategically important. An example of this was the new Lusaka Airport where the highest tender was accepted for part of the contract because the tenderer offered to complete the work considerably more quickly than the contractors who offered lower tenders.

In a sense it was probably asking too much of human nature to expect contractors to be content with 'reasonable' profit margins when there was so much work on offer. This was particularly true of the rural building contracts. Since in pre-Independence days the rural areas had been given tiny sums to spend on buildings, no local contractors of any consequence existed outside the line of rail districts. A certain amount of money, amounting usually to no more than K 10,000 per district per year, was devoted mainly to housing and primary schools, but these buildings were usually constructed under the supervision of government officers and the contracting was limited to Zambian businessmen who provided teams of workers and a certain degree of technical competence and on-site supervision.

In the absence of experienced local contractors in most rural areas, therefore, contractors from the main towns had to be persuaded to take up contracts far from their normal area of activity. They did so, but exacted a high premium in the process. The government's tactics over its contracts contributed to the ease with which the contractors cut the cake to suit themselves. In its haste to have a visible demonstration of its concern for the development of the country, it tried to press ahead with putting out work to tender before proper costing and planning had been completed. In its massive secondary school programme, for example, it called for tenders for twenty-three new secondary schools simultaneously before the bills of quantity and even the designs of some of the component buildings were complete. This allowed the contractors to divide the school contracts amongst themselves and made it difficult for the government to check on the reasonableness of the tenders submitted by the contractors. In one month alone in 1965, the government let building contracts to the value of K 13 million, more than it let in the whole of 1964, and about ten times the monthly average of building contracts let since then.

By 1966, therefore, building prices were 31 per cent higher than in 1964 although since then prices have risen hardly at all. Had the build-up in the government's investment programme been slower there would probably not have been such a large increase in prices, although wage pressures coupled with the government's minimum wage awards, together with a modest rise in profit margins, would probably have caused building prices to rise by around 15 per cent between 1964 and 1966–7. The additional 15 per cent price rise was caused by pressure of demand on a relatively inelastic supply situation.

The surprising feature of this situation is that profit margins did not continue to rise after 1965 although most critics of Zambia's economic planning have tended to assume that the 1964–5 Transitional Development Plan was the 'right' size and that the First National Development Plan, 1966–70, was too ambitious. If 'right' is defined as a level of investment that can be absorbed by the economy without inflationary pressure, then the Transitional Development Plan was a good deal less 'right' than the First National Development Plan. Moreover, it will be noticed that the largest proportionate increase in public sector construction demands took place in 1965: construction investment carried out for the public sector in that year was 105 per cent higher than in 1964. In 1966, public sector construction investment was 30 per cent; in 1967, 51 per cent; and in 1968, 51 per cent higher than in each of the previous years.

Nevertheless, it is somewhat surprising that according to the CSO statistics, profit margins and construction prices have not continued to rise as the annual increase in public sector construction demands have been considerable. They have been paralleled, too, by large increases in private sector demands upon the construction industry. They rose from K 30 m. in 1964, to K 41.8 m. in 1966 and levelled off thereafter.

Moreover, construction in the form of current inputs to other sectors was also increasing during this period so that, in current prices, total construction output rose from K 51.2 m. in 1964 to K 143.5 m. in 1967; even at constant (1964) prices the rise was considerable—from K 51.2 m. 1964 to K 111.0 m. in 1967. At constant prices, output rose by 117 per cent between 1964 and 1967 with the largest increases taking place in 1965 and 1967 when output rose by 55 per cent and 28 per cent respectively.

The explanation of why capacity constraints were not more limiting and inflationary than they were lies in two factors. One was the considerable reservoir of skilled and semi-skilled labour that existed in Zambia as a legacy from the boom days of the 1950s. Between 1956 and 1958 employment in construction averaged nearly 70,000 but by 1963 it had fallen to 25,000. It would obviously have taken some time for the labour force of the 1950s to be reassembled as it had been dissipated into other occupations—in particular, subsistence farming and self-employed occupations in the towns. If this pool of unemployed and underemployed semi-skilled artisans had not existed, then it is doubtful if the spectacular increases in output could have been achieved as rapidly as they were, particularly in regard to the large rural building projects. By 1966, contractors would have been able to produce the additional semi-skilled labour required largely by on-site training and by 1967 it would appear that employment was no longer increasing because of considerable improvements in productivity as the labour force became more experienced. Indeed, in the last quarter of 1967, employment in construction was 2 per cent less than in the same quarter of 1966 and output per worker had risen within the same period from K 1,347 to K 1,765, after having fallen slightly between 1964 and 1966.

The second factor lay in the ability of the contracting organizations, especially those with parent companies overseas, to recruit skilled manpower from abroad. The same is true of firms of architects, quantity surveyors, and engineers established in Zambia. They were able both to recruit personnel and to send work overseas to their parent firm where such existed, or to professional firms with whom they had links, principally in Rhodesia, South Africa, and Britain. This latter practice was extremely important for Zambia since the design and planning stage of a construction project can well be as long as the construction stage, and shortage of design capacity can be potentially as serious a bottleneck as lack of contracting capacity.

Thus construction capacity which was regarded as one of the principal determinants of the size of the FNDP has been considerably less of a constraint than was expected. Indeed, the fact that construction output has not come up to the levels postulated by the FNDP is not because there was not the capacity to execute it but because it would have involved levels of expenditure that would have created a balance of payments deficit and increased the inflationary pressure in the economy. It is really the failure of the food and raw materials producing sectors to expand production sufficiently since 1964 that has limited the expansion of government construction investment at the rates predicted in the FNDP, because that failure forced the government's 'non-productive' cash flows into the purchase of imports and into forcing up the price of locally-produced goods.

Nevertheless, the fact that even a fairly simple construction project such as a housing scheme requires about two years from the first decision to go ahead to the day on which it can be used by the clients meant that the Transitional Development Plan and the first year of the FNDP were notable as a period in which it was impossible to recruit sufficient personnel for the development programme because of a shortage of housing accommodation throughout Zambia.

This bottleneck was partly of the government's own making since it is almost alone in the world as a whole, let alone in Africa, in providing every one of its employees with housing, and, moreover, at rents which are heavily subsidized, with the subsidy increasing with the size of the house. This housing policy certainly inflates the demand for housing and removes any pressure to economize on housing accommodation. In the period from the beginning of the FNDP until the end of 1968, the Zambian government spent around K 34 m. on housing its civil servants. Two-thirds of this was institutional housing, often for people stationed in the rural areas where suitable accommodation for the more senior personnel would not have been available had government not provided it, e.g. at rural secondary schools, agricultural research stations, customs posts, etc. But in Lusaka alone in this brief period, the government spent K 5.6 m. on general civil service accommodation and probably another K 1 m. on institutional housing for police, army, etc. Compared with the K 34 m. spent on civil servants' accommodation, the government provided K 17 m. for low-cost housing, part of which was used by the government for housing the lower echelons of the civil service in the urban areas.

Economic self-sufficiency and the performance of the construction sector

Another of the most important of the government's economic policies has been the pursuit of greater economic self-sufficiency and since UDI this has been particularly associated with making Zambia economically independent of Southern Africa.

Mention has already been made of the close links between building materials suppliers, manufacturers, and contractors with parent or associated companies in Southern Africa and Britain. In the case of the suppliers and manufacturers of building materials there were particularly close links with firms south of the Zambesi. There were sound economic reasons for these links. South Africa produces building materials, particularly steel-made ones which are quite competitive by world standards. Moreover, since building materials generally have a high weight/value ratio, the nearest source of supply is usually the cheapest; hence the fact, too, that in the field of building materials manufacture there exist some of the most fruitful avenues of import substitution.

In 1965, on the eve of UDI, a survey carried out by the Office of National Development and Planning showed that for the government's building programme 47 per cent of the imports required originated from Rhodesia and South Africa. This related only to building materials which required no further processing in Zambia. In addition to such materials, half as much again was imported for use in the domestic manufacture of building materials, and the vast majority of these intermediate imported inputs originated from Rhodesia and South Africa.

Examples were steel sections and fittings imported from South Africa for the manufacture of metal door and window frames. These imports amounted to 53 per cent of the cost of producing the frames in Zambia. In the case of cement, coal and gypsum were imported from Rhodesia and these amounted to 48 per cent of the total production costs.

Since UDI, however, there has been a considerable change in the source of supply of final and intermediate imports of building materials. The first effect of sanctions against Rhodesia was to shift to South Africa much of the demand that had been previously satisfied by Rhodesia. As an indicator of what happened, total imports from Rhodesia were only 52 per cent in 1967 of what they were in 1964, whereas in the case of South Africa they increased by 123 per cent in the same period and have taken over from Rhodesia as the main source of imports to Zambia. This situation is likely to be only a temporary one since with the rapid improvement of communications with Tanzania, the Zambian government has taken measures to step up imports through Dar es Salaam instead of through Beira and South Africa. Thus Statutory Instrument 403 of 1968 gives the Minister of Commerce, Trade, and Industry and Mines the power to specify by which route importers will bring in goods, and he has exercised this prerogative by laying down that most categories of building materials will in future have to be imported through Dar es Salaam. This means that since Tanzania will not accept goods of South African origin, imported building materials will have to come from other sources and in certain cases this may lead to increases in prices. On the other hand, the greater difficulty and cost involved in obtaining such imports may provide a further incentive to produce some of these materials in Zambia and to look for local substitutes in the case of others.

As it is, import substitution has made some progress since 1964. In that year imports of goods and services amounted to 28.5 per cent of total construction output, but by 1966, this had fallen to 20.8 per cent. However, much of this fall was due to the large increase in profits both absolutely and as a share of total output, to which reference has already been made; as it was, the value of the production of domestically-produced building materials as a proportion of total output rose from 17.6 per cent in 1964 to 18.7 per cent in 1966, though part of this rise was accounted for by the fact that the price of domestically-produced building materials rose more quickly than the price of imported ones during this period. Nevertheless, with the expansion of the output of cement and cement-asbestos products, the installation of a clay products factory and the establishment of smaller-scale plants providing the finishing processes for paints, plastic products, and door fittings, the heavy reliance on imports is slowly diminishing. With the coming into production of iron and steel and chemical complexes in the 1970s, albeit high-cost ones, import substitution in the field of building materials manufacturing will be given a much greater impetus.

Until then, the main opportunity for reducing the import content of construction lies in a sensible choice of building designs which deliberately economize on imported materials. For example, a study recently conducted by the writer showed that the cost of imports which go directly into building could, in the case of the government's building programme, be reduced by 27 per cent if the cheapest design already available for each category of building were employed. This is because the import content of a building is determined by the basic technology that is employed for its structure and in the type of finish that is given to it. A reinforced concrete structure, for example, has a higher import content than a brick and mortar one, and a multi-storied concrete frame structure will have a lower import content but a higher skilled-manpower content than a similar-purpose steel frame structure. Similarly the cladding and finishing of the building can produce large variations in import content; as an example, a floor laid with parquet blocks made from Barotse hardwood has little or no import content, while one laid with vinyl tiles has a very high one.

The need to design for the maximum incorporation of local instead of imported materials is very great, since an immense amount of foreign exchange is lost through present construction activities. The inverted 1966 input/output matrix indicates that the total import coefficient of construction is 0.305: i.e. of every K 1 m. that is spent on construction, K 305,000 of imports is generated. This is in addition to the expatriation of profits overseas which would amount to another K 100,000 for every K 1 m. of construction expenditure, on the assumption that two-thirds of the net profits made in the construction sector are exported. If by the judicious choice of existing designs and the use of new designs the utilization of imports were reduced by 5 per cent, a saving of over K 2 m. of foreign exchange could be achieved at the 1968 levels of construction output, though higher import savings should be sought.

From the foregoing, it will be obvious that the huge construction expenditures by the public and private sectors since 1964 have come too quickly for the rest of the economy to experience much advantage from them. This has been true for the various manufacturing sectors that supply the construction industry with materials and services and particularly for those parts of the construction and construction materials industries which are controlled by Zambians, as the next section will show.

The Zambianization of the economy: the performance of the construction sector

In its determination to achieve economic as well as political independence, the government has picked out the construction and retail distribution sectors as the ones which offer most opportunities for Zambians to replace expatriates.

The construction sector was chosen presumably because the capital requirements of small-scale building contracting are quite low. With a few hand-tools and wheelbarrows a man can set up his own contracting business and for K 500 he can have a second-hand pick-up van and concrete mixer. In most countries the construction industry has a few very large and a great many very small firms; in Britain, for example, 80 per cent of contracting firms employ 10 or fewer men while those employing over 250 operatives amount to only 0.6 per cent of the total number of firms. In Zambia little is known about how many very small contractors there are since most of them do not keep books and may have no office or box number to which the Central Statistical Office could send its questionnaires, even supposing the contractors were able to fill them in correctly. There are probably not very many full-time contractors in this category and of the contracting firms who replied to the CSO Census of Industrial Production questionnaires in 1965, only 14 per cent employed 10 or fewer persons, but 15 per cent employed more than 250. Thus in Zambia the average size of labour force per firm in 1965 was 129, compared with 10 in Britain.

In Zambia, therefore, there appears to be a great deal of scope for the establishment of small contracting business. Indeed, with its huge expenditures on buildings, most of which are relatively simple, single-storey constructions, the government provided the type of work with which small contractors could cope.

In 1965, government launched a drive to form co-operatives in the fields of food producing, building, and the manufacture of products for the building industry, such as bricks, roofing timbers, and furniture. There were practical reasons for forming building co-operatives rather than encouraging individual contractors. As a survey carried out by this writer in 1965 showed, in the rural areas there were nearly 400 contractors, responsible for an annual output of K 1.5 m. of the public sector building work. That meant an annual average output of K 3,750 per contractor, which is little more than double the annual output of a single worker in the construction industry as a whole. In fact, only about 20 of them deserved the name of building contractor, because apart from these few the 'contractors' worked under the close supervision of their clients and usually depended on them to purchase and transport the building materials to the site and to provide simple equipment such as wheelbarrows and shovels, while only 10 per cent of these contractors owned their own transport. These contractors were usually artisans with interests outside building who would act as organizers and site supervisors of building gangs and occasionally have the expertise to lay out a building from a building drawing and site plan. In the case of the government contracts which were entrusted to them, two-thirds were virtually under the management of government officers, but despite that 40 per cent of the contracts were not completed on time, 41 per cent were not up to the standard set by the Public Works Department, and 23 per cent were not even constructed according to the specification of the building plans.

There was very little opportunity for this kind of contractor to make a reasonable profit since he was left with only the labour element of the building on which to make his profit. Consequently, most contracts awarded were for very limited amounts of money, the average being K 236.

By grouping these actual or would-be contractors into co-operatives, the government hoped to pool the contracting expertise in each district, and to be able to provide each co-operative with sufficient work throughout the years to enable the co-operative members to rely on building work for their livelihood. With an average of two co-operatives per district this was a perfectly feasible proposition and it meant, too, that the co-operatives' profits should be large enough to pay back the government loans that were provided for the purchase of transport. Moreover, by limiting the number of co-operatives that could be formed, it was easier to provide them with technical assistance and training.

In the event, 95 building co-operatives were formed and provided with loans to buy transport and simple items of equipment. The amount loaned to each co-operative varied from K 2,000 to K 4,000. The Public Works Department established 42 posts of assistant works supervisor and their incumbents were specially assigned to the task of providing the co-operatives with technical advice.

Training was also provided for the treasurers of building co-operatives. The training provision for these co-operatives was extended further with the establishment in the field of four teams, each of two men of works supervisor level, to carry out on-site training, backed up by four engineers to provide more formal training in short courses run for the benefit of the leading members of the co-operatives at provincial centres. This latter form of training was put into action with the aid of the Danish government in 1968 and it is hoped that the Danish instructors will train Zambian counterparts so that the scheme becomes self-perpetuating.

The government attempted to ensure that the co-operatives had ample work by laying down that all government contracts of up to K 20,000 had to be offered initially to co-operatives; in 1968 the limit was raised to K 100,000. In addition, Provincial Development Committees were charged with allocating sufficient contracts to each building co-operative to ensure that each one had sufficient work to keep its members occupied throughout the year.

The building co-operatives only became operational in 1965 and in the three years of their existence there are already successes to their credit. In the Western Province the eleven co-operatives established in 1965 and in 1966 completed projects to the value of K 560,000 in 1967 and by the end of 1967 had paid off one-third of their loans. It appears to be the case that in most co-operatives there are as many non-members as there are members, and on this assumption the output per head was K 1,040, i.e. about two-thirds of the output per head of the construction industry as a whole.

In the other provinces, the tale is rather more dismal, though there are a few cases, even in these, of co-operatives doing extremely well. The outstanding example is the Katete Builders Co-operative which had repaid the whole of its government loan within two years of its establishment and which in 1967 completed contracts to the value of K 130,000. Annual output per head in the co-operatives in the North-Western, Luapula, and Northern Provinces was particularly low in 1967—K 82, K 31 and K 244 respectively, closely followed by Barotse and Eastern Provinces with output per head of K 277 and K 328 respectively. In terms of rate of construction it has meant that in some cases buildings have taken years instead of months to be constructed and it has, of course, meant that rural development projects have been delayed because of lack of housing and offices whose construction was entrusted to the co-operatives.

Lack of success to date also attended the efforts of most of the craftsmen's co-operatives, formed to produce bricks, building timbers, and furniture. In 1966 there were 20 of these co-operatives with a paid-up membership of 397 and a value-added turnover of K 6,462.[5] This has hardly meant great prosperity for most of the co-operatives. An official of the co-operatives department commented recently, 'I am

5 *Annual Report 1966*, Department of Co-operatives, Lusaka.

afraid that the Charcoal Burners, Fisheries, Brickmakers, and Sawyers Co-operatives are not doing as well as they should. But although the flesh is sometimes weak the spirit is always willing to effect efficiency'[6]. The failure of the brickmaking co-operatives has been particularly disappointing because in most districts there are a number of people who know how to make burnt bricks, the technique requires very little equipment, and all the materials are to be found locally, namely clay, water, and firewood for the kilns. It has been estimated by the Central Planning Office that in the first year alone (1966–7) of the FNDP K 672,000-worth of bricks were required for the buildings scheduled for that year of the plan, but the brickmaking co-operatives were only able to meet a small portion of this demand. The remainder was met by substituting concrete blocks and bricks made with imported machinery as in the case of many of the rural secondary schools, or with bricks made by private brickmakers, missions, etc.

It has been said by some that these failures have their origin in the co-operative structure itself, because it does not favour individual initiative and provides no incentive for an individual to work any harder than the slowest member of the co-operative. But against this it can be argued, and with more reason, that where men share the profits of their own labours instead of working for someone else's profit, they are more likely to work hard and diligently. And, indeed, the success of some of the co-operatives within the first two years of their existence seems to indicate clearly enough that where failures have occurred it is not because of the co-operative structure.

The cause of the poor performance of most of the co-operatives to date lies in their lack of proper management and technical expertise. The reason why the building co-operatives in the Western and Southern Provinces have been most successful is because it is there that able people for the past twenty years have sought work because in colonial days the vast majority of development expenditures, and therefore building work, was devoted to the line of rail areas and the Copperbelt. Moreover, on the Copperbelt, the building co-operatives have been able to obtain the help of private quantity surveyors to help them to prepare tenders and cost estimates for the jobs they undertook and they also seem to have been considerably assisted with technical advice by Public Works Department officials.

[6] *Co-operatives Newsletter*, Vol. 2, No. 2, February 1968, Department of Co-operatives, Lusaka.

In the rural areas outside the line of rail, apart from the fairly low-level technical assistance that they might get from the PWD assistant works supervisors, the building and craftsmen's co-operatives are completely cut off from outside technical know-how, and yet it is in these areas that such know-how is particularly needed. The building co-operatives are in great need of an injection of such specialized knowledge since in some cases the co-operative members have too low a level of basic education to enable them to be trained in making building plans, calculating material requirements and costs, and keeping proper records and accounts. Thus an unpublished report submitted to the government by a Danish expert found that:

> Practically none of the building co-operative societies has a proper knowledge of how to make a cost estimate. This will require knowledge and understanding of working drawings and ability to calculate material quantities, and experience of required man-hours for each building operation. The major part of the co-operative groups meet none of these requirements. This implies that the clients of the builders, in most cases a government department, will have to nurse the contractors by estimating the contract sum, by ordering the materials and having them transported to the site and by carrying out thorough supervision.

Unfortunately, most government departments have been too over-stretched by the demands of the development plans and the loss of experienced expatriates to be able to do very much nursing of the building co-operatives and have preferred in most cases to hand the work over to the Public Works Department for planning and construction by the PWD's own labour force, or else have set up building organizations of their own under skilled expatriate supervision. To date, therefore, the contribution of the co-operatives to total building output is not very significant, and in 1967 their output of K 1.86 m. was only 24 per cent higher than the estimated output of the 400 or so rural 'contractors' in 1964.

In 1968, the government established a Federation of Building Co-operatives. The functions of the federation are to act as a buying and stocking agency of building materials on behalf of the co-operatives and to do the 'nursing' that government departments have been unable to provide. It has already (January 1969) begun to prepare properly costed tenders for building co-operatives but it will probably be of chief assistance to the co-operatives which are already amongst the best established as the on-site problems of the worst-managed co-operatives will still remain.

If the co-operative building movement is going to be able to cope with all government projects where the value of the contract sum does not exceed K 100,000—and at present it is only able to cope with 10–20 per cent of these projects—two steps seem to be imperative. The first is to increase greatly the on-site training that is being provided by the eight technicians provided by the Danish government so that there is at least one high-grade technician in each district charged with training the co-operative members in the technical and craft aspects of their work. For it is not only in the elements of costing, book-keeping, and management that the building co-operatives are deficient. As the previously quoted report commented:

> As far as the workmanship is concerned, it differs from group to group, ranging from rather poor to rather good. It seems entirely to depend on the supervision, either by the management of the co-operatives or by supervisors from government departments. The results of poor workmanship can be grouped according to their consequences. Firstly, a poor resistance against the weather, e.g. disintegrating bricks, cracking and loose plaster. Secondly, the waste of materials such as mortar and miscutting of timber, glazing, etc. Thirdly, a general poor appearance due to tilting walls and windows, etc. Of these faults, the first one is considered to be most grave, the second one of limited consequence, and the third one can certainly be endured for the time ahead.

Apart from *external* assistance designed to improve the management and technical ability of the building co-operatives, steps must be taken to provide *internal* management support. There is a great need to improve upon the quality of the present leadership in most building co-operatives and this cannot be done by purely external assistance since the basic education which many of the present building co-operative leaders possess is too meagre ever to allow them to stand on their own feet or to expand the activities of the co-operative. Unfortunately, there is a great dearth at present of Zambians trained in building management and although a start is being made at the Northern Technical College where 22 men are being trained in building management, much more needs to be done.

CONCLUSIONS

The capacity of the construction sector to increase its output and employment since 1964 has been spectacular. At the same time profit margins have increased considerably and have forced the government to pay 15 per cent more for each unit of output than it would have done if profit margins had remained at the 1964 level. The extra output has been achieved by the activities of firms belonging to foreigners or expatriate residents and the Zambian-owned section of the industry has as yet made no significant contribution to the higher levels of output.

The learning effect of the construction boom since Independence on the Zambian sector of the industry has been limited so far since the expansion in the demand for construction has come too fast for the establishment of sufficient training facilities for Zambians in this sector. Therefore, apart from the nationalization of firms in the field of building materials manufacturing and distribution, and the Zambianization of sand, stone, and brickmaking enterprises (which is likely to be hamstrung in the initial stages for lack of Zambians with management experience and technical knowledge to run these enterprises), the construction sector still remains very much under foreign and expatriate control.

Moreover, construction activity is still quite import-intensive and the economy as a whole has received limited benefits from the post-Independence construction boom—and, indeed, some harmful effects in the form of rapidly rising prices and imports—because the large increases in construction activity have come too quickly for investigations to be carried out into local substitutes for imported materials and for their commercial exploitation.

There is a danger that the difficulties being encountered by the building and craftsmen's co-operatives, and the consequent delays being encountered with the small rural building projects, will result in the adoption of factory prefabrication of buildings. This would undoubtedly speed up the building process in the rural areas but would destroy the income-earning and management-learning opportunities that have been presented by the government's building programme.

As far as urban building design and construction methods are concerned, there is a possibility that a concern for appearances, coupled with a desire to imitate European designs and to achieve higher densities of population, will lead to the adoption of multi-storey designs without consideration of the higher costs of such construction compared with single and double-storey buildings, and without regard to their high requirements of imports and skilled expatriate artisans, or of the question of the likelihood of their execution by Zambian-owned contracting firms.

The possibility exists, therefore, that the current boom in construction will dissipate without first enabling the establishment of the basis of a Zambian-owned and -managed building industry and without having established Zambian substitutes for imported materials. This was the legacy of the somewhat similar boom of the 1950s and it is not an experience that Zambia should want to see repeated.

14

Conclusion

CHARLES ELLIOTT[1]

ALL the contributors to this volume have emphasized that the period since Independence has been one in which inflationary pressures have been generated in the Zambian economy. The lower incomes consumer price index, for instance, shows a remarkable constancy from 1960 to 1964 but an increase of over 40 per cent between 1964 and the end of 1968, and in Lusaka at least there was an increase of over 60 per cent in that period in the food index. By 1969 the control of this inflation had come to be recognized as one of the principal objectives of government policy. Thus, within five years the main thrust of government economic strategy had been diverted from development to the control of inflation and particularly the moderation of demand. Perhaps the best indication of the revolution in government priorities is nowhere more clearly demonstrated than in the savage cuts in the budget of the Ministry of Rural Development, originally the spearhead of development, in the 1969 budget.

The inflation had been generated by both cost and demand elements. On the cost side, Table 14.1 shows how the cost of producing copper has increased both absolutely and relatively to the rest of the non-Communist world.

The table shows that Zambian costs rose by a cumulative percentage of 66 per cent over the period 1962 to 1968 and that the real spurt in Zambian costs, which accounted for more than 80 per cent of the whole increase over the period, came in the two years 1965 and 1966. It was this rise that put Zambian costs above average world costs and indeed established her as a vulnerable high-cost producer. It is instructive, therefore, to observe how this rise came about.

---

[1] Assistant Secretary of the Committee on Society, Development and Peace of the World Council of Churches and the Pontifical Commission Justice and Peace; formerly Reader in Economics and Head of Department, University of Zambia.

TABLE 14.1

Cost of producing copper in Zambia and the world, 1962–8
(excluding royalty and export tax)

| | 1962 | 1963 | | | 1964 | | | 1965 | | | 1966 | | | 1967 | | | 1968 | | |
	1	1	2	3	1	2	3	1	2	3	1	2	3	1	2	3	1	2	3
(a) Zambia	281	282	—	—	288	2	2	309	7	10	458	48	63	448	-2.1	59	466	4	66
(b) World	317	324	2	—	337	4	9	360	7	14	400	11	26	392	-2	24	n.a.	—	—
a/b%	87	84	—	—	85	50	22	85	100	71	115	436	242	114	100	246	—	—	—

Notes: Column 1 = Cost per long ton in K.

Column 2 = % increase over previous year.

Column 3 = Cumulative percentage increase over 1962.

The level of capacity at which the mines operated was substantially lower in 1966 than in the latter half of 1967. To the extent that capacity production is characterized by substantially falling costs as capacity working is increased, the large rise in 1966 overstates the rise in factor prices. Similarly the fall in 1967 is explained not by a fall in factor prices but by a resumption of consumption work in that year.

Source: Copperbelt of Zambia Mining Industry Year Book, 1968.

TABLE 14.2
Distribution of costs in copper mining, 1964–8
(K per long ton)

	1964	1965	1966	1967	1968
Royalty	75	94	129	91	98
Export tax	0	0	82	72	101
Transport	47	48	56	63	69
Employees[1]	113	115	157	163	160
Residual	128	146	245	222	242

[1] This figure includes wages, pension contribution, housing subsidy, and some other small items of indirect benefits.

Source: Copperbelt of Zambia Mining Industry Year Book, 1968.

From Table 14.2 it is evident that the reorganization of transport routes has had little *direct* effect, at least as far as the export of copper is concerned: we shall examine its indirect effects in more detail below. The other two elements, namely employees and the residual in the table, account for the great bulk in the increase in costs. For our purposes we exclude royalty and export tax from this discussion. The total cost of labour to the employer shows an increase of 42 per cent in the period 1964 to 1968 and this accounts for almost exactly one-quarter of the total rise. The residual item increased by 89 per cent over the same period and accounts for nearly two-thirds of the total rise. Unfortunately, a detailed breakdown of this residual item is not available and it is therefore impossible to weight the factors that lie behind this substantial rise. However, there can be little doubt that one of the key elements has been the increase in the cost of *imports*, as a result first of increased tariffs on Rhodesia Railways and secondly of the reorganization of transport routes. Associated with this and with the attempt to impose sanctions against Rhodesia is the extra expense incurred by the use of coal from Nkandabwe. Also concealed in the residual item is the rapid rise of prices in industries supplying the mining sector with inputs —e.g. road haulage, construction, and to a lesser extent, light engineering—in which the increasing cost of imports combined with the rapidly rising cost of skilled labour and in some sectors a substantial rise in profit margins.

The extent to which the experience of the copper mining industry in this period can be generalized for the economy as a whole is qualified by the fact that copper production in Zambia is a relatively capital-intensive industry. In industries in which the dependence upon imports and skills was substantially less than in copper, the rise in costs would have been less marked. The only major industry of which this is only partially true is construction, and, as Mr. Christie has shown in Chapter 13, in that sector the rise in *costs* was greatly exaggerated by a sudden, though seemingly discontinuous, rise in profit margins. This is precisely what one would expect in an economy in which a cost-inflationary situation is compounded by excessive demand. In Chapter 11, on manufacturing, Mr. Faber has amply demonstrated the release of enormous purchasing power in the public sector that followed Independence and the simultaneous acquisition of the right to royalties by the Zambian government. Allied with a sustainedly high copper price and a fairly small but not insignificant redistribution of income in favour of lower-income groups this ensured a rise in domestic expenditure from K 366 m. in 1964 to K 830 m. in 1967 (at market prices). In real terms this represents an increase of about 75 per cent in the level of domestic demand in four years. An important feature of this increase in demand is that a considerable proportion of the investment component, itself over a quarter of the total in 1967, was essentially of a long-term character. This was true in transport, in education, in agriculture, and where excess capacity was being deliberately created, as in some sectors of the manufacturing industry and in power supplies. In all these cases scarce resources were being used with little prospect of creating additional supply in the short run.

The other side of the same coin, however, is the fact that precisely because much of the investment undertaken in the period of the First National Development Plan is of an infrastructural nature it follows that the principal bottlenecks that beset the Zambian economy in its first five years of independent existence are on the way to being breached. This is most obviously true of manpower, transport and, to a more limited extent perhaps, domestic inter-sectoral sales. The intense irony of the situation, however, stems from the fact that as these real constraints are loosened so the financial constraints, formerly almost non-existent in the Zambian economy, become tighter. To some extent this is inevitably true since real constraints are breached precisely by the transformation of financial resources into real resources. However, in the Zambian situation the position is more complicated. The rapid rise in domestic costs and the increasing likelihood of a substantial and perhaps sustained fall in the price of copper together imply a much-reduced level of government revenue in the 1970s. In real terms, given the current rate of inflation this is *a fortiori* true. Similarly, Mr. Harvey in Chapter 6 has pointed out that the chances of increasing the level of non-government domestic savings substantially, apart from the

Mulungushi Reforms, are small. By requiring that foreign-owned firms increase their level of domestic saving the economic reforms did something to offset this trend. But at the time of writing, which may well prove to be too soon after the event, it is clear that one of the costs of this increase in domestic savings has been a fall of foreign investment, if not to zero, at least to a very low level. As Mr. Faber has pointed out, the cost of foreign investment in the future will almost certainly be substantial government participation in any project, and this implies that the rate of foreign investment must be determined by the scale of funds that the government is able to make available for partnership projects with foreign investors. If we assume that government revenue will fall in both real and money terms, it is likely that the funds available for such partnership projects will fall by a greater margin. To put it simply then, there is at least a considerable danger that as the supply inelasticities in the economy are removed and the total level of supply which the economy is capable of producing increases, the level of demand is likely to fall or at least to rise very much more slowly than has been the case in the period of the First National Development Plan.

This would be of less concern if it were the case that Zambian industries other than copper could look abroad for markets so that rapidly rising overseas demand could make up the potential shortfall in domestic demand. However, as has been emphasized by many of the contributors, Zambia has become, partly by design and partly by accident, a high-cost producer not only in relation to producers in the developed countries but also, and more significantly, in relation to the producers of East Africa with whom Zambia might be expected to compete.

This makes the current policy of joining the East African Common Market an exceedingly expensive political manoeuvre. For it means that, rather than being able to use the East African countries as markets for domestic production, Zambia is going to find the demand for domestically-produced products much reduced by reason of competition from the East African producers. To the extent that regional investment is diverted from Zambia to the other East African countries intersectoral demand is also affected.

Nor as Mr. Knight in Chapter 4 has shown is devaluation likely to alleviate the situation very much. Given the high import dependency of both consumers and producers and the fact that Zambian exports are sold at a fixed world price over which Zambia has no control, the only substantial effect of devaluation is likely to be a redistribution of income in favour of enterprises. Since this can be taxed away to increase government revenue it can increase the money demand originating from the government sector, but as devaluation is likely to be attended by a sharp rise in the costs of imports and labour the increase in real demand would be much moderated.

It is precisely under these conditions that governments resort to deficit financing. As long as the demand thus created does not exceed the potential supply of the economy, deficit financing *per se* does not imply the generation of inflationary pressure. However, it does imply a strain on the balance of payments since export earnings will have fallen as a result of weakening copper prices and imports will be maintained at the present high level by the creation of demand by an increase in government demand for finance by borrowing.

While it would be foolish to exaggerate the present similarity between Zambia and some of the Latin American economies, particularly Chile, the foregoing analysis suggests that the high level of costs, the ability of urban employees to protect their standard of living, the volatility of export earnings and government revenue, and the small domestic market are fundamental symptoms of the Latin American syndrome which Zambia already manifests.

It is no coincidence that a further symptom is the functional mal-adjustment of the agricultural sector. The importation of a high proportion of food, the failure of the rural sector to generate demand for the output of the industrial sector, the tendency of the rural sector to be a net borrower rather than lender of capital, and the extreme inelasticity of supply of agricultural products all betoken, both in Zambia and in some Latin American countries, a grave weakness in the economic structure that can only be remedied by rapid labour-intensive development of the farm sector. Unfortunately in this respect there is little ground for optimism since the experience of the rest of the underdeveloped world suggests that such structural adjustment can only be achieved very slowly and usually by the diversion of substantial proportions of capital from the urban industrial sector to the rural sector. Yet such diversion of capital merely compounds the difficulties already facing the industrial sector. It is therefore a measure of the challenge facing Zambia along with many other underdeveloped countries that the ultimate pace of development depends fundamentally upon the rate at which the rural sector can be transformed. The fact that it is in the rural areas that the great majority of these populations live adds to a complicated technical situation a political urgency that cannot be ignored.

INDEX OF NAMES

Printed by Kenya Litho Limited, P.O. Box 40775, Nairobi, Kenya and published by Oxford University Press, P.O. Box 72532, Nairobi, Kenya.